Neither Gods nor Emperors

Neither Gods nor Emperors

Students and the Struggle for Democracy in China

CRAIG CALHOUN

University of California Press

BERKELEY   LOS ANGELES   LONDON

951.058
Calhoun

University of California Press
Berkeley and Los Angeles, California

University of California Press, Ltd.
London, England

© 1994 by
The Regents of the University of California

Library of Congress Cataloging-in-Publication Data

Calhoun, Craig J., 1952 –
    Neither gods nor emperors : students and the struggle for
democracy in China / Craig Calhoun
        p.   cm.
    Includes bibliographical references and index.
    ISBN 0 – 520-08826-3 (alk. paper)
    1. China—History—Tiananmen Square Incident, 1989.
2. Students—China—Political activity.   I. Title.
DS779.32.C35   1995
951.05'8—dc20   94 – 9432
                                                      CIP

Printed in the United States of America
9 8 7 6 5 4 3 2 1

Contents

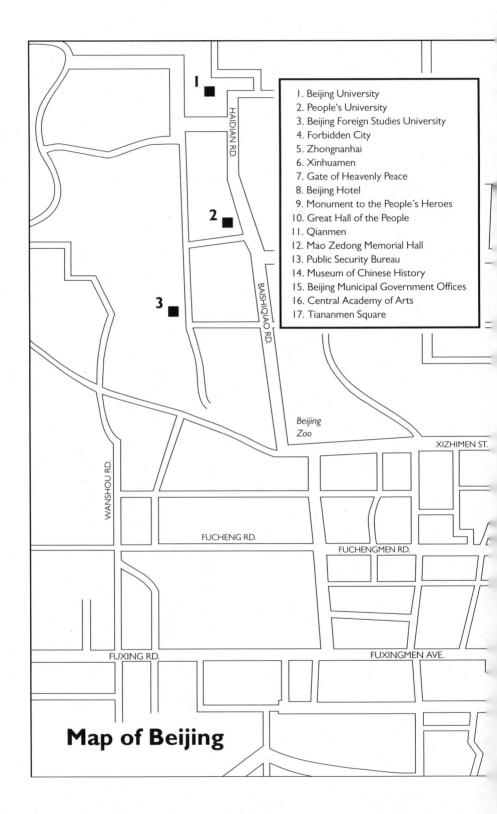

1. Beijing University
2. People's University
3. Beijing Foreign Studies University
4. Forbidden City
5. Zhongnanhai
6. Xinhuamen
7. Gate of Heavenly Peace
8. Beijing Hotel
9. Monument to the People's Heroes
10. Great Hall of the People
11. Qianmen
12. Mao Zedong Memorial Hall
13. Public Security Bureau
14. Museum of Chinese History
15. Beijing Municipal Government Offices
16. Central Academy of Arts
17. Tiananmen Square

HAIDIAN RD.

BAISHIQIAO RD.

Beijing Zoo

XIZHIMEN ST.

WANSHOU RD.

FUCHENG RD.

FUCHENGMEN RD.

FUXING RD.

FUXINGMEN AVE.

Map of Beijing

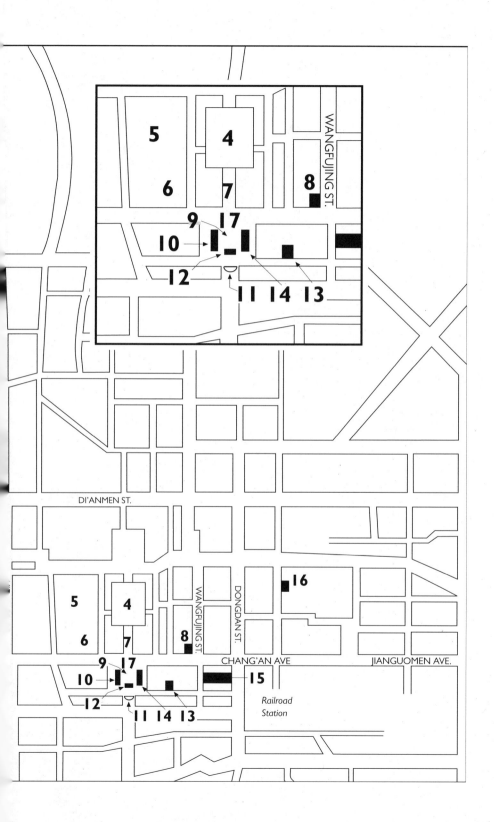

Preface

"There has never been a savior, nor should we rely on gods and emperors," says the Chinese version of "The Internationale." "To create happiness for humankind, we must rely on ourselves." The old socialist song expressed surprisingly well the democratic vision of China's protesting students in 1989. They wavered sometimes, seeking saviors and building a statue to one paradoxical god. But they sang "The Internationale" even as they gathered on Tiananmen Square's Monument to the People's Heroes in the early morning of June 4.

The climax of China's 1989 student protest movement is well known, at least outside China. Troops acting under martial law forcibly cleared Tiananmen Square of protesters. On their way to the Square, they fired automatic assault weapons on unarmed citizens and sometimes shot wildly into neighboring buildings. People were crushed under the tracks of armored personnel carriers on the Boulevard of Heavenly Peace, and tanks smashed the statue of the Goddess of Democracy which had come almost overnight to symbolize the movement. Eyewitness reports emphasized the frenzied activity of the soldiers, their excessive and sometimes aimless violence. Some may simply have run amok, but it is clear that the overall attack was consciously planned and coordinated.

Soldiers also were killed, most dying when crowds torched their vehicles. A few were beaten. Though dead students could not be mourned publicly for fear of reprisals, China's government went to great lengths to honor the soldiers as martyrs, publishing graphic accounts of their deaths. Grisly photographs showed charred corpses strung from lampposts. Student leaders had urged nonviolence, but neither deep cultural roots nor any specific and well-known ideology reinforced their plea. By this point, moreover, the crowds were not composed primarily of students. Workers and other ordinary citizens had rallied in support of the students and against martial law. They fought more openly, and they bore the brunt of government violence.

Though these stark outlines of the massacre are known, it is not clear how to make sense of it. It is just as hard to tell who was making the government's decisions at that point. Various factions had been using the student movement as occasion for their own power struggles. We know that Zhao Ziyang and many of his associates and fellow "liberalizers" had been toppled, though not yet publicly removed from office; we do not know and probably never will know exactly which alliances or events brought this about. We know that the government had been almost incapacitated by its internal struggles in the preceding weeks. But we do not know whether the use of force in clearing Tiananmen primarily represented the policy of factions already in power or whether it was a tactic in the power struggle. Certainly the decision to use violence eliminated the argument that the Chinese government should restrain itself to avoid inflaming world opinion. After the massacre, world opinion was already forfeit.

Since June 4, 1989, despite global sympathy for the students, attention has been focused on the killers more than on the killed, on the Chinese government and not on the protesters. It is important, however, not to let geopolitical considerations or the combat within the Chinese leadership obscure the student movement itself. Even our horror at the massacre and our condemnation of the continuing repression in China should not overshadow just how remarkable this protest was. Nor should we be swayed by those erstwhile protesters who now describe their defeat as inevitable, who believe that the die had been cast by late April or early May and that they (or their comrades) should have heeded the signs. The democracy movement of 1989 was creative, vital, and full of possibilities. It did not succeed, over the short run, in achieving many of its participants' goals. Yet to say it was foreordained to fail is not realism but cynicism. Sometimes social movements do succeed against all the odds; fate speaks only after the fact in human life. For the Chinese people, and for the world, the events of spring 1989 have value as an inspiration, not just as a cautionary tale.

In this book I focus on the movement, not on the massacre that ended it or on its long-term results. I try to show how cultural and political struggle shaped the movement, how contingencies and choices and specific social foundations made it possible. I also try to make clear that the movement of spring 1989 was not monological, did not speak with one voice, express one set of interests, or point in a single direction. It resulted from a confluence of forces as well as of persons and grew amid contestation and diversity of understanding that fit but poorly into established categories. The Western media and the Chinese diaspora alike have objectified the movement—or created a simulacrum of it—in international discourse. But the reigning representations, even those offered by exiled leaders of the movement, are generally too simple.

In their appeals and their actions, the student protesters echoed earlier radical Chinese intellectuals, including those whose struggles helped give rise to the communist government the 1989 students now challenged. The students sought simultaneously a voice for intellectuals, a way to strengthen their country, and a deepening of political participation. Like protesters throughout the modern world, they sought democracy, personal and collective recognition, and an end to corrupt government. But their struggle was also deeply rooted in the cultural crisis of a China embarked on startling economic reforms after years of communism, the trauma of Cultural Revolution, and renewed contact with a West that called China's four thousand years of greatness into question, wounding pride even as it attracted desire.

This book begins with the story of how the 1989 Beijing Spring protests got started, gathered force, broke through the limits of previous rebellions against China's communist government, faltered, found renewal in hunger strikes and dramatic symbols, and finally were ended by military force. This narrative is followed by an analysis of the movement: the dynamics and social bases of its organization; its historical background as part and product of China's halting development of a public sphere and civil society; the role of both Chinese and foreign media; the nature of China's cultural crisis; the meaning of democracy, both for students and for those who watched them from the sidelines in 1989; students' struggles for personal and collective respect; and the sources of their heroism.

Though I challenge the authority of central participants on at least some points, I can hardly claim to be beyond challenge myself. I am not a sinologist, though I have studied Chinese history and sociology and spent time in China before 1989. I am a social theorist and comparative social historian whose work emphasizes popular politics, social movements, and protest. I happened to be teaching at the Beijing Foreign Studies University during the spring of 1989. Not surprisingly, I became a constant observer and ultimately a participant observer in the protest that consumed my students' attention. I owe a great deal of whatever understanding I have achieved to them. I spent literally hundreds of hours talking with student activists, not only from my own university but also from others (especially Beijing University). With the help of my students I was able to meet various leaders of the movement and, by virtue of their translation, to carry on conversations that exceeded my grasp of Chinese. I am especially indebted to the student I refer to in chapter 7 by the famous name of Xu Zhimo. He was my most frequent companion and translator; with his assistance I was able to conduct the survey of movement participants and bystanders that provided some of the data for that chapter.

My debt to these students is enormous, yet I will not name them for fear of jeopardizing their careers in China. My debts continued to mount after I returned to the United States. Chinese students in Chapel Hill and elsewhere have read and commented on all parts of this work and on various essays leading up to it. They have helped especially by translating Chinese sources for me. Some of these students were in China in 1989 and were active in the protest; they have also offered their own reflections. I have further benefited from dialogue with Chinese students and intellectuals at universities across the United States, Europe, and Australia, particularly those (formally or informally) exiled leaders of the protest movement who allowed me to interview them and/or who read and commented on parts of my account.

Fortunately, I do not have to refrain from naming the Western scholars of China who helped me in this work. Before acknowledging specific debts, I should stress that this book could be written only because of the enormous labors of generations of Western students of China. My argument builds at many points on their work. The intertwined histories of intellectuals, social movements, cultural change, and the project of democracy, for example, have been greatly illuminated by writers such as Geremie Barmé, Merle Goldman, Jerome Greider, Leo Lee, Joseph Levenson, Perry Link, Andrew Nathan, Mary Rankin, William Rowe, Orville Schell, Vera Schwarcz, Benjamin Schwartz, David Strand, and Chow Tse-tung (the last a venerable U.S. scholar whose work on the May Fourth movement of 1919 is so much appreciated that China's protesting students hoisted him on their shoulders in Tiananmen Square on May 4, 1989).[1] Studies of earlier student protest have been especially valuable, notably those by Jeffrey Wasserstrom and John Israel. I have tried to connect my more detailed account of the 1989 student protests to precursor movements in Republican China, to the Cultural Revolution and the reform era, and to the organization of China's intellectual field and public sphere. These analyses are possible mainly because so many strong secondary sources have been produced. A number of scholars have also illuminated specific aspects of the 1989 protests through both general observations and analyses of specific aspects. Two of the most helpful book-length reports are Lee Feigon's

China Rising and Michael Fathers and Andrew Higgins's *Tiananmen: The Rape of Beijing*.[2] Useful articles have appeared in a host of places; readers should consult the collections edited by Hicks, Wasserstrom and Perry, Saich, and Unger. Unger's collection is especially valuable for its reports of events outside Beijing. Like most others, I have limited my account mainly to events in the capital. I have done so partly because I was there, partly because Beijing was of central importance, and crucially but regrettably because many fewer observational accounts and documentary sources are available from the rest of China.

Perhaps above all I am beholden to translators. An extraordinary amount of primary source material from the student movement and the years just before it has been translated into English. A few collections have been especially helpful: Barmé and Minford's remarkable *Seeds of Fire* and Barmé and Jaivin's *New Ghosts, Old Dreams*; the invaluable *Cries for De-mocracy*, edited pseudonymously by Han Minzhu; *June Four* by the staff of *Ming Pao News*; the linked collections of Ogden, Hartford, Sullivan, and Zweig, *China's Search for Democracy*; Oksenberg, Sullivan, and Lambert, *Beijing Spring, 1989*; and the combination of documents and commentary in Yu and Harrison's *Voices from Tiananmen Square*. I have also relied on two collections of documents in French translation: *Le tremblement de terre de Pékin* by Béja, Bonnin, and Peyraube; and *L'impossible printemps* by Chen and Thimonier. I have drawn on documents in the holdings of Harvard University and the Center for Transcultural Studies in Chicago, many translated for me by Chinese students in the United States. Not least of all, it has been possible to study the 1989 events in considerable detail largely because they were the object of extraordinary international media attention. Many student leaders knew that journalists and photographers were helping the movement to happen as well as recording it, and these individuals went out of their way to provide interviews, comments, and photo opportunities. These sources are not without their biases, but they are invaluable.

Finally, this study would not have been possible without the Center for Transcultural Studies (formerly Psychosocial Studies) in Chicago. The Center sponsored my teaching in the program on Comparative Cultural Studies, which it helped to found at Beijing Foreign Studies University. Benjamin Lee, the Center's director, has not only provided support but also helped me make connections and avoid errors. I am indebted as well to Leo Ou-fan Lee, Fred Chiu, Prasenjit Duara, Jianying Zha, and other members and associates of the Center who commented on my work and gave me guidance in our repeated discussions. I have also received helpful feedback and suggestions from Tom Gold, Judith Farquhar, James Hevia, and Nan Lin. Jeffrey Wasserstrom did me the great favor of commenting in detail on the penultimate draft of this book. Presentations of early versions of some of this work were also beneficial, and I thank fellow panelists and audiences at the American Sociological Association; the Foreign Service Institute; the Albert Einstein Institution; the École des Hautes Études en Sciences Sociales; the New School for Social Research; Oslo, Duke, La Trobe, and Minnesota universities; the Programs in Asian Studies and in Social Theory and Cross-Cultural Studies at the University of North Carolina at Chapel Hill; and various broader public groups.

Though this book is not an explicitly comparative study, it is informed by comparative research and by theoretical arguments about the relationship of democracy, social movements, culture, and the public sphere. It is also addressed to different sorts of readers. I have tried to write for those with a general interest in this extraordinary movement, but I have also attempted to pursue theoretical and empirical questions rigorously enough to make the study of use to specialists on China, social movements, and political change. Thus, not every chapter will seem equally novel to every reader. Some of the information presented for readers who have not studied China will seem obvious to China specialists. Similarly, not all of the ideas I raise about social movements or the public sphere will seem path-breaking to students of social movements, but they are no less vital for that. It is very hard to write for multiple communities of specialists without seeming a fool or a novice to each. Yet it seems to me especially appropriate to try to reach a broad readership in this case. The movement was born in part out of a rejection of Chinese insularity and a claim that ideas such as democracy and the theorists who fostered them had an international currency. The movement happened on an international as well as a local stage and played movingly to many audiences. This book is a much lesser thing, but I hope that it too succeeds in making new connections. Above all, I have tried simply to be true to the movement itself.

Introduction

Any important event, movement, or set of ideas must have a standard appellation in China. Sloganizing and repetition of set rhetorical formulas is raised to an art, albeit one that sometimes deadens thought. "Turmoil" was the Chinese government's label for the six weeks of student protest between mid-April and early June 1989. The news readers on China Central Television's English service pronounced it with an emphasis on the second syllable, and it figured in every official speech. The now infamous *People's Daily* editorial of April 26 provided this label and simultaneously fanned the movement's flames by insulting the students and threatening government suppression. Li Peng cited turmoil as a key reason for the declaration of martial law. "Turmoil" is an accepted translation for *dongluan*, "to make chaos." Chaos is a perennial fear in China, and the authorities hoped to play on this. The students, however, preferred the label *luandong*, which refers to free-form dancing, the sort of individually creative movement popularized in the West during the 1960s. Beijing students liked the syllabic reversal; they were dancing in spontaneous order, they said, not making chaos.

When former Communist Party general secretary Hu Yaobang, a reformer, died on April 15, it took only hours for students to fill the streets around their campuses and cover the walls with posters. Within two days, marchers had giant photographs of Hu to carry, indicating that there was organization behind the protests. Indeed, activists had been planning demonstrations to coincide with the seventieth anniversary of the May Fourth student movement and simply moved the date up. Student leaders had connections to older reformers and businesspeople who could supply the photographs. They had networks of communication among themselves. However, this organizational basis for protest was not equivalent to a top-down, hierarchical command structure, a formal organization. The broad mass of students were not manipulated by a handful, nor did outside agitators constitute a "black hand" behind the protests; no neat line can be drawn between those who were "inside" or "outside" the organization. Leadership was diffuse and contested, planning informal and rooted in custom—for example, in the common knowledge of where to look for wall posters carrying information or opinion, or in the habitual role of class monitors as leaders. A central theme of this book is that fluid, ambiguous organization gave shape and strength to the student movement. I will try to show that the movement was less the product of central planning than some retrospective constructions—of student leaders as well as government critics—suggest. I will emphasize both the multiplicity of forms of leadership and organization and the extent to which the movement reflected a broader discourse, a wider set of responses to social change and ambitions for China's future.

The movement also had deep roots in Chinese traditions. Students echoed and played with old slogans, protest themes, and national concerns, and these took on new power in a period of cultural crisis. This historical resonance and the movement's relatively open form enabled it to bring in large numbers of workers, officials, and ordinary people—the "old hundred names" (*laobaixing*) of Beijing and dozens of other cities. Such openness also allowed for shifts from one set of issues and identities to another, as a movement specifically of students became increasingly a movement of (or at least on behalf of) the Chinese people as a whole. Ultimately, though, the loose organizational framework and the contests among different leaders and groups of students inhibited negotiations and stalled attempts to withdraw from the occupation of Tiananmen Square. The movement grew beyond its organizational capacity, leading to disorder, disputes, and petty abuses of power.

The student movement of 1989 was truly unprecedented in the People's Republic, yet it was deeply shaped by history and especially by the discourse of intellectuals. It reflected not only an emerging public sphere linked to popular culture in film, television, and other media but also an older sort of communication among elite scholars. Echoes of the past figured prominently. Students began to take to the streets in growing numbers after the death of Hu Yaobang, who had lost his post as Communist Party general secretary during the repression of the 1986–87 student protest. *Dazibao* (large character posters) mounted on the walls of Beijing University's "Triangle Area" listed key dates from previous struggles, especially the May Fourth movement of 1919, China's first major student uprising and symbol of the campaign for New Culture. The seventieth anniversary of the May Fourth protests was the occasion of the second really large march of 1989. That year was also the tenth anniversary of the Democracy Wall movement, which had brought the first massive voice for democratization in post-Mao China.

These and many other anniversaries were a topic of intellectual discussion well before the protest. In an article written early in 1989 and featured in the May issue of Shanghai's *Wenhui Bao*, the prominent writer Su Xiaokang predicted:

> The year 1989 is destined to be a singular memorial year which meets many historical giants: It is the bicentenary of the French revolution; the centenary of the founding of the Second International; the 70th anniversary of the May 4th movement; the 40th anniversary of the founding of the People's Republic of China; the 30th anniversary of the Lushan Conference; the 20th anniversary of the death of Liu Shaoqi; and so on. No one can escape these coming days of the year which may make you happy or unhappy one way or the other.[1]

On May 3, I sat with a handful of graduate students on the Beijing University campus. They stressed the many round-numbered anniversaries repeatedly as they sought to make sense of their movement, which already was beginning to make them feel part of a historical struggle. They cited many of the dates on Su's list, with May 4 the Chinese date that impressed them most. None of them brought up 1949, the year of the communist revolution, so I did. "Yes," said one with little enthusiasm, "but also 1789, the year of the French Revolution and the signing of the U.S. Constitution."[2]

The very scene of this conversation said something about the background to the protest. Of all Chinese universities, Beijing University is perhaps the one that feels most familiar to an American. Its campus was originally that of Yenching University, focus of Harvard's Beijing outreach effort, and it is laid out with quadrangles, spacious lawns, rolling hills, and a pretty lake. No American would need more than a moment to recognize it as a university campus. And in 1989 it looked more familiar than ever. Snazzy ten-speed bicycles were cropping up among the more traditional, utilitarian Chinese designs. Students wore polo shirts with brand-name logos splashed across their chests. Men and women walked hand in hand. One could buy Coke as well as the local orange sodas. A good number of students had earphones on their heads and Walkman stereos at their belts. Oddly, one of the things that struck me as most unfamiliar was the very high percentage of students who smoked ciga-rettes—even though many favored brands from my home state of North Carolina.

Chinese students in 1989 partook of international culture, not only through the sale and consumption of various commodities but also through the mass media, which were making their way increasingly into China. This international culture also had an intellectual side. Students and their teachers were as keen to catch up on the latest trends in Western social theory or literary criticism as Chinese army officers were eager to learn about state-of-the-art computers and weaponry. Habermas, Derrida, and Jameson were all popular to cite, even if only fragments of their writings had been read.

At the same time that icons of Western culture were being imported, key symbols of China's recent past were under attack. Beijing University had previously been home to one of my favorite statues of Mao Zedong. In front of a central building he had stood, his hands clasped behind his back, facing into the wind, perhaps the wind of change. Though Mao was already dead when I first visited Beijing University, it hadn't occurred to me that this statue might be toppled by the time I returned. At worst, I imagined, Mao would simply lose his currency, but I was sure his statue would re-main a landmark—a bit like the Confederate soldier on the front quad of my own campus in Chapel Hill. Yet Mao's statue became a casualty of shifting political currents and a deep-seated ambivalence on the part of young Chinese intellectuals toward their past.

In addition to recent symbols such as Mao, ancient figures of Chinese culture were subject to attack. Students grappled with the challenge of fig-uring out what it did and should mean to be Chinese even as they accepted certain Western influences and proposed innovations of their own. They had not lost their pride in being Chinese, but this pride was coupled, para-doxically, with a humiliation at whatever seemed to have made China weak in the modern world.

Among the bits of Western influence at work in China were partial stir-rings of capitalism. When I gathered with my student friends to talk about the prospects for democracy, it was in a privately owned and operated res-taurant housed on the Beijing University campus. And though there was talk of inflation as a public issue, this restaurant drew praise for providing us with more good food than we could eat—and quite enough beer to drink—for the equivalent of a little over a dollar a head. Even that was an expensive meal for Chinese students, who would ordinarily pay fifty cents or less to eat at the dining hall (carrying their own metal dishes with them and using a spoon rather than chopsticks because it would do for soup and other dishes and because it wouldn't fall through a mesh bag).

Around the table, my new friends praised my handling of chopsticks—a routine sort of compliment for the Chinese to pay a foreigner. They deferentially asked my opinion of and advice for the Chinese student movement. And gradually, after a little prodding, they began to tell me more of what they thought lay ahead. Some expected real democracy in a year or so; others wondered whether they would see it in their lifetime. All thought it inevitable, a matter of historical necessity and popular will. They told me that intellectuals had a central role to play as the conscience of the nation and as the source of a new vision of Chinese culture.[3] They relived inspiring moments from the April 27 march, in which students had broken through ranks of unarmed military police to reach Tiananmen Square, revealing the government's unwillingness to enforce the threats of violent repression it had made the day before. My dining companions speculated on tactical questions: Should the planned May 4 march be the last before a consolidation of gains or one moment in a rising wave of protest? Would the return of Zhao Ziyang from North Korea bring them an important friend in power or end the government's apparent indecision about how to stop the movement? How could the ideas of the students best be spread to other sections of the population? They argued among themselves over such questions and joked about the danger of repression, laughing at the undergraduates who had made out wills before marching on Tiananmen against government orders.

Within six weeks, these students would experience peaks of exhilaration as their movement grew beyond their short-term expectations, troughs of depression as it seemed to falter from ineffective leadership and lack of direction, and rage as soldiers following government orders killed hundreds or even thousands of protesters. By mid-June, some of these students would flee Beijing to the relative safety of family and friends in smaller towns. Others would attend hours of "political study" sessions each week, confessing the number of times they had joined demonstrations, resisting calls to inform on friends, studying the speeches of Deng Xiaoping and Li Peng. All except one (who succeeded in leaving China) would have been silenced, at least for the near future.

Yet they readjusted rapidly. Still bitter at their situation and at China's political silence, they nonetheless embraced the return of calm and the recovery of the economy. With the field of possibilities changing, they shifted the focus of their national and personal aspirations alike. Most again embraced the cause of economic reform and found themselves hoping their erstwhile enemy Deng Xiaoping would outlive the more conservative octogenarians with whom he shared power.

I next returned to Beijing three years after the massacre. The streets were the same, but not the crowds. Though three years is a short time as history—especially Chinese history—goes, it was long enough for the movement to become a matter of history, despite hopes and real possibilities for its resurrection. The return to Beijing of movement leader Shen Tong in the summer of 1992 did cause a stir, and without too much effort he was able to provide the Chinese government with a pretext on which to arrest him, despite its own assurances of safety for returning students and exiles. The winds could shift direction in an instant, I had no doubt, but the winds of 1992 were not blowing the way of 1989. When Wang Dan—perhaps the single most important student leader and the only key activist apprehended by the regime—was released from prison early in 1993, it hardly caused a sensation. The populace of Beijing was worried mainly about how to make money. University professors complained that students wanted only to find connections that could bring jobs in joint-venture companies, that they weren't really interested in serious study. Wang Dan himself announced that he planned to pursue a career in business. The sense of political apathy—or rather, the sense of apolitical eagerness for continued economic reform and its real and imagined opportunities—was indeed striking. I had to remind myself that at the beginning of 1989 professors had made similar complaints that students were apathetic, that they were interested not in doing practical work in China but only in taking the TOEFL test for study in America. People always have more motives than opportunities for action, and in China especially it is important to pick one's actions carefully.

It requires now a considerable effort to recall the sense of agitation and unease about China's situation that was so immediate in 1989. To do so, it is necessary to keep in mind four major conditions that shaped the ground in which the movement grew. I introduce these only briefly here, both as background for those less familiar with China and as reminders for all of the circumstances specific to 1989.

UNDERLYING CONDITIONS
Succession Crisis

Chinese critics of the communist regime are fond of comparing it to its imperial predecessors, pointing out what they call its "feudal" aspects. This is in many ways a problematic characterization, born largely of a crude appropriation of the already simplified historical categories of *The Communist Manifesto*.[4] The particularities of traditional China are poorly grasped by comparing it with medieval Europe; moreover, feudalism was only one aspect, however important, of European social organization. The comparison is blurred further by the translation of feudalism as *fengjian*, a category of traditional Confucian historiography. In the last forty years this term has been used to characterize China's entire past, as though for four thousand years the society was stagnant and unchanging. But *fengjian* was originally intended to describe phases of relatively decentralized rural and military society in alternation with the more centrally governed, urban, and commercial *junxian* system.[5] Instead of seeing Chinese history in terms of large-scale change and internal differentiation, however, many very educated Chinese see it as almost unchanging. Indeed, one of the most prominent criticisms of Chinese culture in the late 1980s was Jin Guantao's argument that it promoted a "superstable" social structure.[6]

For years, the Guomindang government in Taiwan had been fond of claiming that Mao was no more than China's latest emperor. To many in the West this had seemed both a cheap shot and an analytical error. Indeed, blaming the communist system's current difficulties on lingering feudalism was actually a criticism that parts of the government could endorse, as it challenged not official ideology or policy but only premature claims of success. Blaming feudalism only discouraged a more fundamental critique of the current regime.

Nonetheless, in 1989 the government did seem to share a good many characteristics with traditional China. For example, students pointed to the old men struggling to cling to power. Crises of succession were the bane of imperial China. Because each emperor ruled until his death, nearly every transition was marked by a power struggle; as a ruler grew old, his generals, staff, and potential heirs began jockeying for position, creating increasing instability that often culminated in a full-scale crisis after the emperor's death. In the late 1980s, Deng Xiaoping took explicit steps to avoid this pattern. He maneuvered his fellow octogenarians into full or partial retirement, elevating a "younger" generation of leaders (most in their sixties) to power. But ultimately he appeared unwilling to give up the final say on every important policy decision. His stubborn hold on power may have been necessary to avoid open factional fighting. In 1987 Deng engineered the removal of his long-time protégé and designated heir, Hu Yaobang, when the latter had acted too independently in allowing economic reform to extend into the political arena. Deng would do much the same to Zhao Ziyang in 1989. Students sometimes caricatured Deng Xiaoping not just as an emperor but sometimes as the dowager Empress Cixi, who staged a coup against her own son when he took reform to lengths she found intolerable. "Socialist countries," one student placard suggested, "are republics in name only, and monarchies in reality."[7] As a student wrote on one of my questionnaires in mid-May, "This is a life-or-death struggle between democracy and totalitarianism. We want to overthrow Deng Xiaoping because we see him as the last dictator in the centuries-long history of China. This is precisely what the present movement really focuses on!"

In addition to decrying Deng's power, students cited the average age of the party elite as itself an indication of China's failure to modernize. They felt this failure keenly, as it meant that they would have to wait decades, following the dictates of their elders rather than their hearts or minds, before they could have a substantial voice in the highest levels of policymaking. Indeed, one of the sources of Mikhail Gorbachev's popularity in China was his dissimilarity to the Chinese gerontocracy. The Soviet leader was relatively young, and he appeared to listen to and promote still younger voices. A bit of the same had happened in China, to be sure; a few younger economists and business managers had been catapulted to prominence. A Western graduate education helped some overcome the handicaps of youth and enjoy rapid career advancement. But no such person had yet moved into the ranks of central power. The role of the party elders was seen as a drag on China's progress and even as a source of embarrassment, a sign of backwardness itself. That the top party elite generally lacked formal education was also galling to intellectuals and students.

In the spring of 1989, a few people went beyond raising questions about the age of party leaders and wondering who would succeed Deng. Perhaps, they suggested, China was experiencing a succession not just of emperors but of dynasties. Perhaps the communist regime would turn out to be one of China's short-lived dynasties, a reign of decades like the Sui or Yuan rather than of a thousand years, as the traditional benediction has it. Chinese dynasties are thought to have a natural life course: strong and sometimes expanding in their youth, stable and peaceful in middle age, increasingly prone to crises and instability as they grow old. Was communism growing old?

Few students believed that short-term changes were going to end the People's Republic of China. The majority did not even contemplate overturning the Communist Party. They did, however, see the government as weakening and the succession crisis, whether large or small, as playing a significant role in this process. The ordinary work of the government was hampered by poor discipline, increasing corruption, and factional struggles. The latter were waged not just between "hard-liners" and "reformers" but among a wide range of different groups. Though most such groups had ideological positions, these were not necessarily their basis. Many were constructed out of personal loyalties, including kinship, whereas others were marriages of convenience. Alliances crosscut each other, and boundaries shifted. Little of this struggle went on in public or even in full view of the party elite. Jockeying for position seemed the main preoccupation of China's rulers, who remained hidden behind the red door and statuary lions of the Zhongnanhai compound on all but the most ceremonial occasions. As such jostling consumed more and more attention, highly placed people grew increasingly uneasy and uncertain about what sort of government—and ideological line—would prevail.

The succession crisis did not cause all the divisions in government; it merely kept the regime from resolving or papering them over. Differing views of the economic reforms of the past decade; the struggles among generations and among families and cliques; relations between military and civilian leaders; debate over the extent of permissible Westernization; and attempts to stem some of the high-level corruption that ran rampant were all factors undermining government unity. Yet the widespread concern over succession caused the government's near incapacitation when faced with the growing student protest and the evident sympathy much of the broader public felt for it. The movement cannot be understood simply in terms of its own grievances or organizational strengths. It must be seen as flowering in an opening provided for it by the internal divisions and relative weakness of the government.[8]

Material Gains and Their Limits

In the spring of 1989, Chinese people frequently pointed out the various shortcomings of their economy. Inflation was growing; there were periodic shortages of important products; some goods and services could be secured only through bribery; and wages were not only low in absolute terms but also inequitable. Students repeatedly bemoaned their own poverty, which was very real by American standards, and pointed out that even the most senior professors (along with engineers, doctors, and other intellectuals and professionals) made but a fraction of a taxi driver's income.

At the same time, though the students did not always recognize it, their material situation was noticeably better than that of students only a few years before. Bicycles were not a short-supply item, though most students had rather beat-up bikes (a couple told me they had left their fancier ten-speeds at home because they would stand out at the university and possibly be stolen). Most students at the major Beijing universities had radios, and a few had televisions in their dormitory rooms. Undergraduates were crowded four to six to a room, but nearly all ate adequately and owned a few books. Many had cameras (including some fancy Japanese models) with which to photograph their favorite *dazibao*. This was a far cry from the China of the early 1980s, when a tourist might draw stares just by changing film. Beijing students were also better off than those in most of the rest of China; they had tape recorders to play pop songs or to record speeches during the demonstrations, and protest leaders found it easy to buy battery-operated megaphones. In short, even students, who had not shared much in China's economic gains of the last decade, were noticeably better off than they had been five years before.

The gains were much more pronounced for other groups. The *getihu*, small entrepreneurs whose stalls filled markets and sidewalks, often made enough money to be well above manning their own booths anymore. Some, indeed, owned motorcycles and frequented the better restaurants. Of course, some also failed, though this side of capitalism did not yet seem apparent to all Chinese; many assumed that simply being an entrepreneur ensured prosperity. Other beneficiaries of economic reform were the employees of joint-venture companies, from hotels to textile factories to electronics assembly plants. Nearly all these workers could expect to earn a wage at least double the national average. Peasants had benefited most famously from the reforms, largely from the right to raise some animals and market some crops for themselves. The growing big business sector included some well-paid senior managers and an increasing num   of millionaires. Most famous were the founders of the Stone Computer Corporation (Si Tong Company), China's largest privately owned company, which even operated its own think tank (headed by a former sociology teacher who became one of the final four hunger strikers of June 1989) and issued its own publications. Deng Xiaoping's slogan, "to get rich is glorious," had not been ignored.

Since 1987, however, many of the gains had been eroded. The economy had stagnated.[9] Peasants had been paid for their main crops (still purchased by the government) only partly in cash; the remainder was paid in a not-immediately-negotiable scrip. Inflation had eaten up much of the extra earnings of urban workers and may even have led to a fall in real income for the first time in the post-Mao period. Unemployment, hidden behind the euphemism "waiting for work," was growing rapidly, leaving numerous young members of the urban working class with both the time and the rationale for protest.

The juxtaposition of market prices in some areas and regulated prices in others created recurrent supply bottlenecks (though never on the scale of those in the Soviet Union). Where goods were available at both official and (higher) market prices, those who controlled products tabbed at the former always had the temptation to sell at the latter and pocket the difference. In the countryside, the rush to purchase consumer goods had reportedly slowed. The government scrip and consequent shortage of cash was not the only reason for the diminished demand. Peasants had also begun to save for traditional purposes such as weddings and funerals. In July 1989 the government would launch a crackdown on such practices, ostensibly because of their "superstitious" religious foundations but also substantially because of the economic impact of large amounts of money being held out of circulation.

Corruption and profiteering were even more problematic and even more resented, yet both proliferated. Part of the reason lay in the government's loss of control over its own cadres. Inflation exacerbated the problem: Petty officials were generally on fixed incomes, and when inflation squeezed them, they squeezed others. Such behavior likely added to the resentment ordinary people felt toward corrupt officials and the growing prevalence of bribery.[10]

Even though problems had accompanied the economic growth of recent years, the student and popular protest of spring 1989 cannot be understood without noting that gains were genuine. First, many of the popular complaints—most notably corruption, inflation, and inequities in income distribution—were largely products of the economic reforms. Second, the economic changes helped propel the more general opening of possibilities in China. Economic motives had helped to increase Western influences— tourism yielded hard currency, joint ventures brought in capital and technology, and education abroad developed skills. Beyond this, economic reforms had created a sense that career advancement did not depend solely on currying favor with the Communist Party or one's immediate supervisors (though there were still sharp limits to how free from one's *danwei*, or work unit, one could become).[11] Third, and centrally, the very economic ambitions of the Party and government made them newly reliant on highly educated workers, professionals, scientists, and scholars.

A Renewed Prominence for Intellectuals

A very wide range of educated people is categorized by the Chinese term *zhishifenzi*, translated as "intellectuals." In China, all who have a university education and many with technical training are considered intellectuals, not just those who create, criticize, or disseminate knowledge. Deng Xiaoping and other proponents of economic modernization realized they needed such people. This realization had to contend, however, with the ambivalence the leadership of the Communist Party, and for that matter the people of China, had always shown toward intellectuals.[12]

Intellectuals were respected in traditional China as masters of Confucian thought, calligraphy, and classical Chinese style. At the same time, though, they were resented as a dominant, often oppressive elite tied to the imperial bureaucracy. Westernization perpetuated this ambivalence. Intellectual ranks grew, but the role some played as purveyors of Western culture made others uneasy. The struggle to respond to the challenge of Western economic and military power helped to generate reform-oriented intellectual movements. However, the official intellectuals of the imperial bureaucracy by and large proved themselves inadequate to the challenge of reforming their own administration and strengthening China. Far too many remained arrogantly aloof from the needs of ordinary people, the corruption of the late Qing dynasty, and the general crisis of the late nineteenth and twentieth centuries. During the republican era (1911–1949), intellectual life was invigorated by the development of a public sphere and field of discourse separate from the state administration. Intellectuals attempted to reach out to less educated people and reconsidered their own leading role in China.[13] But despite the reform efforts of the New Culture movement, and despite the active role of a number of radical intellectuals, the communist revolution was led by those on the margins of the intellectual elite and oriented to those completely outside it—i.e., peasants and workers. Even during the Yannan years early in the revolution, intellectuals were subjected to repression.

Thousands of intellectuals nonetheless returned from study abroad to help build a new China after the 1949 revolution. Most, however, were treated with suspicion from the start and attacked repeatedly in campaigns of rectification and antirightism, culminating in the Cultural Revolution. They were branded the "stinking number nine," added to the other eight bad social groups: landlords, rich peasants, counter-revolutionaries, bad elements, rightists, renegades, enemy agents, and capitalist roaders. Peasant and worker skepticism toward intellectuals was nurtured and reinforced by ideological campaigns. Though Mao himself was an intellectual of a sort, a proud author of classical poetry, he was unwilling to encourage similar occupations in others.

Deng Xiaoping, by contrast, had fewer intellectual pretensions but was much readier to grant intellectuals an important place in Chinese society. As the main individual agent in ending and undoing the Cultural Revolution, he was deeply appreciated by many Chinese intellectuals. Students and young intellectuals told me in 1984, at a high point of reformist optimism, how Deng had personally saved them from bleak years of working with (and in some cases being tormented by) the peasants and how he had brought a large dose of meritocratic decisionmaking to a university admissions process previously dominated by political, class, and other nonintellectual criteria. Hundreds of professors had been restored to their senior university positions; writers had been able to publish again; scientists had returned to their laboratories. As economic performance and technical know-how were extolled, at least some intellectuals came to be seen as central to China's future. Intellectuals remembered that Deng had not always been their friend, but for the most part they entered into a tacit bargain. In exchange for the chance to be respected advisers to the government and the promise that there would be no return to the persecutions of the past and the chaos of the Cultural Revolution, they offered quiescence and tacit support to the regime.

But as the 1980s and the reforms progressed, the romance between Deng Xiaoping and the intellectuals faded. Deng revealed the limits to his interest in liberalization, especially outside the economic sphere. Technocrats who worked in engineering, demography, econometrics, or other applied sciences moved up rapidly in the bureaucracy and academic hierarchy; humanists and cultural scholars found their work less valued and more controversial by comparison. More and more of them worried that China lacked any real vision of what it meant to be Chinese in this era of reform. They grew not only concerned for China's soul and future direction but also unhappy with their own position and level of influence.

As intellectuals gained in stature and numbers, they began to gain confidence and to push for further liberalizations or even to attack the government.[14] The vanguard of this shift included astrophysicist Fang Lizhi, political scientist Yan Jiaqi, and investigative journalist Liu Binyan. As vice president of the Chinese University of Science and Technology, Fang joined with his colleagues to create a haven for free thought and nurturance of a more Western style of intellectual life. In and out of trouble with the Communist Party (of which he was a longtime member until his expulsion in 1986), Fang traveled the country speaking to receptive campus audiences about democracy and the social responsibility—and importance—of intellectuals:

> As an intellectual, one should be a driving force for society. One major aspect of the effort to push the society forward is to do a better job in our professional field so that we can give more to society. . . . Our social responsibility, so to speak, is for each of us here to work for a better social environment that will allow our intellectuals to make good use of their talent and work more efficiently. . . . One important sign of a developed society is that intellectuals have a say in social development and enjoy considerable influence.[15]

Fang was the Chinese intellectual who came closest to the Soviet and East European model of a dissident and indeed was sometimes called "China's Sakharov." Picking up a theme made prominent in the late 1970s by Ren Wanding, Fang probably did more than anyone else to spread the ideal of human rights as a basis for democracy: "What is the meaning of democracy? Democracy means that every human being has his own rights and that human beings, each exercising his own rights, form our society. Therefore, rights are in the hands of every citizen. They are not given by top leaders of the nation. All people are born with them."[16]

Yan Jiaqi was somewhat more cautious than Fang and more temperate in his arguments—at least before the 1989 protests. In both regards he was more typical of Chinese intellectuals, and he retained his Party membership right up until May 1989. While neither Fang nor Liu was an active force in the 1989 protests, however, Yan was perhaps the single most important senior intellectual publicly to take part in the movement. He was the principal author, for example, of the "May 17 Declaration," by which intellectuals first proclaimed themselves willing to join as a visible, organized group in the protests. In this statement, Yan spoke sharply: "It has been seventy-seven years since the downfall of the Qing Dynasty. Nevertheless, China still has an emperor who only lacks a formal title, and a dictator who is senile and incompetent."[17] As early as 1980, Yan had starkly criticized the persistence of "imperial power" and "imperial position" in communist China and called for reforms to abolish them. But he did not present this as being in any sense an attack on the Party; rather, it was a call for internal reform in accord with the Party's own principles.[18] He had wide contacts in Zhao Ziyang's reformist wing of the Party and stressed the idea that democracy is an "error-correction mechanism."[19]

"Democratic politics" is a kind of procedural politics. Democratic politics does not have to search for perfect "successors," but emphasizes human imperfectability; to err is human. When members of an organization or group disagree on a goal, view, or value, democracy means decision making and revising through predetermined procedures that members agree upon. Democracy cannot guarantee perfect decisions, but it can guarantee that wrong decisions may be corrected by following predetermined procedures.[20]

In the late 1980s, Yan later confirmed to me in an interview, he still thought China could make gradual progress toward democratization without a sharp break with the existing government. (Indeed, he still believes reformers can gain the upper hand after the death of Deng Xiaoping or some other development shakes up the current ruling coalitions.)

Above all, Yan was known in China for his history of the Cultural Revolution, which he wrote with his wife, Gao Gao. Party conservatives tried to repress the book, partly no doubt because it extensively documented the evils of the Cultural Revolution but perhaps more basically because it argued that the Cultural Revolution was not a mere accident or epiphenomenal deviation. The book sold more than eight hundred thousand copies in China and became one of the central works in the reexamination of the Cultural Revolution during the 1980s. This reexamination was perhaps the single greatest source of popular and especially intellectual disenchantment with the communist regime.

The greatest protagonist of the investigation into the Cultural Revolution and its abuses of official power was Liu Binyan. Like Fang Lizhi, Liu was expelled from the Chinese Communist Party (CCP) in 1986 for his increasing dissidence. But unlike Fang, Liu had been a sincere believer in the communist revolution. As a journalist, Liu specialized in documenting the corruption of local CCP officials and the failure of the Party hierarchy to do anything about it. Because he was himself a Party member writing in an officially controlled press, his exposés sometimes carried more weight than those in Western papers; people sought him out to try to get their problems resolved. He maintained voluminous files on investigations all over China, often working with teams of assistants. When he felt he had documented a wrong that needed to be righted, he might send a file directly to a senior Party official such as Hu Yaobang as well as (or instead of) publishing an article about it. Of course, Liu was not always successful, and often his articles backfired, bringing retaliation rather than redress to those whose grievances he documented.[21] Liu had been writing much the same sort of report for more than thirty years when he was finally expelled from the Party in 1987.

Liu Binyan joined the Communist Party as a teenager, five years before the 1949 revolution. He was active in the underground struggle first for liberation of China from Japanese occupation and then for Communist victory over the Guomindang. After the war, he returned to his plans for writing. "I wanted to use my pen to slash the pall hanging over China, to dispel the gloom and open up the mental horizons of the people."[22] Unfortunately for Liu, he thought the gloom could be disspelled through honest reporting on the causes of China's problems. In one of his first major articles, Liu had told of two engineers. One had built bridges entirely according to Party directives, failing to take emergency measures; when floods came early in 1954, the waters washed away the bridge support his team had built. The other refused to wait for orders from above, changed the plans, and saved his construction team's work. The Party promoted the first engineer and demoted the second.

And so it was for Liu, though he continued to exhibit the second sort of loyalty. Liu lost some twenty-two years of his life to labor reform among the peasants and other punishments. He had only been rehabilitated a few months from his condemnation as a rightist when the Cultural Revolution began in 1966 and he was again attacked. Yet even in the midst of his sufferings, Liu could see positive potential in the Cultural Revolution's promise to decentralize China and its attack on bureaucratism, corruption, and special privileges for Party leaders. Though he was one of the most resolute and effective opponents of those who came to power during the Cultural Revolution, Liu was alone among intellectuals in his respect for its ideals. In this, and in having genuinely been a revolutionary, Liu was quite different from Fang Lizhi. He still believed in the ideals that motivated him to become a Communist in the first place. He was not just a spokesman for intellectuals but a man who clearly cared about all sorts of ordinary people; he wanted their freedom and their democracy as well as his own.[23]

For all the personal troubles and sharp criticism visited on Fang, Yan, and Liu, the three maintained a certain optimism, an expectation that China would succeed in reforming itself and joining the world's democracies, a consciousness that their very capacity for voice was a good sign. By 1989 students were more pessimistic and focused on the negative. A poster on the Monument to the People's Heroes addressed Li Peng in April: "You say the 'Number Nines' are only members of the working class; how can we possibly accept this?"[24] Still, it should be noted that a genuine liberalization had taken place. The repression of the 1986–87 dissent had been mild. Publishing was still far more open than it had been during the first three decades of the People's Republic. A variety of think tanks had been founded, some linked to Party reformers, others funded privately. Intellectuals were not just making speeches; they also were organizing in practical ways. This increasingly vital intellectual life in China led students to see a more urgent role for themselves and senior intellectuals as guides and consciences for the country.

The student protest movement of 1989 began with a central focus on issues of concern to students, who saw themselves as young and uncompromised intellectuals. The movement eventually made connections to a much wider range of people, however, through its condemnation of corruption. People whose concerns were primarily economic nonetheless responded to the students' initiative in confronting the government. At its core, however, this remained a student movement, framed primarily in terms of the specific concerns of intellectuals, especially such civil liberties as freedom of speech, publication, and assembly. These ends were sought not just out of selfishness but out of a sense that China needed the advice intellectuals had to offer.

Cultural Crisis

China's intellectuals, scientists almost as much as humanists, were preoccupied in 1989 with a sense of cultural crisis. Some experienced this crisis mainly through comparisons with the West and jointly condemned China's traditions and current leaders. Others focused on the disruption of traditional culture precipitated by late Qing incompetence and corruption, exacerbated by confrontation with the West, and continued by the antiintellectual Communists. For both groups—and all who shared some views with each—the question of just what it would mean to be Chinese in the twenty-first century was of pressing personal importance. It was an issue not just of strategic or optional concern but of basic individual and collective identity. It went beyond the question of whether China would take its rightful place as one of the world's great powers to the question of what China, with any cultural integrity, could *be*.

Nearly everyone wanted to be proud of China and felt at least a twinge of humiliation at its current poverty and weakness, but not everyone was sure it could or should go on being the same China. To say so was still shocking, whether one meant the People's Republic or the traditional China that four thousand years of civilized history had left unprepared for the modern era. Poets and philosophers meditated on cultural identity. Economists and technicians debated whether Chinese culture was a block to modernization. Physicists such as Fang Lizhi and political scientists such as Yan Jiaqi could find common ground simultaneously praising the democratic openness of Western culture and the respect Western political leaders showed intellectual elites.

These concerns spread beyond the intellectual community. The repeated convulsions of the communist era—Great Leap Forward, Anti-Rightist Campaign, Cultural Revolution—had been profoundly unsettling. People felt a loss of personal moorings that stemmed from cultural dislocation as well as from more private injuries—damage to their careers or to their interpersonal networks. The coming of a new level of prosperity and rapid social change only accentuated the anxiety. Television, for example, had spread during the 1980s to even the most remote areas. Parents wondered why their children showed a lack of respect—and why they insisted on wearing blue jeans and strange hairstyles, listening to rock music, and reading incomprehensible poetry. Such concerns were not unique to China, but in China they were widely interpreted as part of a deeper crisis of culture. It was not just that the values of parental respect and poetic form were more basic in China than elsewhere. The crisis of cultural identity challenged individual identity as well. Chinese youths even underwent plastic surgery, altering noses and eyelids, to conform to what they saw as Western standards of appearance.[25]

The sense of cultural crisis was linked to political and economic questions. Were the Chinese people culturally incapable of democracy? Were basic failings in Chinese culture responsible for making the world's most populous and ancient country, once one of its strongest and wealthiest, now both poor and weak? Was there some cultural defect that made Chinese people put up with the evils and abuses of Maoist communism? More than anything else, the crisis of culture at the end of the 1980s was precipitated by the upheavals of the 1960s. The Cultural Revolution was both the greatest of the attacks on traditional Chinese culture carried out by the Maoist regime and the cause of severe psychosocial injury. Children condemned their parents publicly and joined in abusing them. Sisters attacked brothers; wives informed on husbands; and whole communities joined in reviling their own members and revering distant leaders who in retrospect seemed the cause of heartbreak and ruin, not of salvation. How could this have happened if Chinese culture had been healthy? How could it be changed?

Some responded to these concerns with a turn toward introspection. Others became wholesale Westernizers. Still others took up calligraphy or founded institutes devoted to the study of Confucian thought. Whatever the response, however, the widespread feeling that all was not well with Chinese culture fueled a burgeoning discourse that helped pave the way for the 1989 protests. A new magazine seemed to be founded every few weeks in the late 1980s.[26] Original books and translations were published at a startling rate. Leading intellectuals drew enormous crowds when they arrived on college campuses to discuss the links between culture and the contemporary situation, echoing the famous formulation of 1919: science and democracy. For in that formulation—in 1989 as in 1919—science did not mean simply a specialized laboratory pursuit. It meant—much as it had in eighteenth-century Europe—enlightenment. And enlightenment was not just a state of mind; it was a cultural pursuit that involved reforms of almost infinite variety. In 1919 linguistic reform and the promotion of literacy were central. By 1989 reform embraced experimental theater and film—and spread throughout cultural production. At the same time, however, the decidedly mixed legacy of China's greatest experiment in cultural reform—Maoist communism—led many to a positive revaluation of traditional Chinese culture that did not figure similarly in 1919.

THEMES AND PLAN

Underlying conditions make a movement possible, but they do not make the movement happen. In the first place, underlying conditions are relatively continuous; they change more slowly than movements start. People respond to those conditions in a variety of ways, both individually and collectively, but these responses seldom coalesce into rapid growth of coordinated activity. A window of opportunity—often created by some unexpected event or short-term emergency—is generally needed before one of the many potential starts actually becomes a movement. The death of Hu Yaobang combined with the succession crisis and other underlying conditions to provide that opportunity in 1989.[27]

However, movements are products of human action, not purely mechanistic responses to opportunities, conditions, beliefs, or interests. To emphasize action is not necessarily to stress rational choice, calculation, and advance planning, though these may all be significant. The action in social movements consists also of choices made in the heat of struggle, decisions made on the run, and the sort of half-conscious improvisation that allows jazz musicians to harmonize and debaters to utter a verbal jab before they have even articulated it to themselves. In making the 1989 movement, students responded improvisationally to a wide variety of opportunities and stimuli. The ad-libbed nature of such behavior is an important reason it needs to be grasped in narrative context, in relation to previous moves, countermoves, mood swings, and changing conditions. The dynamic nature of students' actions constitutes the first theme of this book.

To form a movement, though, activists' improvisations had to mesh with each other. This was far from a perfect process; clashes were frequent, and in the end the movement was pulled apart from within as well as crushed from outside. But at times different individuals and groups could join together effectively because they had common backgrounds, because they shared certain historical memories, because they had read, listened to, or participated in the same intellectual debates, because they were addressed by the same speeches and posters, because they were actors in the same sociocultural field, and because they were knit together in a dense network of interpersonal relations. A second theme of this book will be the importance of the social and cultural factors that both enabled and shaped the movement.

People always have grievances and desires, but they do not always launch social movements. Movements need to be explained not simply in terms of goals, therefore, but also in terms of how people get them organized and gain support.[28] We need to ask how potential participants find each other, get the material resources they need, identify leaders with necessary skills, and gain access to media and broader publics. This is a question about both the preexisting bases on which they build and their own new mobilization. Of course, we also need to see the resources those who defend the status quo (or who prefer different courses of change) are able to bring to bear in resisting the movement.

Resource mobilization analyses have frequently approached these issues with great emphasis on material and social structural factors and little focus on culture. It is crucial to grasp the social bases of protest (and resistance) but equally crucial to see how cultural patterns and tensions facilitate or inhibit, shape, and channel mobilization. For one thing, as Douglas McAdam has stressed, we need to ask how participants gain the "cognitive liberation" to think they can actually achieve a significant change in the status quo through their collective actions.[29] In 1989 both enduring cultural patterns and specific discussions shaped what students thought possible and desirable and influenced how their deeds. In this sense, culture means broader dimensions of knowledge, understanding, values, and habits, not merely ideology. Moreover, I do not mean to suggest that cultural and social organizational dimensions of collective action can be understood separately from each other. They are closely intertwined in issues such as how a public sphere of open, critical discussion might be constituted.

Though I certainly ascribe causal force to such social and cultural factors, I do not want to suggest that the course of the movement or the actions of individuals can be deduced from such background conditions. Attentiveness to the rich range of possibilities and to the specifics of narrative sequences is one of the very positive trends in recent analyses of social movements. We must not assume that everything that did happen had to happen, and we need to consider how timing and conjuncture, not just background conditions, helped determine the events in the course of the movement. But there is a further reason I have chosen to begin this account with a sustained narrative, even though much of what I describe is well known:[30] The very identities of participants in the student protest movement changed in the course of the events.

I mean "changed" in three senses. First, although the main protagonists throughout (except perhaps during the crackdown) were students, this general term obscures the extent to which different students were involved at different points in the movement. Early leaders faded from the scene, and students from outside Beijing grew in numbers and influence. Second, in addition to such more or less linear changes, the composition of crowds shifted with the specific nature of events. Women figured more prominently in the hunger strike than in the preceding marches. Some occasions drew more students with low commitment; some drew more nonstudents. Third, and I think most theoretically challenging, is the sense in which the identities of the same people changed through and because of their participation in the movement. The movement was marked by wild swings of emotion, euphorias and panics, periods of calm and of intense activity, sleepless nights and midday fainting spells, all of which reshaped the consciousness of its participants. Deeply involved participants were cut off from the more routine schedules and habits of everyday life. As they attempted to absorb their experiences and invested themselves in the emotional intensity of the movement, they were transformed. Such change is part of the meaning of commitment—whether long-term or evanescent—and one of the sources of heroism. It also limits the extent to which a movement can be explained on the basis of the preexisting interests or structural positions of participants. Being attentive to the shifting identities of participants in all three of these senses helps reveal that a movement—even one that lasts only six weeks—is not all one thing, that it has an internal temporal rhythm.

These three themes—actions, social and cultural factors, and changes in identity of participants—inform my narrative account, though I have tried not to break its flow for lengthy discussion of such analytic points. The three themes come together more explicitly in chapter 4, which opens the second, analytic part of the book (though full discussion of the third theme awaits the conclusion). Chapter 4 examines the senses in which the movement was both spontaneous and organized (though not altogether either). As Pierre Bourdieu has shown, to see that an action is a creative improvisation does not mean that it lacks social structure or cultural models.[31] Students were able to do something remarkably new only by appropriating existing ties and organizational roles, templates from historical knowledge, and rhetoric and understandings from widely shared culture. In addition to tapping these cultural sources, students drew on preexisting personal networks and formal associations and created new organizations.

Chapters 5 through 8 shift attention from the dynamic tension between action and structure to questions about the movement's ideological content, cultural orientation, and place in a broader understanding of cultural production. What, for example, did students mean by "democracy," or *minzhu*, a term that was repeated over and over again? Chapter 7 explores this question directly, both in terms of what students said about democracy and in terms of their relationship to other groups of Chinese citizens. But neither this specific question nor broader questions about the meaning of the movement can be handled adequately by looking just within the movement. Student protest was shaped by the emergence—by no means complete—of a civil society in which citizens were linked outside the direct control of the state and of a public sphere not restricted to intellectuals. Television and movies, pop songs and pulp magazines, correspondence colleges and think tanks, even the proliferation of small businesses such as restaurants allowed ideas to circulate widely, providing for ideological connections between the protesting students and other citizens. The attempt to play in this larger public sphere kept the movement from focusing only on students' particular interests but also made it much more threatening to the government. This public sphere gave the movement its crucial, constitutive ability to play to an international audience at the same time that it played to China generally, to urban people more specifically, and to Beijing elites and the government especially. Still, this public sphere was sharply limited, not only in terms of who could participate effectively but also in terms of how well it allowed for rational critical discourse (as distinct from competitive publicity management). This returns us to democracy, which depends on a vital public sphere that nurtures critical discourse across crucial lines of difference. These matters are addressed in chapter 5.

Critical discourse was not the great strength of China's student protesters in 1989. Neither was an appreciation for the range of different social groups in China and how they might relate to the project of democracy. Students acted in a special sense as members of an intellectual elite with a long, if ambivalent, tradition. They sought to be spokespeople for the Chinese nation. They sought, indeed, to save the nation, a task they saw as their special responsibility. This belief helps explain why they took such umbrage at the government's April 26 suggestion that their motives were less than patriotic and why they kept asking to the end of the movement for official retraction of that accusation. It is impossible to make sense of the movement simply by examining the selfish interests of the students as a category of individual actors; they were moved by a sense of national identity and of profound cultural crisis. This is the theme of chapter 6.

The students' sense of cultural crisis and identification with their country linked them in important ways to much of the population of China. It linked them also to earlier patriots who pursued the project of national salvation (*jiuguo*). But the linkage was always asymmetric, because in the students' understanding the project of national salvation depended in a special way on intellectual leadership and cultural production. The Chinese nation could only really be evoked and represented in its full, unitary, and integral sense by China's intellectuals. Businesspeople might pursue fortunes based on networks of kin-relations spanning state boundaries (e.g., from Guangzhou to Hong Kong, Singapore, and Vancouver) and crave any form of political security as much as democratic rule. Intellectuals, by contrast, gained influence from the coincidence of Chinese culture with a Chinese state; not only their personal resources and opportunities for advancement but also their opportunity to act as government advisers and voices of the people made them value an autonomous, unified, and democratic China. Students' understandings of the pursuit of democracy, in short, were influenced by the traditionally privileged role of Chinese intellectuals in politics and public discourse. This tradition limited the extent to which students made common cause with other Chinese citizens.

Assessing such limits is a final theme in this book, but to acknowledge limitations is in no sense to denigrate. For the students made an extraordinary statement, one that moved contemporaries throughout the world and one that will continue to move Chinese aspirants to democracy for generations. A final reason the main text of this book begins with a narrative, then, is simply to let readers grasp some of the sheer excitement of it all. We fail to understand social movements—especially great bursts of activity compressed in time—if we forget how new each day seems amid such drama, how open to disaster or heroism or the making of history. Understanding must involve a narrative and some sense of the movement as process, not fait accompli.

Part One

THE EXPERIENCE
OF THE MOVEMENT
A Narrative

1 Mounting Protest

Through the winter and early spring of 1988–89, groups of young teachers and students gathered on Beijing's university campuses. Six or seven might meet in a dormitory room. Sometimes, as confidence grew, a hundred would gather on a campus lawn for open discussion. At Beijing University (Beida), the favored spot was a patch of grass graced by a statue of Miguel Cervantes—erected, with a symbolism students only half appreciated, in honor of the Spaniard's cultural iconoclasm and his great novel of spiritual quest, which had been very popular among China's early-twentieth-century intellectuals (including those who founded Beida). In all these gatherings, debate centered on democracy and paths for China's modernization.

In the late 1980s, China's students and intellectuals were once again prepared to take up the responsibilities of trying to speak truth to power, of trying to bring enlightenment to the country, of trying to save the nation. These themes had been on the minds of students and young teachers for years. Their expression had ebbed and flowed with the periodic, temporary relaxations of repression that had come every few years since 1976. Before then, such themes had been central to some of the discourse of the Great Proletarian Cultural Revolution (though in a very different context), to the Hundred Flowers flurry of criticism in 1959, and, before communism, to the self-strengthening movement, to Tan Sitong and other rebels of 1895, to Kang Youwei and his critical neo-Confucianism, to Liang Qichao and many makers of the 1911 revolution, and to Lu Xun and all the protagonists of the public discourse that grew as the republic faltered after 1919.

A few worried about the instability of this mixture of intellectual programs. Li Zehou, for example, argued in a widely read essay that Chinese intellectuals should stick to the long, slow struggle for enlightenment and resist the temptation to shift—as their predecessors had too often done—into a blind passion for national salvation.[1] Enlightenment meant the pursuit of knowledge and the growth of rational-critical thought; national salvation (*jiuguo*) signified China's need to be strong and whole in the face of external threat and internal fragmentation. Creating a strong link between the two concepts has been a long-standing dream: Ideally, the truth should not only set individuals free but also make China strong. But Li Zehou worried that if the problems of enlightenment and national salvation were too deeply intertwined, then intellectuals, unable to tell them apart, would once again collude in pursuits that would eventually imprison them. A few even toyed with the notion of a "New Authoritarianism," which was current among some followers of Zhao Ziyang who admired the development of Singapore and South Korea. Wang Juntao, for example, was a Beijing University physicist-turned-professional reformer and social scientist. He had devoted his entire adult life to the cause of democracy but still refused to dismiss the idea of New Authoritarianism out of hand. The reason was largely the disorder into which the reform era had fallen. Using almost the same play on words that students had earlier employed to turn the government's accusation of "turmoil" into a claim of "free-form dancing", some of the social scientists associated with Wang argued that if the Cultural Revolution had been ten years of turmoil (*dongluan*), then the reform era was ten years of aimless drifting (another sense of *luandong*).

Another physicist, Fang Lizhi, had traveled around China's universities attempting to explain the democratic attitude and to motivate China's intellectuals to insist on their role in modernization. "We should have our own judgment about what is right, good, and beautiful in our academic field, free from the control of political power, before we can achieve modernization and true democracy, and not the so-called democracy," he said.[2] Fang's message appealed because it meshed the concern for enlightenment through knowledge with elitist intellectual pride and a strong notion of individual freedom. "It's up to the intellectuals as a class," he argued, "with their sense of social responsibility, their consciousness about democracy, and their initiative to strive for their rights, to decide whether the democratic system can survive and develop in a given society."[3] At the same time, "In democratic countries, democracy begins with the individual. *I* am the master, and the government is responsible to *me*."[4]

Perhaps as important as the content of Fang's message, however, was the very fact that he got away with delivering it. Fang demonstrated that someone could stand up and criticize the Communist Party leadership openly without being struck down, arrested, or simply silenced. A decade before, the Democracy Wall movement had ended in sharp repression. Its most important leader, Wei Jingsheng, remained in prison, incommunicado and perhaps driven mad by solitary confinement. Though students had launched occasional protests during the 1980s, they had attracted little support from more established intellectuals, who had made a kind of peace with the reform-era regime. In 1988 this peace began to fall apart.

A variety of major cultural events and discussions seem retrospectively to have signaled the coming crisis. The most prominent was a television series, *Heshang* (*River Elegy*), which explored the meaning of the Yellow River, the major watercourse of China's traditional heartland. The series suggested that Chinese culture, turned in on itself and cut off from the larger world, was in danger of becoming extinct like that of ancient Egypt.[5] *Heshang* was not alone in expressing anxiety about the vitality of Chinese culture and exasperation that a country with such a proud past could be a comparative weakling in the late twentieth century. One of the effects of the reform era's relative openness was that information from abroad revealed how China had suffered—and perhaps, said the critics, *still* suffered—from government attempts to limit Western influences.

Through most of 1988 the focus stayed on broad cultural questions and themes such as the New Authoritarianism, which the government itself was willing to countenance. But in the late fall, the seeds of a more concrete movement began to be sown. Two foci of organization were crucial.

First, the coming seventieth anniversary of the May Fourth movement, revered as the high point of modern Chinese student and intellectual activism, offered the opportunity for commemoration with a critical edge. In December, several veteran activists from the 1978–79 Democracy Wall protests rented the State Council's Number 2 Guest Hostel at Xizhimen, near the Beijing Zoo, to lay plans.[6] Chen Ziming organized the gathering with his colleague Wang Juntao; the two ran one of Beijing's most active private think tanks, conducting public opinion research on contract and for their own interest. Zhou Duo, an economist with the Stone Computer Corporation (China's most prominent privately owned company), was in the chair, assisted by Zhang Gang, a Red Guard activist during the Cultural Revolution and now deputy director of Zhao Ziyang's main think tank.

Second, the fate of Wei Jingsheng, hero-martyr of the Democracy Wall movement, was once again made an issue. One of his most important colleagues from the movement, Ren Wanding, started a call for Wei Jingsheng's release in December 1988. During the Democracy Wall protests, Ren had been the founder of the China Human Rights League; now he released a letter he had written to international human rights organizations both about Wei and about prisoners being held for their participation in the 1987 student demonstrations. Fang Lizhi followed with a letter to Deng Xiaoping in January linking Wei's cause to the May Fourth anniversary and explicitly placing his own advocacy of science and democracy in both traditions. This was followed on February 13 by another open letter, this one from thirty-three artists and academics (mostly humanists) organized by the poet Bei Dao and former student activist Chen Jun:

> We are deeply concerned with Mr. Fang Lizhi's January 6, 1989, open letter to Chairman Deng Xiaoping. We believe that on the occasion of the fortieth anniversary of the establishment of the PRC and the seventieth anniversary of the May Fourth Movement, the granting of an amnesty, especially the release of political prisoners like Wei Jingsheng, will create a harmonious atmosphere conducive to reforms and at the same time conform with the world's general trend that human rights are increasingly respected.[7]

On February 23 Chen announced the creation of an unofficial "working group to investigate the condition of political detainees," which he called "Amnesty '89."[8] In early March a group of forty-two intellectuals, mainly from scientific and technical fields, followed with yet another petition. These entreaties to free Wei Jingsheng, and more generally to encourage liberalization, marked perhaps the most organized and forceful intellectual challenge to the government in the history of the PRC. As Perry Link comments: "Although the petitions failed to free any prisoners, their very considerable significance was to mark the first time in Communist Chinese history that intellectuals have, as a group, publicly opposed the top leader on a sensitive issue."[9]

When Fang's initial open letter and the two following petitions drew a stern warning that things must go no further, a group of intellectuals responded with a third petition. It was pointedly signed by forty-three scholars, one more than had signed the second, and was again from a group composed primarily of cultural specialists.

Each open letter or petition revealed through its signatures the pattern of both a social network and the categories within the Chinese intellectual field. By alternating groups of natural scientists and technologists in a kind of counterpoint with cultural producers and humanistic scholars, the letters made a subtle point: They neatly represented the diversity of intellectuals addressing the government in a unified protest. At least symbolically, the intellectuals thus overcame the Confucian division of technical skill from cultural essence that had dogged them throughout the modern era; they now spoke as members of a single social field, capable of coordinated action. The government could no longer exploit internal divisions by urging that Western expertise be imported for economic purposes only, without the contamination of "bourgeois individualism" and notions such as human rights.

These intellectuals built on the heroic efforts of standout figures such as Fang Lizhi and investigative journalist Liu Binyan. Crucially, though, they defied the government as an organized group, not simply as courageous individuals. This cooperation marked a break from previous examples of dissent, including those of Fang and Liu. As Chen Ziming reportedly said in April:

> China's independent intelligentsia has risen in history. Its next step to-ward maturity obviously requires a process of organizing, and [it must] move forward from a politically conscious to an organizationally powerful force. . . . The epochal duty of the intelligentsia, of the advanced elements of the intelligentsia in particular, is rapidly to complete the process of organiz-ing the intelligentsia [in order to] form a new source of leadership for the common people.[10]

The early March petition from the group of forty-two intellectuals summed up the widely shared demands:

1. political democratisation to stimulate economic development and end corruption;
2. freedom of speech and freedom of the press;
3. the release of political prisoners and no further convictions on grounds of ideology;
4. increased funding for education and research, and improved remunera-tion for intellectuals.[11]

New institutional bases furthered both political discussions and intellec-tuals' organizing. Coffeehouses and restaurants provided space for this nas-cent public sphere; some even operated on campuses, leasing their facilities from the universities. Future protest leader Shen Tong's "Olympic Insti-tute," for example, met each Wednesday in a restaurant near Beida; when protest came, groups like this could be transformed from mere discussion forums into bases for mobilization.[12] Intellectuals emulated Shanghai of the 1920s (as well as Greenwich Village of the 1950s and 1960s and London of the 1780s) in opening a "New Enlightenment Salon" for tea and critical analysis in the basement of the centrally located Dule (Happiness) Bookstore. The salon also promoted the short-lived journal *New Enlighten-ment*,[13] and the Dule itself was reputed to be the first private bookstore in China since 1949.

Even more important, perhaps, were the proliferating think tanks and research institutes. Many of these were sponsored by the government, particularly by reform factions allied with Zhao Ziyang. A few were set up by major private business corporations such as the Stone Computer Corporation. Others were headquartered on campuses or created as more autonomous academic institutions. Chen Ziming and Wang Juntao had actually bought the Beijing Social and Economic Sciences Research Institute from the government's Chinese Academy of Social Sciences and funded it with revenue from a pair of correspondence colleges Chen had created in 1985.[14] Other intellectual centers remained part of the government's higher education or scientific establishment but were increasingly free from close supervision. These institutes and centers sponsored a rich and complex discourse on subjects ranging from the revitalization of traditional Chinese culture to the development of appropriate business law for the country's emerging commercial sector.

Many of the graduate students and junior faculty members who led the discussions on the university campuses in the winter and early spring of 1988–89 had developed their intellectual positions in the context of these institutes. They were the editors of series of books in translation, makers of television documentaries about China's crisis, authors of sociological analyses of public issues. Some were already well known, others had little public recognition, but all were crucial links between China's emerging public sphere and the specific local discussions on individual campuses. Their audiences were drawn largely from undergraduates. At first, many attendees were simply student fans of popular young teachers; they primarily listened, participating only as disciples. But students quickly grew anxious to take some direct action, not just to talk. Undergraduate student leaders came increasingly to the fore, voicing opinions of their own, laying out their own ideas for China's future and for the role students could play in nudging that better future into being.

Undergraduates were not just passive listeners; some, like Wang Dan, attracted admiration for speaking up in large public gatherings. Many were involved in small discussion groups of their own. Wang Dan met with a "Wednesday Forum" before the "Democracy Salon," which met next to Beida's Cervantes statue, got started. Shen Tong's Olympic Institute drew together a number of Beida science students. Wuerkaixi, probably the most famous of all the student protesters, was involved in a "Confucius Study

Society" at Beijing Normal University. These groups gave undergraduates forums of their own, which helped to nurture both their ideas and their abilities to express them. Many of the most prominent movement leaders came from such groups.[15] Gradually, especially as themes became more daring, undergraduates came to dominate more and more of the big campus assemblies, with graduate students and teachers pushed into the background.

In Beijing, the discussions were perhaps most intense at Beijing University, followed by those at Beijing Normal, People's, and Qinghua universities; they were, however, not limited to these elite schools. Each of these four major universities of the Haidian district saw substantial organizing as well as talking, as did several of the more specialized schools, such as the University of Politics and Law. Outside Beijing there were few comparable centers of dissent and discussion—Tianjin offered one at Nankai University, and Shanghai and Nanjing provided others, though on a lesser scale. Still, universities throughout China shared in the general debate about social transformation, and there were few where the idea of democracy was not voiced. Fang Lizhi's trips took him to teacher training institutes as well as leading universities; he traversed all the major central regions of China. Thus, foundations were being prepared for the public protest that was to come.

That public protest was to come is not just the knowledge of hindsight; demonstrations were already being conceived in that busy winter and spring. The campus discussions often turned to the question of what sort of protest could make the views of dissatisfied students and young intellectuals known.[16] The idea of using the coming May Fourth anniversary as an occasion had gained widespread assent. The famous 1919 student protest movement symbolized both a crucial era in China's struggle for democracy and modernization and the importance of students as the agents of protest and struggle.

In this earlier wave of dissent—the New Culture movement—students from Beijing University had formed reading societies and published magazines; they had taken their message beyond the university gates to give street-corner lectures and make forays into peasant villages. Their message had turned on the ideas of science and democracy and on the need to revitalize China by transforming both culture and politics. The 1919 activists challenged Confucianism and traditional learning as being worn out, hindrances to China's development. Though heavily influenced by Western thought, they sought a specifically Chinese idiom for their speech and writing and shared in a nationalist consciousness that bridled at China's weakness and apparent backwardness in world affairs. When, at the Versailles Peace Conference, China's "allies" in World War I awarded Japan sovereignty over Manchuria and key Chinese ports that had been held by Germany, the students took to the streets in public protest. They attacked the feeble republican government for being unable to press China's interests on the international scene. In producing a partially nationalist protest against domestic rulers deemed responsible for international weakness as well as repression at home, the New Culture movement foreshadowed the events of 1989.[17]

The May Fourth movement had been hailed by the Communist Party as a major step on the path to national liberation. Its seventieth anniversary was to be the occasion of conferences, publications, and a public holiday. Led by Wang Dan, students at Beijing University posted an open letter calling on authorities to honor the movement's memory by encouraging free speech on campus.

> This year marks the seventieth anniversary of the May Fourth Movement. As the birthplace of this extraordinary movement of democratic enlightenment, Beijing University has always held high the banners of democracy and science and marched at the very forefront of our nation's progress. Today, as Chinese commemorate the May Fourth Movement, we, students of Beijing University, the hallowed ground of democracy, continue to hope that we will be able to carry on the distinguished tradition of Beijing University.[18]

The letter recounted their activity:

> Beginning last semester and continuing today, from activity Room 430 in Building 43 to the "democracy lawn" in front of the statue of Cervantes, thirteen democracy salons have been spontaneously organized by students concerned with the future of the country and the Chinese nation.[19]

Citing the example of Eastern Europe as well as China's May Fourth movement, Wang concluded that recent events called to mind "the spirit of 1956."[20]

As the discussions grew, nervous Party and Security Department authorities began to interfere with the salons. In response, the students posted their petition as a big character poster and called for the authorities' support (as indeed the Beida authorities had supported the 1919 movement). The university, they argued, should encourage, not resist, the democratic initiative, which would both serve the nation and "enliven the academic atmosphere." "Beijing University should serve as a special zone for promoting the democratization of politics; it should make a contribution to the progress of Chinese democracy," read their petition.[21] It was posted on April 3, as student organizers geared up for the May Fourth anniversary. This landmark day would afford what they thought to be a perfect opportunity to stage a moderate, but symbolically powerful and widely noticed, protest.

SURPRISE OPPORTUNITY: THE DEATH OF HU YAOBANG

As it happened, events offered the student activists an even more perfect occasion to step off the university campuses, out of mere dialogue and into active, open dissent: the death of Hu Yaobang on April 15.

Hu had been head of the Communist Party during the last major Chinese student protests (1986–87) and had been dismissed for not controlling them more forcefully. His downfall had made him a sort of martyr to the movement, even though he was by no means an advocate of everything the students had stood for. Hu was a long-time Communist and protégé of Deng Xiaoping; their relationship dated back to the revolution and was rooted partly, according to rumor, in a shared passion for bridge. An energetic reformer and proponent of changes that depended on the good will and participation of China's intellectuals, Hu was much more favorably disposed to the West than most of China's leadership. While I was in China in 1984, he had even suggested that the nation abandon chopsticks for forks, condemning China's traditional eating utensils as a feudal inheritance. Hu was in the vanguard of elite sartorial change, abandoning so-called Mao suits (narrow-collared tunics that actually date back to Jiang Jieshi [Sun Yatsen] and the early twentieth-century reformers and revolutionaries) for tailored Western suits and ties.[22]

As general secretary of the Communist Party, Hu had encouraged intellectuals in their growing openness to Western ideas. He had resisted moves by party hard-liners to rein in growing liberalization and talk of democracy but had paid for this stance with a demotion and public confession. Because student protest had been the occasion for Hu's fall from power, students felt a special connection to him. But this affinity should not be exaggerated. Hu was not a supporter of everything students thought important, and he remained a member of the Party, willing to submit himself to its discipline. Shen Tong's mild praise represents student thought more accurately than do the passionate elegies composed in part to goad the government: "I thought old Hu was rather timid compared to the arrogant Deng Xiaoping, but like many other students, I placed a lot of my hope in him, because he had always been one of the more open-minded and honest of the Party leaders."[23] Perhaps Hu's most important distinction from the rest of the Party leaders was that he had something of a "common touch." He was a more lively character than Zhao Ziyang but not dramatically more reformist. Nonetheless, his death provided the crucial impetus for launching the democratic protest movement. As Ren Wanding noted, "Like the April Fifth incident [mourning Zhou Enlai in 1976], people took the opportunity to commemorate a dead man in order to wage an anti-feudal, anti-authoritarian, pro-socialist struggle."[24]

Hu was not mourned with a deep outpouring of sentiment, as Zhou Enlai had been thirteen years earlier.[25] Then, spontaneous displays of grief for Mao's friendlier counterpart had led to massive gatherings in Tiananmen Square. Violent repression had created the April 5, 1976 Tiananmen Incident, which in turn helped catalyze the overthrow of the Gang of Four, the end of the Cultural Revolution, and (after a brief reversal) the return to power of Deng Xiaoping. The mourning for Zhou offered a ritual template to the 1989 protesters; however, Hu's death was a pretext for demonstrations that had their roots elsewhere. Students carried pictures of Hu, some ten feet tall; those at the Central Academy of Fine Arts painted a massive oil portrait specifically for the occasion and laid it on the Monument to the People's Heroes in Tiananmen Square. There were sincere regrets at his death and some suspicion about its causes (he died following a heart attack suffered a week earlier, and rumors attributed it to insults suffered during a Politburo meeting). Posters and placards praised Hu, but the signs are better understood as part of a carefully aimed message for Deng Xiaoping and the hard-liners of the Communist Party. As Wuerkaixi summed up: "The death of a citizen, even of a communist, never causes much excitement; which is perhaps a problem in itself. The fact that the death of this democratic leader has led to such immense chaos shows just how unsatisfactory the situation is in China."[26]

Because students had already begun to organize in anticipation of the May Fourth anniversary, they were ready to respond to Hu's death almost instantly. The first *dazibao* (large character posters) appeared within hours of the news of his death in places such as the Triangle Area at Beijing University. On this campus version of a democracy wall, students proclaimed that the wrong man had died: "Yaobang is dead, but Xiaoping still lives" was not a slogan rejoicing in the older man's continued good health. In case the oblique reference was unclear, others were more blunt. Couplets on Beijing University posters read:

Those who should have died live,
Those who should have lived have died.

A sincere and honest man has died,
But the hypocritical and false live on.

A warm-hearted man has died,
Indifference buried him.

It is difficult for one man to illuminate the country,
But one man is enough to make the country perish.[27]

As students took to the streets in growing numbers after April 15, this message was heard quite clearly by Deng and his cohorts. The protesters were loudly voicing disapproval of their leadership, particularly their failure to listen adequately to students and intellectuals.

The aging leaders initially tolerated the protests for a number of reasons. In the first place, of course, it was awkward to challenge mourning for a deceased head of the Communist Party. Beyond this, they seemed to hope the protests would be easier to contain after they had run their course. Reform-oriented leaders in particular wanted to avoid alienating students and intellectuals any further. Such officials—even those who sought not radical reform but only modernization—knew that the support and enthusiasm of educated people were essential to their plans for technological and economic advancement.

The initial flurry of posters and speeches grew into substantial marches. Perhaps as many as five to ten thousand people marched to Tiananmen Square on April 18 and rallied in front of the Great Hall of the People. Most of these were students from Beijing's elite universities. Organizing was made easier by the fact that several of these institutions were clustered together in the Haidian district of northwest Beijing. Beijing University was the oldest and still perhaps the most prestigious. Qinghua University sometimes styled itself "China's MIT," but though it excelled in the sciences and engineering it also had a variety of first-rate programs in the humanities. People's University (Renda) had grown in recent years both in size and intellectual stature and was an important center of training for both reform-oriented intellectuals and technocrats. Beijing Normal University focused on training teachers but was more elite and central to Chinese higher education than the "normal" label would suggest. In addition to these large schools, several more specialized institutions were also located in the Haidian district, with thousands of students more or less available for mobilization. These academies included the Beijing Foreign Studies University (Beiwai), where I taught. Initially a small college for international studies, then an institute of foreign languages, it had grown (especially during the reform era) into an elite school for the study of foreign cultures and social institutions.

Students at all these universities had high hopes for their own careers; they were an elite selected for the top schools in a country where only about 1 or 2 percent of the college-age population can go on to higher education at all. Their status within the intellectual world, however, was challenged by their uncertainty about intellectuals' status within society at large. They knew they were essential to reform, but they also knew that China was run by old men whose claims to leadership were revolutionary war achievements and personal connections, not diplomas. They knew that ordinary Chinese regarded intellectuals with a mixture of respect and resentment. Students were moved not only by their own personal ambitions, however, but also by ambitions for their country. They were nationalists, even though they admired the West, and they wanted China to gain in world stature.

At first they were cautious, well aware of the penalties that authorities had visited on their predecessors. This was, after all, China's third substantial "prodemocracy" movement in a decade. Participants in the others had been sent to poor jobs in remote provinces or even jailed. The early posters created an environment that encouraged risk-taking and activism; one of the more poetic linked anxieties over individual and national identities:

> The sincere man died,
> The hypocrites live on,
> The compassionate man died,
> Buried by the cold-blooded.
> Empty talk—TOEFL—bridge—Mah Jong
> Despotism and reform,
> Reform lies dead in the heart,
> This world is a new enigma,
> Let me ask you: Yaobang
> Is China still hopeful?[28]

Among other references, the poem harked back to the April 3 poster in which Wang Dan and fifty-five other students had challenged the Beida authorities to reinvigorate the university's May Fourth tradition of pursuing science and democracy. "We cannot help recognizing," they wrote, "the fact that the 'TOEFL School' and the 'Mahjong School' are in vogue, and that business fever has suffocated all other interests. While there can be no doubt that this is the result of many social factors, it also is closely linked to the various kinds of restrictions on students' freedom of thought."[29] The "TOEFL School" referred to students who spent all their time studying English and seeking entrance to U.S. universities, whereas the "Mahjong School" referred to those who spent their free time playing that traditional game.

Though both students and outside observers (e.g., foreign teachers) spoke of apathy on campus before Hu's death, the indifference should not be exaggerated. In addition to the democracy salons and the various small institutes and study groups, there were occasional visits from proponents of democracy and social change. Fang Lizhi, China's most prominent scientist, was by far the most effective and celebrated of these speakers. Not all were famous, however. Shen Tong recounted the impact of an anonymous agitator from Anhui province who spoke with Beida students in March. The discussion was too political—and therefore too frightening—for many, but others were galvanized, spending three days talking nonstop, virtually without sleep.[30] The visitor was a Qinghua University graduate and former activist from the Democracy Wall demonstration of 1978–79. He spoke of the need for a new government and recommended the tactic of a hunger strike, to start April 5. The Beida undergraduates were not ready for talk of a new government, nor were they ready to take such dramatic action. Yet many were not so much apathetic as frightened, and ideas had been planted in their minds.

These ideas bore fruit not just in posters and discussions but also in organizing. Until April 19, activities had been the products of individual decisions, informal ties, and preexisting groups and relationships. All of these remained important, including the structures of everyday student life—classes, departments, roommates, and so forth. But now efforts to create a more formal organizational apparatus began. Posters at Beijing University announced a Students Autonomous Preparatory Committee and a Students Solidarity Committee, and People's University had a Provisional Autonomous Student Union. On the evening of April 19, Beijing University students formed an independent public body: the Beida Solidarity Student Union Preparatory Committee. This was done almost casually: Wang Dan and other student leaders stood up in front of a crowd and announced that "anyone who has the courage to get up, give his name, his major and what class he's in is automatically a member."[31] Though the committee never worked altogether smoothly, it had a crucial symbolic significance: It was a declaration that a group with a public basis and membership might be created outside the realm of official organizations and rules and claim not only autonomy but also the right to lead political activity. The Beijing Provisional Federation of Autonomous Students Associations was formed a few days later. Both coalitions "made it possible for the first time for students to confront the government as a unified body that could legitimately claim to represent the broad student population and, on this basis, demand recognition for their movement."[32] The Beida Preparatory Committee was matched by similar associations at other campuses, providing the basis for coordinated action.

As organizational groundwork was being laid, the numbers of protesting students began to swell and quickly surpassed those of 1986–87. On Tuesday, April 18, a group of students started a sit-in outside the Zhongnanhai compound located close to Tiananmen Square. This old residential area had been built near the imperial palace and Forbidden City for Qing dynasty officials, later was occupied by Republican elites, and was now used to house the top echelon of the communist administration. At its gate—Xinhuamen—stand giant statues of lions flanking military guards and red doors through which ordinary people may not pass. There the sit-in was highly visible to all who passed on busy Chang'an Boulevard. Students chanted, "Li Peng, come out." Slogans such as "down with dictatorship" and "long live democracy" were becoming routine. Groups of students moved back and forth from the universities to Xinhuamen. On April 20, Zhongnanhai guards reportedly attacked the protesting students with belts and clubs. "The peaceful, petitioning people were beaten," wrote a number of "eyewitnesses" in a poster mounted later that day, "and those who did not scatter quickly stumbled and were attacked by several policemen."[33] This action brought anger and renewed determination to the campuses, and reinforcements flooded to the Xinhuamen protest.

The beating at Zhongnanhai was one of a series of government actions that were intended to intimidate students into retreat but in fact provoked further action. Indeed, much of the momentum of the protests was provided by insults, injuries, and threats from the government. Redressing these wrongs became as central a demand as respect for Hu Yaobang or progress toward democracy. Word of the April 20 beating called forth more Beijing protesters and spurred university students around the country, who rallied under the slogan of "Support Beijing."[34]

FROM MOURNING HU TO EXPLICIT CONFRONTATION

Faced with mounting student unrest, the government scheduled an official memorial service for Hu Yaobang. This was to be held on April 22, one week after his death. No doubt the government intended to bring an end to protest as well as to mourning. The funeral was scheduled for the Great

Hall of the People, adjacent to Tiananmen Square. To make sure protesters didn't try to seize the occasion, the Beijing municipal government announced that it was closing Tiananmen Square for the day. However, the tactic failed, as students simply marched in the night before.[35] Starting a couple of thousand strong from Beida at around 10 P.M., they gathered force as they made the eight-mile trek to Tiananmen Square. School and class flags were used to ornament and organize the processions. Crowds of bystanders cheered the marching students on. Thirty to fifty thousand people stayed in Tiananmen Square that night, and more came the following morning. When security forces arrived on April 22, they found a crowd estimated (perhaps overoptimistically) at up to a hundred thousand people and gave up on the idea of clearing the Square.

Everyone still referred to this as the students' protest, and students certainly were still its main protagonists. But if the crowd numbered anything close to a hundred thousand, it must already have included a good many nonstudents. Indeed, people had streamed into Tiananmen from all directions, not just from the campuses to the northwest. Some of these had come from universities in other parts of Beijing, and others were secondary school students, but there were definite signs of support from beyond the student community. These were sources of extra concern to the government and were closely monitored.

An even more immediate concern was the fact that the students were becoming more and more organized, with those at Beijing, People's, and Normal universities in the forefront. As this announcement from the People's University Provisional Autonomous Student Union makes clear, the new organizations were direct rejections of existing *official* student organizations:

> Because the leadership of the original student union is inept, has sold out the students' interests during this April 22 protest movement, and is completely unable to represent the students' wishes, the People's University Provisional Autonomous Student Union has been established in response to the demands of the great majority of students following a meeting of the entire student body. It supplants the [official] student union. It will dissolve on its own initiative when conditions permit.[36]

As the founding of such unions spread rapidly to campuses throughout Beijing, delegates from the more elite and better organized schools in Haidian set out to link up. This was a trickier proposition because it pushed the protesters beyond their existing organizational resources; they could not rely so much on campus networks and reputations. As it happened, several different declarations announced the formation of somewhat different au-

tonomous students unions. Their precise names, memberships, and structures remained fluid for several days, but these amorphous new coalitions,
born of the protests, were significant. No such bodies were recognized in
China. Rejecting the officially sponsored student unions, moreover, meant
rejecting quasigovernmental associations, throwing down a direct challenge to Party and state. Nor was the challenge offered only by university
students. Posters bearing the name "Beijing Autonomous Workers Union"
also appeared as early as April 20.[37]

In terms of both scale and organization, the protests were coalescing into
a movement, and the government could hardly fail to take notice. On April
21, the *People's Daily* ran an editorial with a warning: "Those who take
advantage of the mourning for Comrade Yaobang, and charge, smash, rob
or set fire to offices of the Communist Party or the government will be
condemned by history. Up to now, in dealing with the very small number
of people doing these unlawful activities, the government has been restrained. If some people consider these to be weakness, they will have to
face the bitter consequences."[38] The fears of the leadership were not idle.
On April 22, demonstrations turned into riots in Xi'an, the ancient capital
famed for its terra-cotta warriors, and ninety-eight people were arrested in
the southern city of Changsha. Xi'an is a major university town, and students were involved in protests there, though the rioting seems to have
been more the work of young unemployed workers (described as "lawless
elements" by the official press).[39] It was virtually taken for granted among
students in Beijing that the government had employed agents provocateurs
to turn a peaceful protest into a violent, dangerous one. Fearing the same
ploy would be used against them, they began more carefully to organize
their marches and other activities. After the Xi'an disorder they adopted
the tactic of marching in groups from specific schools and classes, li   .g
arms around the perimeter to clearly delimit their boundaries. This .atter
practice simultaneously kept out agents provocateurs, revealed the students' orderly and peaceful intent, and reaffirmed the solidarity of the constituent groups.

At Hu Yaobang's funeral, the Communist old guard assembled with
President Yang Shangkun officiating, and Zhao Ziyang read an uninspired
oration. If the party leaders intended to convey much of a sense of mourning and thereby reach out to the students on the most easily addressed
of their concerns, they failed. Leaders of the new Provisional Federation of
Autonomous Students Associations one-upped their elders in the theater
of the public sphere.

Students had drawn up a petition and sought to present it to the Party
leaders assembled in the Great Hall of the People. Just after the officials

withdrew from their public performance into the interior of the building, three students, dressed as usual in casual slacks and sports jackets, marched ceremoniously up the steps of the Great Hall, carrying a scroll on which their demands had been written. Self-consciously imitating petitioners to the imperial court, they knelt to offer the scroll.[40] Not surprisingly, no senior official stepped forward to receive it. Unlike traditional petitioners, the students had no recognized status from which to deliver a petition (let alone a list of demands). Their kneeling was prolonged, and their point was clearly made about just who had inherited the mantle of the emperors (and how little their accessibility to the people had changed). I later heard students express outrage that only a minor official came forward eventually to accept the petition, but I don't think the would-be presenters—who included Wuerkaixi in his first major dramatic gesture—really expected a senior Party or government representative to come out to greet them: The point lay in the performance itself. The rumor had spread, however, that Li Peng would come out to receive the petition, and many students thought he should have.

Many, in fact, thought the petitioners should not have knelt, should not have implied, however ironically, that they accepted a lower status than the prime minister. "Our Humiliation Must Be Wiped Out!" was the headline on a poster written by one law student:

> Then came the episode that made everybody stare, tongue-tied: three student representatives knelt down on the doorsteps of the Great Hall of the People. One of them was holding high the students' petition letter. About ten government officials standing in front of the Great Hall totally disregarded them, however, and the policemen lining up were fully prepared to attack the defenseless students. More than twenty minutes passed, and three student representatives were still kneeling on the doorsteps. Yet no government official came to accept the petition letter. By now all the students felt humiliated and indignant. Some choked with sobs.
>
> The national emblem on the front gate of the Great Hall of the People must have now seen how the "masters" of the "republic" were petitioning like slaves, and how the dignified emperor-like officials were treating them with indifference! . . .
>
> This is not our republic![41]

This student went on to suggest a number of measures to wipe out the humiliation—a boycott, the demand that Li Peng step down, popular elections. And, he said: "I have another suggestion: Next time, the student representatives should not make such a self-humiliating petition because we now know that we are facing cold-blooded animals who are not even worth a straw."

Others were even more vehement in condemning those who had

knelt—however ironically—before authority. But a Beijing University poster defended them:

> In the China of the eighties, during a march for democracy, people use a means of petitioning tainted with the stains of feudalism: kneeling! Is this not the tragedy of our age?
>
> Did they disgrace us? Were they begging for freedom? Begging for democracy? No! They sacrificed their own self-respect and human dignity to fulfill a mission entrusted to them by tens of thousands of students. Think about it. As representatives of tens of thousands of students, entrusted with so heavy a responsibility at such a critical moment, after the petition had been ignored over and over again, what else could they do but use the most provocative, most feudal method—kneeling? What self-mockery to use a feudal method of expression in a struggle for democracy in present-day China! And what powerlessness and impotence it implies!
>
> We want to express our understanding and respect to you, the bearers of our petition. Although your action may itself be controversial, it is indeed a microcosm of, a symbol of, the student movement of contemporary China! [42]

Wuerkaixi himself apparently thought the symbolism was problematic and claimed never quite fully to have knelt:

> On April 22, at the funeral of Hu Yaobang, three of the four student representatives got down on their knees in front of the Great Hall of the People—all except one, me. The three of them tried to force me to my knees, but I refused. Democracy is not something you can beg for. There will never be democracy and freedom if you try to get them by begging. It's feudal to get down on our knees to our rulers. It's absurd; is it not ridiculous to fight for democracy and freedom by means of a feudal ritual? [43]

The mock ceremony dramatized a central motif of the emerging protest movement. Most of the students' demands were eminently moderate: rehabilitate Hu Yaobang, end corruption, hold a dialogue, discuss problems. But two demands—one explicit and one implicit—were more problematic. The explicit one was the call for the government to recognize the autonomous students unions. Though seemingly mild, this was in fact a basic challenge, for communist China had never recognized the right of people to form independent representative organizations at will. [44] The implicit demand was equally disturbing. This was the notion that students had a right to address top officials as equals, to demand a dialogue, to expect to be met on the steps of the Great Hall of the People by the prime minister of China.

After the funeral, the pictures of Hu gradually disappeared from the student demonstrations; they were hardly visible by May 4. But the messages of disapproval and the demand for a public voice became ever stronger. Beida students set up a communications center the morning of April 22 with a homemade amplifier and two speakers in the campus's Triangle area. Later the same day this apparatus was moved to Shen Tong's room nearby, and the students apparently began broadcasting at 101 FM, though the signal could only be picked up near Beida.[45] Students used the term "broadcasting" to refer to speeches made over loudspeakers as well as to radio transmissions, both at Beida and later when the equipment was set up in Tiananmen Square. Very few people seemed aware of any radio transmissions, though a number of students I spoke to (including many with no loyalty to Beida) were very proud to claim the existence of broadcast capacity. It seemed to symbolize the ability of the movement to conduct public affairs. Though Shen now makes a point of noting the operation of the FM transmitter, Li Lu explicitly says, "it was a local broadcasting station—not a radio station, but a microphone, amplifiers and loudspeakers."[46] In any case, the important feature was really the public address system in the Triangle area. The first night it blared out news and comment until dawn. The next morning, red-eyed professors came by with a request: "We support what you are doing, but please let us have some sleep."[47] Students dubbed the loudspeaker setup the "Voice of Democracy" or "Voice of the Students."

The work of the communications center went beyond the "broadcasts." It included, crucially, the movement's main (more or less) organized effort to gather and disseminate information. In fairly short order, students found two mimeograph machines and later a Chinese typewriter and went into the news business. Screening their work from prying teachers and administrators, they turned out statements for broadcast, press releases, and leaflets. One widely disseminated item was a chart that listed twenty-seven high-ranking Party officials (including Deng Xiaoping, Zhao Ziyang, Li Peng, and Yang Shangkun) and showed all the positions their children held in the government, the Party, and private enterprise. The staff of an official magazine made secret donations to keep the news center at work, and monetary support came from as far afield as the Chinese students at Kent State University.

On April 23, some ten thousand students gathered on the soccer field of Beijing University to debate the next steps. Similar meetings were held on other campuses. The idea of a class boycott gained the upper hand. This proposal had been mooted in smaller gatherings of leaders, and word spread from campus to campus. The news was conveyed via organized lines of communication set up by leaders, but many students simply began to hop on their bikes and make excursions to read the latest *dazibao* and hear the speeches on other campuses. The Triangle Area at Beida was the most important center, its crowds and *dazibao* augmented by the new broadcast station. Loudspeakers were also set up outside the gates at Beida and Renda. Crowds gathered every evening, and many students went on a sort of regular "patrol" that took them to two or three campuses each night. When they returned, others congregated in dormitories and courtyards to hear the news.

A more formal connection among campuses was achieved when representatives of twenty-one Beijing universities got together on April 24 to form the Beijing Provisional Federation of Autonomous Students Associations (the Beigaolian for short; also called variously the Federation of All Beijing College Student Unions and the Provisional Students Federation of Capital Universities and Colleges—hereafter simply "Federation"). Designed to coordinate the protest activity of the various campus-specific autonomous unions, this became the movement's most important leadership body—at least for the first several weeks of the protest. The mere existence of this unrecognized, autonomous union was a thorn in the government's side, regardless of any actions it took. The initial head of the Federation was Zhou Yongjun of the University of Politics and Law; Wuerkaixi of Beijing Normal University and Wang Dan of Beida were on its standing committee.[48] The Federation's first major action was to call for a boycott of classes.

The boycott began Monday morning, April 24. On the first day, it was observed by 60 to 90 percent of the students at the four "core" campuses and several other universities. By the second day, participation rates were more uniform, and the boycott was being observed throughout Beijing. Two observers reported that by Wednesday only three of Beijing's roughly sixty universities were unaffected: the Public Security University, the People's University for Police Officers, and the School for Diplomats.[49] At least the first of these eventually joined in. Students were urged to stay on campus, not to go home, and to "boycott classes, not studies."

April 24 was also the day Shanghai's *World Economic Herald* devoted its first six pages to remembrances of Hu Yaobang, many of them sharply critical of the government. One theme was the "irregularity" of his forced resignation and self-confession after the 1986–87 student movement. Favorable coverage of that movement could only be seen as encouragement for the one currently taking shape. The *World Economic Herald* was a prominent newspaper at the vanguard of the reform movement. Some of those who contributed to the April 24 issue, such as Yan Jiaqi, had close ties to Zhao Ziyang and other top Party reformers. Nonetheless, the *Her-*

ald's distribution was stopped. The Shanghai mayor who took this action, Jiang Zemin, would later replace Zhao Ziyang as Party secretary.

Thirty-three intellectuals led by Yan responded with an open letter to the Shanghai Municipal Party Committee defending freedom of the press and suggesting that for the Party to close down a paper it didn't publish was to violate the principle of separation of Party and state.[50] Most newspapers and magazines continued to follow the government line, however, at least for the time being. There was scant coverage of the students' activities, and the little that appeared was generally not favorable. Journalists chafed at the restrictions and would later be among the first privileged professionals to join the student protest.

The most striking publication of the week was an editorial appearing on April 26 in the *People's Daily*, China's main newspaper and a frequent source for official opinion. The editorial putatively was based on Deng Xiaoping's April 24 comments during a meeting called to discuss the student unrest. Rumors after this meeting suggested that Deng had threatened military force, saying something like: "60,000 students are boycotting classes, but we have three million troops."[51] Zhao Ziyang was absent on a state visit to North Korea. There has been a good deal of speculation about what impact his presence would have had. That is impossible to say for sure, though Zhao's absence probably did make it hard for the government to take prompt, decisive action. It is worth noting, however, that the very fact of his trip (just after Hu Yaobang's funeral) signaled how readily the authorities thought life would return to normal. They apparently had little idea that the student demonstrations would so quickly redouble their intensity, expand their scale, and proliferate throughout urban China.

By April 26, the authorities were more worried, though they seemed to think that a stern rebuke and warning might still put matters right. Their *People's Daily* editorial (which was also broadcast on Beijing Radio and China Central Television) read in part:

> During the period of mourning, a few abnormal phenomena also appeared. An extremely small number of people[52] used the opportunity to fabricate rumors and attack leaders of the Party and state by name, and to deceive the masses. . . . There were even some other people who yelled out "Down with the Communist Party" and other reactionary slogans. In Xi'an and Changsha there were serious incidents of lawless elements smashing, looting and burning.
>
> Taking into consideration the broad masses' grief, the Party and government took a tolerant, restrained attitude to certain inappropriate words and actions of emotionally excited young students. . . .
>
> But after the memorial was over, an extremely small number of people

with ulterior motives continued to take advantage of the young students' mourning for Comrade Hu Yaobang. . . . In some universities and colleges, illegal organizations were established and tried to grab power from the student unions by force. Some even took over the schools' public address facilities by force. In some universities, students and teachers were encouraged to boycott classes; students were forcibly prevented from going to classes. . . .

These facts demonstrate that an extremely small number of people were not involved in mourning Comrade Hu Yaobang, were not trying to promote socialist democracy in China, and were not just a bit unhappy and letting off steam. [Rather], under the banner of democracy, they were trying to destroy the democratic legal system. Their goal was to poison people's minds, to create turmoil throughout the country, to destroy political stability and unity. This was a planned conspiracy, a riot, whose real nature was to fundamentally negate the leadership of the Chinese Communist Party and to negate the socialist system. This throws down the gauntlet of serious political struggle before the whole Party and every nationality of the whole country.

If we take a lenient, permissive attitude toward this turmoil and just let it go, a situation of real chaos will emerge. What the people of the whole country, including the great mass of young students, hope for—reform and opening, austerity and rectification, development, control of inflation, a better life, opposing corruption, developing democracy and the legal system—will be reduced to nothing. Even the tremendous results achieved by reform over the last ten years could be totally lost. The great desire of the whole Chinese people—to revitalize China—will be next to impossible to realize. A China with great hope and a great future would become a China wracked with turmoil, a China with no future. . . .

Illegal demonstrations are forbidden. Going to factories, to the countryside, and to schools to link up with others is forbidden. Those who smash, loot, and burn must be punished according to law. The normal right of students to attend classes must be guaranteed. The great majority of students sincerely wants to eliminate corruption and to promote democracy. These are also the demands of the Party and the government. These demands can only be realized under the Party's leadership.[53]

The editorial was a pivotal document. Its language revealed the sense of the aging leaders that the disturbances they were witnessing were akin to those through which they had suffered during the Cultural Revolution. The term *chuanlian* ("to link up"), for example, is specifically remembered as the word used to describe the activities of the young Red Guards who traveled around China in the 1960s to make contact with other groups and spread the Cultural Revolution. Though the 1989 student protesters were hardly Red Guards, such analogies were not simply paranoid government fantasies: In a poster of April 23, the students had contrasted current Party leaders' refusal to accept the April 22 petition with the willingness of Mao

Zedong, Zhou Enlai, and Liu Shaoqi to come out even in the middle of the night to talk to a member of the Red Guards.[54]

The editorialist's implication that the broad mass of students were innocent and that only an "extremely small number of people" were truly attacking the government backfired doubly: Students read it as suggesting that they were merely dupes, that the protests were not serious, or both; senior intellectuals read it as an accusation that they were the "black hands" behind the protests. Perhaps most basically, the editorial challenged the students' patriotism, making it sound as if their activities portended the destruction, not the revitalization, of China. As the large character poster of "A Young Chinese Student" put it, "the editorial vilified the present patriotic movement as disorder and agitation. . . . The extremely negative tone . . . has really caused deep, deep shock, disappointment and anger in the nation's citizens."[55]

In short, the April 26 editorial outraged and insulted the students; far from scaring the students off, it only strengthened their resolve. A "Party member and student at People's University" warned of a possible bloodbath but expressed the sense of challenge in a small character poster:

> At present there are only two roads from which we may choose: we may act as conscientious Chinese and as conscientious Party members, and struggle for democracy and the prosperity of China; or we may act as "up-to-par Party members" and actively respond to the call of the Central Committee, in order to preserve our Party membership and secure our individual futures. How are we to choose?
>
> I remember how Zhou Enlai once answered the question of a foreign friend by saying, "I am first and foremost a Chinese, and only then a Party member. . . ."
>
> As a Party member, I no longer wish to weep over governmental corruption and the apathy of the people. I only want to be a true communist, and to let my blood flow with the struggle for democracy and freedom.[56]

BREAKTHROUGH: THE APRIL 27 MARCH

Students were afraid as well as angry. On the night of April 26 they debated whether to go ahead with the march planned for the next morning. At Beida, school authorities had hinted that if the march were called off, they might be able to use their connections to ensure that the government held a dialogue. Shen Tong later reported that he and other student leaders were tempted. Along with other Preparatory Committee members, he helped present the case for a dialogue to a broader group of Beida student representatives. "The students didn't seem to agree with this; they were determined to go to the square. They didn't want to buckle under to the threats made in the *People's Daily* editorial and the government broadcasts, and they were also angry about being called instigators."[57] The prominent literary critic Su Wei also remembered deciding that students should be persuaded to call off the march but then getting caught up in their enthusiasm.[58]

The Beida students came up with a compromise: They would march only a third of the way to Tiananmen, as far as Third Ring Road. This seemed a balance between prudence and the need to act. It would be enough to show that the students rejected the April 26 editorial but would not constitute a major provocation. Still, the compromise only partly assuaged their fear, and some students wrote wills and shaved their heads in anticipation of possible death. Similar fears—and determination—were expressed on other campuses. One "testament" from Beijing Normal University was signed, "the new generation of Liu Henzhen," referring to a student of the great writer Lu Xun. (Henzhen's death on March 18, 1926, had prompted Lu to write a famous denunciation of the government's use of force.) The Beijing Normal author referred to blood already shed—presumably in Xi'an and in the attack on students outside Zhongnanhai compound—as having transformed students' attitudes:

> We depart; we have our cares, our attachments, but we cannot think of them any longer. We come forth as the life force of the Normal University. We throw ourselves onto Tiananmen Square.
>
> Yesterday we were outside observers, indifferent. But the blood of our comrades has awakened us. How can we remain indifferent?
>
> We would have believed that the sky of our fatherland would have remained forever clear; but here today our fatherland is sick! At dawn, before the sunrise, before *Xinhuamen*, where the emblem of our nation is hung, my heart saddened.
>
> What crime did the students commit? We went to Tiananmen for justice and reason! We do not claim the title of martyrs. We demand only to be truly human. The only hope which we will have is that the press can report with honesty the path of our death.[59]

A Beida student wrote more simply:

> Dear Mother and Father,
>
> I am part of this student movement because I love my country. I am not a counterrevolutionary. I am not a lawless agitator. Please understand my actions. Thank you for the money you sent so I could buy food and clothing. I will not be needing it anymore. Rest assured that your son will not bring shame upon you. I will not die in disgrace.[60]

There were real risks in challenging the government, but some graduate students mocked both the fear and the self-dramatization of the undergraduates. If the writing of wills was a form of theater, however, it was also an effective way of issuing public declarations.[61]

On April 27, the leaders prepared for the march with uncertainty about what they would confront and even whom they would lead. As Shen Tong tells the story, he and other Beida leaders expected a small turnout after the government's warning. To their surprise, some eight thousand marchers turned out at Beida alone. Recalls Shen:

> It wasn't long before we ran into our first wall of policemen, who were standing three deep with their arms linked. Wang Dan and I stopped the marchers and went to talk with the head of the police, who was a very old man.
>
> "You know you can't stop us," I said. "You're only three deep, and there are thousands of us. Why don't you let us pass? We're only going to Third Ring Road and then turning back. If you don't let us pass, we're going to rush your line, and after that none of us will be able to control the students."
>
> He didn't say a word to us, just ordered his men to move aside. Wang Dan and I looked at each other and smiled, surprised that it had been so easy.[62]

Thoughts of truncating the march at the Third Ring Road were abandoned, as People's University students expressed their determination to head on to Tiananmen Square. Everyone enjoyed the thrill of marching past the police; apparently the government would not make good its threats of harsh repression.

More police barriers were spaced out every few hundred yards along Chang'an Boulevard, the main road into Tiananmen Square. Again and again columns of students pushed through the token, virtually unresisting ranks of police officers. So the march continued, each successive breakthrough drawing greater cheers than the last, building the momentum of protest. One student later recalled, "During the march, as we saw police lines broken through one after another, our [pounding] hearts gradually calmed down. Only the organizers of the march and those many people who went through the experience can know what it was like to feel such fear and overwhelming relief."[63] Students walked in groups of classmates; those on the outside once again linked arms to keep each unit defined and keep out police and agents provocateurs.[64] The students intended this protest to be forceful but peaceful.

The April 27 march marked at least two crucial shifts in the developing movement. First, and perhaps most important, some students began clearly to speak to and for the whole Chinese people. They self-consciously sought to abandon special-interest concerns as students and intellectuals. As a People's University poster put it: "[A]s intellectuals, we made significant concessions in our banners and slogans. The original slogans that were suggested—'improve the treatment of teachers,' and so on—were only shouted by some marchers from the teachers' colleges. The march's main purpose was changed to 'petition for the people' and 'appeal for redress of wrongs suffered by the students.' "[65] Second, the student protesters encountered their first clear official resistance and overcame it peacefully. In fact, the police lines they had to cross were token or symbolic obstacles more than material ones. The police were unarmed, and only a few ranks were thick; they simply linked arms to block the students. Each time, the surging crowd easily broke through, eliciting a roar of approval and encouraging both onlookers and participants to think it possible to stand up to the army. A crowd-control technique more effective at building the confidence of protesters (and therefore counterproductive for the government) is hard to imagine. But the necessity of breaching the police lines did force the students to explicitly act against the government, even though they refrained from anti-Party and antigovernment slogans.

The April 27 march succeeded beyond even the most optimistic student expectations. Estimates of crowd size ranged from a hundred thousand to half a million. The demonstration was not just successful in gaining publicity or making a point; it was a transformative experience for those who participated, an experience of standing up to the government and claiming (without immediate retaliation) the rights of citizens. As one small character poster put up the next day at People's University began: "Whoever believes in the principles of democracy and who furthermore tries conscientiously to live according to those principles—such were the people who 'went through the experience.' And those of us who went through the experience agree: the march was a great victory in the process of democratization in China, which began over forty years ago. It at least prevented the lords from acting at will."[66] Experiences such as this were personally transformative, reshaping people's ideas about themselves and about what was possible. The will to persevere in the movement grew out of these experiences, not just out of interests that existed before it.

The success of April 27 thus gave the movement new strength and pushed it further beyond the realm of previous exemplars. Only in the very different circumstances of the Cultural Revolution had the rights of a body of citizens to take public action without the approval of the government been so sharply and successfully affirmed. But it was not the Cultural Revolution, with its manipulation from above and its emphasis on class struggle, that served as the movement's manifest antecedent; rather, the uprising of 1919, with its broad symbolism of democracy, modernization, and the leadership of intellectuals, offered the main sense of a historical project renewed. And May 4, the date symbolizing that movement, was just coming up.

On April 28, the Beijing Provisional Federation of Autonomous Students Associations was reconstituted as the Federation of Autonomous Students Unions (though it was still referred to under a variety of similar names), and its leadership was shuffled slightly. Zhou Yongjun had tried to call off the April 27 march—apparently in panic—and was ousted. His offense was a double one: Not only had he tried to retreat instead of pressing forward, he had issued a major public statement without the authorization of the standing committee. Students were determined to adopt clear procedures of legitimate organizational authority. In line with their condemnation of Deng Xiaoping's behind-the-scenes rule of China, they insisted on following clear decisionmaking procedures as prescribed by democratic doctrine. Though they faced recurrent problems with leadership and decisionmaking, the students adhered to this general view to the very end of their protests, even holding votes on the steps of the Monument to the People's Heroes on June 3 to decide whether to flee the Square in the face of the army attack.

Wuerkaixi became the sole chair of the new Federation; Wang Dan was prominent on the standing committee. The recurrent debate over whether to consolidate gains or push further into uncharted territory had claimed its first victim in the leadership; Wuerkaixi and Wang would each become vulnerable later.[67]

Another march took place on May 4. Police and troops kept discreetly to the sidelines, fairly numerous but unarmed. The students basked in the bright sun and felt their new power and freedom. The event had a holiday atmosphere; townspeople turned out to watch and cheer the students on. A quarter of a million people gathered in Tiananmen Square, but there was a strange sense that nothing happened. The march was curiously relaxed and slightly anticlimactic. I watched brigades of students from the main universities marshal in northwest Beijing, carrying banners and signs, a few wearing sashes or headbands bearing slogans. Even more than on April 27, students knew that "the whole world was watching," and they sported signs in French ("Vive la liberté") and English ("Give me liberty or give me death") to attract the television cameras and communicate with citizens in Europe and the United States. They marched the six or eight miles into Tiananmen Square, joining others on the way. I rode ahead on my bicycle.

University contingents from the other parts of town made it to Tiananmen Square first, but once there they had little idea of what to do. It was hot, and people kept drifting away in search of a drink while the crowd waited for its last and most influential components to arrive from Beijing University, People's University, and Beijing Normal University. Occasionally someone drew a cheer by circling the Monument to the People's Heroes waving the blue and white flag of the Federation (designed by Wang Wen, with stripes that recalled those of the U.S. flag, at least to Shen Tong).[68] After the students from the core universities had arrived, Wuerkaixi read a "New May Fourth Manifesto": "Fellow students, fellow countrymen, the future and fate of the Chinese nation are intimately linked to each of our hearts. This student movement has but one goal, that is, to facilitate the process of modernization by raising high the banners of democracy and science, by liberating people from the constraints of feudal ideology, and by promoting freedom, human rights, and rule by law."[69] A few others made speeches, unamplified and audible only to those immediately around them.

The one truly striking event of the May 4 demonstration was the participation of some three hundred to five hundred journalists. They entered the Square late in the day, marching from the east and carrying signs reading, "We want to tell the truth; don't force us to lie," "We want to get the facts out," and "People have the right to know."[70] Contingents came from nearly every major Beijing-based newspaper and news agency. This was the first time any major group beyond the universities had taken part in the protests or manifested its support. Shen Tong reported that a number of journalists had visited Beida the day before, seeking students' help in preparing placards and banners and complaining that they were too closely watched by their supervisors to do this themselves.

When the last marchers arrived, there was a cheer and a pause; then everyone gradually dispersed. The students' repertoire of protest included few dramatic scripts, nothing to focus attention or keep the crowd entertained and motivated. The occasion seemed eerily quiet to me; I realized that in my previous experience such an event had always involved music.

THE QUEST FOR A DIALOGUE

Before May 4, student leaders had put forward a list of ten demands ranging from an end to official corruption to recognition of the autonomous students associations (especially the Federation) and retraction of the April 26 *People's Daily* editorial. Not surprisingly, the government rejected the demands, but even this was better than being ignored, and there seemed to be hints that some leaders listened. Party chairman Zhao Ziyang returned from Korea saying that the protesters were patriotic in intention and that the Party shared their desire to end corruption. Several high officials declared that democratic reform was an appropriate goal but must be pursued gradually. Moderation seemed to be carrying the day. Most students returned to classes, at least temporarily, though some, particularly at Beida, held out.

Calls for dialogue had been a feature of the movement from the outset, and the government wanted to establish one—on its own conditions—as a means of placating and calming the students. As early as April 25, government officials proposed to meet with student leaders from Qinghua University (the less politically active, more technically oriented of Beijing's two most prestigious institutions). This was apparently part of a plan to meet with only a handful of students on a school-by-school basis, emphasizing official units of organization and diverting attention from the Federation. The government might even have hoped it could play different schools off against each other and create rivalries that would undermine future cooperation. A few student dissidents were invited, but invitations went mainly to representatives from the Communist-dominated official student union. Some Qinghua students initially wanted to proceed with the dialogue but backed down in the face of rebukes from their colleagues in the Federation.[71] The student activists declared that "while they welcomed any form and level of dialogue with the government, these had to be with the leadership of the independent student organization as a whole." They rejected the government's "tactic to divide the Beijing students' independent organization."[72]

The government then tried staging a broader but still carefully orchestrated "dialogue." However, government officials met not with protesting students but with leaders from the officially recognized student associations. Presumably, the idea was to show an interest in students, emphasize the availability of "proper channels" for communication, and suggest that the masses or mainstream of students were orderly and supportive of the government. The meeting went so completely according to government script that it convinced no one. Those who participated earned the bitter condemnation of their classmates; the delegate from Beijing Foreign Studies University did not dare to show himself on campus again.

After this failure, to the amazement of most students, the government did agree to a dialogue of sorts with genuine dissenters, to be held on April 29. There was a great deal of debate among the students over whether to participate. The Federation leadership stated three conditions: that government representatives had to be senior officials of the State Council; that the government must deal exclusively with the Federation of Autonomous Students Unions (and not work through the official student organizations); and that the talks should be open to both foreign and domestic press. The government ignored these conditions and proceeded to invite several students individually, rather than as representatives of the Federation (which, of course, it did not recognize). Most of the invitees were representatives of the official student organizations. Because of this failure to meet student demands, Wang Dan, the respected Beida leader, refused to attend. Many students argued, however, that it was crucial for them to be seen as willing to meet the government halfway, that this was a dialogue, even if not precisely the sort they wanted. It could, they suggested, be considered preliminary to a dialogue with properly selected representatives from all the universities in Beijing. Wuerkaixi decided to go, making the somewhat fine distinction that "we are attending as private individuals. Only when the government recognizes our organization as a legitimate association will we have a dialogue with them as representatives of our Union."[73]

Yuan Mu, spokesman of the State Council and a former journalist, met with the students. The exchange was televised but closed to the press. Yuan wasn't quite the top policymaker students had hoped to meet, but the idea of *any* senior Chinese official appearing on TV to be interrogated about policies and the possibility of corruption was a startling novelty. Aided by the absence of some Federation leaders and by the presence of many delegates from the official student organizations, the government was able to seize the initiative.

Yuan Mu proved himself a much more sophisticated performer on camera than the students, easily parrying most of their charges and blandly accepting others—such as a complaint about senior leaders who play too much golf (aimed at Zhao Ziyang)—as worth looking into. Midway through the meeting, Wuerkaixi walked out in frustration (and, he later said, as a protest). It seemed, indeed, that the students were about to be outmaneuvered by the government's superficial hints of openness and repressive tolerance, by which they would be allowed expression but would not be taken seriously. People took heart, however, from the very fact of the government's concession to hold the meeting. And though putatively cooler heads (e.g., young teachers and some graduate students) urged the students to consolidate their gains, others poured contempt on Yuan Mu's slick performance, saying that oily words and smiles were no substitute for real dialogue and demanding that real, responsible leaders, not spokesmen, meet with the students. This was a hard message to get across to a wider audience, however, and the government seemed to have scored a public relations coup (and did so again, to a lesser degree, by staging another meeting with students on April 30).

Exactly what sort of dialogue the students expected was unclear. They wanted a chance to air their grievances publicly and to know they were heard and taken seriously by responsible government officials. At the same time, they sought recognition of their right to bring forward public concerns. This was even harder for the government and Communist Party to accept, because it meant both acknowledging an organization outside their control and granting that such organizations, acting as agents of the public, could legitimately confront the government with a semblance of parity. Consequently, the government preferred the idea of many and varied dialogues "on a small scale, among two or three, or among eight or ten people, in various forms and through various channels."[74] This approach would leave the government in control and prevent any official body of students from claiming recognition and public status.

Though it was only apparently a mild demand, the call for a dialogue was in fact a very radical request. It reflected the students' very high opinion of their own importance as young intellectuals and was based on an egalitarian ideology, offering echoes of young Red Guards interrogating senior officials in the 1960s. The student protesters of 1989 had no intention of acting like Red Guards, but the similarities were quickly noted by others. Undergraduates thought nothing of summoning the president of my university out to a discussion one morning in May, but those old enough to be reminded of China's Cultural Revolution (including some Ph.D. candidates) were slightly chilled by the action. One argued with the undergraduates at the edge of the crowd, but his views were dismissed. The president smiled nervously, declared that he had a heart condition, and said he loved the students but that they must be patient and return to their classes.

In effect, the students were asking for a dramatic change in the constitution of the PRC. Existing arrangements and precedents provided no basis for an autonomous group of citizens to negotiate with the government. Indeed, one of the government's main objections was that the students were seeking not mere dialogue but "negotiation." The students, for their part, complained that they merely got lectures and meetings, not the two-way communication they sought. The key issue was the students' implicit demand to be allowed to organize a group of their own. Aside from its connotations with Western bourgeois democracy and the Cultural Revolution, the idea that any interested group could form its own organization and demand recognition was seen as a recipe for chaos. As Yuan Mu put it:

> If because of one single event some parts of the students declare the establishment of an organization and if the government recognizes it and talks with it, then it will lead to greater disunity among the students. . . . Looking back on the sad lessons of the Cultural Revolution and the extreme chaos during that period, I think a very important cause of that chaos, of that havoc, is that there were usually two, or even three, or even more factions, first in various schools, and then in all social circles, and even in public institutions, and that has resulted in great disunity and division among the general public.[75]

The students, Yuan Mu concluded, were usurping the authority of the legal organizations and sowing the seeds of anarchy.

Questions about the meaning of dialogue ran more broadly through the movement. The Chinese term generally used is *duihua*, meaning "face-to-face conversation." However, it does not carry the built-in reference to multiple, conflicting voices and reasoned argument that characterizes the Greek-rooted Western word. Some Chinese intellectuals were turning their reading of Bakhtin, Derrida, and Habermas into an effort to change the country's manner of public discourse. The prominent critic Li Tuo ridiculed the monological, authoritative discursive form he labeled "Maospeak." Fang Lizhi had urged students to both give and take when debating public issues: "I hope we may all benefit from this interchanging discussion method. I don't want you to listen to me only. . . . I think, if I have said something wrong, you may refute me. Thus, we shall advance toward democracy."[76] But most protesters and certainly most others had at best a vague notion of public discourse as exchange of ideas, even the occasion for change of ideas. Quite often, those who said "dialogue" meant mainly a desire to give, not to take.

On May 5, Shen Tong and others organized a "Dialogue Delegation" charged with preparing for future meetings with the government. They hoped to recover the initiative they had lost to Yuan Mu on April 29. In particular, they sought to respond to the government's success in portraying them as factionalized. One of the students' problems was that they had not agreed on an agenda before entering into the dialogue. Different students competed for attention and raised a variety of issues, some central and some peripheral to the program of the Federation and the concerns of the movement. By contrast, the government leaders had a clear plan, division of labor, and gradation of authority. This put the students at a severe disadvantage. The Dialogue Delegation, however, was also an attempt to prepare for a dialogue with higher-level officials that would bring the movement public attention even without government recognition of the Federation. It was thus maintained as a separate organization, ensuring that the students would not lose all chance to speak to the government by laying too much stress on formal recognition.[77]

Despite these initiatives, the movement settled into a lull for a week after May 4. There were meetings on campuses and a few desultory protests, but momentum appeared to have peaked and dissipated. No one was sure just what to do next, though no one was satisfied with the status quo. In the words of Chai Ling (who would become a key leader in the next phase of the movement):

> On May 4, student leaders announced a declaration that marked the beginning of a new democratic enlightenment movement. So it surprised everyone when a director of the Beijing Student Union proclaimed that the boycotting of classes was over and students would return to school the next day. Many students were very disappointed. This announcement seriously damaged the nationwide student movement. Someone said, "A million-dollar opportunity was ruined by a single decision."
>
> Later the movement dwindled to a low point as more and more students returned to classes. We wasted a lot of energy arguing whether or not to resume our classes. The situation became increasingly difficult.
>
> At that point, we decided that we had to stage a hunger strike. Some from the Student Union were very much against this, but we persisted. We had been contemplating a hunger strike for some time. Marching and boycotting classes had drawn no response from the government.[78]

2   Fear, Uncertainty, and Success beyond Expectations

RADICALIZATION: THE HUNGER STRIKE

On Friday, May 12, word spread from campus to campus that students were calling for a hunger strike. The idea had been vaguely mooted before, but now a large character poster in Beida's Triangle Area declared that the time had come. Students from other schools went to this area near the dormitories, where posters could be displayed on its miniature democracy wall, to get the latest news and ideas. The hunger strike initiative took root rapidly. Within hours, the pros and cons of this action were being debated not just at Beida but also at People's, Normal, and other universities. A few students from Beiwai talked cautiously of joining in. Graduate students were particularly dubious about the wisdom of the new tactic. A number of leaders worried that it would sink the Federation and the autonomous unions. Others, including Shen Tong, thought the focus should be on preparation for renewed dialogue with the government and development of better capacities for public relations. It quickly became apparent, however, that the idea had captured the emotions of many students who were impatient with the lull in movement activity. As one young professor advised Shen Tong, "Many students are determined to begin a hunger strike, so it looks like that's what will happen. Therefore, you should do everything you can to help them make it effective."[1]

By this time Shen was running Beida's communications center and playing a leading role in the Dialogue Delegation, so he was in a position to act. With the professor's assistance, he drafted a short letter of support for the would-be hunger strikers and ran off two thousand copies with space for signatures at the bottom. Several other leaders had also decided it was best to get behind the hunger strike and help put it together. Although the

Federation standing committee had not endorsed the strike, Wuerkaixi, Wang Dan, and several other members joined in a declaration that it would begin the next day in Tiananmen Square.

Even before the strike began, Chai Ling emerged as one of its leaders. A thin, emotionally intense young woman, she was already active in the protests. Her husband, Feng Congde, was one of the key figures in the Beida Preparatory Committee. The night of May 12, she made a speech that helped galvanize support for the strike. With only a few students coming forward, there was worry that the action wouldn't have enough participants to make an impact. Then Chai Ling spoke:

> I am here to tell everyone that I want to go on a hunger strike. Why am I doing it? It is because I want to see the true face of the government. We are fortunate to have parents who raised us to become college students. But it is time for us to stop eating. The government has time and again lied to us, ignored us. We only want the government to talk with us and to say that we are not traitors. We, the children, are ready to die. We, the children, are ready to use our lives to pursue the truth. We, the children, are willing to sacrifice ourselves.[2]

As Chai later recalled,

> People from the Beijing Students Federation desperately tried to dissuade us, but we stood our ground. At the time, there was little common ground between different groups of classmates.
>
> In the evening of May 12, I saw a list of students [who had signed up for the hunger strike]. There were only forty-odd students who had signed up. We posted the list at the "Triangle" at Beijing University, writing on it a few words: "Send off the warriors." I was very depressed and upset at the time.[3]

Whereas some student leaders favored retrenchment and consolidation of gains, Chai Ling sought to confront the government head-on, "to see whether it intends to suppress the movement or to ignore it, to see whether the people have a conscience or not, to see if China still has a conscience or not, if it has hope or not."[4] Those who wanted to propel the movement forward seized the initiative; the others had to join in the new push or be left out.[5]

The next day some three hundred students from Beida and Beijing Normal assembled for a ceremony initiating the hunger strike. They tied on red headbands and wrote slogans on their clothes: "Democracy, Hunger Strike," "Grief," "I dedicate myself to my country, but my powers are limited." Some teachers bought food for the hunger strikers' last meal. Chai Ling and others made emotional declarations of the patriotic sacrifice they contemplated, pushing its dramatic potential to the extreme, and issued a handbill explaining their actions:

> In this bright, sunny month of May, we are hunger striking. In this moment of most beautiful and happy youth, we must firmly leave all of life's happiness behind us. We do this ever so unwillingly, ever so unhappily!
>
> Yet . . . our country has already reached a time when prices are soaring, profiteering by officials runs rampant, power politics hangs high, and the bureaucracy is corrupt. . . .
>
> This country is our country,
> Its people are our people,
> The government is our government,
> If we do not cry out, who will?
> If we do not act, who will? . . .
>
> In the spirit of sacrificing our lives, we fight for life. But we are children, we are still children! Mother China, look earnestly upon your sons and daughters; as hunger mercilessly destroys their youth, as death closes in on them, can you remain indifferent?
>
> We do not want to die; we want to live, to live fully, for we are at life's most promising age. . . . But if the death of one or a few people can enable more to live better, and can make our motherland more prosperous, then we have no right to cling to life.
>
> As we suffer from hunger, Papa and Mama, do not grieve.[6]

The theme of grieving parents was prominent in declarations from the hunger strikers. As one wrote,

> "Perhaps I will not be able to fulfill my filial duty. For thousands and thousands of parents and children, I have tearfully made the choice to go on this hunger strike. . . .
>
> Since time immemorial, it has been impossible to satisfy the demands of both loyalty [to one's nation] and filial duty to one's parents. Papa, Mama, please understand why your son takes this action!
>
> —signed, A Hunger Striker Named Yu, an unfilial son.[7]

Whereas the representatives of the Federation and other existing organizations came across as junior intellectuals desiring to enter into policy discussions with the government, the hunger strikers claimed a rhetoric of innocence and martyrdom. In their presentation, students were not highly educated critics so much as children deserving sympathy.

By the time the hunger strikers had gathered in Tiananmen Square, their numbers had grown dramatically. The core came from Beijing, People's, and Normal universities, though a few from Beiwai and other smaller schools joined at the outset. Some two thousand students had joined the hunger strike by Sunday when I visited them in the Square.

They had formed little encampments, arranged by school, just north of the Monument to the People's Heroes. Amazingly, most had come with no preparation—not even much in the way of extra clothes, protection against either the hot days or chilly nights, or anything to sleep on. Gradually, their classmates (literally organized by class in many cases—e.g., second-year English students) began to supply these needs and to create a new organization in the Square. Back at the universities, the various unions, communications centers, and other groups worked to print handbills publicizing and explaining the hunger strikers' action. These flyers protested "the indifferent and cold attitude the government has taken toward the boycott of classes by Beijing students" and the branding of the movement as "turmoil." The declaration of the hunger strike put forward two demands:

> First, we demand that the government promptly carry out with the Beijing Students Dialogue Delegation a substantive and concrete dialogue based on the principle of equality of the parties.
> Second, we demand that the government set straight the reputation of this student movement, and that it give it a fair and just evaluation, affirming that it is a patriotic student democracy movement.[8]

The hunger strike captured attention and sympathy immediately. The number of participants swelled to some three thousand before the organizers refused to allow more to join. (There was an attempt to start a "wildcat" hunger strike near the Zhongnanhai compound, where protesters chanted at the senior Party cadres who lived inside.) When I went to see the hunger strikers on Monday, the Tiananmen crowd was already back up to a quarter of a million, and it seldom sank far below that; tens of thousands of people were present during the next ten days, even at night.[9] Though I didn't do a careful count, my impression was that the hunger strikers included proportionally more women than did the rest of the movement, certainly more than the leadership of the autonomous student unions and the Federation. If this impression is accurate, then Chai Ling was an especially apt symbolic leader. Still, women were in a minority overall, making up about a quarter of the hunger strikers and a higher percentage of those ferrying blankets from the universities and otherwise providing support.[10]

The hunger strike had important unintended effects. It created a new locus of activity and a new organization to lead the movement. This was a recipe for conflict with the Federation and the various campus unions. As early as May 14, for example, some student leaders were calling for an end to the hunger strike and withdrawal from the Square. Many of these individuals had ties to or sympathy for the reform wing of the government; a few were simply nervous. Others were more interested in building an enduring organization that could carry on a dialogue than in holding symbolic protests. Shen Tong enunciated this position on May 11:

> We see the movement in three stages. The first is to gain attention so that the people of China understand our concerns. The second is to make our campuses democratic castles and strengthen our own commitment to democratic reform, while giving students in other cities and those in other sectors of society—workers, peasants, and journalists—the time to gain their own political awareness. And third, after this has been achieved, we will probably hold a nationwide prodemocracy movement in the fall, to educate people as to what democratic reform is all about.[11]

These leaders—and some who were simply nervous about the prospects for repression—found some support within Federation circles but were unable to sway broader student opinion in the Square. The hunger strikers developed their own leadership structure, centered on the "Hunger Strike Group" and above all on Chai Ling. Though membership overlapped and personal ties joined the Hunger Strike Group to the Federation (particularly in the person of Wuerkaixi), these different centers of power and activity were never more than loosely coordinated. Because public drama was the most important weapon of the movement, the hunger strikers were in the ascendancy. They had, moreover, the organizational advantage of their around-the-clock presence in the Square; Federation leaders were dispersed among several campuses and only in some cases camped in the Square.

In short, the hunger strike had usurped the Federation and bypassed its programs. It was an emotion-charged, highly public declaration that existing conditions were intolerable, that reform was occurring so gradually as to put off democracy and freedom to the far distant future. The strikers' statement was simple: We cannot afford to wait.

ANOTHER ATTEMPT AT DIALOGUE

Even as the hunger strike was being organized, some members of the government were working to try to set up a more balanced dialogue with the students. A number of prominent reform-oriented intellectuals appeared as go-betweens. From May 10 to May 14, officials and intellectuals worked to set up a meeting with Yan Mingfu, head of the United Front Department. Though not the most obviously relevant government office, it was where access was available. Yan was at least a senior official of the sort the students had asked to meet earlier, a member of the Central Committee secretariat with ties in the reform wing of the government. He was joined by Li Tieying, who had succeeded Li Peng as head of the State Committee for Education when the latter became prime minister. Wang Juntao and Chen Ziming worked with other intellectuals to make connections for the students and to try to prepare them for the encounter.[12] They had been charged by Yan with identifying the appropriate students for the meeting.

Acting both as sympathizers and as mediators, these intellectuals brought together all the primary student leaders for a preliminary meeting with Yan Mingfu to agree on the terms of the dialogue. It was clear that Wuerkaixi, as head of the Federation and as the only Federation leader really prominent among the hunger strikers, would play a major role. Wang Dan and Chai Ling were both present, along with a number of others. Shen Tong was there as head of the Dialogue Delegation. He had been trying to position this group outside the Federation so that it might play a bridging role in discussions with the government. Now he would work behind the scenes to negotiate terms while others emerged as more prominent spokespeople for the movement. The key terms were that the dialogue should be one of equality (reflected in both physical arrangements and discourse) and that it should be televised live in its entirety.

As the dialogue approached, the intellectuals tried to give the students a crash course on the factional fighting taking place in the government. Anticipation of an impending visit by Mikhail Gorbachev had powerfully concentrated the authorities' attention, as had the occupation of Tiananmen Square and the hunger strike. The government needed very much to find a way out of the current impasse, and its reform-minded members, at least, hoped this could be done through dialogue. The activist intellectuals advised the students to proceed in a way that would both avoid the potential of a repressive backlash and enable the Party reformers to show they could handle the student threat. No one wanted to see a repeat of the ousting of Hu Yaobang in 1987 or the initiation of a new campaign against bourgeois liberalization (or worse).

While this group worked to promote dialogue, another group of twelve very prominent liberal intellectuals published an "urgent appeal regarding the present situation."[13] They expressed how upset they were on hearing of the start of the hunger strike yet how much they admired the dauntless determination of the students to press the cause of democracy forward. "The people will forever remember the historical contribution you have made today, in the year 1989," the document read. The authors cautioned the students, however, that democracy could only be built gradually and warned against intensification of the conflict. Showing a good sense of what student leaders would need as a basis for calling off the hunger strike, the intellectuals asked the government to publish a statement declaring that the movement was a patriotic campaign for democracy and that the government was opposed to any form of retribution for those who participated. They also called for legal recognition of the autonomous student organizations. Finally, they expressed their opposition to any use of violence against the students: "Whoever acts this way shall be condemned by history."

Shen Tong quoted a curious but revealing statement Yan Mingfu had made earlier, during the preliminary meeting: "Many of you," he said, addressing the students, "believe that there is a distinction between reformers and conservatives in the government. You are in fact wrong about this, but if you believe it, then you are hurting the reformers by being stubborn."[14] Not wanting to weaken the reformers' position, Shen asked Wang Dan and Wuerkaixi "whether they thought it was possible to get the hunger strikers to leave the square by Monday. They said it was, unless Chai Ling opposed the idea."[15] Unfortunately, Chai Ling had left the preparatory meeting early.

The dialogue was scheduled for late in the afternoon on May 14. It may have been the last chance for the reformers in or connected to the government to broker some kind of negotiated solution that would save Zhao Ziyang and the immediate prospects of the reform program.[16] The effort failed. After opening statements from each side, the dialogue began to unravel almost immediately. First, Shen Tong discovered that the meeting was not being televised live, as initially requested. Told that this was not possible, he settled for the promised live radio transmission, with the unedited videotape to be broadcast later. Then the Dialogue Delegation began to move through its planned list of key concerns. This process had barely begun, however, before other students began to pose questions of their own. The delegation had lost control of the agenda by the time a group of hunger strikers turned on a tape recorder playing *their* declaration and statements of "last words." This action raised emotions but also created confusion. The latter was only partially overcome as students tacitly agreed to focus on one issue: getting the government to repudiate the hated April 26 *People's Daily* editorial declaring that the students were instigators of turmoil.

While all this was going on, students outside began to raise a clamor, threatening to charge the building. Finally word got in to their delegates that the meeting was not being broadcast on radio, as promised. Government officials tried to blame faulty equipment, but Shen Tong decided that someone high in the government had overruled Yan Mingfu and that there was nothing the latter could do about it. The members of the Dialogue Delegation were unsure whether or not to try to continue the talks, but reports of the agitation outside convinced them they had no choice but to withdraw. They eventually made their way to the Square and reported on the proceedings, receiving ratification of their decision to walk out.[17]

Ultimate blame for the breakdown of the negotiations probably must rest with the government's failure to broadcast the dialogue—its refusal, in effect, to make it public—but the students' internal discord was also a problem. Some of this discord resulted from simple lack of organization and discipline—too many people tried to ask questions at once. More deeply, just as the government was split between those trying to find a way out of confrontation and those prepared to see it escalate (if only to justify repressing it), the students were split between those looking for a basis to withdraw from Tiananmen and build a long-term movement and those seeking to intensify the current confrontation. The latter were in the ascendancy, with Chai Ling as their official leader—though she may have been riding the wave of emotion as much as producing it. The Dialogue Delegation (and to a lesser extent the Federation itself) faded from prominence. The initiative lay with the hunger strikers.

MIKHAIL GORBACHEV BRINGS THE MEDIA

Mikhail Gorbachev's felicitously timed May 15 visit helped the student movement gain momentum. Western news media flooded into Beijing for the event (some had arrived earlier to cover the Asian Development Bank meeting that began May 4). Their presence gave the students a chance to gain space on various nations' front pages and news broadcasts, which they were not to relinquish for weeks. The powerful visual images of the movement, set against the backdrop of both imperial and communist landmarks, made for effective television and brought enormous international attention, which both pushed the students forward and upset the government.

Gorbachev appealed to the students as a charismatic reformer in another communist country. He symbolized the possibility of change within communism and the validity of political liberalization. Students came to Tiananmen carrying pictures of him and signs in Russian (though Gorbachev's Chinese government hosts did their best to make sure he didn't see them).

This cordiality was a departure from the students' usual contempt for the Soviet Union—seen as a poor competitor with the West—and for Russian influences on China. Though rumors circulated about Gorbachev's alleged rebukes to his Chinese hosts, he seemed rather to have allowed them to save face by making no direct public reference to the demonstrations. Still, students were impressed by his style; it was almost unimaginable that a Chinese leader would stop his limousine, as Gorbachev did, to mingle informally with crowds of ordinary people. (After that incident, the Chinese government tried to make sure his motorcades sped through the city without stopping.)

The presence of Gorbachev and the media inhibited the government from taking harsh action to suppress the student protests. No doubt official anger over the demonstrations was coupled with humiliation. The historic summit marking the resumption of friendly relations between the two greatest communist powers was overshadowed. Gorbachev's arrival parade had to be canceled lest he see the protests or be filmed with them as the backdrop. His schedule was continually readjusted. He had to be whisked ignominiously into the Great Hall of the People by the back door. He was never able to see the Forbidden City.

Some students thought helping the government save face would improve their chances in the long run. On the morning of May 15, Shen Tong took the microphone that had been set up in the Square and urged a tactical retreat: "I'm not saying we have to stop the hunger strike. But we should evacuate the square temporarily. We can't let our emotions make us forget all reason. Gorbachev is leading the Soviet Union to political reform one step at a time. His visit to China could be beneficial and useful to us. By staying here, we are giving the conservatives an excuse to crack down on the reformers."[18] A worker who had come out to support the students accosted Shen. "Are you worthy of being a student leader?" he asked. "You're letting all of the people of Beijing down. You're letting the workers down. To say you want us to leave makes you a traitor to the movement." Students took the microphone away from Shen.

There was great determination but little discipline in the Square. Though the leaders adopted titles (Chai Ling's, for example, was "general commander of Tiananmen Square") the students did not follow their instructions with any regularity.[19] Wuerkaixi, realizing the futility of trying to get the students to leave the Square, sought to arrange them in an orderly camp on the east side; the more order and discipline the students displayed, he reasoned, the less they could be accused of creating "chaos."

And it would be better to have carefully organized student protests as the background to Gorbachev's welcoming ceremony than to have milling masses who might either look incoherent or seem to justify police repression. However, Wuerkaixi was unable to get the all the students to move. The leaders of each group always said, "if the others move, then we'll move too." When some of them did move, others simply poured in to take their place. Moreover, the east side was opposite from where Gorbachev was scheduled to make his appearance. Many students seemed to feel they were being asked to move to the back of the crowd, away from the main attraction, even though they had arrived first. Wuerkaixi was unable to persuade even his own classmates from Beijing Normal to move.

For better or worse, the students had disrupted the first Sino-Soviet summit in thirty years. Though they unfurled a banner welcoming Gorbachev, he never arrived in the Square. He was brought into Beijing by Third Ring Road rather than the usual ceremonial route and greeted at a government guest house rather than in Tiananmen Square. The ceremonial center of Beijing, indeed of China, belonged for the time being to the students, who struggled to develop the capacity to manage their occupation effectively.

THE OCCUPATION SWELLS

Some students wanted to carry things still further, to push self-sacrifice beyond the hunger strike, to stop the waiting in a climactic act of will. One group proposed to burn themselves. No one I talked to was sure who they were or whether they would go through with it, but the Square and Beiwai campus alike were abuzz with the story. The would-be martyrs had written their wills and gone to buy gasoline. Leaders and onlookers apparently scrambled to dissuade them, but even in the absence of the act, the image added to the sense of urgency.

By this time, the hunger strikers' physical condition was becoming serious. Students had started collapsing on Monday, May 15. They were taken to increasingly crowded hospitals all over Beijing, more than two hundred on Monday alone. On Tuesday the numbers shot up as many strikers began to refuse drink as well as food. By Wednesday ambulances were running every fifteen to twenty minutes, by Thursday afternoon every six to eight. Once revived by intravenous drip, students left the hospitals (sneaking out if need be) and returned to the Square to resume their fasts. Several made that round trip ten or twelve times; I heard that the record was fifteen. Six was the greatest number of trips for anyone I knew personally.

Another group of students decided to charge Zhongnanhai compound, the senior leaders' residence, to demand further dialogue and to insist that Li Peng come to the Square to meet directly with protesters. First on Monday, then with more force on Tuesday, Shen Tong and a group of others tried to get the government's attention. Guards were startled that the students were willing to challenge them at the Xinhuamen gate, even to step inside without permission. Just as amazingly, students willingly gave their names, unit identities, and positions within the autonomous students' organizations. Afraid or not, they were not cowering before the authorities. When a couple of minor officials came to speak to them Monday, Shen (somewhat to his own surprise) scolded them brusquely: "I know the two of you are just bureaucrats sent to appease us. You don't have to pretend you're really talking with us. Just get our message to the people at the top. The hunger strikers don't have time for us to exchange niceties."[20]

On Tuesday a few students pushed their way inside the Xinhuamen gate, only to be stopped by People's Liberation Army troops. It was indicative of the students' growing self-confidence that Shen Tong, previously one of the main advocates of proceeding cautiously through established channels, found himself abandoning his role as negotiator and voice of moderation. It was at this point, he recalls, that he began to think the students didn't need recognition from the government to become a legitimate force. Rejecting Yan Mingfu's offer to make himself a hostage in the Square until the government began a proper dialogue, Shen headed off to Zhongnanhai, where he launched a new sit-in and hunger strike. He made this decision abruptly and on his own. It revealed not only the extent to which a variety of students were starting wildcat actions outside of any central coordination but also the extent to which the action had shifted away from the university campuses. If a student leader like Shen didn't want to be relegated to the backwaters of the movement, he needed to be a hunger striker; he needed to be in on the drama and the risk-taking.

The Xinhuamen gate was a nice setting for a protest. It was on the main road to Tiananmen Square, Chang'an Boulevard. The compound was the seat of power (now that the old Imperial City was just a tourist attraction), and the huge red gate made an attractive backdrop, emblazoned with the slogan: "To Serve the People." Shen and his fellow strikers sat facing the gate, waiting for the appearance of government officials, whose very absence was becoming both an issue and one of the symbolic victories of the movement.

While this was going on, Zhao Ziyang met with Mikhail Gorbachev and dropped a seemingly obvious comment that was in fact a minor bombshell: He informed the Soviet premier that Deng Xiaoping was still China's supreme leader even though he had retired from his formal positions of authority, adding that everyone in the government had made a pact to follow his directions on matters of ultimate importance. The implicit message was that Deng, not Zhao, should be held responsible for the way the student protests were being handled.[21] Deng was outraged. The five members of the standing committee of the Politburo—including Zhao and Li Peng—were called into a secret meeting with Deng. Students hoped for several hours that this would result in the high-level dialogue they had long sought. Instead it led to the downfall of Zhao, the reformers, and the soft line on protest, though this consequence wasn't immediately apparent.

What was apparent was the swelling size of the crowds converging on Tiananmen Square. The hunger strike had galvanized support far beyond the ranks of students. A wider and wider spectrum of Beijing citizens came to express their sympathy for the hunger strikers and for the students' cause. Vendors selling sodas from pushcarts arrived to offer free drinks. Clerks from government office buildings in the surrounding area came out surreptitiously on breaks or stopped on the way to and from work to offer quiet encouragement. The students' attitude of self-sacrifice proclaimed that this was not a movement of privileged youth complaining about their own situation but of China's children worried about its future. In a culture that made much of the importance of food, not eating was a potent symbolic act. But, as Han suggests, "it was the extremity of the act that shocked ordinary Chinese: influenced by a traditional culture that esteemed moderation, living in a highly repressive society where experience soon taught that individual will or desire had little impact on one's environment, citizens were deeply moved by the youths' willingness to stake their lives, as well as by their faith that the sacrifice would ultimately alter Chinese society."[22]

Normally cautious senior intellectuals were also moved by the students' protests. On May 16, more than a thousand signed a declaration that started with a recollection of the May 16 Circular, by which Mao Zedong and his supporters had opened the Cultural Revolution. The 1989 declaration echoed Mao's statement that "history has proven that those who suppress student movements will come to no good end." The intellectuals challenged the April 26 *People's Daily* editorial and called for recognition of the students' organizations. They ended, however, with a lightly conciliatory note: "Long live a free, democratic, socialist motherland!"[23]

MARCHING REACHES ITS PEAK

Wednesday, May 17, was another turning point. More than a million people converged on Tiananmen for perhaps the largest unauthorized protest ever, exceeding in size even Zhou Enlai's funeral in 1976. Once again, marchers came not in amorphous masses but in delimited groups. Most were identified by banners naming their university (or other official unit). Some of the groups were highly specific, representing a particular department or field of study, and each was proud of its participation in an historic event. Part of what made the event so historic was the enormous, open participation of workers. The relatively conservative head of the All-China Federation of Trade Unions (ACFTU) was out of the country, and in his absence Hu Yaobang's liberal protégé, Zhu Houze, tacitly encouraged ACFTU participation.[24] In addition, a group of twelve well-known intellectuals led by Yan Jiaqi released a declaration directly blaming the hunger strike on the intransigence of senior Party leaders and throwing down something of a gauntlet with its strong language:

> [D]ue to the absolute power enjoyed by a dictator, the government has lost its sense of responsibility and its humanity. Such a government is not truly the government of the Republic—it is a government whose existence is possible only because of the power of a dictator. . . .
>
> Down with the dictatorship of the individual! Those who are dictators will come to no good end! Reverse the April 26 editorial! Government by old men must end! The dictator must resign![25]

But the intellectuals also sought to defuse the crisis and get the students out of the Square by proclaiming them already victorious: "Today, we declare to all of China, to all of the world, that from now on the great fight the students have been waging, their hunger strike of one hundred hours, has won a great victory. The students have used their own actions to proclaim that this student movement is not turmoil but rather a great patriotic democracy movement to bury forever dictatorship and the imperial system."[26]

The Beiwai contingent bicycled within a mile of Tiananmen and marched the last stretch of Chang'an Boulevard.[27] At the northeast corner of the Square we turned south, following a path monitored by lines of mostly male students called "pickets" (with reference to fence posts). We marched in a sort of "U" around the core of protesters, were led into what I later learned was the second but not innermost circle to pay our respects, then headed out to one side for a rest and refreshments. We then made another circuit and headed back to our bicycles. (However, it proved impossible to cross the crowded street to ride in the right direction and we had to return by a roundabout path, heading south to go north.)

All manner of people had turned out to protest. Students from Beiwai and Beida kept commenting that they never knew there were so many universities in the city—universities of iron and steel, travel and tourism, broadcasting, commerce, and public security. This was also the first time that students from outside Beijing were present in large enough numbers to make an impact as a distinct group. A large contingent from the nearby port city of Tianjin was most prominent. The open appeal of the twelve well-known intellectuals had helped generate new enthusiasm; several of them marched openly with the students for the first time. Even more impressive was the fact that the protesters included a few soldiers and policemen, as well as a great many officials from various government offices—the Ministry of Trade, the Foreign Ministry, the Xinhua News Agency, and the railways. There were small entrepreneurs and owners of large businesses; the latter arrived in an air-conditioned bus with a banner across the back reading, "We are rich but we still want justice."

The next night I was invited to join a group of student leaders in the Square. We had a "passport" that enabled us to enter the inner circle. In addition to marking off routes for marchers (something not done on May 4, when people milled about in confusion), students had cleared paths for ambulances and strung plastic ribbons between human pickets to keep these thoroughfares open. Similar cordons marked off two approximate circles. The outer housed the bulk of the protesters actually camped at Tiananmen, organized by school; only individuals from the appropriate university were allowed into each section. The inner circle housed the hunger strikers, also divided into separate groups for each school, with a spot for the core leadership. This system enabled those in the outer circle to care for those fasting inside; it also kept the massive crowd at bay and allowed some freedom of movement and circulation of air where the strikers slept. Moreover, the inner circle provided a place for midnight organizational and strategy meetings. This physical layout extended the students' earlier tactic of marching with linked arms to prevent the penetration of agents provocateurs or other unwelcome elements into their midst.

The elaborate security system was largely the work of a Beida graduate student named Zhang Lun. Its purpose was both to shield the hunger strikers and to maintain order in the Square. In addition to the corridors—"lifelines"—that allowed ambulances to come and go, there were paths for arriving protesters; student ID cards and/or passwords were the condition of entry at various checkpoints. Members of the press were identified and given access to students for interviews, but they were prevented from badgering the weakening hunger strikers. Many journalists found themselves frustrated in their efforts to reach the inner circle. Shen Tong even found himself excluded once when he left his ID in his jacket and forgot the password.

It was getting harder for students to maintain an organizational structure. Hunger strikers and Federation leaders were fighting over control of the movement and the Square; the Dialogue Delegation was yet another focal point. At the same time, the rapidly increasing numbers of students from outside Beijing brought new organizational challenges. Tens of thousands of provincial university students—and some high school students and workers—had come to Beijing to be a part of the great democratic movement, but many had only vague ideas of the policies developed by the Beijing students. Nonetheless, the outsiders clamored for a greater voice in decisionmaking about the occupation. They had reason. Thousands were crowded into an underpass at the north end of the Square. It was squalid and smelly, poorly ventilated, and lacked toilet facilities. Yet the security arrangements of the Beijing students were tight enough at first that it was hard for other students—let alone workers—to penetrate and join in the occupation.

Meanwhile, a group of workers had set up a headquarters near the west reviewing stand at the edge of Tiananmen Square. The organization was never large, but the mere hint of concerted working-class mobilization was extremely threatening to the government. A few of the workers were veterans of earlier mobilizations. Zhao Hongliang, who became a leader, had been active in a strike of bus drivers and conductors in 1985. One of the most important worker-activists was Han Dongfang, a peasant's son and onetime assistant librarian and refrigeration engineer, who now con   :d the new Beijing Workers Autonomous Federation. When he went to .nake speeches, he recalled later, he often heard catcalls both from workers, who thought he sounded too well educated to be one of them (though in fact he was self-taught), and from students, who yelled "What right do you have to tell us what to do? You're just an ordinary worker!"[28] Han and his colleagues persevered, however, at one point even placing their banner on a bus and driving it around the city center to announce their existence. Though only forty or fifty workers had signed up as members, many more stopped by the headquarters or cheered the bus on. The workers announced their program with rhetoric indebted to the *Communist Manifesto*: "The proletariat is the most progressive class in society. Through the democracy movement, we have nothing to lose but our chains, but we stand to gain the whole world."[29]

Gradually accommodations were made for the out-of-town students, but tensions remained high, and the newcomers formed their own association. Only one non-Beijing student, Li Lu from Nanjing, came to prominence within the leadership of the Hunger Strike Headquarters.[30] Li had traveled to Beijing by himself at the end of April and gravitated to Beida, where he listened to speeches and the announcements on the Voice of Democracy.[31] Eventually he made contact with some of the student leaders, though many remained suspicious of him. He was hampered especially by his lack of a student ID, which he had left behind in Nanjing, he said, in order to travel anonymously. He won the confidence of Chai Ling, however, and through her gained entrée into the leadership circles. He was thus in on the hunger strike from the beginning. Even so, he continued to have difficulties with the Beijing activists—particularly those who had been prominent in the original federation. On May 15, for example, he tried to chair a meeting of representatives from different schools in the Square. "People did not know me," he recalled. "They asked me who I was. The former student leaders were especially uncooperative. Chai Ling introduced me as the deputy commander of the headquarters. She told them I was in charge of the day-to-day business. I was temporarily accepted, though I knew that sooner or later they would realize I was from out of town, and their suspicions would revive."[32]

Shen Tong's account of hearing of Li Lu's leadership reveals the tensions and suspicions between the long-standing activists and the newcomers:

> I didn't know anything about Li Lu. I had heard that he was from Nanjing, which made him the only person from outside Beijing to assume a top leadership role. People were a little worried about him because no one had ever seen his student identification card. When I heard about this leadership, I became concerned. Our movement was about democratic reform, but a lot of people in the square had lost their vision of what we were after, which was going to make it more difficult to accomplish our goal.[33]

An articulate young man who spoke good English, Li Lu did express a strong sense of direction and goals when I interviewed him.[34] Though he revealed an overwhelming commitment to the immediate leadership of the occupation in the Square, he possessed little knowledge of the organizing work or political arguments that lay behind the initial mobilization of the Beijing students.

Still, with all the difficulties, the May 17 demonstration was full of enthusiasm. In addition to the huge march, other developments buoyed spirits. The All-China Federation of Trade Unions—China's only recognized labor organization—publicly gave 100,000 yuan to help the hunger strikers. Letters of support poured in from a variety of groups—women's associations, art and literary circles, the so-called "independent parties." One of the most important features of these was that groups that had always been controlled by the Communist Party were acting independently of any orders from the top.

MEETING WITH LI PENG: THE FINAL FAILURE OF DIALOGUE

The high spirits of Wednesday gave way to an air of crisis on Thursday, May 18. Round-the-clock activity was wearing on everyone. Not only students were meeting at 2 A.M.; the standing committee of the Politburo was in action late at night and at the crack of dawn. At around five in the morning, four standing committee members (Zhao Ziyang, Li Peng, Qiao Shi, and Hu Qili) went to visit hunger strikers in Beijing Xiehe Hospital, and senior Party and government leaders visited exhausted students in other hospitals. The bed-ridden students repeatedly asked their eminent visitors to go to Tiananmen Square to talk with the hunger strikers there, but the officials merely expressed their sympathy and their desire to end the suffering and the risk to the students. The rumors that a group of radicals had to be restrained from burning themselves started up again.

In the midst of this frustration and anxiety, Premier Li Peng agreed to meet with student representatives. The hastily called meeting promised to offer the high-level dialogue students had so long sought. No members of the Dialogue Delegation could readily be found, however, so it was not represented. After hearing how the encounter went, Shen Tong said he wasn't sure a delegation presence would have made a difference.

Li Peng sat back in an overstuffed armchair, flanked by colleagues and aides and facing a broad oval that included a dozen students. Wuerkaixi had come direct from the hospital, still wearing the pajamas he had been given there. Li opened the meeting paternalistically, saying all parties needed to focus on one subject: how to make the student hunger strikers stop fasting.[35] The Party and government, he said, were very concerned about the strikers' health. He emphasized the students' youth, noting that his own children were older than they (and adding that none was involved in *guandao*—official profiteering). As he seemed to settle into lecture mode, Wuerkaixi broke in: "Time is running out quickly. We're sitting here comfortably while our fellow students are starving outside, so please pardon me for interrupting. You said just now that we should focus on just one subject. We're not here because you invited us, but because of the hundreds and thousands of students in the Square who invited you to talk to us. We must decide the number of topics, not you." Li Peng must have been angry, but he controlled himself as the students took over the meeting. Wang Dan, claiming the support of several million demonstrators, suggested that "to end the hunger strike, the government should first meet our demands."

WUERKAIXI: It's very clear that the question is not how to persuade us who are present here to leave the Square. I'd like to state that, first, we know better than anyone else that the students need to leave as soon as possible. Second, it won't help if all of us at this meeting are persuaded because we consist only of one tenth of a percent of the students in the Square. It's not a matter of subordination to the majority. I believe that if there is one single student who decides not to leave, the rest will keep him company.

WANG DAN: This isn't an opportunity to convince us, but to respond to our requirements. First, the government must acknowledge that the current student campaign is patriotic in nature, not "troublesome" as it was called in the April 26 editorial. Second, dialogues must start as soon as possible. If you can give us a satisfactory response to our demands, we'd like to return to the Square and do our best to persuade our fellow students to go back to school.

Several other students made short speeches of their own. Some tried to placate the government with declarations that they shared the goal of fighting for communism. One claimed (against all evidence) that the students harbored no personal animosity against Li Peng: "We're dissatisfied with you not because we're against you personally but because you're the premier." A student from the University of Politics and Law brought forward the widespread but ungrounded view that the government's failure to respond to a hunger strike within seven days was a violation of accepted international practice (one of a series of claims throughout the movement that international law was on the students' side). Nearly all the students echoed the theme that accepting the students' demands—retraction of the April 26 editorial, recognition, and dialogue—was the only way to prevent the situation from getting worse.

Li Tieying (head of the State Committee for Education and a reformer) offered an ambiguously worded attempt to mollify the students without guaranteeing any structural changes:

> We in the education committee have a lot of experience in setting up different kinds of channels to listen to the faculty and students. I don't want to see the student movement remain at the present level. It is in fact a national event; its demands have gone beyond educational areas. There are more political demands, and the situation is still developing.
>
> If you ask me my opinion of the student movement, . . . I would say that the students have demonstrated their patriotism through their criticisms, suggestions, and proposals. But many of their decisions aren't in line with our thinking. I think history is the best judge of this movement.
>
> The movement could become inconsistent with the students' initial ideas. Both of us are against turmoil. Nothing will ever get done if there isn't a stable environment in China.

Yan Mingfu, another broadly sympathetic reformer, spoke more directly (and revealed a fairly penetrating understanding of the current situation of the movement):

> I'm confident that we'll find a resolution to the problem. Right now we need to send those who are very weak to the hospital. I suggest we reach an agreement on this. We must resolve the two problems separately.
>
> As I said in a conversation with Wuerkaixi and Wang Dan on the thirteenth of the month, things have gone far beyond what people can control. At that time, I raised three points. First, the students should leave the Square immediately and the hunger strikers should be persuaded to receive hospital treatment. Second, the Central Committee has authorized me to assure the students that they will be safe after they return to school. That was our response to the students' question about "squaring accounts after the autumn harvest."[36] Third, if you do not trust me you can take us to your schools as hostages until the People's Congress begins its session. I was told that, after I left, Wang Dan and several other students presided at the meeting, and that some there agreed to my proposal but the majority did not.
>
> Meanwhile the government and Party leaders made quite a few attempts to visit with the students at the Square, but because they could not get in touch with student headquarters, they were unable to enter the center. You may know of this already. More and more evidence shows that the three spontaneous student organizations are no longer able to influence the surging crowds. It's not likely that the crowds that keep pouring into the Square will listen to you. The direction this whole thing is going worries people. It seems the only thing that you can do is to persuade the hunger strikers to leave. Then we of the Central Committee and the government sincerely want to resolve the issues you students have brought up. An immediate problem is the safety of these kids. It concerns everybody. We must handle it with great care, as we want to be responsible to them.

The more conservative Chen Xitong, mayor of Beijing, added a strange twist by claiming to have more concern for the hunger strikers' lives than they had themselves. He also implied that the students he was speaking to were somehow manipulating the others. Chen voiced the recurrent government claim that people from all walks of life were writing and calling the government and Party to complain of traffic and other problems caused by the protests: "Although some workers have joined your demonstration in support of your petition, many more want to end the confusion." Paramedics and doctors had asked the government to make rescue of the hunger strikers a top priority: "They wanted us not to play with the students' lives, or to use them as bargaining chips. I want you to understand this too. We must guarantee the health of the hunger strikers. Fasting is unhealthy; it can even be deadly. After all, what's the point of suicide if there are other ways to resolve the problem?"

Under the guise of providing needed care for the hunger strikers, Li Peng proposed that the Red Cross be charged with moving them immediately to hospitals. He seemed oblivious to the fact that doing so would end their protest, and he offered no material concessions. He did, however, go what he must have thought was some distance toward meeting one of the students' key demands:

> The second question I want to address is that neither the government nor the Party has ever referred to the students as rioters. We have always emphasized the value of your patriotic enthusiasm. There were quite a few things you did right. Among the suggestions you made, I found that a lot are on the government's agenda and will be solved soon. One thing is certain, you people have taken a positive step toward pushing the government to get these things done in the future. . . . However, things are not developing in accordance with your kind-hearted wishes, imaginations, and patriotic passion. Beijing is now in total disorder, and the confusion is spreading to the rest of the country.

Li said he didn't blame Wuerkaixi or Wang Dan for what had happened but was simply concerned with ending the hunger strike. Acknowledging that perhaps the student leaders couldn't make the decision to stop others' fasts, he asked that those present carry his petition to the hunger strikers. Wuerkaixi assured him the matter rested with the hunger strikers in the Square and suggested that if even one insisted on staying, the others would want to stay, too. He reminded Li that the students had made quite clear the conditions under which they would leave and suggested that if the government wasn't willing to meet those conditions, then it wasn't sincere in its expressions of concern. After a couple more comments, someone handed

Yan Mingfu a piece of paper, from which he read aloud a request from the Hunger Strike Group that its representatives return immediately. Wuerkaixi fainted, falling to the floor dramatically, and the meeting broke up.

Based on its manifest content, this meeting might have started a real dialogue had it been held in late April or the first week of May. But now the government was offering too little, too late. In retrospect it does seem that Li Peng and others were looking for a nonviolent way out, but, as one student charged, "he wants us to leave the Square, but he doesn't want to give an inch." No doubt Li thought the students should appreciate the very fact that he met for dialogue, not to mention his repeated acknowledgment of their patriotic intentions. But the students did not regard this meeting as a real dialogue. As Wang Zhixin said at the meeting, "This wasn't a dialogue, but an introductory meeting." Yan Mingfu even acknowledged as much. The transcripts also fail to bring out the participants' tone—either Li Peng's stiff body language and smug, patronizing non-engagement with the students or the confrontational style of Wuerkaixi and others. The Dialogue Delegation promptly issued a statement, read over China Central Television's English service, denouncing the morning's meeting.

At the same time, it should be noted that at least the more reform-oriented officials did try to reach some sort of accord. Yan Mingfu, for example, went out of his way to describe the students' organization as "spontaneous" (and he was certainly right that leaders could not control the crowds, though they were not altogether without influence). Li Tieying, and even Li Peng, stressed the students' patriotism—albeit perhaps a little disingenuously.

The hunger strikers were indeed in bad shape. Rumors circulated that the police might move into the Square as soon as Gorbachev had left for Shanghai. Worst of all, at least in the short run, it rained. Students erected makeshift tents, throwing plastic sheets over sticks lashed together with string. The hunger strikers themselves were better protected, as buses had been brought in to house them; most were Beijing city buses donated by their drivers or by bus companies, perhaps with the organizational aid of the local Red Cross.

The Beiwai students were particularly demoralized because they had expected a visit of solidarity from their teachers, but nearly all the latter had backed out when one of their number (a Party member) returned from an official meeting with the claim that the government had agreed to a dialogue and that leaders would be convening with the students at midnight. Once again, members of the Party elite huddled late into the night to try to decide their policy. As always, their goal was that the Party speak with one voice. This time, with Li Peng fresh from the abortive attempt to persuade the students to leave the Square, the hard-line approach was apparently gaining strength.

Midnight passed without a dialogue, to no one's great surprise. A few minutes before 5 A.M., however, the few hunger strikers who were awake were surprised to learn that Zhao Ziyang had come to the Square after the all-night leadership meeting. Not wanting to seem out of touch, Li Peng had followed hastily. Both shook hands with students on their arrival, but Li stood stolidly and silently behind Zhao as the latter took a megaphone and spoke to a small crowd. Li stayed only a minute or two and left without any real conversation or statement. Zhao lingered. He signed his name on t-shirts and spoke with hunger strikers on a bus. Tears in his eyes, Zhao declared that "we have come, but too late." He begged the students' forgiveness and reiterated that the hunger strikers' health was the most important issue. Zhao's words were not so far different from Li Peng's of the day before, but his tone was a world away:

> [A]s you know, everything is very complicated. A process is needed [for resolving the problems raised by the movement]. You cannot any longer insist on this point after seven days of strike. You insist and insist again on obtaining a satisfactory response before stopping your strike, and at this moment it will be too late. The irreparable will be done. You are still young, student friends, still young, you still have time. You must live, remain healthy and safe, until the day when you will see China realize the Four Modernizations. You are not like us: we, we are already old. This does not concern us.[37]

Zhao seemed above all sad and tired, and he earned strong student support for his show of sympathy.

Unbeknownst to the students, Zhao had been sharply outvoted in the standing committee hours earlier, spelling his apparent downfall; the tears in his eyes might have been for himself as well as the students. Reportedly, his decision to visit the students had been condemned, but he insisted on going anyway, violating the discipline of the Party of which he was chair. Li Peng was thus forced to rush out to visit the students as well, lest Zhao seem the only sympathetic leader. However, as Li did not linger to talk to the students in their buses, he would be remembered for his earlier talk in the Great Hall of the People, lecturing students sternly and arrogantly from an overstuffed chair. The next day film clips of the two visits were shown on TV almost hourly (though the insulting end to Li's was edited out). Seeing one after the other reinforced the contrast between Zhao and

Li and lifted the latter even further in viewers' esteem. However clear the popular preference, it was largely irrelevant to the top Party leadership.

RUMORS IN THE SQUARE

Thursday night the Square reminded me of a battlefield. It was damp and lit mainly by the moon. Sirens sounded from ambulances heading off in various directions. Occasionally a white-clad Red Cross crew would rush by carrying an unconscious hunger striker on a stretcher. I thought first of the Crimean War for some reason, but it could equally have been Napoleon's invasion of Russia or the War between the States. Students froze in their makeshift tents and put on layers of ill-fitting (mostly donated) clothing, half of it the vaguely military kind favored during the Maoist era. When the sirens were particularly loud I thought of science fiction renderings of the world after a nuclear explosion. Of course, such associations were exaggerated; I was responding both to the surreal scene and to the general mood of the place. But moods were important, shifting quickly, often for no apparent reason or because of a rumor one's conscious mind discounted.

There were rumors in plenty, not least about the student leaders. As various new waves of students declared themselves part of the leadership, so suspicions circulated about the old leaders. I was told repeatedly how Wuerkaixi had been seen eating with foreign reporters when he was supposed to be on hunger strike, how he always had foreign cigarettes they had given him, and how his desire to find a negotiated way out of the Square was a sign of cowardice. Shen Tong reported hearing similar stories about Wang Dan.[38] On that rainy Thursday night, even the gift of shelter could look suspicious as the bus drivers who drove their vehicles into the Square learned:

> Everyone was talking about the thunderstorms that were predicted. We
> could feel them in the air; the wind had already started blowing. We began
> moving the hunger strikers into the buses, but many of them didn't want to
> leave their makeshift tents. Their leaders were afraid that this was a trick
> set up by the federation to drive them off the square, so the drivers were
> booted off their buses and some of the hunger strikers, weak from fasting,
> punctured the tires.
> "How are we going to explain this?" the drivers cried.[39]

I was not surprised when students suspected a government trick, but their suspicion of the other students shocked me. The weak links between the out-of-town students and those from Beijing were a central factor. Relations were further strained at this point by the creation of the Federation of Students from Outside Beijing (Waigaolian), which formalized the non-Beijing students' separateness and reinforced their determination to stay in the Square. Divisions among the students exacerbated the ever-present problem of rumors. Suspicions about leaders or about what the Dialogue Delegation was doing behind closed doors spiraled out of control; there were no established relationships to ensure trust or create skepticism about the wilder stories. The Dialogue Delegation—composed entirely of Beijing students active in the early days of the movement—faded completely from prominence as the Waigaolian grew. The Hunger Strike Group, still controlled mostly by Beijing students, largely displaced the older Federation as a leadership structure.

The dependence on rumor was greatest, of course, when there was least to be learned from any reliable source. And Thursday night was not the worst of such times; on Thursday there was still real news. For a remarkable week, the Chinese press defied all precedent (as well as current orders) and actually reported what was taking place on the campuses, in the streets, and especially in the Square. On May 8, the *People's Daily* had begun publishing editorials supportive of the students and democracy (presumably under the guidance of reformers linked to Zhao Ziyang). On May 12 (perhaps partly in response to the students' targeting of the press on May 10), one paper after another began to carry accurate and sympathetic spot reporting of the protests. For a few unprecedented days, the Chinese press was full of news of opposition to the government, denials of official reports, and so forth. The *People's Daily* ran a two-page photo spread, including a shot of a mother worrying over the health of her hunger-striking son. Television footage showed Tiananmen and protesters being fed intravenously in hospitals. There sometimes remained a hint of caution, an implication that journalists still considered a few topics too hot to touch, but the reversal was remarkable.

Effective, apparently uncensored Chinese media coverage began with the hunger strike and continued through Gorbachev's visit. Television and print reporters from around the world were also most active during this period. This coverage had a significant impact around the universities—for example, in persuading cautious professors to look more carefully and sympathetically at the students' actions. The papers were read assiduously by ordinary people all over Beijing. Ironically, the information they contained was perhaps least accessible in the Square itself. Though those in the

Square had the best location for getting the latest rumors, they had a hard time getting the newspapers and couldn't see television. Whenever I brought a newspaper into the Square, there was an eager scramble to see it.

Moreover, the movement lacked an effective internal communications channel. The communications centers on campus had been outstripped by the developments in the Square. There, a small "broadcast center"—once again, mainly an amplifier and loudspeakers—was established, providing a mixture of news and commentary, instructions from students leaders, and rumors. This system was called the "voice of the students," but it was inadequate to the task. The students were more effective at getting their message to the public than at organizing communications among themselves. In late April and early May, Shen Tong and his Beida colleagues had briefly formed a newspaper, the *News Herald*, but that was short-lived and mainly aimed at the broader public. Had it been sustained, it might have provided a flow of more or less reliable information, perhaps muting the effects of the wilder rumors and offering a basis for greater unity among the protesters. Hand-operated printing presses and mimeograph machines were used to produce single-sheet flyers, but there was no journal for news reports from the students' point of view, let alone for discussion. The 1979 Chinese democracy movement had formed several of these. Its 1989 counterpart mobilized more effectively and found deeper popular sympathy, but it fell behind on both theory and communication.

The Beijing students at least had a steady flow of friends and family moving back and forth between campus (or home) and the Square. These visitors brought reasonably accurate second-hand summaries of the news. The out-of-town students were more completely cut off. A few had radios and could hear their own actions and broader events discussed on Chinese radio, the Voice of America, and the BBC. The foreign news media thus played a major role not only in informing the world about the student protests but also in presenting to the students a somewhat larger picture than they themselves could see, camped in Tiananmen Square.

MARTIAL LAW

On Friday, May 19, the rumors ran particularly hot and heavy. They were fueled not just by uncertainties over the government's actions but also by conflicts between student leaders and questions about who spoke for the movement. The careful attempt to maintain regular internal decision-making procedures as a key dimension of democracy had broken down, and the lack of communications capacity was becoming an acute problem. Both on campuses and in the Square, a debate raged about whether to end the hunger strike or even to withdraw.

Intellectuals associated with Zhao—administrators, think-tank members, and professors—visited students at their Tiananmen headquarters throughout the day. They passed on rumors of Zhao's fall and urged students to withdraw before the leadership decided to "adopt strong measures such as military control. . . . This bleak prospect is something that the people of China, having suffered for a decade during the Cultural Revolution, cannot possibly accept."[40] Through a thousand different channels, students heard that a declaration of martial law was imminent. Even Wuerkaixi returned to the Square to argue once again for an immediate pullout. "It was related to a very dangerous piece of news I got later that night," he explained, recounting how he too had received a warning of the coming imposition of martial law.[41] As the students knew well, rumors were not always false; they were the Chinese people's main early source of information about policy debates and shifts within the Party leadership. No published or broadcast news on such matters would be available until everything had been settled.

Zhao gained enormous sympathy and popularity when, shortly after his early-morning meeting with the students, word spread of his imminent political demise. At the same time, some activists—particularly workers—grumbled about how naively impressed the students had been with the mere gesture of Zhao and Li's visit to the Square. "What is it with you students?" one member of the Beijing Autonomous Workers Union said to Shen Tong. "What did they think they were doing, getting the autograph of the enemy?"[42]

Autograph collecting became a craze that day. To an American this fad possessed something of the tone of the last day of school, when students sign each other's yearbooks, or of the exchange of addresses and photos at the end of summer camp. Students wanted souvenirs of their great moment. At the same time, there was a growing grimness in the air. Martial law threatened the end of the occupation of the Square, quite likely of the movement as a whole. Though students occasionally contemplated the possibility of violent repression, however, few really expected it. After all, Party members and others with ties to the leadership had gone to great lengths to offer advance hints of military action. The government clearly had no intention of catching the students by surprise; it wanted them forewarned—and thus out of its way—when it moved its army into Beijing.

Student leaders called a series of meetings during the day. There was never any doubt that the majority favored ending the hunger strike; the questions were whether this could be a unanimous (or near-unanimous) decision and whether the broader mass of protesters would support it. Those in favor of ending the strike pointed to the student leadership's increasing difficulty in maintaining order, security, and control over the burgeoning crowds and cited the threat of martial law. In one sign of the growing confusion, only Chai Ling, Zhang Boli, and Li Lu could be found to represent the Hunger Strike Group in the most crucial meeting, discussions with representatives of the various universities. Eighty percent of those present voted to end the hunger strike. The occupation of Tiananmen Square would continue, it was decided, but henceforth would be a "sit-in."[43] When this decision was announced, around 9:30 that evening, it astonished not only the thousands of protesting students but also several members of the leadership itself. Feng Congde heard this startling news from other students in the Square, even though he was Chai Ling's husband, the "vice commander" of the Hunger Strike Headquarters, and one of the strongest links between this newer group and the old Federation. As Li Lu reports:

> Feng Congde was hysterical. He said the students were accusing us of having sold out to the Government, just as victory was around the corner. He grabbed the microphone and wanted to announce that the previous resolution was invalid. "How could you have made the decision without me?" he asked.
> "You weren't there," I said. We couldn't find you anywhere."
> Chai Ling went over to snatch the microphone from her husband's hand. They started to fight and I went over to pull them apart.[44]

Li and Chai even discussed the possibility of having students from the "picket line" security brigade use force to take Feng to the hospital. Feng was one of the few hunger strikers who had not fainted and thus had not been taken to a hospital, where intravenous drip and a bit of rest, as Li suggests, might have revived his energy and calmed his nerves. Indeed, just as Feng went to call another leadership meeting in order to demand a new vote on the question of withdrawal, he fainted and was taken to an ambulance.

While this was going on in the Square, similar debates were being held on the various university campuses. Friday evening I rode up to Beijing and People's universities with a friend. Before great crowds, speakers were debating whether or not to withdraw from Tiananmen Square. Those urging moderation got polite hearings at best and were applauded only when they praised the overall goals of the movement. Later, at Beida, others said, "This is time for actions, not words; march to Tiananmen," and the crowd was off with little hesitation. It picked up more people at Renda and headed for the Square. However, this enthusiasm for continuing the occupation came from supporters, not from the hunger strikers themselves.

My friend and I rushed back to Beiwai to report what was happening. We knew that some students were debating similar questions at the graduate student dormitory—and debating they were, as perhaps only graduate students (or faculty) would do at such a moment (in this case the faculty had already decided to stay home in caution). We had expected the Beiwai students, like those at Beida, to move en masse toward the Square, but they dithered; they hesitated; they argued for three hours about what to do. Around 10:30, news came of Chai Ling's announcement that the hunger strikers had decided to end their fast.

The rumors that Zhao had been toppled raised questions about the wisdom of returning to Tiananmen. Some of the leaders of Beiwai's rather more affluent students, with better career prospects at risk, suggested that because the students from Beida and Renda had marched, there was no need for marchers from another, smaller school. Several hundred Beiwai students had already lined up, carrying water, bits of food, and something to keep them warm if they stayed the whole night. But nobody would call for the march to start, and the marchers were unwilling to go without a leader. Some wept, half in sorrow over the apparent crisis of the movement and half in anger over their own failure to move, yet leaders continued to stall and to find excuses for staying put ("maybe we should see what the news is on TV"). For all the students' vaunted individualism, they were very Chinese in needing to move as a whole group or not at all.

Li Peng solved the problem. Near midnight, Chinese Central Television broadcast his speech, made before a selected gathering of senior cadres. He was ill at ease, occasionally muffing his lines, reading woodenly, though with periodic angry emphasis, from papers in front of him. The speech was arrogant and hostile and could not have been more provocative to the students, whom Li ordered to quiet down. The capital, Li claimed, was "in a grave state of anarchy that is going from bad to worse. . . . The hunger strikers are being used as 'hostages' by a few people trying to force the Party and the government to yield to their political demands. These people do not show a single sign of compassion. . . . The student representatives admit that they are no longer able to control the situation; crowds keep pouring into the already packed Tiananmen Square, shouting their own demagogic slogans." This was "chaos," Li said, "turmoil," and it was spreading.

> The Party and the government have stated again and again that the majority of the students are kind and honest and did not mean to cause such

turmoil. They are patriotic and democratic. . . . But such activities as demonstration, protest, and class boycotts will damage social stability. They will not solve the problems but will rather cause a turn for the worse. The seriousness of the matter tells us that things in the Square are not developing the way the students intended.

It has become more and more clear that a very small handful of people are using the situation to reach their political goals, that is, to negate the leadership of the Party and the socialist system of China. They openly shout slogans saying that bourgeois liberalization must not be opposed. . . . They spread rumors, smear Party leaders, and call the leaders names. Their purpose is to overthrow the leadership of the Chinese Communist Party and the people's government that was lawfully elected by the National People's Congress, and to completely destroy the people's dictatorship. They stir up trouble, set up secret ties, organize various kinds of illegal associations, and try to force the government to recognize them. It is obvious that they are making preparations for opposition parties in China. If they should succeed, everything we have worked so hard to accomplish in reform and open policy, in democracy and law, and in socialist construction will all come to nothing. Chinese history will show this to be a time of great retrogression; the hopeful China will become a hopeless, futureless country.

We must be firm in exposing the handful's political conspiracy, so that we can differentiate between the majority of the students and those who want to stir up trouble.[45]

Li concluded by announcing that the People's Liberation Army had been called in and that martial law would be imposed.[46] If this hadn't made things clear enough, Yang Shangkun then spoke, less in his ceremonial capacity as China's president than as a representative of the hard-line old guard and the army leadership. "Recently," Yang said, "Beijing's normal work and production, order, and daily routines have all been thrown into chaos; in essence, in many aspects, [Beijing] is already in a state of anarchy. To maintain social order in the capital and restore normal routine, we have had no alternative but to move some troops from the People's Liberation Army." This deployment was intended only to help police carry out their public security duties, Yang said; "it absolutely is not directed at the students."[47]

After Li and Yang spoke, it took three hundred Beiwai students less than ten minutes to achieve unanimity and depart amid tears of anger into the face of what they were sure was imminent military repression. They urged me not to come, fearing a bloodbath. (My appointed guardian and other personal friends did not want the responsibility should "their" foreign expert become even a minor casualty.) They were relieved when I decided to stay at the university. None of us imagined that the spontaneous action of the people of Beijing would stop the army.

THE PEOPLE'S BARRICADES STOP
THE PEOPLE'S ARMY

Beginning Friday night, the citizens of Beijing repulsed all attempts by the army to clear Tiananmen Square. In fact, only a few soldiers made it as far as the Square, and then only by using the subway tunnels (though not the trains—workers had shut them down). Trucks of soldiers entered the city from a variety of directions, only to be stopped by impromptu barricades and crowds. Buses and bicycle-lane partitions were drawn across the road, and troops were unwilling, if not precisely unable, to move forward against such opposition. Having been kept in the dark about the nature of events in Beijing and apparently about the purpose of their own maneuvers, they seemed bewildered and chagrined by the popular resistance. They were greeted as friends by the crowds but denied privacy and subjected to never-ending "education" about the current situation.

I saw one such incident on Xisanhuan Avenue Saturday morning. Five open trucks and one bus of military police drove south in moderate traffic. Students with banners and flags moved into the path of these vehicles to stop them, halting other trucks and cars in front to make a roadblock. A substantial crowd of local people formed instantly. Drivers got out, and all joined in talking to the soldiers, telling them they had been brought to Beijing by a corrupt government and urging them not to attack the students. The soldiers said they knew nothing of such a purpose, claiming to have been told they were going to the city for "military maneuvers." They agreed to turn back, to great applause from the crowd. Similar scenes were reported from all over Beijing.

On this occasion I was with a Beiwai Ph.D. student in English literature who was a nineteen-year veteran of the army now employed as a teacher at one of the military colleges. The spontaneous blockades of the soldiers and the troops' refusal to breach them moved him to tears. This level of emotion was not uncommon. Part of the genius of the hunger strike was that it tapped into very strong popular sentiments. People felt an emotional bond with these students, who were risking their lives to protest a government all agreed was corrupt. Acting out of a desire to protect them, citizens crowded into the streets, even in the middle of the night, and built barricades to stop the soldiers. Over and over, individuals told me how inspired they were, first by the students and then by the actions of "the people." This sense of inspiration seemed set against a background of shame about the passivity of the Chinese people in the face of repression. Some students quoted Lu Xun's comments on this submissiveness from seventy years ago and suggested that only now were the Chinese people beginning to come alive. The students were quick to embrace the support of Beijing's citizens, which came as a surprise but was deeply moving and invigorating.

The production of handbills and posters never stopped. However, the messages shifted decisively away from the particular concerns of students to the broader appeals of patriotism and democracy and to specific responses to the imposition of martial law. Expressing their newly affirmed solidarity with the masses, students said that military control was an insult to Beijing residents. "The capital is in danger! China is in danger! The nation is in danger! The Republic is in mortal danger!" screamed the first characters of one handbill, which declared itself to be an "emergency declaration from the people of the capital to the people of the nation."[48] "Faced with the democratic struggle of millions of patriotic students and people from every level of society," the handbill went on, "the current ruling clique in the government has brazenly stirred up disturbances, announced military control, and branded the patriotic movement of millions in the capital as 'turmoil.' All this stands in flagrant violation of the Constitution of the Republic." The writers were not above hyperbole: "Now is the darkest, bloodiest, and most inhuman time in the history of the Republic, a time that like none before causes one billion people to completely despair. The Republic now faces its most severe trial ever." The student movement had become, at least in the speeches, handbills, and posters of Beijing, the "people's democracy movement."

By Saturday night, barricades had been set up on most or all of the major roads into Beijing, backed by others on the main internal thoroughfares. I spent all night at one, but, though there were several alarms, the army never arrived. A crowd of close to a thousand people stayed consistently in the street, blocking one of the main roads in from the west. When alarms were sounded that troops were near, the number quickly doubled or tripled. People appeared seemingly out of nowhere. Nearly all were local residents and workers, though a group of secondary school students was the best-drilled contingent and the only one to try leading songs to help pass the time. I spoke to staff from the nearby Shangri-La Hotel (one of the many new, relatively luxurious joint-venture establishments in Beijing), a geological engineer, a truck driver, and others.

This range of occupations indicates the breadth of the public's support for the students and its opposition to the government, to martial law, and especially to Li Peng personally. Beyond this, people's goals and desires were varied and rather vague. Keeping the army out, protecting the students, and expressing distaste for Li Peng seemed the most concrete reasons to be out in the street. It is hard to overstate the revulsion people felt toward Li Peng after his speech. He seemed not only to oppose their interests but also to deny the legitimacy of their desires and opinions, even of what they saw with their own eyes. They took his manner as a personal insult.

The young hotel workers spoke mainly of the high incomes of Li Peng's children in contrast to what they considered their own low pay (though by Chinese standards these teenagers in fact had very good jobs, earning between 300 and 400 Renminbi (RMB)—around $100—a month when the average urban wage was 220 RMB a month). They spoke longingly of Western consumer goods, rattling off names of cars, brands of cigarettes, and various Western currencies. The engineer, by contrast, mentioned corruption but stressed democracy, by which he seemed to mean mainly the people's right to free expression and to a government responsive to their will (though not necessarily elected by them). He spoke angrily and bitterly of Li Peng's speech as proof that the government didn't care about its citizens. When I conversed with other Beijing residents present at barricades or demonstrations, nearly all expressed strong support for the students, though a few voiced concern that the protests would simply bring a crackdown and worsen the current level of repression. A number identified prices as a key issue, one businessman stressing the need to move ahead with opening the economy; several made direct comparisons to what they took to be Gorbachev's greater openness and desire for reform (though they did not use the Russian terms "perestroika" or "glasnost"). Bringing wages and prices into balance seemed the most important long-term goal to nonstudents; next most frequently mentioned were stopping official privileges and corruption and "having the government listen to the people." These seemed rather strikingly not to embody the whole democratic view of Lincoln's phrase "government of the people, by the people, for the people." Students often repeated this phrase to me, but only as a sort of claim to plebiscitary consultation—their assumption was that government would always be something sharply different from "the people."[49]

The barricade at which I spent Saturday night was constructed mainly out of erstwhile bicycle-lane dividers, concrete posts, steel bars, and some concrete pipe from a nearby construction site. Drivers had to slow down to negotiate this zig-zag course and could be stopped by the crowd for examination and interrogation. Later a couple of buses from the city's electrified lines (so-called "trolleys") were pulled over by the crowd to supplement the barricade. During the day they were parked by the side of the road, at night dragged back into service. A gang of motorcyclists—snazzily attired, prosperous small entrepreneurs calling themselves "Flying Tigers" (*fei-hudui*)—sped from barricade to barricade reporting on troop movements and conveying other news. They never failed to draw cheers and fervent praise, even when they roared by without stopping. People who might have complained about these nouveaux riches a week before found them inspiring now, and the motorcyclists seemed to be having a ball (not imagining, presumably, that they later would be singled out for early arrest).

Though I saw no troops that night, they did arrive by the thousands at other barricades. Most remained stuck in place for days. Nearly all told the same story of being tricked by the government, never knowing they were moving against the people. They said they had been denied newspapers and TV for up to a week. The soldiers were young boys, most from peasant families, it seemed. In the April 27 protest, the marching students had taunted the armed police, also largely of peasant background, with shouts of "go back to your fields; this is not your business." But by mid-May, such open class bias had disappeared (though one of the basic weaknesses of the student movement remained its almost complete absence of ties to the countryside). The troops were greeted warmly, made to feel that they and the Beijing students were of the same people. The implicit message, of course, was that one should not shoot one's fellow citizens or block their protests. Most of the soldiers I saw at this point appeared bewildered and tired, though sometimes a little flattered by the attention and kind words they received from the city dwellers. For the most part, they were unarmed.

Few people imagined that the stalemate between government and citizens would last as long as it did. Most expected the army to move in greater force at almost any time. Over the next two nights the rumors spread—"they're coming now; things are coming to a head." These rumors had proven false so many times that even with the army in sight I doubted them. At the same time, I felt the tightening sensation and quickening of gattention that was part of the expectation of attack.

It was generally accepted that if the army were to move with force, it would overwhelm the civilians quickly. Tanks were available, after all, to smash through the barricades. The questions were about the leaders' willingness to risk a bloodbath and the soldiers' willingness to create one. Only gradually during the next few days did we begin to realize how deeply divided both soldiers and Party leadership were. The troops in most places neither moved forward nor retreated for four days. When I visited those at Liuliqiao Bridge on May 21, they were still stuck. Eleven truckloads of soldiers were drawn up in a line before a barricade anchored by two buses. A crowd of perhaps fifteen hundred people surrounded them. The troops looked very hot and a little baffled. Citizens climbed all over the open trucks the soldiers were in, occasionally offered them food, and constantly harangued them, teased them, jabbered at them. An English TV crew filmed them, and dozens of locals snapped pictures. The student friend I was with gave a page of "news" from the protesters' point of view to each truck. Though the soldiers had guns—a few were cleaning them, perhaps to pass the time—they did not seem very threatening. They did seem very tired of having no place of refuge, sleeping in or under their trucks, baking in the hot sun, and being lectured at.

Members of the government also began to think these troops were both tired and insufficiently threatening. The longer they remained in close contact with civilians, the less likely they would be to take up arms against them.[50] Eventually orders came for them to pull back and make camp a little outside Beijing. (When things did finally come to a head at the start of June, the government seems to have replaced these troops—who had been subjected to popular discussion and seen the people they would be asked to fight—with others brought in from remote provinces.) Halting the military was considered a victory by the demonstrators, but the mood became increasingly grim afterwards, with only intermittent new bursts of enthusiasm. Though many hoped the government was about to break down, and rumors to that effect periodically circulated, few really expected it. Still, most remained convinced that severe repression would not be tolerated by the population and perhaps not by a large part of the leadership. Various senior officials and government offices were alleged to have condemned the prospect of violence and/or Li's seizure of power. In the latter scenario, Deng was always considered the key behind-the-scenes actor (though it later became evident that various other senior officials, particularly President Yang Shangkun, had played important roles). On the barricades there were reports that one of the surviving marshals (the top military rank from the 1949 revolution) had said that if the troops were going to fire on the students, they should shoot him first. The Foreign Ministry (or some unidentified people speaking for it) was said to have denied the legitimacy of the new leadership.

After news spread that Wan Li (the chairman of the National People's Congress) had sent a telegram from Canada questioning the martial-law decree, great hope began to be placed on the prospect of his return.[51] Wan had given a speech in Canada that could be interpreted as distancing him from the martial-law regime, though its phrasing was ambiguous: "We will firmly protect the patriotic enthusiasm of the young people in China. All these problems should be settled through democracy and the legal system. We should adopt a rational and orderly way to settle these problems."[52] To place a great deal of faith in the National People's Congress was, however, to forget the very analysis the students themselves had brought forward—that power was extremely centralized despite constitutional provisions to the contrary. There was plenty of evidence of discontent with martial law—even in high places—but no sign that anyone could overturn it.

Everyone I talked to agreed that Li and Yang's new regime was illegitimate and should be ended. The curious story spread that, according to "international law," martial law had to be enforced within two days of its declaration; otherwise it was not valid. At least a dozen different students told me this or asked me if it were true. I could never figure out what difference it would make. It seemed, however, to be a significant idea to the students, perhaps reflecting their general notion that China was being governed by the whims of its rulers, not by laws, and that better procedures were standard elsewhere.

Martial law didn't stop the marches, though shouting at the blank Xinhuamen gate now seemed perhaps a little more futile. "Li Peng, step down" and "Down with Li Peng" were the main chants of May 20; the popularity of Zhao Ziyang, the government's scapegoat, remained high. But a week before, protesters had emphasized that the problem was systemic, not merely a matter of individuals. Just when I was beginning to think this was being forgotten, that I would not again hear "Long live democracy!" as a slogan, the student leadership at Beiwai held a rally aimed at shifting the focus back to ideals and away from individuals. Still, there was a common tendency to see both evil and salvation in terms of individual personalities. It was very easy for the protesters to slip from talking of real democracy to implicitly calling for the replacement of a bad dictator by a benevolent one.

BEIJING WORKERS JOIN THE MOVEMENT

A variety of other groups besides students had created formal organizations by the time martial law was imposed. The most visible group was the Flying Tigers (also sometimes called "dare to die" brigade).[53] These were mainly young entrepreneurs (*getihu*) whose small businesses had earned them enough to enjoy the great luxury of a motorbike. These vehicles seemed to connote a sense of greater power. Shen Tong reported asking a Flying Tiger from his old neighborhood why he had gotten involved:

> "I had nothing better to do at night," he joked. Then he became very serious. "People like me have never had any status in this society. We have no money, we have no education, we are the lowest class. The people who work with me got together and donated money, but we couldn't even buy respect. We want the same things that you students are after. The officials are corrupt, but we're the ones who are looked down upon. This is the first time that the people of Beijing have recognized us," he said emotionally. "They actually respect us and like us. Everywhere I ride, the people yell, 'Long live the Flying Tigers!' It's worth dying for." I understood then that the Flying Tigers were not just joy-riding around town; for the first time in their lives, they believed they were doing something good and right for the country.[54]

Perhaps more accurately, for the first time in the bikers' lives, *others* saw them as good. Entrepreneurs such as those in the Flying Tigers were subject to suspicion and constant envy. They were not as penurious as Shen's acquaintance claimed (a motorcycle was no small consumer durable in China in 1989), but neither were they all as rich as their neighbors suspected. Part of their problem was that they made money without education or employment in a prestigious job; the rationale for their modest affluence was not apparent, and there was a vague suspicion that their gains must be ill-gotten. At the same time, corrupt officials subjected them to never-ending demands for bribes, which both cut into their hard-won profits and primed them for protest against government corruption.[55]

Annoying as it must have been to see these young businessmen join the movement (they *were* all men, though occasionally their girlfriends rode on the back of their bikes sporting chic biker outfits), the government no doubt found the formation of the Beijing Autonomous Workers Union (BAWU) much more ominous. Actually, workers formed at least three independent organizations, though only the BAWU developed into a major ongoing force. One effort focused on the First Beijing Iron and Steel Factory, among the country's largest and most prominent industrial companies. This campaign gained a significant response, but most workers who got involved in the protests did so by coming down to the Square on their own.

Individual workers had expressed support for students from early on, and those at the iron and steel factory had even contributed money to the hunger strikers. Formation of the BAWU was reported as early as April 20, though it did not become continuously active until martial law was declared.[56] At this point it was relaunched as the Beijing Workers Autonomous Federation (BWAF). The new name gave a nod to the existence of other unions that might be incorporated into the Federation, which called itself "a spontaneous and temporary organization formed by the workers of Beijing in response to the unusual current situation."[57] According to some reports, about 5,500 Beijing workers joined the BAWU or BWAF.[58] Workers faced much more immediate regulation of their lives than students did and were much more likely to endure repression. Women accounted for only a handful of the new union members and activists; they may have felt especially vulnerable or perhaps simply less optimistic, and they were constrained by gender roles that discouraged public leadership by women. One woman, Lu Jinghua, did become prominent as the microphone voice of the workers after the students refused them access to the central loudspeakers and they acquired their own equipment. Initially drawn to the protests out of curiosity, Lu had begun to bring small packets of food to the pickets guarding the strikers. Providing such support seemed to be a more general and legitimating path for female involvement.

The implementation of martial law sparked widespread outrage and brought a rapid upswing in the numbers of both male and female workers in the Square. Organization of workers remained limited, however, even though it frightened the government. Early on the morning of May 20, for example, the BAWF called a general strike intended to last until the troops had been withdrawn. Most workers in Beijing continued to report to their jobs, however—partly, no doubt, because attendance was closely monitored. Many of those who did leave work did so as a body, with even supervisors accompanying them. One of the most distinctive features of the BAWF was that it sought to organize workers from a variety of different enterprises throughout the city of Beijing—to be autonomous not only of government and Party control but also of internal division, to link workers laterally to each other for greater strength. In addition, the BAWF appointed "worker-marshals" to cooperate with the Federation in order "to protect the students' lives and safety and the stability of social order in Beijing. . . . [T]he worker-marshals, while preserving public order, should protect the transport of all types of material goods and articles of daily use for ordinary citizens, such as vegetables and grain."[59]

Though the Chinese government claimed the "turmoil" had caused all sorts of hardships and privations, such consequences were not apparent and were vehemently denied by nearly everyone—including people interviewed on TV. One foreign reporter who wrote of shortages of eggs, vegetables, milk, and other staples was mocked locally, the assumption being that she must have based her account on government news releases. I looked all over Beijing and saw no shortages at any time before June 4; one could choose duck or chicken eggs; plain or chocolate milk; apples, pears, or oranges; and beans or cauliflower. Prices did not inflate until hoarding began after the massacre.

Traffic was often snarled because of demonstrations and gawking crowds, particularly near the Square on Chang'an, Fuxingmen, and Jianguomen boulevards. Throughout Beijing, it became a little more difficult to navigate intersections, as the policemen who normally direct traffic from pedestals in the center had disappeared. At peak times, however, these officers were replaced by students and neighborhood residents. The barriers that separate bicycle lanes from motor traffic had been moved in many places. Motor traffic was greatly reduced, however; motor vehicles were largely the privilege of state and Party officials, many of whom had either left Beijing or ceased going to meetings and appearing in public. Some bicyclists actually found relief from ordinary congestion by taking over the whole street. In general, people took the added hassles with good humor; only rarely did someone yell out a complaint at the inconvenience (and complainers were as apt to blame the government as the students).

Absence of buses was probably the biggest problem for ordinary people and workers. Those with bicycles could still get around (Beijing is relatively flat), but traveling long distances was difficult. Many workers used the lack of buses as an excuse to stay home. This form of truancy helped to resolve a tension many felt. To fail to show up was not just to risk ordinary discipline but to court identification as a protester or sympathizer. No one doubted that the Party had ordered its agents in every enterprise and work unit to keep attendance records, though everyone knew that some lacked the will to be diligent about this. Most workers, however sympathetic to the protests, chose not to tempt fate by joining in openly, especially during working hours. But when lack of bus service and other obstacles began to provide both a genuine disincentive for work and a cover for absence, workers could safely stay away, knowing that the number of others doing the same thing would protect them. Many of these joined protests or the crowds watching them, though others—probably more—stayed at home or visited the Summer Palace and other parks, enjoying an unexpected holiday. Meanwhile, taxi drivers, short on paying fares, offered cut-rate transport to students shuttling between the Square, campuses, and various government offices, where they still sought dialogue. What the taxi drivers lost from the absence of tourists, however, they almost made up from the influx of journalists.

AFFIRMATIONS AND ANXIETIES

There was little outward change during the next few days, except that the student movement, aided by donations from workers and from Hong Kong, installed better loudspeakers in Tiananmen for music and speeches. Rumors veered from positive (Zhao was fighting back) to negative (old leaders to the right even of Deng Xiaoping and Li Peng were seizing power).

In the midst of all the confusion, anxiety, and intermittent enthusiasm, several students staged an affirmation of life and "ordinary happiness."[60] Li Lu's girlfriend from Nanjing, Zhao Ming, had found him in Tiananmen Square just before martial law was declared. He had told her to leave because of the danger (and because his vision of life with her clashed with his sense of involvement in big and complex issues in the student movement), but she had stayed. Now, after ordering her once again to leave, Li softened. Chai Ling and Feng Congde had just been talking about their upcoming wedding anniversary; now Li kissed Zhao, then made a short speech. "I'm twenty-three years old," he said. "In my short life, I've experienced everything but sex and marriage. I may die at any time. I owe myself this pleasure."[61] As the little knot of students laughed, Chai Ling suggested that the two lovers ought to go ahead and get married, and so the leadership circle staged an impromptu wedding ceremony. Zhang Boli prepared a marriage certificate, complete with the stamp of the Hunger Strike Group headquarters to make it official. Bread donated by local people replaced traditional wedding sweets, and saltwater substituted for wine. After all, as someone said, "without it we would not have lived until today." The ceremony was held at the Monument to the People's Heroes, with Chai Ling as bridesmaid, Feng Congde as best man, and Zhang Boli as justice of the peace. A few people tried to sing the "Lohengrin Wedding March," but the crowd shifted to the better-known "Internationale." News of the marriage swept the Square, bringing some levity and pleasure. As people crowded in to see the event, Li made a short speech declaring his new slogan: "We have to fight, but we must marry too."

Later he reflected on the why the event stirred people and what it stood for:

> I understood why people responded so strongly to our wedding. It was the
> symbol of their longing and hope. And many certainly knew the story
> from fifty years before, of when a young couple were arrested because their
> beliefs offended the Government and later executed. At the execution
> ground they announced to the whole world that they were married. They

wanted to show that though they could be killed physically their beliefs and their unity could never be eliminated from their souls. People were shouting, "It's a wedding on the execution ground." Many more corrected them, "No, it's a wedding on the square. The square is not an execution ground. It's still in our hands!"

The political symbolism went even further, perhaps. By staging the wedding, the students usurped yet another prerogative of the government. In a seemingly apolitical dimension of life, they suggested once again that the government was not needed, that the stamp of approval could come from the people, that social life could be self-organizing, and that they were up to the task.

The night of May 22 and morning of May 23 saw perhaps the most concerted effort to achieve linkage between the students and the host of other groups that had arisen in the course of the protests. Chen Ziming, a veteran of the Democracy Wall movement and head of one of Beijing's most important private research institutes, helped to draw the various parties together. Chen and other prodemocracy, reform-oriented intellectuals had been watching the student movement with a mixture of excitement and anxiety. They were impressed by the students' sincerity but worried by the innocence and impetuosity that went along with it. They were afraid the students would push the government too far, leading to a crackdown that would reverse the progress of the reform era and their hopes for a gradual transformation of Chinese government and economic life. They were almost equally afraid that the students couldn't keep their own ranks organized, let alone deal with the rapid increase of nonstudents in the Square. And they were aware that communication between the students and the government had completely broken down and that Zhao Ziyang had lost his power.

A Beida sociology graduate student, Zhang Lun, had become an important bridge linking Chen and his network of young intellectuals (most in their thirties) with the students. Zhang had become indispensable to both groups by coordinating the workings of the "pickets" that maintained security in the Square. At Chen's behest, on May 22, Zhang called a meeting at the monument at 10 P.M. Representatives came also from the Beijing Intellectuals Union (formed by Bao Zunxin and Yan Jiaqi), the Flying Tiger motorcyclists, a new group calling itself the Beijing Citizens Autonomous Federation, and the Beijing Workers Autonomous Federation. Though student representatives came, the top leaders were not present; they were at another meeting, trying to deal with their own leadership crisis. Zhang and Chen's group agreed to continue dialogue the next day.

The morning of May 23, Chen sent a large van to pick up the various representatives. They met in the offices of the Institute of Marxism-Leninism-Mao Zedong Thought—an ironic setting but also an indication of how different parts of the government had very different relationships to the emerging movement. The representatives agreed on a strategy of trying to get Wan Li, chair of the National People's Congress, to convene a special emergency session of that body—nominally China's paramount constitutional authority—so that martial law might be overturned. Accordingly, they set up yet another new organization, this one with the cumbersome name of The Joint Liaison Group of All Circles in the Capital to Protect the Constitution (Capital Joint Liaison Group for short). Gan Yang, a young political philosopher who had been instrumental in creating the wave of translations of foreign political thought during the 1980s, drafted a statement: "The Final Showdown Between Darkness and Light." The group felt, Gan said later, that there was no longer any possibility of lobbying factions within the government; the decision to use violent military force had already been made. The only hope was to outflank the Central Committee and other top Party leadership through the NPC. Otherwise, there would certainly be not only a crackdown but also, as the statement suggested, reprisals; a "settling of accounts after the autumn harvest" would certainly ensue, and a wide range of prodemocracy activists would inevitably be its targets.

This gathering of delegates from so many branches of the population was unprecedented in the People's Republic, even if not all of the constituencies were equally well organized. However, the meeting was unsatisfactory in at least two respects. First, many participants thought it had come too late; it would have been much more effective before martial law, when there was still a possibility that dialogue with the government might work. Second, the students still occupied center stage; they exercised a kind of veto power over everyone else and didn't think they needed the advice or collaboration of other groups. The student leadership, moreover, was losing its ability to lead, especially to lead in the direction of lessening the confrontation with the government. Leaders were like surfers, needing to stay on the front side of the wave or be toppled. Already, the split between the Federation and the hunger strike leadership was apparent; so was the increasing distrust of anyone not taking part in the hunger strike (which included all of the adult intellectuals).

Despite these rifts, another major march took place on Tuesday, May 23, this one billed as a march of intellectuals. It was announced on large character posters at a variety of locations, and the news was passed on by word of mouth. The instigation seems to have come from the new Beijing Intellectuals Union, founded by Bao Zunxin and Yan Jiaqi. By this time marches were being enlivened by singing and ever more creative slogans. The "Internationale" was by far the favorite song; close behind came doggerel rhymes to tunes such as "Frère Jacques" ("Down with Li Peng, down with Li Peng, Deng step down, Deng step down . . . "). Slogans were welcomed for their clever puns and tongue twisters, whose complexity far exceeded my limited command of Chinese. This march of "intellectuals" was particularly keen on that game.

Hundreds of marchers left Beiwai about 2:30; the student friends with whom I walked were especially enthusiastic because of the turnout. By the time it reached Fuxingmen Boulevard, this group had joined up with several other contingents, thousands strong. Still others converged on Tiananmen from other directions (although I think the Chinese news agency's figure of one million was an exaggeration based on wishful thinking and perhaps on a desire to send a message to Li Peng). However, more remarkable than their sheer numbers or their diversity—professors, journalists, bureaucrats, foreign ministry officials, librarians, translators, school teachers, lawyers, doctors, foreign experts (an occupational category of its own)—was the marchers' perseverance.

By the time Fuxingmen turned into Chang'an Boulevard (perhaps a mile from the Square), a bitterly cold, very heavy rain began to fall. Winds gusted so strongly it was hard to walk straight. Undaunted, we marched past Tiananmen to Taijichang Street, where we turned south and stopped to chant outside the People's Government of Beijing—"Li Peng, step down!" "Down with Li Peng!" "Down with dictatorship!" and a variety of stronger slogans (which made the pacifist in me uneasy) suggesting that people would not sleep until Li Peng committed suicide, that they would laugh when he drank poison, and so on. Then we marched back west to the Qianmen gate and into Tiananmen. In the hour since we had passed through before, someone had covered the giant portrait of Mao on the Gate of Heavenly Peace with a canvas tarp. We later learned that vandals had thrown paint to deface it. There was much suspicion that this was the work of agents provocateurs sent by the government. Later, it was announced that the vandals were disgruntled people from Mao's home province and that they had been apprehended by students, who interrogated them briefly before handing them over to the police. They seem simply to have been seizing the occasion to add their protests to others, but the students neither felt much commonality with nor wanted to be seen as disorderly vandals.

Thoroughly soaked by then and facing the bitter wind, our bedraggled group of intellectuals headed back to the beginning of Chang'an Boulevard, where we had left our bicycles near the Xidan intersection. Already freezing, we had to ride home without the benefit of the periodic singings of the "Internationale" that had cheered us on the way in and with no slogan-shouting to warm us. But spirits were high. Our group of protesting students and teachers went off to a late dinner of Xinjiang noodles.

LEADERSHIP CRISIS AND REFORM

The general good mood lasted through Wednesday, May 24, continuing to bely the leadership crisis in the Square and the anxieties of older intellectuals. Though confident of their victory, students and other people still manned barricades at night in case of a "desperate move" by the government. But people were back at their jobs, traffic was pretty much normal, and policemen reappeared on their stands to direct traffic. Ominously, however, the heads of all the military areas outside Beijing and the general offices of the People's Liberation Army, the navy, and the air force issued public announcements of support for martial law. Copies of Yang Shangkun's and Li Peng's speeches were distributed for soldiers to study.[62]

On that Wednesday the students occupying the Square announced a re-organized leadership. Eighty-nine university groups had sent representatives to the meeting of May 22. The organizers of the hunger strike, easily the most visible of the activists, were again chosen as leaders. This group had met with members from a variety of other organizations to try to create a consultative body. Now, at a rally in front of the Monument to the People's Heroes, Chai Ling took an oath of office, trading her role as "general commander" of the hunger strikers for that of "commander-in-chief" of the newly formed Tiananmen Square Security Headquarters (or Protect Tiananmen Headquarters). Feng Congde (her husband), Zhang Boli, and Li Lu were once again her chief deputies.[63] As Chai Ling noted, organization was a problem:

> I felt that the Hunger Strike Group should take the lead, having been present throughout. Since adopting a leadership role I had noticed that various organizational tasks were not being carried out. There had been 182 people in various positions; meetings were convened without serious thought or purpose; the health of the students deteriorated; requests for food got less response; and sanitary conditions became terrible. Worst of all, the students were becoming short-tempered as tension mounted in response to events.[64]

It was affirmed that Chai would report to a joint conference of the Hunger Strike Headquarters, the Federation, the Dialogue Delegation, representatives of the main colleges and universities involved in the protest (including a few from outside Beijing), and several nonstudent groups. Signatories of one broadside version of the statement included the Patriotic Association of all Parts of the Capital for the Defense of the Constitution, the Federation (Beigaolian), the Federation of Students from Outside Beijing (Waigaolian), the General Command for the Defense of Tiananmen Square, the Beijing Intellectuals Union, the Beijing Workers Autonomous Federation, the Beijing Citizens Autonomous Federation, the Beijing Workers for the Maintenance of Order, the "Dare to Die" Brigade (as the Flying Tigers now styled themselves), and a similar brigade made up of urban citizens.[65] As Li Lu worried, however, many of these organizations existed virtually in name only—and even the names kept fluctuating.[66] Wang Dan, named moderator of this joint conference, made a speech on behalf of the whole, but it was something close to a swan song: No matter how the student movement ended, he said, it would certainly be one of the most glorious events in Chinese history. Unfortunately, the joint conference never became a very successful basis for mediation among the competing leaderships; the initiative lay mainly with Protect Tiananmen Headquarters.

In addition to addressing their need for reorganization, the student leaders declared their renewed commitment to stay in Tiananmen Square and enunciated plans for more propaganda, or "educational activities," with the public. Actually, the "public" was almost always called "the people" (*renmin* or *laobaixing*) and understood as a collective unity, distinct from the three estates of intellectuals, government, and army.[67] Educating the people, it was hoped, would build support in the general population, establish specific links to other groups, and arouse the Chinese nation. The Capital Joint Liaison Group continued to meet (Wang Juntao ordered out for a lunch of Kentucky Fried Chicken on May 24), but its more educated members had a hard time figuring out how to talk to workers, let alone peasants.

The Capital Joint Liaison Group issued a statement on May 25 describing itself as "a mass organization of the workers, intellectuals, cadres of the state apparatus, young students, patriotic-democratic elements, peasants, and people engaged in business."[68] That description not only covered a broad range but actually suggested a civil society of diverse, interconnected interest groups, the emergence of real citizen organization.[69] Chen Ziming and Wang Juntao were much taken with the language of citizenship, but it was not clear that they were much better than the students at taking the workers seriously. Han Dongfang was not impressed with the meeting he attended. "I hear you talking a lot about the 'citizens' [*shimin*, or 'city people'] who are out on the streets, when what I think you mean is 'workers' [*gongren*]. I don't know if that's a deliberate evasion on your part, but it's important to call these people by their true name."[70] Han approved of the workers' having a union of their own to represent their concerns rather than "virtual representation" by intellectuals claiming to speak and think on behalf of workers.

> You theoreticians can go on acting as the brains of the movement, and the students can give it its emotional spark. But unless the workers are the main force, the struggle for democracy will never succeed. . . . Only if they think of themselves as workers and band together in a new trade union will they develop the strength that is required. Otherwise the movement will be too loose, too formless to succeed—as it has been this time.[71]

Like the students, Han and the workers sought first and foremost official acknowledgment; they wanted their new union legally registered. The BWAF not only claimed the same sort of autonomy as the students' unions but also suggested that workers had class-specific claims and grievances of their own, even in the communist state. The provisional statutes of the union were pointed: "[T]his organization must have the function of monitoring the party of the working class—the Chinese Communist Party."[72]

GROWING REPRESSION

Though people remained well fed and the markets were bustling, the waiting seemed strained on Thursday. Nothing in particular happened; a sense of tiredness just seemed to spread. People stopped building barricades because no more soldiers came. In fact, most of the soldiers pulled back to make better camps just outside the city on Wednesday night and Thursday. But by Thursday the rumors were running in Li Peng's favor, suggesting his power was now secure. He consolidated this mood shift with a televised appearance (on the occasion of greeting three new ambassadors) during which he claimed to be firmly in control and confident that his government could deal with all disturbances. I watched with two Chinese graduate students and teachers, who mentioned that they didn't like Li's apparent self-assuredness but didn't make much of it.

After a visit to Tiananmen that day, I made a note to myself saying that for the first time I recognized "clearly a shift which in retrospect I thought had been taking place all week. The students from Beijing are wearing out, becoming demoralized and worried. But students from outside Beijing are replacing them in the Square. The proportions have reversed." This shift continued and became more prominent on May 25, when the students from the rest of the country announced a new version of their own independent students' association.

The same day, a meeting of representatives convened in the Square to discuss the future of the movement. The possibility of withdrawal and consolidation was raised again and put to a vote, along with three other proposals: 1) to stay in the Square while holding talks with the government, offering to withdraw if student demands were met; 2) to stay in the Square but maintain distance from any political power struggle, concentrating simply on winning negation of the April 26 editorial and recognition of the movement as democratic and patriotic; and 3) "to stay in the square, but to consider the Government our enemy, to launch strikes, call for special meeting of the Party and the National People's Congress, and try to stage a coup within the army, the Government, or the Party."[73] Of 288 votes, 162 were for the strategy of all-out attack, 80 for continued dialogue, 38 for maintaining distance from power struggles, and only 8 for withdrawal. The students began to push for action by the National People's Congress and declared their intention to stay on in the Square at least until it met on June 20.

By Friday morning, May 26, the consensus was that Li was coming out on top in the Party power struggles. Zhao was rumored (by large character poster) to be under house arrest; Hong Kong newspapers ran accounts of his ouster based on the testimony of unnamed "insiders" (though Zhao apparently had not yet been formally dismissed). Wan Li's return from the West was an anticlimax. Though he seemed healthy enough when he left the United States (to which he had traveled after Canada), he was detained, allegedly for medical care, when his plane stopped in Shanghai. Whether Wan came freely to the conclusion that the student movement was a source of chaos that had to be stopped or whether he was simply persuaded that his own future depended on following the Party line, Wan threw his support behind martial law. He did agree to convene a meeting of the People's Congress on June 20 to discuss problems raised by the students, but his statement offered little hope that he intended this to be an occasion for challenging the government. "All sorts of things," he said, quite in line with Li Peng, "have indicated that a very small number of people are engaging in a political conspiracy, making use of student strikes and deliberately creating turmoil."[74]

Most people I talked to after Wan's statement said, "It's over," though they thought students would remain in Tiananmen and declared their own readiness to march. The mood was gloomy, full of talk of reprisals and persecution. More and more military and political leaders from throughout

China reportedly reaffirmed their loyalty to Deng Xiaoping and thus to the Li Peng regime. Some observers, including students, commented on how slowly this show of support had come, seeing in this a sign of reluctance. Nonetheless, there were few indications of weakening resolve or open conflict at the top. Newspapers published a string of endorsements from other high-ranking officials. Though many seemed to have moved grudgingly, none spoke out in public opposition.

Facing the growing depression in Tiananmen, student leaders debated what to do. Loosely linked in the joint conference, they decided on a ten-point program, which Wang Dan read at a press conference May 27.[75] The statement reiterated many of the long-standing goals and claims of the students, including recognition of their movement as "spontaneous, patriotic and democratic." This declaration was more explicitly oriented toward concrete political action than many earlier ones, calling for Li Peng's removal and suggesting that Zhao Ziyang should remain in office because he was supportive of the movement. Most important, the ninth point called for withdrawal from Tiananmen Square after a mass rally on May 30.

The leadership that adopted this resolution was composed primarily of Beijing students. They underestimated the determination of students from outside Beijing to continue their protests in Tiananmen Square. Though Chai Ling attended the joint conference discussions and was present when Wang Dan read the ten points to the press, she was ambivalent, alternately denouncing all attempts to withdraw as "capitulationist" and expressing her own fears and desire to pull back. On May 28 she sought out Phillip Cunningham, a University of Michigan graduate student who was helping the BBC cover the movement, at the Beijing Hotel. She struck him as "tired, dusty, wounded, and angry," and suggested that some kind of threat had been made against her; she was thinking of running away, ar ie wanted to talk. Cunningham turned on a tape recorder, and she beg in to blurt out her story, her fears informing the opening phrase, "I think these may be my last words." Though admitting that "if we withdraw, the only one to rejoice will be the government," she expressed her desire to leave:

> I had a conversation with a plainclothes cop on April 25. I asked him what the sentence was for counterrevolutionary activities. He said that it used to be three to five years, but now it is seventeen. I'd be forty after seventeen years in prison. I'm really not willing to do that.
>
> Yesterday I told my husband that I was no longer willing to stay in China. I realize that many students won't understand why I'm withdrawing from this movement and I will probably be criticized for this. But I hope that while I can no longer continue with this work there will be others who can.[76]

More acutely than many of her cohorts, Chai Ling appreciated the dilemma in which the students found themselves—trapped between a withdrawal that was hard both to accomplish and to accept and an almost certain catastrophe if they pressed ahead.

By May 29 the student leaders realized that it would be impossible to withdraw the next day, as called for in the ten-point plan. Thus, the withdrawal was postponed until June 20, when the National People's Congress was scheduled to convene. Having lost all hope of uniting the various groups of students, especially of reconciling the Beijing and provincial students, several of the top student leaders, including Chai Ling and Wang Dan, resigned their positions. Chai Ling's resignation was short-lived, as she never left Protect Tiananmen Headquarters for long, but Wang Dan, a strong advocate of withdrawal, had reached the end of his central leadership. In the midst of this wrangling, Li Lu and other students from outside Beijing pressed for a more decisive confrontation with the government. Most of the Beijing students became increasingly glum. As Chai Ling commented: "I have felt depressed many times. Some of the students have such a poor understanding of democracy. On the day that I suggested the hunger strike, I knew in the back of my mind that it would be futile. There are certain people and certain events in history that are destined to fail. In spite of all this, I have always tried to come across as a strong role model for the students and let them know that some day we will win."[77]

THE GODDESS OF DEMOCRACY

By now the search for a savior inside the government seemed futile. But no sooner did pessimism seem to take root than a sign of hope came from outside the system. On May 25, a replica of the Statue of Liberty had been carried through the streets of Shanghai by demonstrating students and set in front of City Hall. A young man traveled from Shanghai to urge the Beijing demonstrators to follow suit. This notion caught the imagination of a number of students; the protests had lacked a visible symbol since Hu Yaobang's portraits had fallen out of currency in late April. The leadership of Protect Tiananmen Headquarters sent emissaries to the Central Academy of Fine Arts offering 8,000 yuan for materials. The academy had already been active in producing images for the protests, most notably the enormous oil painting of Hu Yaobang that had been placed on the Monument to the People's Heroes on April 19.

The students at the Central Academy of Fine Arts undertook the project but decided not to make a direct replica of the Statue of Liberty. This, they thought, would be taken as too explicitly pro-American and in any case was not quite original. "Copying an existing work," said one sculptor at the academy, "was contrary to their principles as creative artists."[78] Instead, without abandoning the reference to the Statue of Liberty, they created a new figure, the Goddess of Democracy. Building from a partially finished statue of a Chinese peasant in their workshop and with the assistance of a student model, they changed the male figure to female, the pole on which the peasant leaned to a torch held aloft, and the peasant clothes to a flowing robe. Thus they created a symbol original to the movement, Chinese yet linked to the West. The Goddess was made of plastic foam, wire, and plaster and built in four sections so she could be transported to the Square. She was carried there on rented bicycle carts, those ubiquitous Chinese conveyances with a bike in front and a flat wooden bed on two wheels in back. When finally the Goddess stood in Tiananmen Square, face-to-face with Mao, gripping her torch of freedom in both hands, her debt to the Statue of Liberty was not lost on anyone. In fact, that name was in common usage alongside "Goddess of Democracy" for days. Only gradually did the label shift decisively to Goddess of Democracy in order to counter criticisms of overt Americanization and to encourage resonance with traditional folk goddesses. Later some would complain that the statue's facial features seemed remarkably Western, but that was a debatable judgment call, and in any case this bothered almost no one in the crowds.

When word of the statue reached our campus the evening of May 29, I joined some fifty students and rode off at breakneck pace for the Square, trying to get there in time for an "unveiling" ceremony rumored to be planned for 9 P.M. We were nearly an hour late and waited for three more hours before learning that the statue would not be completed until the next morning, apparently because of some difficulties in getting the components into the Square. Still, flags waved from a large scaffolding, some students did a dragon dance, and the mood began to lift. But the crowds were a little more surly than they had been during the previous two weeks. There was pushing and shoving, just teetering on the edge of danger. A girl from a remote provincial town (visiting Beiwai for an English refresher course before her TOEFL exam) was in our group for her first visit to one of these protests; she had been scared even by the crowds of cyclists and now grabbed hold of my hand and held on tightly as we were tossed about. Shen Tong also noticed the changed mood of the crowd: "This was the first time that I felt afraid of being trampled."[79] I felt exactly the same. Students dominated the gathering, but there were many more nonstudents (and possibly students from outside Beijing) than usual, people who refused to submit to the discipline of organizers. Groups were asked to sit down in rings around the scaffolding, but some refused and surged in the direction of those sitting. Fortunately, no harm was done.

The next morning, May 30, a mood of jubilation spread. The statue was a much-needed dramatic move. It gave a new rallying point to the protest and put the positive message of democracy back on center stage, alongside the calls for Li Peng to step down. It also brought relief from the succession of calls simply to march to or gather in Tiananmen, activities that had become boring and were producing ever smaller crowds. With the erection of the statue, crowds instantly swelled again (though not to their earlier sizes—perhaps to a couple of hundred thousand). And the statue was visible to pedestrians, cyclists, bus riders, and other passers-by.

The thirty-seven-foot-tall, pure white Goddess was situated in a superb symbolic position, facing not only Beijing's main street but also the gigantic official portrait of Mao Zedong.[80] Holding up her torch toward Mao in a two-handed gesture of defiance (or perhaps homage, though that wasn't the general interpretation), she also challenged imperial China: Mao's portrait hangs on the front of the Gate of Heavenly Peace leading into the old Forbidden City. Behind her spread the tent city of student protesters, divided by a seemingly ceremonial pathway leading to the Monument to the People's Heroes, and behind that were Mao's mausoleum and the Qianmen gate. The whole series lay along a neat north-south axis. The Goddess stood on a low platform and dominated the space between the Monument to the People's Heroes and the entrance to the Forbidden City. Visitors arranged flowers and laid poems at the statue's feet. On May 31, the scene was further brightened by fresh new tents—bold red and blue igloo-style shelters around the statue, olive green ones with red flags on either side of the path to the Heroes' Monument. These were donated by supporters from Hong Kong. Under the direction of Guo Haifeng, a member of Protect Tiananmen Headquarters, they were arranged in very neat, precise rows to give the lie to Li Peng's accusations that chaos and anarchy reigned in Tiananmen Square.

The statue gave the protest a focal point and drew a continuous flow of ordinary people and other visitors into the Square. Everyone wanted their picture taken in front of it. People asked each other, "Have you seen it?" It galvanized the flagging spirits of the demonstrators, even though it went up at a time when many students from the elite Beijing universities were returning to their campuses. The Goddess of Democracy was a moving symbol to every student I knew, even those who thought it imprudent. Indeed, a number of student leaders, especially from the original Beijing groups, doubted the wisdom of erecting the statue. They were looking for a way to avoid violence, yet the statue accelerated confrontation. It is possible that some activists pushed for the statue in order to force the hand of others and to forestall any attempt to withdraw from the Square.[81] The statue also represented an attempt to raise the stakes for the government. One of the sculptors said they had made the statue as large as they could so that the government would not be able simply to remove it: "If they decide to do this they'll have to smash her into pieces, thereby exposing their antidemocratic faces."

The erection of the statue was the latest and perhaps the most dramatic in a series of innovations in protest. Some of these, such as the practice of linking arms to delineate groups, drew on earlier Chinese models. Others may have been borrowed from the international repertoire of collective protest—for example, the slogan "power to the people," which echoed the Philippine revolution of 1986 as well as the 1960s dissent throughout the West. Whereas early rallies had been quiet, students later bought battery-operated megaphones (occasionally abused in arguments over strategy) and put up somewhat distorting but effective loudspeakers, which by the last week of May blared sound constantly over the Square. They mixed speeches with music—Chinese pop, Beethoven's "Ode to Joy," and Western music from the 1960s (though the latter was not the music of protest but "bubblegum" pop). Meanwhile, the hunger strike had focused attention and built support. The protests had steadily grown, and each time they lost momentum a new source of energy and inspiration was found. Sometimes the government itself provided the occasion for renewal: Popular opposition to martial law had taken the protest to a new level. And now protesters had the statue. But the sense of renewed exuberance the Goddess brought to some was matched by a jittery anticipation of repression. Surely the authorities would not let her stand.

3 Crisis, Climax, and Disaster

WAITING FOR THE BALANCE TO TIP

As heavy news coverage showed the world, the imposition of martial law was a failure. Though massive, the initial troop movements were somewhat tentative. Soldiers made no attempt to force their way through resisting crowds. Instead, commanders allowed troops to be stopped on the periphery of Beijing by the *laobaixing*, who took it upon themselves to act as citizens rather than the government's masses. To the surprised and deeply moved students, it seemed that in every neighborhood there was an old woman who placed herself in front of troop trucks, saying they would have to run over her if they were to move against the protesters. Students and other protesting groups tried to turn the soldiers' loyalties from their government to their nation. But if the popular story was one of citizen power, it was apparent that the regime had not exhausted its resources: It made plans to bring in fresh troops and to use force.

From May 20 to June 2, life in Beijing was an emotional roller coaster.[1] Popular participation in the movement ebbed and flowed. At first people stayed up all night on barricades, waiting to defend the city against the army. The Paris Commune sprang to my mind; similar thoughts occurred to Beijing citizens, especially older ones who had read a bit more Marx than today's students. Later people grew tired, and the immediate military threat seemed to pass. Rumors spread simultaneously of popular victory and an imminent crackdown, of a military coup and a siege of the city. As the stalemate continued, eyes turned toward the internal power struggles of the government. Would Zhao Ziyang lead reformers to a new and secure dominance? Or would the old guard and its protégés (including Li Peng) oust the others as too sympathetic to students, capitalism, and the West?

As the balance of evidence and opinion turned toward the latter possibility, fears of repression grew. There was no clear sense, however, of whether the government would take action in a week or a month, and hopes remained strong in many quarters that the protesters would eventually regain the initiative.

By this time, people from various parts of Chinese society had joined the original student activists in Tiananmen. Provincial students outnumbered those from Beijing, and most of the people packed into the Square were ordinary Beijing residents. Some were active in the protests themselves, though the actual occupation remained mainly a student affair; most were simply curious, generally supportive onlookers who swelled the size of the crowds. Entrepreneurs catered to them with Tiananmen Square t-shirts, souvenir photographs taken in front of the Goddess of Democracy statue, and an array of snacks and drinks.

In the meantime, the government tried staging demonstrations of its own. The biggest progovernment manifestation was a march in the suburbs of Beijing on May 31. Several thousand peasants, cadres, and others marched in Ro, Fengtai, and Daxin counties just south of the city. Their slogans gave a suggestion of how the government wanted to interpret the events (though the words sounded implausible in the mouths of peasants). "Down with Fang Lizhi!" shouted the demonstrators, referring to the prominent physicist and human rights activist. Fang was not only condemned as a conspirator but even burned in effigy twice. The Hong Kong paper *Ming Pao* identified one Zhou Xing as organizer of the march and quoted his explanation: "[S]ome troublemakers want to put pressure on the government. Fang Lizhi is one of them."[2] This terse summary of the official line was as deep an explanation as any reporter could get from the participants for their actions.

The government was also now a continuous presence in Tiananmen Square and its vicinity. Its loudspeakers were mounted on lampposts throughout the area and blared a continuous stream of warnings. Less noticeable, but not overlooked by most locals, were its security cameras. And although uniformed police had disappeared from Beijing, various plainclothes police were active in the Square, sometimes identifying themselves openly. Last but not least, the soldiers who had been smuggled into the center of the city days before were coming out more and more often, sometimes in uniform, to look around.

The government's security agents did not always stay in the background. A little after 1 A.M. on May 30, for example, they arrested Shen Yinghan.

Shen was a founder and leading member of the Beijing Workers Autonomous Federation; at the time of his arrest he was carrying notebooks reporting, among other things, the disposition of funds raised by the union. The organization's leadership immediately issued a public protest, describing the action as a "kidnapping" rather than an arrest and calling "on the great mass of workers to take action and demand that workers' representative Shen Yinghan be released at once. Workers also have the right to be patriotic. Save our workers' representative!"[3] In fact, the government was much more worried by workers' attempts to claim and exercise their "right to be patriotic" than by the students' actions. It is no accident that arrests began with workers rather than students. In the short run, though, they seem to have brought the BWAF attention and sympathy; its roster reputedly swelled to some ten thousand members in the days just after the arrest.[4]

In a rare show of solidarity, students rushed to join the workers in protesting the apprehension of Shen Yinghan. On the day of the arrest, Han Dongfang led the group to the Public Security Bureau's nearby office. Later that day, the student leadership even allowed the BWAF to use the steps of the Monument to the People's Heroes—which the students considered their turf—for a press conference. This event went smoothly at first as Li Jinjin, a Beida doctoral student–turned–worker, spoke, denouncing the Public Security Bureau's action. But when Han Dongfang took the microphone and began to speak about the BWAF itself, students began to shout, "Who is this guy?" "We are the vanguard!" "Get down, leave!" Solidarity was precarious.

The BWAF was mainly composed of employed men (and a very few women), but many of the working class people in the Square were unemployed. These young men roamed the streets in bands of a score or more, sometimes styling themselves "dare to die" squads, and were among the most bellicose of the groups in and around the Square. Their presence gave the crowd a much surlier tone and greatly diminished the students' ability to maintain order and ensure a peaceful response to military provocation. A "dare to die" squad trashed a jeep that someone claimed had been used in seizing Shen. This was one of the first acts of real violence in the protests. Students wondered whether some of the cyclists or unemployed workers were agents provocateurs; however, emotions were running so high and hostilities were so open that no agents provocateurs were needed to rouse the crowd. And perhaps the six weeks of protest, capped by the raising of the Goddess of Democracy statue on May 30, offered more than enough provocation to the government.

THE BEGINNING OF THE END

In retrospect, the end moves of this Beijing struggle seem to have begun late on Thursday, June 1. A few more policemen had gradually become visible on the streets, though not an alarming number. The soldiers who had been camped in the Beijing train station came out for brief public forays—jogging around Tiananmen between 6 and 7 A.M. on Friday, for example. On campus, pressure was stepped up to get classes meeting again. The vice chancellor of Beiwai reported that 60 percent of undergraduates had returned to the university. The claim seemed plausible from just looking around, though it was not clear that the returning students considered themselves no longer on strike. Central education authorities seemed to have told campus officials and faculty that they must increase efforts to resume normal activities. At the same time, the government began to reiterate the martial law decrees prohibiting foreigners from associating with, reporting on, or being in the vicinity of any people committing banned activities. Such activities were defined sufficiently broadly that they included virtually all gatherings of any groups, critical discussions of the government, even the reading of posters. In short, an effort was being made both to get foreigners to stay home and to minimize journalistic coverage of the struggles. New regulations aimed specifically at foreign journalists were promulgated, calling among other things for all non-PRC reporters to apply to the municipal government for a new permit if they intended to report from Beijing and specifically banning coverage of the activities in and around the Square.[5]

June 1 was China's Children's Day. This is usually celebrated with great pageantry in Tiananmen Square; children are bussed in from all over the city. This year the government demanded that the Square be cleared for celebrations, attempting to tug on the students' heartstrings (or those of broader audiences) by reminding them how they had looked forward to Children's Day when they were younger. Similar propaganda blared out over the north end of the Square on high-powered loudspeakers; the students competed with their own, somewhat weaker sound system. Throughout Beijing, the government made a new effort to recapture public attention. Hotels and office buildings were draped with banners early Thursday morning. Properly printed rather than handmade, these bore slogans such as "Take a firm stand against bourgeois 'democracy' " and "Support the great, glorious, and correct Chinese Communist Party."[6]

Students made their own Children's Day entertainment plans for any youngsters who might come to visit. Many did arrive, even after the government canceled the official celebration. Most of these were brought by their parents, though a few classes attended, accompanied by their teachers. The schoolchildren, perhaps prompted by teachers, told the protesting students they believed in democracy and offered small collections of money—90 yuan from one group I saw—for "their big brothers and sisters." Some students put on a song-and-dance show to entertain the youngsters. The atmosphere was relaxed but the enthusiasm desultory. Picking up garbage was the day's dominant activity.

Thursday's strangest event was the botched kidnapping of Chai Ling. Coming on the heels of the arrest of Shen Yinghan, this was quickly interpreted as another provocation from the government. The rumor spread like wildfire but (at least in my hearing) always with a note of puzzlement and sometimes skepticism. The latter was well founded, for by the end of the day it was learned that the attempt to kidnap Chai had been engineered by some of the provincial students, apparently upset about rumors that funds had been misappropriated. The would-be abductors had grabbed Chai and her husband, fellow student leader Feng Congde. When Feng resisted, the kidnappers ran away. Chai later named some of the provincial students she thought she recognized and suggested to reporters that they might have been bribed by the government. It must be noted, however, that the stories about misappropriated funds were not entirely without basis; the record keeping of Protect Tiananmen Headquarters was chaotic at best, and tens of thousands of yuan went unaccounted for.

The sense of internal conflict was increased by Li Lu, who accused student guards of having been drunk on duty. This lapse, he said, enabled the government to infiltrate the occupation and cut off the telephone used by the headquarters and two loudspeakers on the monument. Verification of this sabotage was impossible; some other students suggested there was no telephone to cut off. The different views reflected, among other things, different levels of access to the various inner circles of leadership. Students had apparently commandeered space under the Monument to the People's Heroes for their communications center; it likely had a telephone, though I personally did not notice. Whatever did happen, trust and organization were both wearing thin. There were increasing quarrels between Beijing and provincial students, and the Beijing Federation itself underwent a change of leadership. An announcement on June 1 said that both Wang Dan and Wuerkaixi had been replaced the night before.

The three main student groups—Protect Tiananmen Headquarters, the Beijing Federation of Autonomous Students Unions, and the Federation of Students from Outside Beijing—held a joint press conference on June 1.

Once again they stressed their willingness to resolve disputes through dialogue with the government. They indicated that their patriotic and democratic movement was not to be influenced by the power struggle within the Party and stated four demands: an end to martial law, withdrawal of occupying troops from Beijing, an end to news censorship, and a guarantee that student protesters would not be subjected to reprisals. As some observers noted with surprise at the time, the statement of demands did not call for retraction of the April 26 editorial. This omission may indicate as much as anything the passage of time and the absence from the leadership of many of the original organizers at whom the editorial was aimed.

The pace picked up on Friday, with the soldiers taking a higher profile. The army took control of the Beijing television and radio stations, as well as the telegraph and post offices. Early in the morning several thousand troops pushed toward Tiananmen Square up Chang'an Boulevard from the west, but they were easily stopped in front of the Beijing Hotel by bystanders and retreated after minor scuffles. The soldiers were clad in combat uniforms and helmets but scantily armed. Rumors spread of an assault on Tiananmen to topple the Goddess of Democracy. Government condemnations of the protest focused even more on the statue than the students themselves did. The official media called it an insult to the people's heroes and martyrs and an affront to the solemn dignity of Tiananmen Square; the government merely described it as an unauthorized permanent structure. In fact, as Wu sums up, "The statue of the Goddess of Democracy was a monument that was *intended* to be destroyed, because its monumentality would derive from such self-sacrifice. In this way, this statue separated itself from those permanent 'revolutionary monuments' whose photo images fill a tourist guide or a textbook. These permanent monuments are consequences of revolutions—like the Monument to the People's Heroes built to mystify a glorious past—but not revolutions themselves."[7] This analysis makes sense, but we should not let it obscure the equal truth that the statue was an act of theater, presenting the student movement as the monumental equivalent of a government. Though some two hundred thousand soldiers were said to be stationed around the city, the statue remained in place—for the time being.

Friday morning the government sponsored another counterdemonstration, a rally by peasants on the outskirts of Beijing. A variety of foreign journalists were rounded up, but the event seemed so obviously staged that few of the reporters were impressed. The crowds were neither large nor terribly enthusiastic; peasants readily admitted that they had been paid to participate. This event brought the government less press coverage (and distracted less from the students) than the demonstration it staged two days before.

A NEW HUNGER STRIKE

The big event planned for June 2 was the initiation of a new hunger strike. This time it would not be students but four established young intellectuals who would take the lead. None had been among the leading democratic activists earlier, though all were public figures. By far the most prominent was Hou Dejian, a singer and composer whose popular song, "Descendants of the Dragon," was among those most familiar to the university students. The song posed the central dilemma of modern China—how could a country with such a rich history be so poor and weak? As Hou said:

> The song just talks about the Chinese. We are a very ancient and very historic people, but our quality of life is still very poor. Can anyone tell us why? Have we ever thought about these questions—deep in our heart? The major power to destroy the family, or the people, or the nation, is not from foreigners. It comes from ourselves. With that song, I wanted to make it clear that everybody should be thinking from the inside; that we should take a good long look at ourselves.[8]

Hou (thirty-two in 1989) was a particularly intriguing figure because he had been born and raised in Taiwan and moved voluntarily to the PRC in 1983, describing his move as "choosing liberty." Though he was appalled by the conformity and other aspects of life in the People's Republic, Hou felt he had come home and needed to confront the problems of collective and personal identity in mainland China. Though he had encountered a variety of difficulties in communist China, his return had been an important enough propaganda coup to the Party that Hou could count on an element of protection and freedom of action. This liberty didn't last long, however; because of his refusal to submit to authorities in his work unit (a matter of organizational rather than national politics), he was fired from the musical troupe he had originally joined and blacklisted for a time. His wife, a mainland musician, helped to support him. Eventually, however, he found a work unit willing to shelter him and provide him a base, and he began to build a successful career singing and producing videos. Royalties from sales to overseas Chinese helped to make him rich, and by 1989 he was back in Beijing, driving a red Mercedes.

The other three hunger strikers reflected diverse dimensions of the intellectual culture of China. Like Hou Dejian, however, all were relatively privileged and successful, beneficiaries of the transformations of the 1980s but frustrated and caught in the broader search for a new Chinese identity. Liu Xiaobo, thirty-five, was the enfant terrible of Chinese literary critics. A brilliant young Ph.D. and extremely popular lecturer at Beijing Normal University, Liu had made his reputation more as a somewhat cynical challenger to the elites of his profession than as an activist. He had been in the United States for a conference at the outset of the student movement and, after initially stating his doubts that it could amount to anything, returned in order to participate. Indeed, Liu challenged the intellectuals pontificating about the student movement from the comfort of California: "Either you go back and take part in the student movement [or] you should stop talking about it."[9] Liu was the principal author of "Our Suggestions," a tract passed out by the hunger strikers calling for immediate goals such as an end to martial law and urging that organized autonomous groups be elected by different sectors of society to represent their interests. Liu argued for rationality, democratic procedures, and the development of "civic consciousness."[10]

Forty-year-old Zhou Duo, a sociologist by training, was the head of the general planning department of the Stone Computer Corporation. This department was in effect a think tank closely allied to Zhao Ziyang's faction of the Party leadership and to even more radical reformers. Zhou was one of the social scientists most prominent in suggesting the practical reforms necessary for the continued modernization of the PRC. The fourth hunger striker, thirty-year-old Gao Xin, was a former chief editor of the magazine put out by Beijing Normal University and a member of the Communist Party.

At 4 P.M. that Friday, Hou, Liu, Zhou, and Gao mounted the Monument to the People's Heroes and declared the commencement of their hunger strike. "Our purpose," they wrote in a prepared declaration, "is to protest, appeal and confess. We are not looking for death, but for a real life."

> In the face of the mounting pressure of military violence by the Li Peng government, which has lost its ability to reason, Chinese intellectuals must end our "osteomalacia," which we inherited from the ancestors of our ancestors over thousands of years. We have indulged ourselves more in talking than in doing. Now we are taking action to protest the martial law, to call for the birth of a new political culture, and to confess the mistakes we made in the past because of our "weak knees." We are all responsible for China's being left behind by the rest of the world.[11]

Though they offered their protest and their confession as intellectuals, the four protesters argued for a political culture that replaced ideas of class division and struggle with a more general notion of citizenship. In the first place, they suggested, the communist emphasis on class struggle created a tendency toward violence and division, a tendency that had also produced the current martial law. This predisposition had to be countered with a recognition that democracy was built out of tolerance, cooperation, and the participation of the whole society: "Democracy is a political form excluding enemies and hatred; it requires mutual respect, forgiveness, and cooperation in making its decisions after discussion and voting." This more peaceable attitude was to be extended, they suggested, even to Li Peng: "Li Peng made serious mistakes in the office of premier; he should step down according to democratic procedures. However, Li Peng should not be considered our enemy. When he is out of his office, he will enjoy the rights that a citizen does. He can, if he chooses, hold onto his wrong political ideas." In the new political culture, class and other hierarchies would not dominate over citizenship: "The Chinese people must know that in the democratic process of politics, everybody is first and foremost a citizen, then a student, teacher, worker, cadre, or officer." Yet this was not a traditional Chinese appeal to unity or sameness over difference. On the contrary, in defending the importance of independent organizations, these new hunger strikers articulated as clearly as anyone in the movement the idea that no new "good emperor" could save the day and that democracy in its essence depended on practical decisionmaking procedures rather than transcendently noble leaders or pure ideologies: "What we need is not a perfect savior but a good democratic system," they wrote, alluding to the "Internationale." "We would rather have ten contending devils than one omnipotent angel."

Six weeks after the protests began, established intellectuals had finally offered a sustained discussion of its the movement's direction. They chided the students for using

> non-democratic means to fight for democracy. They announced democracy as their theory, but they did not use it in coping with day-to-day routines. They lacked the spirit of cooperation, so their strength was wasted in conflict. Their decisions were temporary and inconsistent. The student leaders did not know how to manage money and materials. They were more emotional than rational and more involved in exercising their individual power than in practicing the democratic idea of equality.

However, the four acknowledged that the movement itself was an education in democracy, for the government and the Chinese people at large as well as for the students.

It is hard to know what might have come from this belated effort to deepen the movement's discourse about democracy. Certainly the government was past heeding any discussions of democratic practice or even any calls for tolerance and cooperation. And though Hou, Liu, Zhou, and Gao declared, "We have no enemies! Do not allow hatred and violence to poison our wit," they were a tiny group. A few prominent figures, such as political scientist and Zhao adviser Yan Jiaqi, appeared in person to wish the hunger strikers well. But among the students, though there was respect for the intellectuals' action, there was little discussion of their statement. To the original protesters and to the bystanders in Tiananmen Square, the four new hunger strikers were a curiosity alongside the rump of the occupation, not the center of a renewed movement. There were scoffers, too. The hunger strike was only symbolic: The four announced in advance that they were only forgoing sustenance for seventy-two hours—and Hou Dejian was leaving after forty-eight because he had to go to Hong Kong to cut a record. The Beijing Municipal Party Committee thought it safe to mock this "two-bit so-called hunger strike."[12]

The last student initiative was the attempt to create a "Democracy University" to give a longer-range focus to activities in the Square. This, too, was a response to the notion that understandings of democratic theory needed strengthening. It was also an answer to the suggestion of many graduate students and activists from the old Federation of Autonomous Students Unions that it would be best for the students to give up the occupation of Tiananmen and return to their universities for further study of democracy. Students from Hong Kong—especially the Chinese University of Hong Kong—were instrumental in organizing the Democracy University. It was to be an open forum for discussion, a "public sphere" that would nurture discourse not just among students but among people from all walks of life. Indeed, the plans for Democracy University were among the most clearly egalitarian of any launched by the protesting students. Organizers talked of how democratic discourse had to be an exchange among equals, not just a series of speeches from platforms. Democracy University was also explicitly proposed as a link among the various Chinas—Taiwan, Hong Kong, and the PRC. This proposal was a public recognition that all three lacked democracy in 1989 as well as a claim to equal Chinese identity by protesters from Hong Kong and Taiwan. One organizer, Fred Chiu (Ah Fei to most acquaintances), embodied much of this cosmopolitan mixture. A Hong Kong resident who had been educated at the University of Chicago (but also imprisoned on Taiwan for his activism), he was as devoted to the struggles of workers for free and effective unions as to those of students for a voice in public affairs. The organizers of Democracy University invited Yan Jiaqi and Liu Binyan to be its honorary presidents and planned an inauguration ceremony fatefully for 8 P.M. on June 3.[13]

THE ARMY MOVES — TENTATIVELY

Friday night the initiative passed from the protesters. Shortly after midnight, a military jeep ran over four pedestrians in the area called Muxidi, west of Tiananmen; three were killed. It's still not entirely clear how the presumed accident happened. The official story was that the jeep was on loan from the army to China Central Television and that its military driver was on his way back to his barracks after dropping off the film crew when he lost control.[14] According to the mayor of Beijing's report, the accident "was deliberately distorted as a provocation by martial law troops. The conspirators attempted to seize the bodies and parade them in coffins, stirring up the people and making the atmosphere extremely tense. After this incitement and uproar they lit the fire of the counter-revolutionary rebellion."[15] Eyewitnesses estimated that the driver was going 100 kilometers an hour, however, and in the midst of martial law and the progressive military occupation of the city, many people were ready to believe the worst. The driver was taken into custody, but the stage was set for further confrontations. Many people seemed almost to be spoiling for a fight. The mood had not been altogether cheerful for some time, but before the accident it still had been fairly relaxed. Sightseers mingled with the crowd and had their pictures taken first with the Goddess of Democracy as backdrop and then with the giant portrait of Mao and the gate to the Forbidden City. A few vendors sold buttons proclaiming "Victor[y], Tiananmen, 1989," and others hawked t-shirts with the two-fingered victory salute on them. But after Friday no one was entirely at ease.

Early Saturday morning a small column of troops—most guesses are in the range of fifteen hundred to three thousand men—tried to enter Tiananmen Square on a forced march, half-running at times. They were unarmed, and they were repulsed by the crowd. Some students called after them, "We love the People's Liberation Army, the People's Liberation Army loves the people." But other protesters stripped soldiers of their tunics, helmets, and boots and sent them back humiliated.

At about the same time, other troops began moving toward the center of the city and Tiananmen Square from other directions. They, too, failed to reach their objective. Just as on May 19–20, crowds of citizens and protesting students surrounded them and built barricades to stop them. There were a few instances of gunfire from the soldiers and a few cases where the crowds attacked the soldiers. Some students thought they had actually turned back the army; more puzzled over why the military would launch such a halfhearted assault and wondered what would come next.

At Zhongnanhai compound, from which China's senior leaders had hardly emerged for a month, protesters were teargassed shortly after midday and responded by throwing stones at police. When I passed by later, two rows of soldiers stared straight ahead and refused to make eye contact with students and workers who tried to talk with them from their own more ragged lines, just inches away. A protester told me they were new guards who had been brought in from Inner Mongolia and were unable to speak the Mandarin Chinese (*putonghua*) prevalent in Beijing. I never saw them speak at all. A student held a spent tear-gas canister as he made a speech denouncing what he claimed was the first use of the substance in the history of the People's Republic. Cracked bits of paving stones lay all about.

The eruption of violence caused near panic at Protect Tiananmen Headquarters. The leaders broadcast a final urgent appeal to mobilize against the government:

> History will show that this day will be a symbol of shame, a day that the people will always remember. On this day, the government has ripped off the last shred of the veil covering its hideous visage. It has dispatched thousands of brutal troops and police, who have frenziedly attacked totally unarmed students and people, to suppress the students and people. They have used every type of weapon, from tear gas to electric truncheons. We no longer hold out any hope whatsoever for this government. We now solemnly declare: if Li Peng's government is not brought down, China will perish and the people will no longer have any right to existence whatsoever. Thus, we solemnly state that our rallying cry is: Down with Li Peng's government.
>
> We call on the entire people to take action: Workers, strike! [People of Beijing], go on general strike! Resolutely resist the ruthless rule of Li Peng's government! We appeal to all of our classmates to return quickly to Tiananmen Square to defend our position. In the future, the Square will become the clearest banner of the triumph of truth over evil, of the people's triumph over fascism. We appeal to all patriotic soldiers with a sense of justice: please arise! Resolutely refuse to be the sacrificial objects of dictators! Do not open fire on the people!
>
> We also appeal to all patriotic, peace- and freedom-loving people and

nations across the world: please give your utmost support and aid to the Chinese people's struggle for justice.

The people will be victorious! Truth will be victorious! Long live democracy! Long live the people!

Long live the Chinese nation!

All Beijing residents and students, join together!

Victory is near! [16]

The students at the headquarters overestimated the willingness of their fellows to return to Tiananmen for a last-ditch stand. More fatefully, they greatly underestimated the government's willingness to use "every type of weapon" against them.

A few students had ridden back and forth from Beiwai to the Square in the morning, keeping tabs on the situation but not returning to the occupation. When I decided to make the same trip, no one tried to stop me, though the government had been at pains all day to tell foreigners that they were forbidden from the streets and would be made to obey the decree by "any measures." Before I left Beiwai, a student claimed that the entire area around Tiananmen was sealed off by troops. His report, like those on the radio, implied that the soldiers had been rather more successful than turned out to be the case. Citizens were far more in evidence than soldiers, and the latter were not faring very well.

The citizens had set up a barricade at Muxidi, scene of the recent auto accident and a prominent residential area, near a major intersection on one of the main routes from the Haidian district to the Square. A big, articulated bus was now blocking Fuxingmen Boulevard. Further along, another bus was torn in half and combined with more of the ubiquitous iron and cement bicycle barriers. Beyond this were two captured military vehicles, one still occupied by half a dozen soldiers. The crowd closed tight around it; some people climbed all over it, pounded on the sides, and pressed up against the windows. The soldiers had been closed in there for six to eight hours by this point. A protester on the roof displayed weapons, clothing, and helmets taken from them. A little closer to the Square men, were disabling a couple of military trucks, working under the hoods and throwing out parts of the engines over their shoulders like characters in an old cartoon. Behind the Great Hall of the People, the crowd at another barricade held off several hundred soldiers trying to beat their way into the Square with belts. Glass was everywhere from broken windows. People had armed themselves with, among other things, branches torn from the trees that lined the avenue, and they beat the buses that had brought the soldiers until they were battered hulks. People's need to vent their anger was evident everywhere. The crowd had also captured a few weapons from the troops, which boded ill for the future.

The largest capture of arms occurred at Liubukou, just south of Zhong-nanhai compound. A crowd of perhaps a thousand people swarmed over four military buses and a jeep. Youths jumped up and down on the buses' roofs and jeered at their occupants until taunting the helpless soldiers lost its novelty. From inside the buses, youths took several rifles, some am-munition, and a variety of other gear. The soldiers, outnumbered five hun-dred to one, offered no resistance. Every now and then, bystanders looked over their shoulders at Zhongnanhai compound, where thousands of troops were known to be billeted. Amazingly, none of these came out to rescue their fellows. Finally, at around 2 P.M. Saturday, some two hundred armed police staged a counterraid to retrieve the weapons. They fired tear-gas grenades as they charged out of Zhongnanhai's west gate, fought the crowd—principally young working-class men—with billy clubs, and fi-nally reached the stranded buses, where they seized the ammunition and freed the trapped soldiers.

Students counseled nonviolence, for the most part, but they were not in the majority of this crowd; most evident were workers and ("waiting for work") youth. (Indeed, workers continued to arrive at BWAF headquarters to register as late as 6:30 the evening of June 3.) [17] Gangs of men in hard hats roamed the streets with hammers and wooden clubs, shouting at the soldiers. Students worried that these were agents provocateurs, and people on the street joined in trying to calm the workers. I saw enough such groups at various points around the city, and they seemed genuinely angry enough, that I doubt whether all were out to do the government's bidding. However, some students reported stopping trucks carrying helmeted work-ers near Tian Tan (a temple south of Tiananmen) and others near Jianguo-men. These workers allegedly confessed to having accepted a bonus of two weeks' pay to come into the city to "help the soldiers." [18]

Did the soldiers need help? They certainly appeared to, as they were stopped time and again in their advances on the Square and forced to sub-mit to badgering by the crowds; officers even asked openly for coins and went to use public telephones to call their superiors for instructions. But was this military incompetence? Was it popular strength? Or was it a plan? The recurrent forays of the troops had inflamed Beijing's population—could this have been part of an effort to create a pretext for the use of actual force? The soldiers were humiliated by their treatment and frustrated at being sent on missions they couldn't accomplish. Was an effort underway to get them angry enough to carry out violence against unarmed civilians?

Or was all this military activity just an elaborate series of feints designed to throw students and civilian defenders of Beijing off their guard? All these possibilities were raised at the time, though some, especially the last, have seemed more likely with hindsight.

Though the peaceful protest had begun to turn violent and people sensed that a confrontation was coming, few had any idea how brutal it would be. I didn't. I stopped to buy an orange soda from a street vendor. A group of students from my university passed by, marching under their familiar white, green, and rose banner. They smiled as I waved. I walked into Tiananmen Square to check on the Goddess of Democracy. She still stood, bedecked with flags and flowers. Some onlookers struck up conversation. "You like our Statue of Liberty?" they asked. "Just like the U.S.?" When someone asked about the original's provenance, my listeners doubted my claim that it had been a gift from France. A young man asked pointedly why, if the United States was the model democracy, President Bush hadn't issued any statement of support for democracy in China. Unable to answer, I moved on. That was the last time I saw the statue.

Just west of the Square, behind the Great Hall of the People, soldiers and the crowd were still facing off. Every now and then violence erupted, as it had done intermittently all day. Troops beat protesters with belts and truncheons; the crowd fought back with limbs pulled from the trees along Chang'an Boulevard. Though violence never entirely subsided, the troops were kept at bay (to what must have been their growing frustration). The conflicts were confined enough that a surprising number of families with small children came out to enjoy popsicles and the entertainment that street fighting offered. Around 7 P.M., I bought a crepe from a street vendor less than three hundred yards from a barricade behind the Great Hall of the People where troops were still challenged by protesters, occasionally flailing away with their belts.

THE ONSLAUGHT

New troops had been brought to Beijing. The often-repeated rumor that because they were from Inner Mongolia they could not speak with Beijing locals was likely false. However, they had not been worn down by days of student propaganda, had not had doubts raised by chance conversations or observations or by reading the *People's Daily* during its period of sympathy for the students. For whatever reason, the new soldiers were impassive in the face of student taunts and imprecations, surer of themselves than earlier troops had been.

The government succeeded in getting a substantial number of soldiers to at least three locations close to the Square: Zhongnanhai, the central railroad station, and the old Imperial Palace museum—the Forbidden City. Students in the occupation headquarters received frequent bulletins on these troops. When a few thousand advanced on the Square the morning of June 3, some students thought the final onslaught had come, but the soldiers were enveloped by the crowd and never fired their guns. They were repulsed with light fighting; such skirmishes continued throughout the day. Even tear gas was used only once, as far as I could tell, at the gate to Zhongnanhai compound. These nearby troops were not those charged with the major action.

The army's biggest concentration was in the west. A substantial force had been gathered near a prominent landmark, the "Princess's Tomb," which lay five miles due west of Tiananmen Square and about as far south of the Haidian district.[19] This area was near a number of military facilities and home to many officers of the Beijing garrisons. The buildup had been underway since the day before, local residents told me later, though it was only early Saturday evening that the soldiers came together in a large formation. Many had flowed in from the western suburbs where they had been camped. A similar, though apparently smaller, force had massed on the eastern fringe of the city.

Around 8:30 or 9 P.M. the army began a concerted movement toward the Square from both east and west. They fired a few times into the air as they began the push into Tiananmen Square. For those coming from the Princess's Tomb, the chosen path was a broad thoroughfare; a single continuous street, its first section was named Fuxing Road, the second Fuxingmen Boulevard, and the third Chang'an Boulevard, the Boulevard of Heavenly Peace. Residents would soon dub it "Blood Boulevard." The soldiers encountered civilian resistance almost as soon as they started moving. Perhaps emboldened by their successful blockage of the halfhearted military forays of the last two days, crowds surged around the troops; men, women, and children jammed the street in front of armored personnel carriers (APCs). Only a few of these people were actively trying to fight the soldiers; sticking iron rods into the tracks of the APCs, hurling stones, tossing Molotov cocktails to try to set fire to the military vehicles. Most people simply blocked the street, relying on their very presence to stop the troops. Over and over again people told me—and nearly every other interviewer—"I didn't think they would use live ammunition."

Yet the shout went up—"*Zhendan!*" ("Live fire!")—just west of Muxidi. Armored personnel carriers moved to the vanguard and demolished the makeshift barriers citizens had erected. This happened first, apparently, in front of Gongzhufen, a traffic circle on Third Ring Road, adjacent to Muxidi.[20] This upper-middle-class neighborhood was home to a number of Party officials and professional elites (including Deng Xiaoping's personal cardiologist). Most of these residents stayed inside. Some had been given intimations that a crackdown was coming. Others were shot when the fire from soldiers' AK-47 rifles raked their windows.

The idea that barricades and crowds could stop a determined modern (even semimodern) army was quickly dispatched. The APCs flattened the barricades under their tracks and crushed more than a few citizens with them. A wide range of ordinary people were in the street. Most probably lived nearby—a few in Gongzhufen, more in the various other, less prestigious neighborhoods on either side of Fuxing Road. Men outnumbered women, youths outnumbered the elderly, but virtually every group was represented. These were *laobaixing*, the "old hundred names" of Beijing, ordinary people.

Though the army routed the civilian resistance, the *laobaixing* kept fighting back. An APC was stopped where Chang'an Boulevard meets Tiananmen Square and set alight by Molotov cocktails.[21] Two Canadian journalists described the scene:

> [A]nother armoured personnel carrier was fighting its way over extra blockades which had been dragged across Changan on the north side of the square. Long guard rails made of concrete and steel blocked the street, along with an iron fence. Some protesters hurled sticks and steel pipes like javelins, trying to jam the carrier's tread mechanism. It began to slow, lurching forward in jerky movements. When it tried to climb over another barrier, the vehicle got caught. A huge roar went up and the crowd moved in. The carrier rocked back and forth, then pitched forward and began to move. A shower of sparks flew from where a pipe was caught in the treads. The APC got perhaps five metres before it ground to a halt. The mob pounced on it, smashing steel pipes against the pillbox-style windows. Shattered glass sprayed into the air. A man in shorts and an undershirt jumped on top of the vehicle and began pounding it viciously. Others joined him. Before long, more than ten people wielding sticks and iron bars were hammering the vehicle. Molotov cocktails were readied and the assailants jumped down. A couple of the firebombs hit the rear of the APC's roof and caught fire. The man in shorts took a blanket soaked in gasoline and laid it on top. A thick cloud of orange smoke began to rise. The crowd surrounded the rear door of the carrier, pounding on it and chanting for its occupants to get out. Many were waving sticks and steel bars. The door finally opened; a flurry of rocks was thrown in its direction. The driver jumped out.[22]

According to several reports, students intervened to save at least one of the APC's occupants. Witnesses elsewhere also reported that students negotiated the safe flight of trapped soldiers. Given the chance, many soldiers appear to have been eager to flee; indeed, thousands may have vanished into the night, deserting temporarily rather than facing the wrath of the crowd or shooting the citizens. A few of those pulled from stalled APCs were not so lucky. A Finnish journalist who had stood nearby told me with revulsion how they were literally torn to pieces. Other soldiers were burned inside their tanks and other vehicles, and some were hanged, providing footage for the films the government prepared later to bolster the claim that the troops acted in self-defense to put down a violent rebellion.

The government itself openly admitted that its army encountered massive civilian resistance; indeed, this resistance was cited as evidence of the severity of the "antigovernment riot" and the need to repress it.

> From 10 P.M. to 11 P.M. [June 3], at Cuiweilu, Gongzhufen, Muxidi and Xidan, 12 military vehicles were burned. Some people threw bricks at soldiers. And some rioters pushed trolleybuses to the crossroads, set them on fire and blocked the roads. When some fire engines got there, they were also smashed and burned.
>
> Around 11 P.M. three military vehicles were wrecked and one jeep was overturned at Hufangqiao and military vehicles on Andingmen overpass were surrounded. In Chongwenmen Street, a regiment of soldiers were surrounded, and on Jianguomen overpass 30 military vehicles were halted by barricades and another 300 military vehicles were halted to the west of the Beijing Coal Industrial School.
>
> Trying to persuade the rioters to let them through, PLA men from warrant officers to generals were beaten up or kidnapped.[23]

The worst bloodshed came as the soldiers fought their way past barricades at Muxidi. Crowds were particularly thick here, both because this is a densely populated part of Beijing and because the three locals had been killed there by the jeep the night before. Two of the apartment buildings at Muxidi—numbers 22 and 24—were among the most exclusive in Beijing, housing officials with the rank of vice minister or higher.[24] Once again, their residents had no protection against the wild firing of the soldiers. This gunfire was taken by many locals as evidence that the army was out of control, that the soldiers must have been drugged or otherwise goaded beyond normal endurance. Over and again, Beijing residents reported the arbitrary, even random nature of the violence and their shock when they encountered it. One met "a girl whose body was covered with blood. I asked if she was wounded but she said no. An old watermelon peddler had been bayoneted to death by a soldier; she had blood on her because she had tried to save the old man."[25] The shock was equally great for a graduate student from Wuhan University:

> I left Beijing University at 11:30 P.M. When I reached Baishiqiao [the area near the Beijing Library, perhaps half the way to Muxidi], I sensed that something was wrong. I ran into someone going in the opposite direction. He cried as he told me, "They're killing people; many were killed around me." Others began to cry with him as they heard the news. . . . During the movement we had talked often about dying for democracy, but that was purely hypothetical. We never dreamed we would actually have to lay down our lives; it couldn't be true. I had to see for myself. . . . Flames lit the night sky as I got within a few hundred yards of Muxudi [sic]. Soldiers, wielding machine guns, crouched behind armored personnel carriers. I couldn't believe that this was Beijing. . . . I saw a young girl walking toward me along the sidewalk. She was weeping while murmuring to herself: "What is this all about? Why? Why?"
>
> Then, at 12:30 A.M. on June 4, I saw the first corpse: a twenty-year-old man wearing a headband and a mask. He was lying on the concrete divider between the bicycle and automobile lanes, 200 yards from Muxidi.[26]

Though some students were in the streets at Gongzhufen and Muxidi, it is crucial to emphasize that they were a tiny minority of any crowd and there almost by accident. These were neither crowds of students nor crowds mobilized by students. The violence was at its most severe when its targets were the workers and ordinary people of Beijing.

It is not clear why there was such an eruption of violence, a "paroxysm of killing," as Robin Munro has called it, specifically at Muxidi. One factor was probably accidental. The troops coming from the west were to meet at Muxidi with a unit of six hundred officers of the local People's Armed Police (PAP). These officers would have been much more familiar than the soldiers with the local layout and situation. But the PAP contingent was stopped—indeed, surrounded and ultimately dispersed—a mile and a half away in the *hutongs* (alleys) near Yuetan Park.[27] The provincial troops thus were on their own at Muxidi and confronting sharp—albeit mostly unarmed—resistance. We will never know for sure whether their violence was premeditated, brought on by the tensions and false starts of the last several days, motivated by anger at the crowds that challenged them, or simply the result of panic.[28]

Whatever the explanation for the frenzied aggression of the troops, there can be no mistaking the intentions behind their deployment. The movement toward Tiananmen Square was a determined military operation, with troops coming from the east at the same time as from the west. Those coming from the east met less opposition but also fired repeatedly on civilians and into buildings. It may be that the violence was greater than top officials intended, but there is no doubt that they planned the taking of Tiananmen Square to end the protests and authorized violent means. Indeed, General Xu Qinxian, the commanding officer of the elite Thirty-eighth Army (garrisoned at Beijing), had been relieved of duty and arrested in late May for failing to carry out martial law forcefully enough; he was later court-martialed. This treatment offered a warning to officers who might hesitate to attack as instructed. It is quite possible, in fact, that many troops did fail to fire on their compatriots. The Chinese government claimed as much in propaganda distributed after the massacre, indicating that this restraint was one reason many soldiers had died. The troops these officers commanded were primarily peasant youths, eighteen or nineteen years old. It is not hard to imagine that they panicked as they attacked their own capital, in some cases after being stuck on its outskirts for days. The most convincing explanation for the violence, however, is not that the soldiers were drugged or deranged but that they were ordered to shoot and to advance at any cost. Their heavy-handedness may also have been a result of their lack of experience in or preparation for urban combat (let alone crowd control). They were trained for conventional military clashes; their officers had gained experience by deploying tanks against Vietnamese forces.

The military operation to retake Tiananmen Square was massive: the divisions that fought at Muxidi were backed by tanks, armored personnel carriers, and more than two hundred thousand additional troops. It is as though government and Party leaders felt they had to retake not just the Square but Beijing itself. Indeed, this level of force, shockingly high for a mission allegedly to restore order in China's own capital, was more in line with an all-out invasion to capture the center of a city deemed hostile. Responsibility for the designation of Beijing as a hostile city must rest with the government, not the soldiers. It was the government that apparently ordered the military to secure the city at all costs rather than to protect the lives of civilians. It is possible that the violence was entirely intentional, sought by factions in the Party and state leadership to decisively defeat and intimidate democratic opposition. Excessive force may even have been deliberately used to alienate world opinion, thereby weakening the claims on power of those whose strength was their ability to relate to the West.

Analogies to the Paris Commune were popular on the barricades during the first days of martial law, and apparently the analogy still held: the invasion of the rebellious city and reprisals against the insurgents were comparable to those occurring after the defeat of the communards.[29]

LAST STAND IN THE SQUARE

While the bullets flew at Muxidi, students in Tiananmen Square proceeded calmly with the inauguration of Democracy University at 10 P.M. A small crowd gathered around the statue of the Goddess of Democracy for the occasion. Zhang Boli, one of the vice commanders of the occupation, was named president. Yan Jiaqi, the honorary president, almost missed the opening. As he recalled later, "On 3 June, I thought that the idea had been abandoned, when at 10:30 I received a telephone call asking me to come offer the first course. I went then to Tiananmen at 11:30. The one and only course of this university lasted for thirty minutes: I explicated the concepts of the rights of man, of liberty, of democracy and I addressed an appeal to Li Peng."[30] At this moment, there was still hope in the Square. As Yan explained later,

> no one had the feeling that it was dangerous, because we never believed the troops would fire. Therefore, when at 10:30 I took my bicycle to ride into the Square, I felt myself in complete safety. There were tens of thousands of people in Tiananmen but no one was afraid. When I had finished, I decided to return home since I had a lot to do the next day. At midnight in Tiananmen, one could not hear the gunshots. Thus, I had no realization of anything. An hour after my return home, I heard shots and I understood that everything had changed.[31]

Word of the killing and the troops' advance reached the students in Tiananmen Square. Wuerkaixi spoke over the student broadcast station: "The government has now placed itself in complete opposition to the people. Li Peng has become the universal enemy of our people: he will be judged by history, and he will be nailed to history's pillar of shame. We, the Chinese people, are now called upon to sacrifice ourselves for the sake of a beautiful tomorrow."[32] Students gathered to offer a pledge, reported later by Chai Ling:

> In order to push forward the democratic process of our motherland, to realize prosperity in our country, to avoid a handful of conspirators draining our great motherland, and to save the 1.1 billion Chinese from losing their lives in the white terror, I pledge to use my young life to defend Tiananmen and to defend the republic. My head may be cut off, the blood may flow, but Tiananmen Square must not be lost. I will fight until the last person falls.[33]

Wuerkaixi was even more incendiary, according to Black and Munro, yelling into the microphone, "The citizens have a right to defend themselves, and the only way to do so is with force." An anonymous BWAF member pleaded with the students and other protesters to carve out their place in history by remaining faithful to the highest pacifist principles of the democracy movement. "When the Dare-to-Die squads find themselves face-to-face with the soldiers," he shouted hoarsely, "the first thing they must try is persuasion. With our songs, our truth, and our sense of justice, persuade, persuade, and persuade again."[34]

For two more hours, the soldiers' approach and their violence were still matters of rumor. As a Beijing lawyer reported, "Around 11:00 P.M., as I walked westward away from the square I saw people on bicycles rushing toward it, shouting hysterically, 'Soldiers are killing civilians!' No one could believe the killing had started."[35] The occupation leadership attempted to hold a news conference in the Square, but, as Chai Ling summarized, "unfortunately there were very few foreign correspondents, probably because they had been confined to their hotels by the military. We were also told that their rooms had been searched. Only one or two foreign press personnel managed to enter the Square."[36]

The advancing troops reached the Xinhua gate outside the Zhongnanhai compound a little before 1:30 A.M. There they encountered the last real resistance of their push to Tiananmen Square. Now there were no more barricades. The advance guard set about clearing the area while the columns of troop carriers and tanks gradually caught up and deployed themselves around the intersection at the northwest corner of the Square, where The Beijing Workers Autonomous Federation had set up its tents; the first contingent of soldiers to arrive allegedly set fire to these. Several people were apparently shot in the area. The last obstacle before the army could enter the Square was a thin line of people with their arms linked. Perhaps a hundred gathered to make this last symbolic stand. Some told me they still had not absorbed the fact that the soldiers were killing those who stood in their way. Students returning to the Haidian district told of how a group of people linked arms in front of soldiers on Chang'an Boulevard and were shot down en masse. A second row of students (or, some said, workers) took the place of the first. Other reports suggest that students and workers were intermingled from the beginning and mention no second line.[37] It is still not clear to me whether this happened, at least with the dramatic staging described, though there is little doubt that both students and workers were killed and that both groups were unprepared for the deadliness of the military onslaught.

Gradually the troops took control of the northern end of the Square. There, a bus drove straight at the soldiers, its driver seemingly suicidal in his defiance. Automatic weapon fire raked the bus until it smashed into an

APC temporarily stopping the line of armored vehicles. A Hong Kong student leader, Kenneth Qiang, reported that "the driver was dragged out by soldiers and clubbed to the ground with their rifle butts. The crowd was incensed, and they ran forward to within fifty meters of the troops, throwing glass bottles at them. I heard two separate gunshots. The driver fell to the ground dead."[38]

Other soldiers poured out of the Forbidden City through the Gate of Heavenly Peace. Government loudspeakers played a warning over and again:

> The Beijing municipal government and martial law headquarters urgently announce that a counterrevolutionary rebellion is now taking place. Ruffians are violently attacking PLA soldiers, confiscating arms and ammunition, burning army vehicles, setting up roadblocks, and kidnapping soldiers. They aim to overthrow the People's Republic of China—to overthrow the Socialist system. PLA soldiers have shown a great deal of restraint in the past several days. Now we must crack down on this counterrevolutionary turmoil. All Beijing citizens should observe martial law and cooperate with the PLA to protect our laws and our great Socialist motherland. All citizens and students now in the square should leave immediately and let the troops carry out their tasks. We cannot guarantee the safety of those who disregard our advice. They will be completely responsible for anything that happens to themselves.[39]

Students struggled to make their response heard over the din by loudspeaker and broadcast:

> Fellow students. We bear a historic responsibility. We must decide for ourselves whether to defend the monument. We should stop those who are trying to resist the army. Stop anyone trying to fight back.
> All students guarding the square, please return to the monument. We must protect the monument. Protect our banners of democracy.[40]

WITHDRAWAL FROM TIANANMEN

Most of the students who had remained in the Square gathered around the Monument to the People's Heroes, near Mao's mausoleum toward the southern end. Some three thousand, perhaps as many as five thousand, were still there to gather around Chai Ling and the four hunger strikers. There they waited "stoically," according to American journalist Richard Nations. The army continued to move in around the northern perimeter of the Square. Several thousand troops, each armed with an AK-47 automatic rifle and a long wooden cudgel, were massed at the steps to the Museum of Chinese History.[41] Soldiers had arrived earlier from the east and blocked

Chang'an Boulevard in front of the Beijing Hotel; they were met by others moving out of Tiananmen Gate to seal off the northeastern entrance to the Square. There was a prolonged pause in the confrontation as the enormous army that had fought its way from the Princess's Tomb massed before Tiananmen Square. In Munro's summary:

> After the arrival of this main force, only a sprinkling of people— apparently not students but ordinary residents and workers—remained in the northern part of the square, between Changan and the monument. The statue of democracy looked more dramatic than ever, facing Mao's portrait and the troops beneath it through the flames and smoke that still billowed from the crippled A.P.C. At around 2:15, there was a terrific burst of AK-47 fire, lasting several minutes, from the vicinity of Tiananmen Gate. I hit the deck. Most of the crowd fled southward, toward the monument, but I saw no one injured.[42]

Chai and other student leaders urged those who gathered at the monument to remain peaceful. Earlier they had persuaded a group of students to surrender guns they had taken from captured vehicles, lest they provoke an attack or provide fodder for government propaganda. Hou Dejian reiterated the appeal. Students turned over a machine gun, two semiautomatic rifles, a pistol, and a box of Molotov cocktails. A group of workers manning a machine gun at the top of a flight of steps on the monument were also persuaded to surrender their weapons. Liu Xiaobo and others destroyed the weapons in front of reporters, who took photographs.[43] Now, said Chai Ling, nicely mixing prudence and principle, "We were ready to receive the butcher's knives in peace. It was a war between love and hate, not between violence and battle forces. We felt that the patriotic democratic movement, which was based on the principles of peace, would fail if the students tried arming themselves with gas bottles and wooden clubs to resist the machine gunners and tank drivers, who had already lost their ability to reason."[44] Protect Tiananmen Headquarters' sound system still worked, and loudspeakers played Hou Dejian's "Descendants of the Dragon." Some students hummed or sang along.

As 3 A.M. approached, Chai made a short speech, often quoted since:

> I said there is an ancient story in which about 1.1 billion ants lived on a hill. One day a fire broke out on the hill, and the only way to safety was to go down to the foot of the hill. To save themselves from the fire, they all clung to one another in a big ball, and tumbled down the hill. The ants that were on the surface of the ball were killed by the fire, but the majority were saved.
>
> I told them that we were standing at the forefront of the nation, and we were all aware that only sacrifice could bring life back to this republic.[45]

Holding hands together, Chai said, the students sang the "Internationale" over and over again. Three of the four older hunger strikers pleaded with them to withdraw rather than add to the horrendous sacrifice that had already been made. As Hou Dejian recalled it, of the older group, only Liu Xiabo insisted on defending the Square to the death, but in the end even he gave in.[46]

It was not clear at first whether the students would be swayed by the prudence of Hou, Gao, and Zhou or by the passion of Liu. One self-declared leader of the Beigaolian argued for staying: "Students! We must on no account quit the square. We will now pay the highest price possible for the sake of securing democracy in China. Our blood shall be the consecration."[47] A few minutes later a leader of the Beijing Workers Autonomous Federation argued the contrary position: "We must leave here immediately, for a terrible bloodbath is about to take place. There are troops surrounding us on all sides and the situation is now extraordinarily dangerous. To wish to die here is no more than an immature fantasy."[48]

Two Red Cross doctors suggested that someone try to negotiate with the soldiers to secure a peaceful withdrawal from the Square. Though no collective decision had yet been made to leave, Hou Dejian and Gao Xin decided to see if the troops would cooperate.

> When we reached the corner of the square we saw a mass of troops. We got out of the ambulance and ran toward them. As we approached, we heard the clicking of rifles and the troops shouted to us to stop.
>
> Their political commissar, Colonel Ji Xinguo, listened to our request and then asked us to put an end to our hunger strike. We replied that we had already done so. Then, in a very gentle manner, the officer said he had to consult headquarters. Within five minutes of his leaving us, the lights in the square went out. We were very frightened. The soldiers were impatient. Some clicked their guns, some shouted, others stamped on the broken bottles that littered the area. The four of us stood there, not daring to move. The doctors called on the troops to hurry.
>
> Finally Colonel Ji reappeared and told us that headquarters had agreed to our request, and that the safest route for withdrawal was the southeast.[49]

A German journalist taped Hou and others speaking to the students gathered around the monument:

> HOU DEJIAN: We cannot remain here anymore. Students and citizens, I dare to say that our movement has succeeded [*cheers and applause*], but we have not won today. Students, all the people here now are outstanding citizens of China [*applause*]. None of us fears death, but our deaths should serve some purpose. Speaking on

behalf of four of us who are hunger-strikers, we didn't consult with you students for your permission to take a certain action. A moment ago we went to the north side of the square to talk to the soldiers. We found their commander. We were hoping that no more blood had to be shed. We spoke with the political commissar of troop 51048, Colonel Ji Xinguo, and he reported to the command post of the martial law forces. We all agreed that all citizens of the People's Republic of China should leave the square in safety.

MALE VOICE: No! No!

ZHOU DUO: Students! If we can save even one more drop of blood now, there will be that much more hope for the future of our march toward democracy.

[*Sound of tanks passing*]

MALE VOICE: Please be quiet!

ZHOU: We have agreed to lead the students away from the square as quickly as possible. The soldiers told us that they have orders from their commanders to clear the square before dawn. That means they are going to use any means necessary.

Students, we cannot use fists against soldiers armed with rifles and bayonets. There are no more conditions for further negotiations. We must now try our best to save ourselves. They have agreed to leave a path at the southern corner of the square for us to withdraw. We hope we can withdraw in an orderly, safe manner, at once.

LIU XIAOBO: If we want to achieve democracy, we must start now, with ourselves. The minority should listen to the majority. That is a basic principle of democracy.

HOU DEJIAN: Friends, no matter what you think about what I have done, I hope we can leave safely and peacefully. I personally shall remain in the most dangerous place of all until the last of you have left.

[*Applause*]

LIU XIAOBO: What Hou just said represents the wishes of all four of us. We will stay until the last one of you leaves.

FIRST MALE VOICE: What's wrong with these guys?

SECOND MALE VOICE: You Fascist running dogs!

MALE VOICE (OVER LOUDSPEAKER): They've stabbed the people in the back. If we stay, we'll die needlessly. Some students want to stay because they have delusions about the government not using force on them. But it's absurd to risk our lives. We should preserve our forces. Now, I beg you to withdraw from the square immediately.

LIU XIAOBO
(OVER LOUDSPEAKER):

Let's hold each other's hands. Let's be quiet and think about the situation carefully, and about what we should do next. The decision on whether to leave or not depends on everyone here.

MALE VOICE:

If we must die, let's die together!

LIU:

Students! Students! Throughout the movement, the citizens of Beijing and the workers gave us great support. We cannot win the movement without their support. Now I'm sure the students in the square can leave together safely, but I cannot guarantee the citizens' safety. At this important moment, I appeal to all the students to try your best to protect the citizens and leave the square from the south corner in an orderly manner.

MALE VOICE:

Hurry, let's go!

ANOTHER MALE
VOICE:

Sit down!

THIRD MALE VOICE:

Point your guns at us! Go ahead!

[*the "Internationale" is sung*]

CHANTING CROWD:

The People's army does not fight the people! The People's army does not fight the people!

MALE VOICE:

If I had a gun, I would not be afraid to use it.

STUDENT BROADCAST:

Soldiers and officers, you are the sons of the people! Don't point your guns at the people!

CROWD:

Don't point your guns at the people!

MALE VOICE:

What are they doing?

[*Gunfire*]

MALE VOICE:

They're shooting at the loudspeakers!

ANOTHER MALE
VOICE:

Those are real bullets!

THIRD MALE VOICE:

Don't shoot at the monument!

CROWD:

Don't shoot at the monument!

FEMALE VOICE:

Don't shoot at the monument! . . .

MALE VOICE:

Protect yourselves—they're going to fire tear gas!

[*Sound of tanks and gunfire*]

MALE VOICE:

Drag her! Pull her into line!

ANOTHER MALE VOICE:	They're going to hit us. Stop it! Stop!
MALE VOICE:	I told them to leave their tents. They wouldn't follow my advice.

[*the "Internationale"; machine-gun fire; screaming*]

MALE VOICE:	Let's hold together tightly.

[*the "Internationale"*]

FEMALE VOICE:	Don't panic!
ANOTHER MALE VOICE:	Don't push! Don't push!
MALE VOICE:	Don't hit people! Don't hit people!

[*Cursing; a babble of different dialects*]

MALE VOICE:	Don't panic!
ANOTHER VOICE:	My glasses!
MALE VOICE:	Let's go! Let's go!
MALE VOICE:	Stop pushing, stop pushing. . . . I'm falling![50]

The students and citizens began to withdraw, heading to the southeast as requested. The soldiers began to press in. The recorded shooting had occurred when an advance contingent charged up to the monument, leading Chai Ling and other students to think they had broken their promise to allow safe passage. Chai recalled:

[A]s the students were leaving, soldiers wearing combat helmets and armed with machine guns charged to the third tier of steps at the platform of the Monument. Before the Headquarters had a chance to announce the decision to withdraw, our loudspeakers had been strafed into shreds. This was the People's Monument! It was the Monument to the People's Heroes! The were actually shooting at the Monument. Most of the rest of the studer s retreated, crying as they retreated.[51]

Despite some reports of slaughter, the soldiers do not seem to have killed students at the monument. Their charge did, however, add to the confusion of the withdrawal. Hou recalled that he and Zhou moved to the northeast to roust the remaining protesters there:

People were still sitting on the ground there. Zhou Duo and I pulled them up whenever we could. "Blame me, curse me if you like, but move!" we said. Some extended their hands without saying a word. Others stood up and explained, "Teacher Hou, we don't blame you."
"Thank you," I cried aloud as I pulled at them.
Before the last group of students arose, troops pressed us from the west

in a human wall. They moved in quickly and squeezed us like water in the neck of a bottle, barely able to move. I could hardly breathe.

All around me plainclothes antiriot police were waving thick wooden sticks and beating people on their heads and bodies.

Students were bleeding. The crowd stumbled over iron railings that had been scattered on the ground. A whole row of people fell. Those behind fell over them, and the next wave over them.[52]

ASSESSING THE DAMAGE

An armored vehicle eventually toppled the statue of the Goddess of Democracy. The action was captured on film and seen repeatedly around the world.

> Pushed by a tank, it fell forward and to the right, so that its hands and the torch struck the ground first, breaking off. It must have been quickly and easily reduced to rubble, mixing with all the other rubble in the square, to be cleared away by the army as part of its show of cleanliness and order. The statue, however, could not be so easily destroyed. It was intended from the beginning to be ephemeral, and yet to endure as an image of the desire of the great mass of Chinese people for the ideals it symbolized. I envision a day when a replica, as large as the original and more permanent, stands in Tiananmen Square, with the names of those who died there written in gold in its base.[53]

There is no shortage of martyrs to the Chinese government's repression of the protests of 1989, but the preponderance of evidence suggests that if any students were killed in Tiananmen Square that night, they were few. Though widely circulated, the idea of students being taken by surprise as they slept in their tents is implausible.[54] Very little carnage, if any, seems actually to have taken place in the Square. That millions of people around the world were virtually sure there had been, and almost thought they had seen it, was due largely to the deceptiveness of television reportage and editing. This illusion was generally unintentional but systematically produced by standard TV news practices and pursuit of the most exciting presentation. Robin Munro summarizes one instance:

> Correspondent Richard Roth of CBS had time to file one last report before soldiers arrested him and took him into the Great Hall of the People. "Soldiers have spotted CBS News cameraman Derek Williams and myself and are angrily dragging us away. And a moment later it begins: powerful bursts of automatic weapons, raging gunfire for a minute and a half that lasts as long as a nightmare. And we see no more." The film was confiscated. Roth's dramatic commentary, aired on the June 4 *CBS Evening News* and accompanied by footage shot two hours earlier, left the clear impres-

sion that troops had opened fire on the students as they evacuated the monument.[55]

Reports from putative eyewitnesses confirmed the supposed slaughter. The most prevalent one initially appeared in a Hong Kong paper and has been reprinted and excerpted many times since. Its author identified himself as a "twenty-year old student of Qinghua University." His account agreed in outline with those of Chai Ling, Hou Dejian, and Western journalists who were on the scene. The student claimed to have "witnessed the whole incident in which the army shot the students and the citizens." His recollection was similar to Chai Ling's up to the attack on the loudspeakers the students had set up at the Monument to the People's Heroes. He described this action as being more violent, with more physical attacks on students:

> When we reached the ground the machine guns opened fire. Some soldiers knelt down to shoot, and their bullets just flew over our heads. But others aimed low, and their bullets hit the chests and heads of the students. We had to go up the Monument again, then the machine guns stopped firing. But the soldiers there forced us down again. Once again we were shot by the machine guns. . . . More than thirty armoured vehicles were driven at people. Some students were run over . . . thus the whole Square was in a state of chaos. I couldn't believe that the students were so brave. They rushed at the vehicles. Many were killed. Others stepped over the dead bodies and ran forward again. At last there was a gap, and something like three thousand students dashed out, reaching the Historical Museum. Only a little more than one thousand of these were to survive.[56]

This is not an implausible story; the violence used by the army elsewhere in Beijing shows that it *could* have happened. But the only footage of the actual evacuation shows no slaughter. Says a member of the Spanish film crew that shot it: "There was absolutely nobody killed at the monument. Everyone left and no one was killed."[57]

The killing took place mainly on the streets around the Square and those leading to the center of Beijing. Most of the videotape of military attacks on citizens seems to have been shot either in Muxidi or in front of the Beijing Hotel, just east of the Square. The early press reports inaccurately describing the Square as the scene of mass slaughter, as running with rivers of blood, gave the government the pretext for denying that such violence took place anywhere. The government's official account left out the violence elsewhere and the tension and clashes in the Square, but it was essentially accurate, if misleadingly bland, about the actual withdrawal. Indeed, it seemed to gain credibility by comparison with the exaggerated reports of the foreign press, which officials denounced as "a rumour spread by the

Voice of America and some people who deliberately wished to spread rumours. . . . During the whole operation no one, including the students who refused but were forced to leave, died. Tales of 'rivers of blood' in Tiananmen Square and the rumour-mongers themselves 'escaping from underneath piles of corpse' are sheer nonsense."[58] Saying "there was no killing in Tiananmen Square" became a cagey rebuttal to all accounts of a massacre, possibly true but hardly the whole story.

One crucial subtext was the fact that government violence was directed mainly against workers and other nonstudents. Recall Liu Xiaobo's statement at the Monument to the People's Heroes: "Now I'm sure the students in the square can leave together safely, but I cannot guarantee the citizens' safety. At this important moment, I appeal to all the students to try your best to protect the citizens."[59]

By the small hours of Sunday morning the troops had cleared the Square, but the protesters, students and citizens alike, refused to give up. Throughout Beijing troops encountered surprising resistance. Some protesters threw rocks and Molotov cocktails. Others used weapons captured earlier from the army. Surprisingly often they managed to set a tank on fire, usually after persuading its occupants to surrender it but occasionally with the soldiers still inside. This opposition came less from the students—who had retreated to the campuses, their homes, or out of Beijing—than from local residents. No one attempted a frontal assault on the occupying troops, as far as I know, though many unfortunate soldiers perished or suffered beatings when they found themselves cut off in narrow alleys in the close-knit residential neighborhoods of Beijing. There, gangs of local youths turned violent, encouraged by their neighbors and knowing that potential witnesses were their relatives and friends. Torching a trapped tank offered an occasion for symbolic resistance and release from frustration. Such acts made the city look perhaps more war-torn than it was, as columns of smoke rose over a wide variety of neighborhoods.

DEFEAT, SHOCK, ANGER

For two days after this massacre, the people of Beijing moved about in a state of shock. Some retreated to their homes. Others scurried about the town trying to get a clearer sense of what had happened. Hospitals were overflowing with wounded. Sporadic shooting continued, and vehicles burned throughout an unusually hazy Sunday afternoon and much of Monday; occasionally an explosion indicated that another had been set alight. Everyone seemed uncertain of what would happen next.

Each time I ventured more than a mile or two from the university, an explosion or burst of gunfire—usually coming from somewhere out of sight but always sounding nearer than I liked—would frighten me back. I walked out Sunday night about 2 A.M. to find a crowd gathered around the burned carcass of a tank. I also saw what appeared to be a truck full of bodies (most covered with a canvas tarp). The army drove them out of town, I was told, to crematoria, where they could be made to disappear. Gunfire and cries could still be heard occasionally, though I was several miles from the heart of the struggle. And the sirens sounded all too often.

I resisted the urge to go to the center of Beijing, though many of the students I knew were braver. Instead, two expatriate friends and I checked in to the Shangri-La Hotel to use the phone and fax machine and to see the news updates every thirty minutes on CNN's Headline News, which was beamed in on satellite TV. The government had ordered these transmissions stopped, but someone had temporarily "forgotten" to shut the system down at the Shangri-La. My Chinese students came and watched the television reports. They used the phone to call friends around town and nearby, trying to verify various reports. We sent and received faxes; we cabled in reports to London newspapers and held telephone interviews with American television stations. We were, according to these reports, "eyewitnesses," yet what we could see on the streets was a small if powerful piece of the action.

As it happened, the Shangri-La was the base of the CBS television crew, which occupied an entire floor. It was also the hotel to which Fang Lizhi and his wife, Li Shuxian, China's most famous dissident intellectuals, briefly retreated under fear of arrest. They were brought in by Perry Link, one of the United States's leading specialists on Chinese literature. (Ironically, Link had been with Fang when the latter was turned away from a dinner to which George Bush had invited him while visiting Beijing the year before.) The Shangri-La is luxurious, tall, and modern, with a sleek, climate-controlled interior; it could be found in any of the world's major cities, but for a few decorative gestures toward China. Now, purely by chance, it was the meeting place for a handful of straggling tourists, late in fleeing the country; journalists torn between the exhilaration of an enormous story and the horror of what they had witnessed; Chinese staff in a state of shock; a few relatively anonymous Westerners such as me; and two of the most visible people in the background of China's democratic movement.

Professors Fang and Li were faced with a hard choice. To stay in their apartment or appear at Beida, where Li taught, was to court almost certain arrest and trial as the putative "black hands" behind the movement. But staying in the Shangri-La or the Jianguo, another Western hotel (to which they moved because it was closer to the U.S. embassy), was disorienting and not a long-term solution. Yet to seek safety in the U.S. embassy, as they ultimately did, was a very bitter choice. Link managed to hustle Fang and Li into the embassy on June 5, before the PLA guards realized what was happening. The embassy offered "temporary refuge" but could not guarantee enduring political asylum or transit to the United States. Fang and Li took a day to consider the embassy's offer, but they finally concluded they had no alternative, even though it might mean an extended stay in very cramped quarters. Fang and Li were confined to the embassy for over a year before the Chinese government finally allowed them to go into exile. That Monday, before accepting the U.S. offer, Fang told Perry Link, "I think it would be good if the American Embassy gave protection to some ordinary people—a worker, a student, or just a regular townsperson like the ones who were killed last night. It would be a good statement about human rights—much better than taking in a famous person."[60]

The students, workers, and *laobaixing* of Beijing were in retreat in their own ways, though a few brave souls spoke to foreign reporters. Some of these were arrested—one after the Chinese government intercepted the unedited ABC news footage of his interview from its satellite transmission back to the the United States. But most local residents simply stayed inside as much as they could, venturing out to stockpile essential foodstuffs in case of prolonged disorder. Many students returned to their parents' homes, but others talked of defending their campuses; a few said they were stockpiling weapons or preparing Molotov cocktails. And there were still some urban crowds, mostly small neighborhood gatherings around a smoldering military vehicle or one of the burned bodies the government left hanging from trees and lampposts as grisly reminders of the "counterrevolutionary rebellion."

One gesture of resistance from these days stands out. On June 5 one young man, a twenty-six-year-old printer, placed himself in front of a column of tanks seeking to move down Chang'an Boulevard, etching the image of his defiance into international memory. The tanks stopped rather than run him down. When they tried to go around to the left, then to the right, he stepped sideways to block their path. Then he clambered on top of the first vehicle and argued with its driver. Eventually, when the soldiers lost patience and made more threatening moves, the young man's friends dragged him out of harm's way (though he apparently was arrested several days later).

That morning I joined in one of the most widespread activities of the aftermath: the search for those who had disappeared. One student I knew had never returned from the center of town after the massacre. Twenty-four-years old, she was a bright, vivacious student of foreign languages. She had become involved in the movement gradually and was never a central activist. Yet she shook with anger after Li Peng's arrogant, hostile speech declaring martial law. She knew that protesting might lead to future reprisals against her, though I think she feared a bad job assignment or denial of a passport more than slaughter. But she did not discount violence altogether and helped talk me out of joining the march just after Li's speech. Now several of us focused our anxieties on looking for her. But hospitals were overflowing with victims of the massacre. The wounded lay on mattresses in the corridors, and there were too few staff to clean up the blood. Trying to find a particular individual was hopeless. The horrors we saw were never personalized on the faces of those we knew. Our friend turned up the next day after spending the night in another hospital, not as a patient but as a volunteer helping to care for the wounded. Thousands of other missing students had not been found by the time campuses began to empty on Tuesday, June 6. The majority had probably slipped off home, but not all; many parents would never know for sure how their children perished. The government took little responsibility. Chen Xitong, the mayor of Beijing, said that "among the non-military casualties were rioters who deserved the punishment, people accidentally injured, and doctors and other people who were carrying out their various duties on the spot. The government will do its best to deal with the problems arising from the deaths of the latter two kinds of people."[61]

At midday on Tuesday, I visited some student friends. Their anger was like a dose of amphetamines; they punched the mattresses on their bunks or stood, shaking, unable to sit down as they talked in a jammed dormitory room of their different experiences. Some had been on barricades, others in hospitals. Friends standing next to them had been killed. They all repeated over and over that they never believed this would happen. Some, on hearing the shooting begin, just assumed the army was using rubber bullets. One said he was talking with an acquaintance on a street in the Muxidi area and turned his back when he heard shots, imagining that a stray rubber bullet would hurt less on his back. Then his companion dropped to the ground; a pool of blood formed, and "he died instantly; his eyes were still open."

A few called for revenge. One said that he was a true Marxist and that the time had come for violent revolution. "I can shoot a gun," he said, "I can throw a grenade fifty meters if I need to." Of course, a successful armed rebellion without the support of a large part of the Chinese army seemed as improbable as this boast. But that did not diminish the intensity of his anger. The rage that seemed to fill the room, more powerful than any I have ever seen, occasionally lapsed into numbness and depression, only to flare again. The young friend for whom I had been searching, just back from spending all night in the hospital, put a black band around my arm. Like others, she kept saying that this repression, this massacre, was unprecedented. What really was unprecedented, however, was the momentum the students' popular protest had gained. Unfortunately, the repression and violence had all too many precedents in China and around the world—though perhaps few had been quite so dramatic. But the immediacy of anger breeds a foreshortening of historical perspective. And it was true that, although the Chinese government had killed its own civilians before (and in much larger numbers), the Communists had never done so in this kind of publicly recorded pitched battle.

At lunch Tuesday in the nearly empty dining hall, breathless students announced that Li Peng had been shot. The story was quite developed: A young man had set out to avenge the death of his girlfriend (or, in one version, his sister) and killed the premier. As more reports arrived it appeared, to widespread disappointment, that the shooting was not fatal (and eventually, of course, that it had not happened at all).

Many people expected the Thirty-eighth Army to move against the Twenty-seventh Army, which had run amok and attacked the city and the students. The Twenty-seventh assumed defensive postures and dug in with extra tanks at major intersections, but there was no military engagement. In fact, the commander of the Thirty-eighth Army had already been relieved of duty and arrested for failure to enforce martial law.[62] In any case, such fighting would have meant civil war, and it is doubtful that anyone really wanted that. We will probably never know how close it came to unfolding. Amid all this carnage, it occurred to me that a tank battle in Tiananmen would probably mean the destruction of the Forbidden City, perhaps the most important relic of imperial China. It was also suggested that the campuses might be occupied at any time. Such rumors were plausible, though I thought the army probably felt a more pressing need to defend itself against military threat—if or as long as that proved real. At any rate, by Tuesday evening only about 10 percent of the students were left at Beiwai. The situation was much the same at Beida and, I am told, elsewhere. A new slogan spread: "Empty the universities." It was designed in part to make the campuses less attractive for military occupation and in part to get students out of the most obvious places, where they could be rounded up when the repression came. The more hopeful suggested that emptying the Beijing campuses would send "seeds of fire" around the country. Students would tell people the truth, countering government propaganda, perhaps even organizing protests.

I had dinner in a student dining hall with a couple of Ph.D. candidates. Supplies of food were dwindling, hoarding had begun, and many shops were closed. At that time, students bravely assured me that they were not much worried about repression. If it came, they thought, it would take the form not of guns or prison but mainly of bad job assignments or refusal of visas for study abroad. "There are too many of us," they said. Still, wherever I went, people stopped me, nodded at my black armband, and said, "You are very brave." I could never think of a good reply and only mumbled a denial or said it was not I who was brave but the students. What impressed people, I think, was that a non-Chinese, someone who didn't have the same moral obligation they did, someone who could opt out, should care.

Beijing remained tense, and people braced themselves for repression, but now there were more substantial confrontations in other Chinese cities. Indeed, it was only during the first days of repression that those of us involved in or closely observing the movement began to realize how completely our attention had been focused on Beijing. The same was true of the Western press, which acted as though China could be reduced to the capital, with occasional snippets of Shanghai and bustling Guangzhou. But there had been protests around the country. The occupation of Tiananmen Square had gotten national attention, and students flocked from all over China to participate in the great, central event. But after the massacre, the activity outside Beijing assumed more prominence.

Memorial meetings were held across the country, "from Harbin in the north to Guangzhou in the south, and from Shanghai in the east to Lanzhou in the west," according to the Hong Kong newspaper *Ming Pao*.[63] Protests and violence were perhaps most extensive in Chengdu. On June 4 the armed police moved violently against demonstrators, killing at least a dozen and possibly many more.[64] Three buildings were reportedly burned on June 8.[65] Shanghai was all but shut down for three days. Students from its major universities organized barricades almost immediately after the massacre; the local media reported that 123 intersections were blocked.[66] Worker militia teams removed the barricades the night of June 6, only to see them replaced the next morning. Most dramatically, a train plowed into a crowd of people and was set ablaze. No satisfactory explanation ever emerged, though both the government and protesters interpreted the incident as significant. The government cited it as one more bit of evidence of the chaos that made forceful intervention necessary; students thought the government instigated the crash to make precisely that propaganda point. Some claimed the train had carried photos and documentary evidence of the Beijing massacre and that these had been intentionally destroyed by guards when students tried to rescue them from the mail car. The most widespread rumor was that those killed were protesters lying on the tracks in front of the train; after the train rammed into them, other protesters attacked it and set it on fire.[67] As late as June 9 and 10, Shanghai students were still protesting publicly, holding a memorial service for those killed in Beijing and rallying in front of the Municipal Security Bureau. They were scolded but not attacked. At the same time, however, several members of the Shanghai Autonomous Federation of Trade Unions were arrested, and their organization was declared illegal. On June 15, three of the seven workers charged with burning the train were sentenced to death.[68]

AFTERMATH

By late on June 7 it was clear that China would not endure civil war; whatever tensions may have divided the Thirty-eighth and Twenty-seventh armies—if any—had been resolved. The government began to recompose itself, the hard-liners and their associates consolidating their victory over more liberal Party forces. Still, public protests continued around China and often met with little response from local authorities. By June 9, the Li Peng government had consolidated its authority enough to begin to demand sharper action. Repression now entered a new phase, going beyond the mere crushing of open protest, establishment of "public order," and control of the streets and Tiananmen Square. Students were arrested on campuses, and a "tattletale" hot line was set up for those who wanted to turn in "counterrevolutionaries"; people on the street turned their faces to avoid Western reporters. The apparent leaders of China had themselves filmed, and the footage was broadcast on China Central Television to demonstrate their solidarity and control. Deng Xiaoping delivered a major speech to senior commanders of the martial law troops. "You comrades have been working hard," he began, and after expressing his condolences for their losses he suggested "that all of us stand and pay a silent tribute to the martyrs."[69] His analysis was simple and recalled the April 26 *People's Daily* editorial: The problem was indeed turmoil; many young students were well-intentioned though misguided; a minority of bad people mixed with them and manipulated them. This is what made it difficult for the government to know how to act.

> Some comrades didn't understand this point. They thought it was simply a matter of how to treat the masses. Actually, what we faced was not just some ordinary people who were misguided, but also a rebellious clique and a large number of the dregs of society. The key point is that they wanted to overthrow our state and the Party. . . . They had two main slogans: to overthrow the Communist Party and topple the socialist system. Their goal was to establish a bourgeois republic entirely dependent on the West.

Slogans about fighting corruption were just a front, Deng continued. This was a test, and the Party passed, thanks to the leadership of so many senior comrades. He concluded, "As determined by the international and domestic climate, it was bound to happen and was independent of man's will. It was just a matter of time and scale."

The scale of arrests undertaken after Deng's speech was massive, though hard to gauge precisely. Perhaps the most distinctive fact is that students were not those most targeted. Although students such as Wang Dan, Chai Ling, and Wuerkaixi topped the government's "most-wanted" list (the first was captured and the latter two escaped to the West), the main repressive effort was directed against workers and ordinary citizens. According to Black and Munro, "Workers, isolated in their workplaces, had fewer connections than anyone, and the BWAF and its counterparts in other cities were the first targets of the post-June 4 crackdown."[70] The Beijing municipal government announced the arrest of more than four hundred people on June 10. The crackdown was at least as severe, if not more so, outside of Beijing. In Xi'an, for example, the authorities began making arrests around June 11—over two hundred people in a week, including both student leaders and workers.[71]

One of the saddest arrests, and the one that most evoked disturbing chapters in China's past, was reported over and again on television. Zhou Fengsuo, a twenty-year-old physics student at Qinghua University, was apprehended in Xi'an. He was turned in by his sister. The government reported the sister's "honorable" act over and over again, perhaps in the hope of inspiring more such informers but more likely as a moral message in itself. Yet everyone assumed that her action had been coerced, a product of the near-total control the government had over the lives of individuals. At the same time, the events stood out as exceptional. Unlike the Cultural Revolution and other previous campaigns, this crackdown had to be accomplished almost entirely by direct application of military and police power.

Ordinary citizens showed little interest in informing on their neighbors; university deans displayed little desire to punish students; and, most worrisome for the government, the cadres in charge of workplaces carried out only the minimum level of persecution and "rectification" necessary to keep up appearances.

On June 6, government spokesman Yuan Mu had offered an early official version of the military operation. Twenty-three counterrevolutionary thugs and hooligans—some of them possibly students—had died after attacking the People's Liberation Army, sent to keep order in the capital. A thousand soldiers had perished, he said, making one wonder what kind of marvelous Shaolin masters these counterrevolutionaries must have been to inflict with their bare hands such disproportionate damages on heavily armed troops. But by Thursday, June 9, that ratio was not enough. The official media upgraded the official lie: An army general declared that no students had been killed on June 4.

Such extreme untruths never had much chance to work in the West, where television footage was too graphic (even if commentators were imprecise on the details). Neither did they have much potential to persuade citizens of Beijing; too many saw the peaceful protest and the massacre, and too many bullet holes and bloodstains remained. But perhaps the deception was effective in parts of China where news had not flowed very fully and where the Party and PLA retained more authority. Or perhaps the government believed it could repeat the official claims often enough that some of them would eventually seem true even to doubters. In any case, the government gradually developed an official position that acknowledged some deaths but treated them as the by-product of riot and rebellion rather than as massacre.

There was at first some confusion among top officials. It was not a question of whether to protest the official story; none did, at least not openly. Perhaps some covertly signaled their displeasure by dragging their feet slightly in sending congratulatory telegrams to military leaders. But even among those who supported the government's action, there was the question of how to describe it. It took a few weeks to work out the formula. Eventually, Chen Xitong, the mayor of Beijing, published what has become the main, authoritative account of the government's position, a small blue pamphlet entitled *Report on Checking the Turmoil and Quelling the Counter-Revolutionary Rebellion*. It recounts the toll of the final repression:

> In the several days of the rebellion, more than 1,280 military vehicles, police cars and public buses were wrecked, burned or otherwise damaged. Of

the vehicles, over 1,000 were military vehicles, more than 60 were ar-
moured personnel carriers and about 30 were police cars. More than 120
public buses were destroyed as well as more than 70 other kinds of motor
vehicles. During the same period, arms and ammunition were stolen. More
than 6,000 martial law soldiers, armed police and public security officers
were injured and the death toll reached several dozens. . . . During the
counter-attack, some rioters were killed. Because there were numerous bystanders, some were knocked down by vehicles, some were trampled on or
were hit by stray bullets. Some were wounded or killed by ruffians who had
seized rifles. According to the information we have so far gathered, more
than 3,000 civilians were wounded and over 200, including 36 college students, died during the riot.[72]

Chen's account is full of specifics, and much of it is accurate, even if one
regards it as incomplete and/or misleadingly presented. The government's
version of events has come to be called the "Big Lie," a reference to the
strategy that a wholesale distortion, by its very audaciousness, may be
more successful in redirecting public and historical attention than a series
of small untruths, which dissenters would be able to quibble with and perhaps disprove. But the official line is not simply a blatant lie. It is a historical construction, an interpretation of events not altogether different in kind
from those that give the student protesters martyrs' crowns or saints' ha-
los.[73] It makes sense, within its own frame of reference and evaluation, of
a great many accurate empirical claims. It is, however, a construction in
which a peaceful protest is a "riot" because it disrupts "public order,"
which in turn constitutes docile adherence to the wishes of Party leaders.
It is a paranoid vision in which the protest can only be explained by the
presence of behind-the-scenes organizers who first premeditated turmoil
and then exploited it. For example, the enumeration of death and destruction in Chen's *Report on Checking Turmoil* comes in a section headed,
"How did the counterrevolutionary rebels injure and kill People's Liberation Armymen?" This passage not only focuses on the harm done to the
PLA (rather than to citizens) but also explains how the army suffered such
large casualties.

Such heavy losses are eloquent testimony to the restraint and tolerance
shown by the martial law troops. The PLA is an army led by the Chinese
Communist Party and serves the people whole-heartedly. They are ruthless
to the enemy but kind to the people. They were able to defeat the eight million Kuomintang troops armed by US imperialism during the war years
and able to defeat US imperialism which was armed to the teeth, and to effectively safeguard the sacred territory and territorial waters and air space
of our country. So why did they suffer such great casualties in quelling the
counter-revolutionary rebellion? Why were they beaten and even killed,

even when they had weapons in their hands? It is just as Comrade Deng Xiaoping pointed out: "It was because bad people mingled with the good, which made it difficult for us to take the firm measures that were necessary." It also showed that the PLA love the people and are unwilling to injure civilians by accident. The fact that they met death and sacrificed themselves with generosity and without fear fully embodies the nature of the PLA. Otherwise how could there be such a great number of casualties and losses?[74]

This is not a fair account. It is intended to promote a favorable view of the military and the government and to minimize both the killing of civilians and the plausibility of the protest. But as a more or less *complete* interpretation, factual wherever possible, it has much more potential for influencing Chinese popular understandings and history than a simple lie or denial.

Nonetheless, the 1989 student movement showed the limits on the Chinese government's ability to control its own media, let alone the networks of gossip that also shape public opinion. Records of the movement have been archived, and discussions proliferate among exiles. The government's account may have an effect, but it will hardly prevail unchallenged. The protests of 1989 will live in Chinese memory.

Part Two

THE SOURCES AND MEANINGS
OF THE MOVEMENT
An Analysis

4 Spontaneity and Organization

The 1989 student demonstrations came about suddenly. Students turned from seeming apathy, games of mah-jongg, and study for TOEFL tests to concerted protest with startling speed. Organization was imperfect but still sufficient to mobilize hundreds of thousands of people and to maintain more than a minimum of order in the occupation of Tiananmen Square. Protests reached beyond Beijing and beyond student and intellectual ranks, gave rise to a number of tactical innovations in dissent itself, and produced the largest popular uprising independent of the government that the People's Republic has ever seen. How was this possible?

Even more puzzling, how could such an extraordinary movement have lasted only six weeks? A crucial answer to both questions lies in what researchers call the "political opportunity structure."[1] Social movements do not happen simply when people want them to or when groups have an interest in certain outcomes. They happen when there are openings for them. This movement flourished within a window of opportunity produced largely by the conjuncture of the government's internal division over potential succession to Deng Xiaoping and contingent circumstances such as the death of Hu Yaobang. Both factors helped bring about the string of inept government responses that enabled the movement to grow in its early weeks.[2] Within that window students were able to act very creatively, and with the help of their supporters in Beijing (and to some extent elsewhere) they may even have enlarged the window. But they did not create the opening for their movement; they only seized the occasion.

The students' ability to do so had a great deal to do with their own leadership capacities and their use of organizational resources others had not fully recognized. But if students were able to mobilize beyond anyone's expectations, they could not keep their mobilization effectively organized, especially when it came to achieving a tactical withdrawal from the Square. And though the government was initially too factionalized to offer either modest concessions or a firm enforcement of its bans, this disunity didn't last; after the regime regrouped, it was able to crush the movement handily.

In this chapter I focus primarily on the question of how students were able to act as effectively as they did and secondarily on the limits of their effectiveness. I offer less analysis of why the regime was weak and how it regained its strength, maintaining the perspective of the movement rather than of the regime. Remarkable as it was, the movement was not an act of pure creativity, molded out of nothing; it drew on existing organizational bases, established roles, and historical precedents. Students made their own history but not their own conditions.

TWO ILLUSIONS

In looking back on their movement, student activists have often fallen prey to two widespread, though opposed, illusions. The first is fatalism. In my interviews I repeatedly encountered former Tiananmen protesters claiming that they knew in advance the denouement of the movement. In this account, the die is usually said to have been cast by April 26, when the party leadership (minus Zhao Ziyang) issued the *People's Daily* editorial asserting that the students were about to cross the line of creating "turmoil." Students threw down a challenge of their own by marching in massive force through police lines and into Tiananmen Square the next day. "From that time on," one former student leader now studying in the United States told me six months after the movement's end, "I knew that the massacre was inevitable." We need to allow for a little rhetorical overstatement here; this very intelligent philosopher certainly didn't mean that he knew every detail of what would happen. But he did mean that he knew the government would crush the movement with violent force. I want to dispute this claim; it is an after-the-fact reconstruction. This student called for an end to the public protests and a consolidation of gains in early May. He was worried about repression from early on, but his very call for withdrawing to the campuses suggests that in early May he did not really believe the fatal die had been cast. And by May 17, he was once again caught up in the excitement as intellectuals moved to center stage by issuing a collective declaration and marching as a group. The point is that the narrative development of the movement was not in fact fated but open to creative action.

The students who made it happen believed *any* outcome was possible; they were constantly engaged in discussions about strategy and tactics for this action, not following a predetermined course. Each new round of events, each escalation of the confrontation with the government, did constrain future action, pose problems for students to solve, and raise the risks. But until the last play, the game was still open.

There is some evidence that the government began discussing forceful repression as early as late April and that it had activated the military almost as soon as hunger strikers occupied Tiananmen Square. On May 22 Li Peng announced that "we have come to the stage where there is no retreat. If we retreat still further, we shall have to give China away to them."[3] These facts, however, make fatalism no less illusory. The fatalist illusion depends on a kind of teleology, a reading of history from its end, and is thus fundamentally a denial of action and contingency. The issue is not when options were open and when they were closed off but what options were open when; there were *always* options. It doesn't matter whether one says the crucial date was April 26, or May 19 (when Zhao Ziyang's defeat seems to have become final), or May 22. Even in the early hours of June 4, the course of events was still open to change; indeed, the choices made by Chai Ling, Liu Xiaobo, Hou Dejian, and Colonel Ji Xinguo may have been crucial in avoiding a greater bloodbath.

The attraction of the fatalist illusion is not limited to the opportunity to claim personal foresight or wisdom. It includes the chance to construct the narrative of the protest in the form of a tragedy or a romance of doomed heroes.[4] This view offers a kind of honor to the actors, each of whom played his or her role to the fullest even though the dramatic structure was fixed in advance. It also offers a kind of absolution: because the end was fated, the actors need not shoulder blame for having failed to head it off.[5] The fatalist illusion also places the movement within a larger narrative of Chinese history, one that stresses the extreme difficulty, even the impossibility, of effecting real change.[6] Even where the narrative is one of heroic romance rather than tragedy, the fatalist illusion displaces the "foreordained" victory into the distant future, outside the reach of immediate practical action.

In direct opposition to the fatalist illusion is that of radical spontaneity. In many tellings of the Tiananmen story, student narrators find it important to claim a kind of "virgin birth" for the movement. Determined to accent hope and a sense of the possible, these narrators also challenge the government's accusation that the movement was directed by a "black hand"—someone such as Fang Lizhi or, worse, foreign agents or overseas

Chinese agitators. The government's conspiracy-theory account of the movement makes the students into marionettes whose strings were pulled by offstage powers, honest but naive dupes of political manipulators. Such a charge was implicit in the April 26 editorial, which suggested that a "very small number" of bad elements were pushing the movement in an unpatriotic direction.

One of the rhetorical effects of such attacks was to deprive the students of ownership of their movement. If somebody else was the *real* actor, then the students were not truly making the movement happen, not truly making history; they were just pawns in someone else's game. This sense of being mere pawns was very real to the students—it was how they felt in regard to Party power struggles and many other factors affecting their lives. But they were not prepared to accept that they were being controlled by others even in their own movement of resistance to domination.

This context made it important to claim altogether spontaneous origins for the movement. Such claims were not made only in retrospect, like the fatalist ones. On May 12, the hunger strike was announced as having been "spontaneously organized by some students."[7] The Beijing Autonomous Workers Union began its "Public Notice No. 1" by declaring, "The BAWU is a spontaneous, transitional organization formed by the workers of Beijing at this extraordinary time."[8] In a *dazibao* of April 3 addressed to the authorities of the Beijing University, Wang Dan and his colleagues used the term "spontaneous" four times in the space of a paragraph. The students added that if the authorities were to accept their proposal for a public event, "two days in advance of a scheduled democracy salon, the organizers of these spontaneous meetings will furnish to university authorities for registration a list of the persons invited."[9] Obviously "spontaneous" was largely a code word for something such as "free of manipulation." In the Chinese communist tradition, the term usually translated as "spontaneous" (*zifa*) referred to activities not organized by the Party or one of its rivals but rooted immediately in popular self-organization. The term was used also to contrast the 1989 movement to the Cultural Revolution, which students understood to have been manipulated from above. Yet clearly Wang Dan and his colleagues were organizing fellow students; "free of manipulation" should not be taken to mean "free of leadership and advance organization."

Part of the attraction of claims to spontaneity was their affirmation of the distinctiveness and individual freedom that the movement itself proclaimed. Jia Hao, for example, couched his account of the movement in a critique of the "so-called 'scientific laws' . . . that Marx and his followers imposed on human society as universally applicable and predictable. . . . In reality, almost all major social events and historical conditions in human societies are unique."[10] Words like "spontaneous" also carried connotations of authenticity and naturalness; these were celebrated attributes of the movement.[11] Students expressed a strong sense of novelty, repeatedly describing both their own actions and those of the government as "unprecedented."

The illusion of spontaneity was reinforced above all by the notion that the movement sprang into existence in direct response to the death of Hu Yaobang. But, as described in chapter 1, the movement did not spring from a single event or at a single moment. For weeks and months before Hu's death on April 15, students and intellectuals had been meeting in their democracy seminars, enlightenment salons, and other forums for discussion of precisely the sort of issues that became central to this movement. Intellectuals had petitioned the government to free Wei Jingsheng. Students had planned protests for May 4, and this groundwork enabled them to spring into action when the opportunity for demonstrations came earlier. Like all important mobilizations, in other words, this one had a "prehistory." It also drew enormously on preexisting organizational bases. The idea of spontaneous self-organization obscures both these facts.

The illusions of fatalism and spontaneity are not opposites but sometimes exist side-by-side in single narratives. "We did this entirely ourselves," students say, "and it was fated that blood would be shed." But whether taken separately or together, the two rhetorical tropes suggest a spurious dualism: deeds are either predetermined or voluntary, manipulated or self-directed. The two illusions keep us from recognizing how complexly interwoven structure and agency, constraint and action always are—with a good deal of chance mixed in. We make our own histories, then, but only partially, and not under conditions of our own choosing.

AUTHENTICITY AND MISRECOGNITION

The immediate occasion for protest was indeed the death of Hu Yaobang. Though more than a pretext, mourning Hu was not the central factor in producing the movement. Indeed, we should be skeptical about the suggestion that this grieving was simply a deep, spontaneous, and heartfelt outpouring of sadness over the death a beloved figure. Hu was, after all, a Communist Party leader, a relatively—even remarkably—benign one but not the perfect role model some enthusiastic mourners made him out to be. Su Shaozhi's comment captures the mild and somewhat ambiguous tone of the underlying feeling students had for Hu:

> In 1986 when we discussed the seventh five-year plan for the social sciences Hu Yaobang met with us and said that since the Third Plenum, the party's Central Committee has never used the stick. Many people said, and as I recall Li Honglin was the first to speak up, "What do you mean you never used the stick? Some people have been expelled from the party." Wu Mingyo added that some even lost their jobs. And I also added that some were even expelled from Beijing. But Hu Yaobang did not object to being interrupted by so many people. He took their opinions very seriously, and said, "Write a report and I'll approve it if it's correct." This sort of broadmindedness is unusual among our leaders."[12]

Unusual though it may have been for Party leaders not to resent being interrupted, that level of broad-mindedness did not fulfill every hope intellectuals had. Their feelings for Hu as a person may have been less significant than their sense that his dismissal from power marked a turning point in the reform era, diminishing their faith that it would really bring greater freedom.[13]

When students said, "The one who died should not have died; those who should have died live," the emphasis was primarily on the second clause. Elegies for Hu made a variety of similar points in veiled and indirect fashion. The pervasive rhetoric of authenticity through which students claimed to be moved simply by grief should not be taken quite at face value. Hu provided a powerful, multivocal symbol. His death provided the students with a splendid opportunity, and they made the most of it.

Of course, successful use of Hu's death depended on the protesters' refusal to admit that it was being "used" at all, rather than simply mourned. It was important that students "misrecognize" their own strategic aims and commit themselves to an ideology of spontaneity.[14] Students thus were able to understand their actions as pure and innocent, to claim spontaneity yet also take pride in their organization. Emphasizing the planned, strategic character of collective action would invite others to see it as calculating and instrumental rather than a genuine expression of moral outrage. The rhetoric of spontaneity pressed the theme of authenticity and the absence of ulterior motives.

However, to adhere to it in retrospective analysis is to make the movement seem less than it was. It serves the government's desire to underestimate the extent of organized, thoughtful opposition and to suggest that (beyond the "very small number" of "black hands") student protesters were merely acting emotionally, expressing their grief at Hu's death, their indignation at corruption, or their anxiety about the process of reform. Such analysis devalues the self-disciplined character of the movement and obscures the importance of both existing and newly created means of organization.

From the beginning, the Beijing Spring of 1989 bore testimony to the fact that even a relatively spontaneous movement depends upon organization; neither feature necessarily contradicts the other. Spontaneity is not always a radically individual phenomenon, some of the current Western-influenced ideology of Chinese youth notwithstanding. Students' spontaneous participation was nurtured in group discussions. Small clusters of friends and classmates had discussed their complaints about the government and the state of Chinese culture for months; they had debated various ideas about what could be done in the privacy of dormitory rooms and in semipublic gatherings at restaurants and campus hangouts. When they came forward they did so arranged by schools, and within schools by classes. Indeed, one of the striking features of the protest movement from the very beginning was its ability to generate organization without requiring much bureaucratic apparatus or a formal leadership hierarchy.

In order to make sense of the mobilization of the Chinese students, we need to consider several different, partially complementary ways in which action can be organized. Though all challenge extreme claims to spontaneity, they need not support the opposite illusions of fatalism or determinism, on the one hand, or external manipulation, on the other.

PRECEDENTS

The 1989 student protest movement was not China's first, and historical precedent was among its most important bases. Prodemocracy protests had flared in 1986 and been much more sustained in 1978–79. The mourning of Zhou Enlai in 1976 was itself a dramatic, veiled protest centered on Tiananmen Square. The Chinese revolution of 1949, the student protests of the republican and warlord eras (including the May Fourth movement of 1919), the republican revolution of 1911, and the examination candidates' remonstration and repression of 1898 all figured in the imaginations of students and other Chinese who tried to understand them.

These precedents offered two main advantages. First, they provided students with a positive identity through which to understand and plan their actions and through which to be understood by others. Students adopted an established role when they embarked on a protest movement, identifying themselves with earlier Chinese heroes such as Tan Sitong, the martyr of the 1898 examination candidates' remonstration. Tan was in Beijing along with other students and young intellectuals to take the traditional imperial examinations of the old *keju* system. But this was also the era of self-strengthening; Tan, along with other young intellectuals, argued that continuation of the traditional, closed bureaucratic attitude toward the challenges of modernization would be fatal for China. The remonstrances of the examination candidates were linked to the abortive Hundred Days of Reform, ending with a sharp return to the authority of the dowager empress Cixi. Rather than try to escape, Tan chose to press his challenge to the end, which (perhaps predictably) entailed government repression and his own execution. Tan has been celebrated as a hero of the struggle against feudalism in China, a precursor to both the student radicals of the May Fourth movement and the rise of the Communist Party. He offered a familiar model for both protest and heroism. The students who protested on May 4, 1919, were even more direct exemplars of the role into which students stepped in 1989.

Second, historical precedent offered students a variety of tactical examples, scripts, and repertoires for collective action. Historical dates were thematized in the new protests, most obviously May 4 but also May 16, the anniversary of the opening of the Cultural Revolution, which was marked by a declaration from over a thousand intellectuals.[15] The "dare to die" squads formed by students at the time of the repression and by *getihu* motorcyclists immediately after the declaration of martial law took their name from anti-imperialist struggles of the late Qing and republican eras. Students in 1947 had put radical new words to the tune of "Frère Jacques," just as their successors in 1989 did.[16] The idea of writing "last testaments" in blood, as some students did before the April 27 march, echoed an older idea of "records written in blood."[17] Students did not have to think up the ideas of using caricatures or large character wall posters, forming autonomous organizations, issuing declarations, wearing arm or headbands, or displaying bloodied clothing. All these acts were part of a repertoire of protest with which they had been made familiar by accounts of earlier movements.[18] May Fourth movement students had delivered street-corner lectures in 1919; so did those in 1989. The "Internationale" had been sung by generation after generation of Chinese protesters.

In a sense, the student protesters of the Beijing Spring were descendants of a lineage running from the May Fourth protesters of 1919 through the Beida Demonstration Corps and Petition Corps of 1931–32, other republican-era protesters, the communist youth organizations, and the Cultural Revolution to the various protests of the 1980s. Most immediately, much smaller Beijing university demonstrations had taken place in 1988, helping to set the stage for 1989. These protests accustomed a number of activists to taking risky action and gave them practice in organizing.[19]

The depth of historical background was not always immediately apparent. For example, along with many other foreign observers in 1989, I was impressed by the students' tactic of linking arms and marching in units to maintain order and solidarity during protests. This procedure became widespread on April 27. Students I asked about it stressed their desire to keep out agents provocateurs. Only much later, in interviewing exiled activists, did I discover the practice was not an invention but an inheritance from republican-era protests (preserved for 1989 demonstrators by its reproduction in communist-era films). Similarly, when the hunger strikers occupied the Square, cordons of student guards, termed "pickets," were posted at intervals to keep the crowd organized and protect the inner circle of strikers. This, too, turned out to be in imitation, taken from anti-Japanese protesters in 1919.[20]

Creating a kind of shadow bureaucracy that mimicked and appropriated official forms was another long-standing tactic that figured prominently in 1989. The students had a "general commander" and various deputy commanders; similarly, protesters during the republican era claimed military titles for themselves and announced elaborate structures of departments and officers in charge of propaganda, demonstrations, finances, and so forth.[21] Like rebels of the 1920s and 1930s, student activists of 1989 occasionally subdivided into groups of ten, echoing not only communist cell structure but also imperial organizational forms. Well before that, the Taiping rebels of the 1850s had created an almost exact replica of the government's formal structural hierarchy.[22]

The appropriation of bureaucratic forms had several functions. It made the protesters appear maximally organized (and thus rebutted the fear of chaos). It challenged the state's monopoly on "official organization." At the same time, it mocked the state's pretensions, revealing how easy it was to claim an august-sounding title. Theatrical performance, not just practical organization, was at work when students created their elaborate hierarchical structures (which they were in any case unable to implement fully). The hunger strikers in Tiananmen Square had a series of "bureaus," with vice commanders for each. Other groups, such as the Joint Liaison Group of All Circles in the Capital to Protect the Constitution, consisted of "departments for theoretical research, strategy and countermeasures, information, fundraising, propaganda and agitation, liaison, coordination, reinforcements, editing, publishing the *People's Voice*, and security."[23] The impetus to announce elaborate formal structures was linked to protesters' experience in school and official contexts and was backed by a genuinely impressive capacity for organization. Support from the Beijing Social and Economic Sciences Research Institute and other think tanks and networks of more established intellectuals may have given this bureaucratic system a chance to succeed had not the pace of events overtaken it.[24] The group did publish a single issue of *People's Voice*, edited by Bai Hua. As head of its security section, Zhang Lun was able to achieve some level of coordination among the student, worker, and citizen picket teams. Nonetheless, the declaration of a formal structure was largely a theatrical device for conveying organizational solidity.

In addition to imitating official organizational forms, students picked up bits of rhetoric and symbolism promulgated by the Communist Party and turned it to their own purposes. They repeated Deng Xiaoping's 1980 arguments for an end to lifetime officeholding and rule, quoted Mao Zedong on the fate history holds for those who suppress student protests, and laid claim to protection under the constitution.[25] From the time martial law was declared, students repeated over and over again, "The people love the People's Army, the People's Army protects the people." This slogan of the communist era was itself an updated saying from the *Analects of Confucius* cited prominently by the Yongzheng (Yung-cheng) emperor in the eighteenth century: "The people support the soldiers and the soldiers protect the people."[26] Jeffrey Wasserstrom's point about the republican era holds equally well for 1989: Student protesters were empowered by their ability "to appropriate and subvert the meaning of official rhetoric, forms of action, and organizational techniques."[27]

Part of the students' advantage was that the communist government had itself kept alive memories of a broad range of previous protests. These were part of the glorious history of communism and more generally of the Chinese people's struggles against feudalism, imperialism, and foreign aggression. They were themes of schoolbooks and popular films, revolutionary operas and television documentaries. As such, they offered examples of tactics and provided links to a heritage of protest—once one established the similarity of the communist government to the bad regimes of the past.

LIMITATIONS TO CONTINUITY

The protesters' ability to establish links to past protest was extremely important. However, the links were mainly symbolic, though they sometimes involved knowledge of specific tactics. They did not include the capacity to maintain organizational continuity or even sustained opposition to the Party. Previous struggles with the communist regime were not studied for what they might contribute to a cumulative development of opposition. Continuity with past prodemocratic activism was provided only by the relatively small number of individuals who bridged the Cultural Revolution, the Tiananmen incident of 1976, the Democracy Wall movement of 1978–79, the 1986–87 student activism, and the 1989 events. The influence of these individuals was considerable. Among the most important were Wang Juntao, Su Xiaokang, and a few others of the so-called "in-between" generation of young intellectuals who had been activist youths during the Cultural Revolution.[28] But the very importance of the handful suggests the absence of a more substantial organization or a more widespread and active historical memory.

One of the most pernicious effects of totalitarian government is the destruction of historical continuity.[29] This process may start, as it did in China, with a radical revolutionary condemnation of traditional culture, but it often extends beyond that. History has been subject to constant attack in postrevolutionary China. Photographs of great events are constantly brought under the retoucher's airbrush, for example; after the Cultural Revolution Jiang Qing had to be removed from Mao's side, just as Liu Shaoqi had earlier been removed from pictures of the founding of the People's Republic. As policy lurched from mass campaign to bureaucratic clampdown and back again, it was hard to maintain a sense of continuity; the fact that each campaign might subject individuals to "thought reform" only amplified this effect.[30] Few unofficial sources of information could surpass the level of gossip, and even that was undercut by the dangers inherent in loose talk (when neighbors and even family could be persuaded to turn into informers). It is no surprise, then, that the students of 1989 were not well informed about the Democracy Wall movement or even about the Cultural Revolution. Copies of Wei Jingsheng's discussion of democracy as "the fifth modernization," for example, were hardly in circulation or available in school libraries. It is significant, in this connection, that the student protesters' demands were almost identical to those of the intellectuals whose open letters and petitions had helped start the protests in late winter. The main exception was that the students hardly ever mentioned Wei Jingsheng or called for the release of political prisoners.

A sense of historical continuity is not only important to individuals but is a resource for oppositional movements.[31] For one thing, the visibility of ongoing dissent reveals that opposition is possible. This is a crucial source of "cognitive liberation," the freedom introduced by the realization that the world does not have to be just as it is.[32] It is also a source of tactical knowledge and substantive ideology. However, students' understandings of democracy in 1989 were limited by the suppression of their recent forebears' ideas (Western "bourgeois democratic" writings were more accessible than those of many earlier Chinese dissidents, whose ideas circulated mainly by word of mouth, if at all). Repression has tended not only to restore the government's control over ideological discussion but also to prevent development of unofficial organizational bases and communication networks. To some extent, therefore, each new movement has had to start from scratch, including that of 1989: It could rely on personal networks but not on more complex formal organizations.

Lack of visible, continuously functioning oppositional groups has led some commentators to stress the absence of existing organization on which the 1989 democratic movement might build. Oppositional organizations, however, were not the only bases for a movement; to focus too much on explicitly nonstate formal organizations is to miss much of the genuine foundation on which the 1989 movement rested. Zhou Xueguang, for example, has described the problem of collective action in the People's Republic as one of mobilizing a large, disaggregated mass of people linked primarily by common interests, a common enmity to the state, and common responses to state actions. In his analysis, "collective action in China is less a process of purposive and rational organizing than an aggregation of large numbers of spontaneous individual behaviors produced by the particular state-society relationship."[33] Zhou offers a stark contrast between an unorganized "civil society" and a highly organized state, drawing on the rhetoric of Eastern European resistance to communism and a number of more recent Western analyses. But though Zhou's argument offers insights, it is potentially simplistic in that it tends to pose a set of false dichotomies: state versus civil society, organized versus unorganized, consciously engineered versus spontaneous.

Though it is important to consider the extent to which social institutions and networks are organized outside the control of the state, and though it seems accurate to suggest that there was less such "civil society" in China than in most of communist Eastern Europe—let alone Western Europe or North America—it does not follow that in China "society consists of unorganized interests."[34] Common culture and state power are obviously central in China, whereas in the West both the impersonal capitalist economic system and the web of nonstate social institutions play larger roles. But when we ask about how people are mobilized for specific collective actions, neither "state" nor "market" is a fully apt answer anywhere.

Though markets contribute to large-scale societal integration in the West, for example, specific collective actions in relation to markets are accomplished through businesses, trade unions, chambers of commerce, and a host of other organizations (including branches of the state apparatus). In China, *danweis*, branches of the Communist Party, and special-interest associations are nearly all integrated into the state in some sense, but they also organize action on the basis of their internal structure, including networks of interpersonal relationships. Indeed, various such "state" units often contend with each other and may pursue a variety of different policies so long as the central power of the state has not been mobilized behind the definition of one of these as "correct" and the others as "erroneous."

In short, even if a wide range of units of concrete social organization are sponsored by the state, they are not always effectively under central government control. Excluding the Chinese Academy of Social Sciences or Beijing University from "civil society" because they are officially and financially part of the state is misleading. The 1989 protest movement was possible because students were able to deploy existing organizational networks for purposes quite contrary to official state policy. They were able to do so partly because individuals and groups within the government and Party encouraged them, protected them, or turned a blind eye to their activities. Large numbers of middle- and upper-middle-level officials chose not to act, or at least not to act forcefully, on the explicit or implicit wishes of those at the top of the state hierarchy.[35] These middle-level officials were central to the organization of "society," and though they did not build institutions entirely outside the purview of the state, they were able to limit the capacity of those in power to govern the immediate activities of their units. They were, in a sense, buffers, equally important in making dissent possible and in moderating the impact of repression after the movement was crushed.

This kind of organizational structure did not afford the protesters an adequate basis for resisting the government's concerted effort at repression. However, this need not mean the end of the story, as the example of Poland makes clear. The Polish workers of Solidarity were similarly unable to resist government repression at the time of the Gdansk strike; the initial repression that brought the Jaruzelski government to power was temporarily effective. But the Solidarity activists ultimately succeeded in enlarging the scope of organization outside the control of the state and in laying the groundwork for further expansion. The latter came about because the Polish government, after repressing the protests, felt obliged to generate new economic activity to compensate for the political losses suffered by the Polish people. This effort created "free spaces" outside immediate state control that were later available for antiregime collective action. It is entirely possible that the same sort of thing will happen in China, where the government has also sought to encourage economic activity by allowing more activities to be conducted outside its purview. Though ostensibly apolitical, this action nonetheless generates nonstate organizations and a "civil society" less fully penetrated by the state.

It is important to separate the questions of whether particular organizational bases are internal to the state and whether they are able to resist the exercise of central power. The two variables are correlated, no doubt, but not perfectly. Zhou thus expresses a "principle" of communist regimes, but one not fully put into practice, when he writes that "the Communist state eliminates the traditional intermediate strata between the state and society—it directly links each citizen with the state and thus reduces all social groups to a similar structural position subordinate to the state and its bureaucratic organizations."[36] Mao attempted to achieve this kind of structure during the Cultural Revolution—indeed, it is an important reason for the leadership's habitual recourse to "mass campaigns," designed to reach people directly rather than through the intermediate layers of party and government—but it is not an adequate description of the state of affairs in China during the 1980s. Though nearly every individual arguably was linked directly to some part of the state, not all were linked with equal directness to central power. The state was both represented symbolically as a singular whole and manifested in a variety of specific institutions, many of them local. Moreover, despite forty years of communism, personal connections remained one of the most important means of access to those in power.

Though his sharp state/society division is misleading, Zhou does make a very good point about another aspect of popular mobilization in the PRC: the "large numbers" phenomenon. According to Zhou, "the institutional structure of state socialism reduces the barriers to collective action by producing 'large numbers' of individuals with similar behavioral patterns and demands that cut across the boundaries of organizations and social groups."[37] Put another way, the circumstances in China generate categories of individuals with similar interests and similar predispositions to action. Zhou assumes that such categories have few internal network linkages and that the actors are therefore primarily individuals rather than organizationally coordinated groups.[38] He refers, thus, to the metaphor of "swarms of bees."[39] He might have echoed Marx's image of peasants as being like potatoes in a sack, for he has much the same model of action as that Marx employs in "The Eighteenth Brumaire of Louis Bonaparte."[40] In Marx's view, because of their disorganization and disconnection, peasants could only react to changing circumstances of state power and economy; they could not be protagonists of revolutionary change. The latter role could only be played (at different stages) by the bourgeoisie and the proletariat—each concentrated in cities, internally differentiated and organized, and capable of creating autonomous political associations. Marx's model is a bit unfair to peasants (who, after all, have been central actors in most of the world's great revolutions), and it rather exaggerates the extent to which revolutionary action depends on the creation of new social organization rather than the redirection of existing ties, rational choice rather tradition.[41] However, Zhou's use of a similar framework illustrates a key reason why every shift in state policy produces such strong responses (positive or negative) in the population. Large categories of people, whether linked directly or indirectly to central power, stand to be affected in similar ways by the various policies. This is so regardless of whether they are linked directly to central power or indirectly through many layers of bureaucracy. The crucial point is that the population is not so differentiated as to be affected in many different ways, and that each category is not crosscut by others to such a degree as to reduce its salience. Were either of these situations true, policies would not induce such widespread propensities for similar action.[42]

At bottom, Zhou suggests that students in China were mobilized because, as members of a single category, all of them were affected similarly by government action. This assertion seems accurate and important for understanding the breadth and magnitude of Chinese students' participation. All were subject not only to the same state actions but also to the same market forces (increasingly significant in the 1980s), the same media influences, and the same concerns about Chinese national identity. However, they were not effectively knit into a lateral organizational structure. The absence of such a structure, indeed, is one of the reasons for the difficult relations between the Beijing and provincial students who shared the occupation of Tiananmen Square (and, for that matter, for the tensions *within* each of those groups). It also helps explain how there could be simultaneous protests in a wide range of cities throughout China without the existence of any centralized organization to coordinate them, and it helps explain why they did not evolve from many "seeds of fire" into one large brushfire of rebellion. Workers, too, formed a category of people with similar interests yet relatively weak linkages across the boundaries of work units (let alone cities or regions). The salience of these categorical identities made it possible to address and mobilize large numbers of people but hard to organize and sustain their activities once they went into the street.

This is an important point, but it applies most strongly at a relatively large scale. That is, categorical identities were the main connection among students or workers, but within each of these large categories there were significant *local* concentrations of denser, stronger, lateral network ties. Taken as a whole, the students of China might constitute a category without much of a network, but those within the Haidian district were better linked, and those within each school were quite strongly linked, both by informal relationships and by participation in officially sanctioned organizational units. Thus, categorical similarities largely explain the simultaneous occurrence of protests in many cities, but local networks were important to the internal organization of each protest. Local network ties helped *mobilize* students in Beijing, but these protesters sought to *represent* the category of Chinese students on a national scale.

FRIENDSHIP AND FREE SPACES

At the level of face-to-face relations and personal networks, students had a wealth of organizational resources. Every class had its monitor, for example, and they were as prepared to support the hunger strikers as arrange for circulation of course materials. Students planned marches and organized the occupation of Tiananmen Square by school, class, and often major. Such patterns of organization have been important since China's first universities were created—and since the first student protests. Chinese cultural traditions encouraged this sense of the primacy of the group, and it was reinforced by students' need to rely on informal connections to manage many of life's problems and opportunities. In other aspects, this q-uity of organization was an achievement of Chinese communism, the *danwei* being the supreme example. Intraparty units also often facilitated organizing. They gave students not only connections and sometimes material resources but also experience in mobilizing their classmates.

In 1989, however, mobilization also drew on a more novel factor that helped change the meaning of solidarity itself. This feature was, simply, friendship. Personal ties among individuals, created voluntarily rather than by the system, were highly valued and emotionally charged. Students debated, for example, whether the friendship bond—something perhaps closer to the strongest senses of Australian mateship than to the usual American sense of the word—should take primacy over marriage.[43] They stressed high ideals of loyalty. They shared everything. Students, well aware that the black market rate for foreign exchange was some 50 percent above the official rate, nonetheless exchanged money among friends at face value. They did so even though foreign exchange was an extremely prized commodity for those who hoped to go abroad, as everything from tests to application fees had to be paid for in foreign exchange certificates. One student I knew, eventually a minor leader in the protest, housed a friend in his dormitory room, even paying for his friend's meals out of his own meager income (a standard tiny stipend augmented by income from teaching English to students preparing for TOEFL exams). The friend was a graduate student at another university but came to think of himself as a "professional revolutionary."

The institution of friendship has by no means always overridden ascribed group membership—kinship, work unit, class—in China. Previous policies of the communist regime had in many ways specifically undermined it, calling for a commitment to ideology and party above personal ties, creating powerful ritual occasions for friends and relatives to betray and criticize each other. The struggles of the Cultural Revolution offer extreme but not unique examples. Of course, in 1989 cynical manipulation of connections coexisted with ideals of friendship. Family loyalty still retained great force. Yet friendship seemed of central importance to students' lives. And even kinship was reinterpreted in much discourse as a matter of affectionate, mutually supportive interpersonal relationships—not only obligation and ascription.

The students' discourse and practice of friendship were poorly explained by either the notion of individualism or the equation of society with the state. Students identified strongly with various aspects of individualism, from Western writings on capitalism and freedom to belief in the primacy of romantic self-expression (personified in China by the poet Xu Zhimo and reflected in Su Rui's popular song lyric, "Follow your own feelings"). They shared a vaguely Rousseauian (or Californian) idea of the ultimate value of expressing one's internal feelings; the government's common taunt of "bourgeois individualism" seemed rather accurate in this sense. But the strong feeling for friendship—including a level of loyalty that put most Westerners to shame—was not individualistic but truly social. I wondered how many students thought about whether their own espousal of individualism might be at odds with the fundamental value of friendship and asked a few. They were puzzled, for the most part, and as we talked I realized that a key aspect of friendship was to regard friends as individuals, not as representations of classes or categories. In any case, the resurgence of friendship was one of the most basic manifestations of society beyond the reach of state manipulation—even if it sometimes developed in the very midst of state institutions. It offered an important resource for insurgency. Friendship networks were a genuine form of organization, if one of only limited capacity.

Personal friendship networks overlapped largely with institutions, of course: friends were apt to attend the same school. Friendship thus reinforced ties based on membership in the same class, study in the same department, residence on the same dormitory floor, and so forth.[44] One of the most important functions of friendship networks, however, was to provide students with access to other university populations. Beiwai was linked to Beida, thus, by personal ties that facilitated the passage of news, the introduction of new bits of organizational procedure or rhetoric, and even the development of loyalties to one or another of the prominent student leaders. (At Beiwai, for example, Wang Dan was considered a "friend of friends" and was therefore supported by most Beiwai students in his sparring with Wuerkaixi.) Such crosscutting ties were strongest among elite Beijing schools, weaker among the capital's more specialized and/or less prestigious universities and among the provincial schools. This is one reason that organizational effectiveness declined as the movement expanded beyond its original base.

The cross-institutional networks were also influenced by characteristics specific to each university. For example, because Beiwai focused primarily on the humanities, its students were more likely to connect with their counterparts at Beida than with those at the heavily science-oriented Qinghua. These crosscutting friendship networks also reflected students' backgrounds outside the university; for example, students at Beida and Beiwai (at least by reputation) come from more elite families than, say, those enrolled at the equally first-rate Qinghua University—a pattern that has persisted for seventy years. Many personal links were rooted in hometowns—individuals from the same community often wound up at different Beijing universities.[45] In this there is an echo of the native-place associations that shaped much mobilization—and that helped unite students and workers—in early-twentieth-century Chinese cities, especially Shanghai.[46] In 1989, hometown bonds joined students to each other but not to Beijing workers. Moreover, students generally had dense and solidary personal networks within schools. The ties between schools were crucial supplements to these but perhaps never quite effective enough to limit rivalries and mistrust.

The local networks that helped students organize their protest also served to mediate their responses to government actions or other major events. Students did not form their opinions of Hu Yaobang's death, the April 26 editorial, or Zhao Ziyang's visit to the strikers in Tiananmen Square in isolation or linked only by their similarities as members of the category of students. Their views were developed out of intense discussion and vigorous gossip. This is another sense in which the notion of "unorganized interests" is misleading. The local nexus of social ties was also a vehicle of opinion formation; interests were not simply fixed by membership in an objective category but were constructed through discussion and debate. The movement itself was an occasion for extending the exchange of views. In addition to arguing with a knot of friends in a dormitory, students used speeches and posters to make the discourse public. Conversations that would ordinarily have been held only in more or less private settings were held among a wider range of students. All were already in the Square and therefore had taken a risk larger than that posed by anything they were likely to say.

The reform era saw an increase in "free spaces" for discussion—for example, the private restaurants that proliferated on or near university campuses. But the most important institutional spaces for the nurturance of protest were the universities themselves. This fact suggests again the difficulty of trying to explain the movement as one of civil society versus the state. Although the 1989 movement gained from the emergence of new, independent organizational bases outside the official purview of the state, the protest was rooted much more fundamentally in institutions run as part of the state apparatus. The "civil society" that mattered was not altogether distinct from the state but had roots deep within it. And the public sphere—however limited—that emerged depended not only on the support of new structures but also on changes in the significance and use of state-sanctioned entities.

THE DIFFICULTIES OF LEADERSHIP

The student protesters were not limited to existing organizational bases; they also established new associations, such as the autonomous students unions on individual campuses, the interuniversity Federation, and Protect Tiananmen Headquarters. In addition, they forged new informal connections of friendship and collaboration. Collective action in the movement always involved both these dimensions; formal organizations were complemented by informal relationships. Sometimes, leaders spoke directly to crowds and relied on word of mouth to spread their appeals.

The April 27 march pushed many of the early activists into the background. It was the first of several occasions on which quasiformally recognized leaders found themselves faced with a popular momentum to which they had to either adapt or succumb. The leaders who weathered this storm and emerged in the front ranks of the Federation remained central through most of the movement. However, new waves of activity and risk-taking brought new leaders to the fore, and the older ones had to share prominence and influence. The April 27 march was particularly decisive because it marked the point at which the movement as such became the central object of widespread concern. No longer were students from different campuses focused on their own autonomous unions and wondering just how much to invest in shared activities. Whether or not they thought the Federation an adequate vehicle, after April 27 most were committed to a movement that was clearly much larger than any one campus and that had a momentum of its own.

The April 27 march also brought student leaders into a new level of interaction with the press, especially the international press. They now actively courted foreign journalists and photographers, carrying signs in English, French, and other Western languages. Use of the slogans "Vive la liberté" and "Give me liberty or give me death" established links to the year's two famous bicentennials (albeit loosely in the second case, since the reference was revolutionary and not constitutional) and created images that were more likely to hold the attention of Western citizens than were signs in Chinese. Some student leaders began to become much more visible in the press than others, precisely because they made themselves more accessible; Wuerkaixi's dormitory room at Beijing Normal University became a regular stop for journalists. At the same time, a few leaders from smaller schools—including the very active University of Politics and Law—began to chafe a little at the appropriation of the spotlight by students from Beijing Normal and Beijing universities. Wang Dan, somewhat more reflective and reticent than Wuerkaixi, never achieved comparable celebrity in the international press; his advocates regarded Wuerkaixi with suspicion. The latter was an astute and mediagenic figure, as he showed in his countless interviews during May, his pointed questioning of Li Peng in the "dialogue" of May 18, and his press conferences from Paris after his escape (where he played ably on the fact that his arrival coincided with the revolutionary bicentennial). Wuerkaixi was also a self-promoter, and his colleagues were frequently irked. As Chai Ling remarked in late May: "I have also been irritated at Wuer Kaixi all along; he has at times used his own influence and position in ways that have caused great damage."[47]

If April 27 challenged leaders to stay in control of a protest that expanded beyond anyone's expectations, the period after May 4 posed the opposite sort of challenge: how to maintain momentum that seemed to be flagging. For a week after that date, students watched the movement dwindle as they waited to see what response the government would make to their demands. Most returned briefly to classes. The protest was the constant topic of discussion on campuses, but no one seemed to know what the next move was.

The next move was unclear for three main reasons. First, the protest had moved beyond the range of lessons available from experience. Though protesters had posed implicit challenges to the government before, none within living memory had acted against direct instructions—instructions backed by military force—and gotten away with it. Students talked frequently about possible courses of action with teachers and others who remembered earlier movements; the latter gave advice, but this mobilization escaped their expectations and experience. Second, it was not clear what the government was going to do; the possibilities ranged from harsh crackdown to massively accelerated reform. Uncertainty about the government's actions stemmed from lack of knowledge of which factions were ascendant; most students were not even sure just how deeply divided the government was. Partisans of the reform faction may have talked with student leaders or communicated with them indirectly through senior intellectuals (on the other side, Li Peng met with senior professors to try to get them to encourage calm and faith in the government on campuses). Such contact may have affected actions at various points, but it does not seem to have been extensive enough that the movement was substantially aided by any party faction or helped by access to significant inside information.

The third reason for the movement's temporary confusion was that the student leadership was somewhat amorphous and unable to make firm decisions and communicate them widely. Students had initially become leaders primarily by leading. In some cases, leadership was ratified—typically after the fact and by acclamation—at a large meeting. Only in a few cases were there formal elections, and most of these were uncontested. Chai Ling's account of how she rose to prominence seems plausible and reveals her frustration with some of the other leaders. The specific leadership vacuum into which Chai stepped was created in part by wrangling and ego clashes between the two most prominent male leaders, Wang Dan and Wuerkaixi. Chai says she first became involved on April 22, when she attended the funeral for Hu Yaobang and watched the futile effort of Wuerkaixi and other students to present their petition to the authorities. Angry, she made her first speech, a brief call for the officials to heed the students. Shortly thereafter she offered the proposal that all the Beida students join hands and leave the Palace of the People.

> Before the end of that day, I had enlisted in the Beida preparatory committee. . . . In working thereafter on the preparatory committee, I gained experience and realized that my comrades on the committee had an unsuspected ardor and devotion and were completely sincere by every test. There were also, however, these egoistic men who pursued a personal end and who sought glory above all, ambitious men who proved questionable whenever their vanity was at risk.[48]

In the wake of the hated April 26 editorial and successful April 27 march, Chai became more active and vocal in pushing for further action. She was in the forefront of the small group that forced the hand of the larger leadership by initiating the hunger strike while others were still debating the issue. With some forty others, Chai issued the widely circulated declaration of the hunger strikers on May 11. From that time on she was at the center of the protests, especially because she became the focal point of leadership in Tiananmen Square. Her allegiances and energy were focused on the occupation of the Square, not on negotiations with the government or on the older organizations rooted back on the campuses. Increasingly, her Hunger Strike Group transformed itself into the core leadership of the occupation:

> The heads of the Autonomous Association of Beijing Students [the Federation] had desired to control the situation, but, in the Square, there was always disorder. Several of the leaders were far from being irreproachable, and I thought it was better to count on the Hunger Strike Group. It alone had persevered to maintain the occupation of the Square. Therefore, I volunteered to be the president of the Group. It was after having taken over these functions that I discovered the deplorable state of the situation.[49]

By mid-May there had been, according to Chai's count, 182 personnel changes in the student leadership. By the end of the month, she was becoming all but paranoid—and certainly apocalyptic—about the desire of various "capitulationists" to secure a departure from the Square. "[O]ur presence here and now at the Square is our last and only truth," she argued. "If we withdraw, the only one to rejoice will be the government. What goes against my inclinations is that, as commander-in-chief, I have again and again demanded the power to resist these capitulationists, while the Beijing Students Federation and the Non-Beijing Students Federation are also anxious to have the power to make decisions."[50]

Even where there were elections among the students, the outcome was seldom in doubt by the time the voting took place (internal elections at Beida and one or two others at large and active campuses were the only exceptions).[51] The polling merely ratified a decision that had already become more or less consensual (not unlike many Communist Party elections). In any case, despite being nominal "commander," Chai Ling had little opportunity to command, for there was little real hierarchy of authority. Moreover, even duly elected leaders could be unceremoniously sloughed off if they no longer seemed to represent the opinion of large numbers of active students. Such sackings happened mainly when leaders counseled moderation to students who wished to accelerate the pace of confrontation.

In addition to being less official than Western media reports frequently suggested, leadership was spread widely through the movement. Many different groups of students made innovations in the protest simply by deciding that some particular slogan or line of action was a good idea, putting it into practice, and seeing if it caught on. Important decisions were often taken by small groups that were not identical to or part of a centralized leadership. It is important to realize how rapidly the movement grew from limited bases on university campuses to include hundreds of thousands of participants from various backgrounds and with varying degrees of knowledge and commitment. Given this swift expansion, the level of organization achieved was quite remarkable. Marches were orderly, not rag-tag affairs; in mid-May there was a notable increase in pageantry, with new banners and flags and matching t-shirts for a few groups. In the Square itself crowds were well behaved, there was virtually no crime, health services were set up, and paths were made so ambulances could reach the hunger strikers when necessary. A system of passes was devised and enforced fairly effectively by student guards. Much of this organization came through the diffuse and widespread borrowing of templates from other settings (as with the role of class monitors) and from lateral interactions among groups; only a portion was centrally initiated.

As time went on, however, central leadership became simultaneously more important and harder to provide. In late May, for example, leaders tried repeatedly to move slogans from an almost exclusive preoccupation with persons—"Down with Li Peng," "Deng Xiaoping step down"—to a renewed emphasis on democracy and other systemic changes. They failed. The early emphasis on institutional themes was all but lost as the movement broadened, anger grew, and confrontation intensified.[52] At the same time that such ideological leadership was relatively ineffective, organiza-

tion remained fairly strong. There was a crisis over the handling of donations from abroad, but this was a minor problem considering the pressure
the students were under, the fact they could not even open a bank account,
and the fact that the sums were huge by the standards of their daily lives.
Donated supplies were circulated fairly effectively. Tents from Hong Kong
were distributed and arranged in orderly ranks. Couriers maintained contacts between students in the Square and their home campuses. Loudspeakers were set up. Troop movements were monitored.

There were two great triumphs of inspirational leadership. The first
was the decision on May 11 and 12 to begin a hunger strike; the second
was the erection of the statue of the Goddess of Democracy exactly two
weeks later. Each involved a widespread sense that something needed to be
done, initiative from particular individuals and/or small groups, and a sort
of unofficial ratification by the core leadership of the movement. In the case
of the hunger strike, the initiating and ratifying groups were closely linked,
heavily overlapping at the major universities—Beijing, Beijing Normal,
and People's. With regard to the statue, however, key roles were played by
a newcomer from Shanghai and students at the Central Academy of Fine
Arts, people for the most part outside the "established" core of student
leadership. Yet both the hunger strike and the statue were splendidly successful symbolic acts. They bolstered the flagging enthusiasm and commitment of student activists and communicated the movement's message to
far-flung audiences.

The hunger strike was the more important of the two, though the statue
became the movement's enduring symbol. Several tactical considerations,
as well as emotions, guided the hunger strike. Most obvious, perhaps, was
its timing: Those who planned the action were well aware of the impending
visit of Mikhail Gorbachev. His presence would inhibit the Chinese government from taking overt repressive action and bring a flock of international reporters. The protesters' message would be heard (and seen) by the
world, which itself might have an impact on the Chinese regime. Moreover, the hunger strike provided dramatic events and photo opportunities,
as students collapsed and were carried unconscious to hospitals while others rallied to their support. It was during the hunger strike that the largest
of all the protest marches was held, with more than a million people converging on Tiananmen Square on May 17. The impact of its sheer scale was
multiplied by the diversity of banners proclaiming the different units in
attendance and offering witty or piercing slogans. And the marchers wore
a rainbow of colors; delight in more expressive clothing was one of the

most visible signs of the sense of freedom they felt in the midst of this brief relaxation of government control.

The hunger strike also aroused enormous sympathy on the part of ordinary Chinese. Scenes from the hunger strike were broadcast on China Central Television and described in the *People's Daily*. Chinese citizens felt drawn to and protective of the hunger strikers, whom they were prepared to see as suffering on their behalf. They were moved by the spectacle of relatively privileged university students worrying not simply about their personal careers but about China's future, putting their health, future prospects, and possibly lives at risk. Moreover, they could identify readily with some of the students' complaints, notably those about corruption. And although political democracy was apparently not a highly pressing concern outside intellectual ranks, the economic concerns raised by the student protest were widely shared.

The hunger strike quickly turned into an occupation of Tiananmen Square. This ultimately became problematic, as student leaders found that they could not end the occupation in a way that saved face, satisfied the full range of participants, and still avoided a violent confrontation with the government. But at the start it was a fine tactical move. The occupation of Tiananmen Square gave the movement a focal point, a symbol of success and an object of defense. This was important not just for those reporting on it from outside but also for the protesters themselves. Previously there had been no "neutral" turf on which activists from all the different universities gathered to discuss their plans and ideas. Now the Square became the setting for nightly meetings of the student leadership. These midnight sessions (only one of which I observed firsthand) seem to have involved an average of about thirty people, though I was told that at some points they were constituted as a "council" of nine members and that at other points a considerably larger crowd joined in (particularly after the number of student contingents from outside Beijing had swelled).

Discussions focused on tactical and logistical issues but were hampered by a problem almost endemic to student movements—the attempt to make decisions by consensus. This became a major issue when proposals to withdraw from Tiananmen Square began to be put forward by the most prominent leaders of the movement. A substantial minority indicated that it would not depart, and it was clear that a complete and orderly retreat could not be achieved. Leaving a rump occupation behind could only weaken the movement, so the students stayed (ostensibly all of them, though in fact a good many drifted away until the statue of the Goddess of Democracy rekindled enthusiasm). On all sorts of occasions, students spent hours debating the right course of action, with little clear mechanism for making decisions and moving ahead.

Closely related to this problem was the fact that the student leaders generally did not have a strong conception, still less a habit, of pluralistic public discourse. They favored pluralism in the sense that they wanted their voices to be heard and not squashed by the government. But they also felt a strong need to speak unanimously; in this they were just like the government they opposed. They sought to be the "voice of the people" and understood themselves as speaking for the country as a whole. They did not often consider that there might be competing but equally valid points of view or solutions to a problem.[53] Though they tried to respect minorities, they did not see nurturing an internal discourse across lines of significant difference as one of the goals of their movement—and still less as an immediate priority. As a result, rank-and-file protesters occasionally complained that movement leaders behaved toward them just as the government behaved toward the people. Certainly leaders made no systematic effort to ascertain the views of ordinary movement participants. They reached their own conclusions, announced them, then hoped they would be followed. When they were not, they felt abandoned and tended to become passive.

Different contingents of demonstrators acted with considerable autonomy, guided as much by constant observation of each other and lateral communication as by any directives from top leaders. This independence did not prevent a high level of organization in the protests, but it rendered certain difficult decisions almost impossible to make and implement.

MOVEMENT GROWTH AND CONSOLIDATION AS MANAGEMENT PROBLEMS

On May 22 I sat in Tiananmen Square with a group of the occupying students. The sun was mercilessly hot, and the pavement absorbed the heat and radiated it back at us. The Square had been occupied for ten days, and garbage disposal was a problem (though students worked hard to keep it under control). Banners that had been bright and fresh a week before were a little bedraggled. So were the students. On the plus side, the chronic water shortage was lessening. Pedicabs wheeled around the Square with barrels on their backs; protesters came and filled their own bottles, usually the one- or two-liter plastic soda containers ubiquitous in the West but new to China. Merchants were now donating food in abundant quantities. I ate steamed rolls with my student friends, then shared their disappointment when a more tempting meal of sliced pork over rice arrived after we had taken the edge off our appetites. The pork dishes arrived in styrofoam containers, just as they might from any Chinese take-out restaurant in the United States, fifty at a time. Only three days before, many of these same students had ended a week-long hunger strike. One had made six trips to a hospital to be revived by intravenous drip, returning each time to the Square to continue his fast.

Now he ate well but talked of disarray and discouragement in the leadership. The previous day had seen crisis atop the movement, even while the broad masses of students were savoring the support of Beijing's *laobaixing* and the government's inability to impose martial law. The three most prominent leaders—Wuerkaixi, Wang Dan, and Chai Ling—had set their differences aside enough to agree that it was time to call for a withdrawal from Tiananmen Square. From the massive and festive May 4 demonstration to just before the massacre a month later, students occasionally suggested, "It's time to consolidate our gains; let's declare victory and return to classes." They didn't intend to give up, of course, only to step back from the most provocative tactics and put the ball in the government's court for a response to the democratic challenge.

At first this suggestion came mainly from older graduate students, somewhat less radical and more cautious in their overall approach. This is one of the reasons graduate students lost the prominence they initially had in the Federation and several of the autonomous campus unions. By the end of May, however, a similar argument for caution and consolidation of gains had been voiced by most of the key leaders at Tiananmen. Some thought a declaration of victory and a withdrawal would bolster Zhao Ziyang's chances to stay in power and thus enhance the forces of liberal reform. Others worried that if the occupation were too prolonged, crowds would grow smaller and the movement would look gradually weaker. Still others simply wanted to avoid violent repression. However, student leaders knew it would be difficult to gain a consensus in favor of withdrawal; they recalled how much conflict there had been over the less dramatic decision to end the hunger strike.

In the May 21 midnight caucus of the leadership, those seeking a tactical withdrawal were outvoted by a substantial majority. Wuerkaixi retreated to collect his thoughts and recover his strength. Wang Dan sat for hours with his head in his hands, sometimes crying in frustration. The problem was not just that the leadership was losing its efficacy but also that there was no coherent alternative. The decision had been made to stay in the

Square, but there was no particular plan about what direction the continued occupation should take.

What would the Students for a Democratic Society (the prominent American protest group of the Vietnam War era) have done under similar circumstances? the main student leader of one of the smaller Beijing universities asked me. I wasn't sure, I said. In retrospect, however, it seems to me that the SDS quite likely would have done, and over the long run did do, pretty much the same thing the Chinese students did. Though comparisons between the Western student movement of the 1960s and the Chinese students' struggles in 1989 were often misleading, there was a striking similarity in this instance. The SDS dissolved in factional fighting and lost its ability to lead a movement that had grown rapidly beyond the core members who initiated it, outstripping its organizational capacity.[54] So, too, in Beijing. There were clashes of egos and ideologies among the leaders. Protesters from outside Beijing surpassed the number of those from the capital by the third week of May. Those who came later often felt a need to demonstrate their commitment to the struggle by taking stronger positions or engaging in more extreme tactics than those who began the fight. At the same time, their understanding of the slogans and goals that guided the movement was often fuzzier and shallower.

Here, too, the Chinese student uprising shared much with other reform coalitions, including the U.S. civil rights, student, and peace movements of the 1960s. It is common for such movements to grow in waves. Each major thrust taxes those already mobilized, often raising the risks of participation and leading some to drop out; a lull often ensues while activists grope for new tactics and chart new courses. When these capture the attention and galvanize the enthusiasm of still more recruits, absorbing them can be difficult. Existing organizations are often overwhelmed. Long-standing activists may look down on their new colleagues, may do a poor job of blending them into the movement, and may feel threatened by the erosion of their own familiar milieu or their own leadership. Latecomers may stage coups within existing organizations, form organizations of their own, or simply remain cut off from much of the center of action. However well or poorly the new recruits are absorbed, however, as each wave recedes activists feel pressure to top their previous performance, to bring out more marchers, to take deeper risks, to escalate confrontation. Keeping the momentum rolling in this way is one of the few dependable ways to maintain some control over the movement. The press accentuates this need because it is interested only in new developments, events that are bigger and more dramatic than those that went before. Moreover, because new activists are generally less well integrated into organizations and networks than are old, leaders are tempted to address them en masse (e.g., through the media) rather than by relying on direct relations.

THE PRESSURE TO ESCALATE

The declaration of the hunger strike and the erection of the Goddess of Democracy gave the movement momentum even though neither was initiated by the reigning leadership. At various points, other students tried to push the movement ahead by taking still more radical measures. The most striking of these was the declaration of a handful of hunger strikers that they would burn themselves to death if the government did not meet key student demands. This threat was issued repeatedly during the week after May 13. On at least one occasion the would-be martyrs apparently got as far as dousing themselves with kerosene before they were prevented by other protesters from completing their threatened immolation.

This incident made me think of the comments Lu Xun made on the death of Qiu Jin some eighty years before.[55] Qiu Jin had been one of the first women to rise to importance among China's radical modernizers and had studied in Japan at the same time as Lu Xun. There she developed a reputation as a fiery orator and drew large and admiring crowds. Her fame continued to grow when she returned to China in 1906. She played a key role in building the Datong school and secret society and joined her lover and others in planning an insurrection. Eventually their plot was uncovered; her cousin Xu Xilin succeeded in shooting the Manchu governor of Anhui province but was captured and executed. Warned by friends that the army was coming for her, Qiu chose to remain at her school, hoping to make a dramatic last stand with the arms that had been stockpiled there. She was captured and ultimately beheaded. Lu Xun, however, said that she had been "clapped to death." In other words, the crowds that had urged on her speeches and applauded her protestations against the government had implicitly pushed her to ever more radical positions. She could neither pause to consolidate her gains nor escape when the troops came without suffering humiliation and betrayal of her own ideals. The complicity of the crowd in her death went further. Their applause signified not just agreement with her complaints but pleasure in the entertainment her protest provided. A crowd also gawked at her execution.[56]

The same effect operates during all protest movements. A crowd of a quarter of a million people is impressive when observers and participants expected only a hundred thousand, but it quickly establishes a new norm.

To sustain interest, activists must constantly heighten the drama of their movement. Though attention is generally focused on the apparent leaders and the core activists, the crowd on the fringes shares implicitly in responsibility for the actions taken. Those who cheer encourage those who demonstrate; those who merely watch still swell the crowd. Simply by attending, every person in Tiananmen Square, Chinese or foreign, raised the ante for the protesting students.

Almost invisibly, then, the stakes kept getting higher throughout the month of May and the first two days of June. The government tried concessions, the most obvious being the series of dialogues initiated by government spokesman Yuan Mu, but these were not open enough to satisfy many people. Even when leaders began to acknowledge students' patriotic intentions, it was too late to mollify most protesters. Concessions encouraged further action, in fact, not just by failing to satisfy the demonstrators but also by seeming to prove that protest could bring results.

When concessions did not work, the government condemned the movement and eventually imposed martial law. Li Peng's speech declaring martial law, however, simply fanned the flames of student anger. Those who previously were unsure of how far to go immediately took to the streets, insulted by his tone and infuriated by his denial of everything they called for. When troops were stalled on the periphery of Beijing for two weeks, the students felt they had achieved another triumph. But the standoff only raised the tension yet another notch. However orderly they might be, the students and their allies among the citizens of Beijing were now engaged in what the government would clearly see as a sort of illegal occupation of the city.

The flow of students from outside of Beijing into Tiananmen Square contributed to the radicalization of the movement in a different way. These students had started arriving shortly after the hunger strike began. Because they had not been involved in the early stages of protest, they may have felt an extra need to prove their commitment to the cause, to match or top the actions taken by the Beijing students. They were also cut off from various potentially moderating influences. Whereas local students constantly mingled with less radical classmates, those from outside Beijing had few such contacts; only those most committed to the struggle had made the trip to the capital. Local students also talked more often to family members and teachers. Perhaps most important, the students from outside of Beijing were not well integrated into the leadership of the movement. Li Lu was their only prominent voice, and he became closely linked to Protect Tiananmen Headquarters rather than continuing to represent the non-Beijing students. The creation of their own organization (the Waigaolian) on May 19 affirmed their separateness from the Beijing protesters. Personal network ties and flows of communication spreading information, views, and instructions among the non-Beijing students were not nearly as dense as those among the students of the capital.

The students from outside Beijing played a central role in the decision not to withdraw from Tiananmen Square at the end of May, a few days before the massacre. They had not been in the occupation as long as their Beijing colleagues and so perhaps were not as tired of it. More to the point, withdrawing from the Square meant returning to their own homes or campuses, where they might be exposed to retaliation from local officials (many of whom were less sympathetic to the protests than were leaders of some of the Beijing campuses, nearly all of which had prominent large and powerful pro-reform factions among professors and administrators). It would also cut them off from any meaningful form of prodemocracy activism. Beijing students could stay intensively involved after a withdrawal, but those from other cities would have to try to carry on their protests out of the limelight and away from the main lines of communication.

Many of the non-Beijing students did leave during the first three days of June, but those who stayed may simply have been all the more radical. In any case, on the fateful night of June 3, as the army approached Tiananmen Square, the students from outside of Beijing are reputed to have been the most determined to stay put.

LIMITATIONS

In the end, some of the movement's strengths contributed to its undoing. Organization based on friendship and interpersonal networks facilitated rapid expansion but inhibited cohesive leadership; participation of broader elements (workers, non-Beijing students, *laobaixing*) gave the movement a less exclusive character but made unified action and expression virtually impossible to achieve; and the dramatic and risky actions the students undertook brought them worldwide admiration and sympathy but placed them under constant pressure to raise the stakes, lest the Beijing Spring be dismissed as old news. Most crucially, perhaps, the occupation of Tiananmen Square—initially a focal point and a powerful symbol for the movement—left the students in a double bind: They could afford neither to hold on nor to let go.

When these problems became apparent to student leaders, efforts to end the occupation mounted quickly. Those who favored leaving the Square were not just trying to avoid a massacre. At the time, no one anticipated an attack of the sort unleashed on June 3 and 4; students generally expected nothing worse than tear gas and rubber bullets. The real issue was how to reorient the movement toward long-term reform and away from short-term protest. The point here is not to judge whether withdrawal would have been the right or wrong move but rather to note how hard it is for a movement like this to sustain an ongoing struggle, shifting from what Gramsci called the "war of position" to the "war of maneuver"—or in this case back again.[57]

However, the Chinese student protesters in 1989 lacked the luxury of building a movement gradually. China's lack of nonstate social institutions inhibited the development of a public discourse in which a range of views—heterodox and iconoclastic as well as orthodox—could be aired over a period of months or years. The late-1980s surge in the creation of "free spaces" for open discussion helped make the movement possible, but compared even to the Soviet Union and Eastern Europe of the 1980s (let alone to the West), China was still very short on the institutions (for example, a free press) that could nurture such discourse.[58]

One final organizational issue undermined the movement: the difficulty the students had forging ties outside their own ranks.[59] Not all free public spaces hold the potential equally to empower—let alone to join—intellectuals (including students), workers, and peasants. The 1989 protest was an urban movement, with almost no resonance in or connections to the countryside (except on the fringe of major cities like Beijing). This is not to say that China's rural population is without grievances or uncritically supportive of all government policy. But word of this protest spread in the countryside much less extensively than in the cities and primarily through official government media.[60] It is still the case that few peasant children go to universities, and so the informal communications network that spread unofficial and "insider" views of the protest did not work effectively in rural areas. Links between students and peasants also were inhibited by class bias: The former shouted to soldiers, "Farmers go home; you have no business here," whereas the peasants—like rural people everywhere—had suspicions about "city slickers." Moreover, in some respects urban and rural populations were pitted at least superficially against each other as consumers versus producers. Higher food prices (even in the form of an end to the scrip payments by which peasants were forced to loan money to the government) would have furthered the inflation that worried urban folks.

Students and urban workers found a measure of common cause in the protests, but few organizational linkages united them. Though the ideas of sending student delegations to visit factories or of forming a joint student-worker committee were sometimes mentioned, little action was taken on this front. Indeed, the students often actively rebuffed workers who showed an interest in joining *their* movement. On April 19, student pickets kept a group of workers from joining their march; the day after martial law was declared and ordinary people stopped the troops in the streets, students refused the Beijing Workers Autonomous Federation permission to read its declarations over the loudspeaker set up at the Monument to the People's Heroes. (However, students were happy enough to accept money from the All China Federation of Trade Unions.)[61] Ties between students and workers may have been even weaker outside Beijing.[62]

Occasionally activists mentioned the model of Poland's Solidarity movement.[63] Emulating Solidarity was popular, and certainly it was one of the nightmares of Deng Xiaoping and other aging Party leaders, but the rise of such a coalition faced several hurdles in China. Solidarity was rooted in stronger, more independent workplace organizations than exist in China. It was enhanced by links between intellectuals and the workers' movement, which prevented intellectuals from completely dominating the leadership. Polish society had more social arenas free from close state supervision than China. And China had no institution like the Polish Catholic Church to bring together urban and rural populations.

Without either free public spaces or deeper popular unity, democracy is unlikely to get very far. It is possible that reform will bring more of each to China over the next few years, and there almost surely will be more flowerings of dissent similar to the student movement of 1989. But until deeper roots are laid, Chinese protests are apt to continue to echo the old Confucian idea of the people (or the intellectuals) remonstrating with the ruler. They will not be manifestations of alternative bases for government so much as attempts by the powerless to remind those in power of their true responsibilities. The 1989 student movement was designed not so much to supplant the government as to deliver it a kick in the rear. The government responded mainly by kicking back. It has also tried somewhat to clean up its act—for example, by policing corruption more closely—and to foster rapid economic growth, partly as a distraction.[64] Such concessions are the most that this kind of popular movement usually can achieve. Its strengths lie in the ability to make life difficult for top officials and especially to exploit divisions within the party and government. If the crises provoked by such a movement actually topple a government, the movement by itself is unlikely to provide the basis for a new regime.

5 Civil Society and Public Sphere

REPRESENTING "THE PEOPLE"

Tiananmen Square has replaced the adjacent Imperial Palace of the Forbidden City as the metaphorical center of China. Unlike the palace, a ceremonial court closed to commoners, Tiananmen Square is traditionally used for ritual expressions of popular government.[1] During the forty years of Communist rule, it has been the place to which "the people" have come in large crowds to witness displays of leadership and to grant leaders authority by acclamation. Especially during the Cultural Revolution, Tiananmen Square played a crucial role in Chinese politics. Here Mao addressed favored groups of Red Guards and reviewed the army. The displays and performances in Tiananmen Square frequently signaled shifts of policy; true believers went there for inspiration, for a glimpse of Mao, for the most Durkheimian of collective representations of social membership.[2] Appropriately (on symbolic if not architectural criteria), Mao's mausoleum was placed in Tiananmen Square.[3]

In this way, Tiananmen Square has straddled traditional modes of authority and novel, more popular ones. During Mao's life, Tiananmen was used for ritual displays of the sort by which the European monarchs reached their people:

> Representation in the sense in which the members of a national assembly represent a nation or a lawyer represents his clients had nothing to do with this publicity of representation inseparable from the lord's concrete existence, that, as an "aura," surrounded and endowed his authority. When the territorial ruler convened about him ecclesiastical and worldly lords, knights, prelates and cities, . . . this was not a matter of an assembly of delegates that was someone else's representative. As long as the prince and the

estates of his realm "were" the country and not just its representatives, they could represent it in a specific sense. They represented their lordship not for but "before" the people.[4]

Much the same was true of ritual performances by Chinese emperors—for example, the procession to the Temple of Heaven (Tian Tan) to pray for good harvests. The emperors represented the country to heaven before the people. Though Mao's rhetoric was decidedly more populist than the emperors', he, too, claimed to represent the Chinese nation (in his case, to history and the world) *before* the people rather than to represent the people in the mode of an elected legislator. In such a model, the Chinese nation was greater than the sum of the Chinese people. China preceded them and would endure after them; it was a singular being, whereas they were plural.[5]

Mao did represent the people in government to an extent, but he represented them as a unitary whole, not as a differentiated body with diverse views or interests. When Mao addressed "the masses" in Tiananmen Square, he spoke for the general will in Rousseau's sense, not for the will of any individuals or even of all.[6] Mao's speeches to the people were monological, not part of a polyphonic discourse; they were top-down communications. Both Mao and the traditional monarchs occupied the public space with a uniquely authoritative claim to represent "the whole" of society— in relation not only to the forces of gods and nature but to the members of society itself. This claim was at the heart of the authority they represented when they performed before the people.

However, Mao and the traditional monarchs had different constructions of "the people." For the Chinese emperors (and in varying degree the European kings), this was a very unfocused category. The ranks of the people might swell or shrink with the latest military adventures; borders were not sharply defined (Great Wall notwithstanding) but rather vague frontiers. The people were defined mainly as those lacking in any significant form of authority. Mao's "masses," by contrast, were the ultimate source of authority; the general will for which he spoke reposed in them. But this conception of "the people" constructed a categorical identity in which each individual was a member of a set of equivalents; the set was bounded by membership in the Chinese nation.[7] Though Mao's authority derived from his capacity to speak for the Chinese people, he spoke for them only as masses, not as citizens. He spoke about what was right for everyone, not about what was fair to a range of competing interests.

Western ideas of democracy, by contrast, are rooted substantially in the idea that "the people" are differentiated, that as citizens they have a range of interests and the right to represent them *to* the government and to have their representatives *in* government take them seriously. It is fair to say that in calling for democracy in 1989, the student protesters and ordinary people of Beijing were demanding to be treated as differentiated citizens rather than as the government's masses.

We must ask, therefore, how society produces individual and collective actors capable of playing the role of citizens. In Western discussion, this notion is tied up with that of "civil society." Civil society is conceptualized typically as the realm of organized activity outside the immediate control of the state but not entirely contained within the private sphere of the family. It includes economic activity, voluntary associations, religious groups, and literary societies. Ideally, for democratic purposes, it includes a public sphere in which a rational-critical discourse can take place about how the interests of different groups are related to each other and to the actions of the state. This is the basis for a form of authority that ascends from citizens rather than descending from rulers and that presents a range of different identities, interests, values, and perspectives on public affairs.[8]

Though the eighteenth-century European public sphere that informs most theorizing understood itself as universal, it was in fact an upper-class, male domain: Workers and women were excluded. Indeed, the universalistic language of discourse actually hindered the recognition of differences between elites and workers, or between men and women, as significant issues *internal* to the public sphere.[9] The workers' movements in many countries, including China, brought class issues clearly into the discussion; the presumption that public life was a male preserve has been only more slowly challenged. Radicals of the early twentieth century addressed gender issues with calls for women's education and an end to foot-binding and to arranged marriages. The government of the People's Republic went to some lengths to end the traditional subjection of women, enabling them to gain education and positions of responsibility. Yet the PRC itself, particularly since the Cultural Revolution, was generally ruled by men. The lone woman to reach the top levels of the Chinese power structure was Jiang Qing, Mao's wife and the leader of the ultraradical Gang of Four. The reform-era vilification of Jiang seemed to symbolize a reversal in the fortunes of women. "Corrections" of the errors of the Cultural Revolution seem especially often to have involved replacing female local cadres who allegedly abused their authority. The "literature of the wounded" (narratives by the Cultural Revolution's victims) tended to present women either as innocent victims (or the mothers of victims) or as particularly rapacious petty bosses. Such presentations did not grant women many strong roles in the action of the public sphere.

Gender exclusion was not one of the themes of the protesters in 1989, but gender did figure in the protests. By my count, approximately 80 percent of the students who occupied Tiananmen Square were male.[10] I do not mean to suggest that women were either uninvolved in or unsupportive of the movement. However, the predominance of men was more than a reflection of the skewed gender ratios at Beijing's elite universities. During the hunger strike, for example, men were more likely to refuse food and drink, women more likely to provide hunger strikers with care and support. The vast majority of core leaders of the protests were men, as were most speech makers; Chai Ling was in this sense an anomaly.

Gender, class, and other differences rooted in the institutions of civil society and private life pose a double challenge to the ideal of rational-critical public discourse. First, they raise the question of whether any particular public sphere excludes important voices from its discourse. Second, and perhaps more insidiously, they pose the question of whether certain kinds of difference can themselves be made the object of attention in the public sphere. For example, when the language of public discourse is universalistic but equates men with humanity, it is hard to get issues of gender foregrounded. The same is true in slightly less universalistic terms for claims to national identity when men may be represented as potential martyrs, women as mothers, or differences of class and region are similarly repressed.

A somewhat related issue for Chinese intellectuals was their tendency to cast themselves as voices of the people, insisting on the need to restrict public discourse to those with the appropriate educational background. Intellectuals were prepared to speak for the people and even for differentiated groups of people—for instance, entrepreneurs, workers, or peasants. But they were ill-prepared to recognize their own interest in framing the public discourse in a way that uniquely empowered them.

The formation of diverse identities and the empowerment of diverse voices were basic issues for Chinese public discourse in the late 1980s. A "passion for studying culture" (*wenhua re*) swept through China's intellectual community in the late 1980s.[11] If any single theme dominated the public sphere, this was it. Yet this theme also poses a challenge for theories of the public sphere that ignore identity politics and the transformation of culture.[12] The (mostly young) people who joined in this searching exploration of Chinese culture were not engaged in an abstract deliberation of policy, interests, or anything altogether external to themselves. They were seeking to make sense simultaneously of their collective predicament, the resources available for constructive action, and their personal identities as Chinese intellectuals.

Perhaps the most important version of identity politics has been the pervasive modern reliance on the idea of "nation," commonly brought forward in the claim that certain cultural similarities should count as *the* definition of political community. Nationalism was a central feature of new social movements in many nineteenth-century settings, and issues of national identity have been crucial throughout modern Chinese history, particularly since the mid-nineteenth century.[13] Moreover, despite repeated academic expectations that it would soon vanish into the mists of the archaic past (from which it was allegedly a survivor), nationalism has proved itself integral to the present era; indeed, it is all the *more* important today because of globalization, not neutralized by it. In this broader sense, as Li Zehou argued in the 1980s, problems of national identity have been basic to Chinese intellectuals ever since European contact. But intellectuals have not offered a simple Chinese identity, to be developed and settled in advance of participation in public discourse. On the contrary, according to Li Chinese intellectuals have always been caught between two ideals— patriotism versus enlightenment—and vacillated between the different implications of each. The former implies the need for unity, an anxiety about foreign threats, and the importance of seeking national salvation; the latter implies rationalism, an emphasis on science and democracy, and an opening to the rest of the world.[14]

The goals of national salvation and enlightenment were not strictly opposed; students wanted both. Intellectuals had long seen strengthening of the nation as one of the benefits of enlightenment. But national salvation emphasized a technocratic role for intellectuals, whereas enlightenment placed more value on their role as producers and disseminators of culture.[15] In 1989 students and intellectuals thought about national salvation in ways that stressed the unity of the entire nation, but they also thought about enlightenment in ways that reflected their desire for more individual freedom. The discourse of national salvation tended to repress many forms of diversity, demanding that "individuals or any interest groups conform to the people's will embodied in the movement."[16] It also carried gender biases. Posters encouraging a reinvigoration of the "national essence" often criticized Chinese men as effeminate.[17] Deng Xiaoping was doubly mocked as both feudal and female when he was caricatured as the Empress Cixi. The national essence was presented as primarily male.

A civil society that allows for a variety of individual and group identities—and even a variety of *kinds* of different identities and groups—is helpful in encouraging the inclusion of diverse perspectives in public discussion. In such a civil society, people differ not only on a handful of officially recognized dimensions—gender, occupation, region—but also on whichever of a myriad of possible factors they regard as salient. Moreover, identities and perspectives are not fully formed in advance of participation in the public sphere. On the contrary, when political debate and broader cultural discourse are really effective, they have the potential to shape the identities and the perspectives of their protagonists.[18] Thus, for the Chinese students in 1989, participation in the public discourse of the social movement was not just an occasion for articulating established interests or expressing the identities with which they began. It was an occasion for trying on new identities and for shifting their interests and the bases of their dialogue. For example, the identity "Chinese patriot" became increasingly salient and more strongly linked to the specific identity of "student/intellectual" the longer students participated in the movement; the students' discourse shifted away from special-interest demands and toward broader populist and nationalist claims.

But if we are interested in democracy, knowing people identify with the whole of society is not enough. Such identification fails to distinguish mob rule from democracy and genuine popular decisionmaking from mere conformity; it is, for example, the basis of Leninist substitution of the vanguard party for real democratic procedures. Emphasis on society as a singular whole—a tendency typical of nationalism—makes recognition of difference problematic. But difference is not the enemy of democracy; unequal access to power is. It is crucial to the democratic ideal that conflicts be settled in the public sphere on criteria of reason and critical inquiry—competition among ideas—rather than on the hierarchy of authority attached to the various identities of participants.[19]

Thus, a political public sphere is successful in distinguishing democracy from mass compliance when it provides for a discourse about shared societal concerns that takes place across lines of significant difference and that is both rational-critical and influential. Such a public sphere depends on a favorable organization of civil society. It is not enough that there simply *be* a civil society more or less autonomous from the state.

TOWARD A CHINESE PUBLIC SPHERE

The discourse of public sphere and civil society addresses three basic questions:

1. What counts as or defines a political community?
2. What knits society together or provides for social integration?
3. What opportunities are there for changing society by voluntary collective action or democratic decision-making, and how can that action be organized on the basis of rational-critical discourse?

It is common to answer at least the first two questions with "the state." In the People's Republic of China, indeed, "the state" has been the normal answer to all three questions. The government and corollaries such as the Communist Party define the political community, provide for social integration, and determine what opportunities people are to have for collective action. But the state is not the only possible answer to these questions. For national minorities, especially for Tibetans, the Chinese state clearly does not define the relevant political community. There is obviously a tension involved in the Chinese tendency to include the Chinese diaspora, scattered all over the world and subject to multiple states, in what remains a single-state-centered notion of national identity.[20] As China adopts more capitalistic economic reforms, some aspects of societal integration turn on an economic system that is not under the direct control of the state. Finally, discussion of the public sphere raises the possibility that people can knit themselves together in ways not directed by the state, whether through social movements, the formation of political parties, the exercise of cultural persuasion through the media, or other means. The task of democratization is to create a range of institutions outside state control that support a lively critical culture about topics of political significance. Only such institutions can provide the necessary linkage between face-to-face gatherings like those of Tiananmen Square and the "metatopical" spaces opened up by modern communications media, and only such institutions can make both into effective vehicles of sustained democratic participation.

It has recently become commonplace to observe that communism everywhere stifled the development of "civil society."[21] This is one of the most meaningful senses in which communist rule was (and in some senses still is) totalitarian. We should also note, however—especially in regard to China—the extent to which the state not only dominated the public realm and prohibited nonstate organizations but also penetrated the putatively private realm of the family, undermining the very distinction between public and private.[22] In China, moreover, democrats and modernizers faced the problem of the absence of civil society well before Mao and his fellow communists rose to power. As the opening article of the *New Tide* monthly, a leading publication in the New Culture movement of the May

Fourth era, put it in 1919, "Our society is very strange. Western people used to say that China has 'masses' but no 'society.' "[23]

By the late 1980s, "civil society" was becoming a front-rank piece of international jargon. It had been picked up in China from both Eastern European and Western sources. Chen Ziming told public opinion researcher Bai Hua in 1986 that he was reading a "fascinating new book on civil society. It's just been translated. I'm thinking of writing a book on the subject myself."[24] Many of the Chinese reformers and dissidents of the 1980s, in fact, saw themselves largely as building a civil society, a realm of social organization and activity not directly under state control. Civil society became the institutional counterpart to the discourse of enlightenment (*qimeng*); it might make possible, the reformers thought, a new sort of public discourse and eventually spread enlightenment beyond the elite sphere of intellectuals to a broader public.[25]

This theme is central to any consideration of the social foundations of democracy. It reveals, to start with, the extent to which rituals of popular sovereignty fail to enable true popular political representation. The very nature and history of Tiananmen Square as a public place suggests as much. It was a square built for popular political gatherings, to be sure, yet it was not a place of discourse. It was not an Italian piazza; it did not house a New England town hall. It occupied over a hundred acres and could accommodate crowds of perhaps a million people;[26] but once there, the people were addressed as a mass, not a differentiated body of interlocutors capable of discourse among themselves or with the government.

In Tiananmen Square, in short, the Chinese government used the imagery and representations of popular sovereignty to elicit acclamations of nondemocratic party rule. In this sense, Tiananmen is a striking metaphor for the problems that gigantic scale and weak intermediate associations pose for democracy throughout the modern world.[27] The West is no exception: We have the external attributes of popular rule far more than the capacity to carry it out, not least because we lack the institutional bases for vital, effective, and democratic public discourse. Manufactured publicity "sells" politicians to the people; the latter respond as consumers, "spending" their votes and their support on the most appealing candidates, rather than as creative, autonomous participants in public debate. In a society of millions of people, let alone one of more than a billion, such debate must be carried out through the media and in quasiautonomous communities and associations.[28] In occupying Tiananmen Square, students turned a vehicle of nondemocratic political representation into an effective means of protest. The demonstrations gave impetus to expansion of the public sphere and empowerment of public discourse, but real democracy would have had to rest on a more deeply transformed social structure.

When students seized Tiananmen Square, they seized a powerful, multivocal symbol. The Square spoke at once of the government, which used it to display its power, and of the people, who gathered there to acclaim official leaders. It linked the Imperial Palace to revolutionary monuments; it represented the center of China. But by their actions the students transformed the meaning of the Square: Its popular side became dominant. Correspondingly, the "government" side became diminished, a challenge the regime well recognized. For a time, the students also made Tiananmen Square into a genuine place of public discussion. They met in small groups of friends, addressed large audiences in speeches, and even convened a more or less representative council to debate collective strategy and carry out self-government. Though these arrangements were ad hoc, they presaged the development of stronger, more enduring institutional bases for a public discourse.

The official authorities of China were forced out of the reviewing stands and back behind the closed doors—figuratively, at least—of the Zhongnanhai compound. A line of elite troops held back a constantly heckling crowd at the ceremonial front gate, much as their predecessors held back crowds outside the Forbidden City in previous generations. In fact, most of the Chinese leadership had apparently fled Beijing for military command posts in the western hills. But in the drama of the event, this retreat didn't matter. The very seizure of the Square and the sequestering of the government made a powerful (if generally unconscious) statement that the Party was merely a continuation of the old imperial tradition rather than any form of modern, popular rule.

THE BEGINNING OF A NEW CIVIL SOCIETY

The student protest movement challenged the government in the name of the Chinese people and with a claim to act as citizens. It is not surprising, then, that many analysts locate the social bases of the protest in the emergence of new civil society institutions—small entrepreneurs, think tanks, poetry journals—yet simultaneously suggest that insufficient development of these institutions helps explain the failure of the protests.[29] The 1980s saw a substantial proliferation of such institutions in China, and they contributed not only to the protest but also to the development of democratic ideology and a new critical consciousness about the country's present and future. But we need to be cautious both about attributing too much to civil society and about slipping into a sharp division between "society" and "the state," particularly in regard to the 1989 protests in China.[30] Though new nonstate institutions certainly mattered, the protest was also organized largely through the institutions of the communist state, above all *danweis* and universities.[31]

Analysts have often invoked the concept of civil society without sorting out whether it means the capitalist free market, social movements like Solidarity, or the sort of public sphere once thought to exist mainly in cafes and coffeehouses.[32] Though conceptually distinct, all three dimensions matter and are connected. Cafes and coffeehouses are, after all, generally businesses. In China, economic reforms played a crucial role in the formation of civil society by enabling entrepreneurs to create such businesses. Larger-scale enterprises also contributed to the emergence of civil society; for instance, Chen Ziming and his colleagues built one of the most important think tanks of the reform era (the Beijing Social and Economic Sciences Research Institute) and financed a newspaper primarily with revenues from their commercially run correspondence schools.[33] The existence of such independent or quasi-independent organizations, associations, and gathering places mattered more to the creation of a politically significant civil society than did markets as such. Markets do not directly facilitate political action or political discourse, though they may do so indirectly.[34]

These indirect effects were evident in China during the 1980s. For example, small entrepreneurs, many of them merchants, were multiplying in number and filling every free market (and quite a few sidewalks), their capital limited to the merchandise they could fit on a single table or the back of a pedicab—pots and pans, books and magazines, belts, bicycle bells, or postcards. A few of these *getihus* came to be owners of substantial businesses, operating a chain of market stalls, for example, or entering the wholesale trade. Increasingly, peasants were now also entrepreneurs, bringing their vegetables, pigs, and chickens to the private market. Cultural critics Xie Xuanjun and Yuan Zhiming looked to the entrepreneurs (even before some *getihus* supported the student movement) for a needed complement to intellectuals: "Possessing greater practical strength than these [intellectuals] is perhaps the plain-faced, soft-spoken new breed of entrepreneurs. Even amongst the owners of these small shops, among these businessmen hurrying along the road, among these peasants who have left the land to make their living all over the country, there is building up a new social energy and a new vitality, none of which should be underestimated."[35]

Other kinds of enterprises contributed more directly to the beginnings of a public sphere in Chinese cities. Restaurants, for example, flourished at all price levels, bringing a range of regional cuisines into Beijing and providing at least partially free public spaces. Some of these were operated on university campuses, using buildings leased from the institution. Perhaps not surprisingly, they offered the best (though not the cheapest) food on campus. Others, often much smaller, were located nearby, providing the opportunity for free discussion over Xinjiang noodles or Szechuan soups at four or five tables. Still others catered to a more upscale clientele—businesspeople, Party officials, and foreigners—and charged prices that kept most students away. Owners of all these sorts of businesses contributed money to the protest movement; many of them joined the marches in late May.

Though rarely seen in the protest marches, large capitalists also contributed to the development of civil society in China. Most could not have cared less about building a public sphere, but a few, notably the founders of the Stone Computer Corporation, devoted a good share of their profits to the establishment of think tanks and other institutions encouraging critical thought and public discourse. At least a few large capitalists invested in the nascent nonstate publishing industry.

The motives of private publishers may have been mostly pecuniary, but the growth of a private market in publications was a powerful influence on the rise of dissenting, pluralist thought. Since the early 1980s, independent booksellers had gradually carved a major niche for themselves in China's intellectual life. To be sure, their most popular publications were sex manuals and salacious or gory novels. On the same tables, however, one could sometimes find such provocative foreign works as Freud's *New Introductory Lectures*, C. Wright Mills's *The Power Elite*, or Locke's *Second Treatise*. One could also find—in between the government's periodic campaigns to purge the market of such counterrevolutionary materials—texts by Chinese thinkers on questions of national identity, the problems of bureaucratization, and the possible virtues of stock markets and private ownership of industry. The most influential books were probably works of fiction, which could raise controversial questions in less than explicit forms, pose problems without having to advocate solutions that might be at variance with Party policy, and express individual feelings (thereby encouraging the idea of their primacy).

Various journals made a similar impact, both introducing Western ideas and providing for an independent Chinese discourse.[36] Those that were too independent were often short-lived, flowering mainly during such periods of democratic activity and apparent government openness as the 1978–79 democracy movement. They were especially likely to be suppressed, or to fail of their own internal problems, if they were published without institutional sponsorship and/or were aimed at a relatively broad readership. Shanghai's *World Economic Herald* was one of the longest-lived journals of this type, perhaps partly because it stressed economic rather than political or cultural issues. It was suppressed after a symposium honoring Hu Yaobang in the early days of the 1989 movement. Academic periodicals were more stable. Though their openness to free expression varied with the political climate, they continued to offer discussions of new and often controversial ideas fairly continuously through the 1980s. Journals of philosophy called tenets of official Marxism into question, encouraging a flowering of interest in Western Marxists and critical theory. Sociological publications examined the nature of stratification in Chinese society.

Perhaps the most influential publications were literary journals. These not only reinforced the influence of some fiction writers but also sponsored a discourse on the problems of Chinese culture, a discourse heavily influenced (in its more academic versions) by Western postmodernists, rhetoricians, and new-wave literary scholars. Jacques Derrida, Wayne Booth, and Fredric Jameson all had Chinese fans, though these audiences usually had only a fragmentary understanding of their French or English works. However, at the same time that it sought currency by international standards (or almost pathologically pursued Western trendiness), this discourse also sometimes found new inspiration in older (but for the most part still modern) Chinese writings, especially those of Liang Qichao, Lu Xun, and the protagonists of the May Fourth movement. It addressed in original and important ways the problem of how Chinese culture—traditional and communist—would and could fare in the twenty-first century. What were the cultural implications of importing Western technology? Was China's generally postulated economic and political backwardness due to fundamental cultural weaknesses? How would Chinese culture have to be strengthened to provide for modernization, perhaps including democracy?[37] These questions were not always posed straightforwardly, but they were raised and debated by readers. Even popular music was a very important medium for transmission of political dissent. Singers did not attempt to develop major social analyses in their lyrics, of course, but they did give expression to feelings that moved many others. Movies and the performing arts played similar roles.[38]

However, as a tool for analyzing the social foundations of democracy, civil society can only take us so far. The concept is too general. We need to look more specifically at the extent to which any civil society nurtures a "public sphere," institutional bases for discourse, voluntary social action, and political participation. Above all, it addresses the development of an effective rational-critical debate aimed at the resolution of political disputes.[39] Though real public spheres are multiple, overlapping, and variably rational or egalitarian, the ideal suggests an inclusive discourse that joins various smaller, constituent publics and that is decided by arguments rather than by the statuses of actors. Something of this idea was implicit in the protesters' central demand for a dialogue with senior government officials. The students were insistent on having not just an exchange of views but a give-and-take discussion in which the weight of their arguments would be matched against those offered by officials. The more sophisticated protesters used the term *duihua* to signify this sort of give-and-take discussion, not merely "face-to-face conversation," which might be an equally apt translation.[40] It was in this sense that Wang Zhixing announced after the students' discussion with senior party leaders on May 18 that "this was not a dialogue, but a meeting."[41] The government, for its part, recognized the force of this idea and offered its own challenge: The students, Beijing mayor Chen Xitong asserted, wanted not dialogue but political negotiations.[42]

Civil society provides as readily for private meetings and negotiations as for politically effective public discussion. We need to look further, therefore, to understand what forms of social organization offer adequate foundations for a democratic public sphere. A wide range of groups, networks, and organizations can stand between individuals and the state. These can also provide the social context for discourse, both internal and external. Unions, voluntary associations, political action groups, religious organizations, and social movements all have the capacity to empower their members and bring their diverse voices into the public forum. Most such entities were minimally developed in China even in the late 1980s.

Danweis, part of the state but not of the central government apparatus, stood out as the major form of intermediate association joining individuals and families together. They were the crucial building blocks in a nested hierarchy of associations and mechanisms of "block recruitment" for protest.[43] However, *danweis* were limited as institutions of civil society and even more so as vehicles of a potential public sphere. They lacked autonomy, first of all, in discourse as well as practical decisionmaking (though universities and research institutes enjoyed much more independence than others in the public sector). *Danweis* had long been vehicles of tacit censorship. Within their confines nearly all conversations were public, and memories were long; with recurrent "criticism campaigns," possible informers were everywhere. Moreover, other than the Chinese Communist Party and organizations it governed (e.g., the All-China Federation of Trade Unions), no associations crosscut *danwei* affiliations on a wide basis; thus, people lacked the protection of countervailing group membership and the capacity to link up effectively in protest or other mobilizations.

Intellectuals had more cross-*danwei* affiliations than people in most other social categories. First of all, they joined topical professional groups and attended conferences. Moreover, they were relatively mobile, moving from one *danwei* to another more frequently than other Chinese (starting with the transfer from one university to another with the shift from undergraduate to graduate study). Where once there had been no possibility of leaving a disagreeable job assignment, both the growing number of jobs with private employers and the increasingly prominent "quasi–labor market" among *danwei*s in need of key services (such as translators) gave people new options and reduced the authorities' control. The proliferation of think tanks and similar organizations providing consulting services on a contract basis and doing other part-time work greatly added to the cross-*danwei* connections between intellectuals.

The relative absence of crosscutting linkages outside the intellectual realm placed severe constraints on the movement. Proliferation of entrepreneurial businesses and reliance on markets by themselves did not (and will not) remedy this deficiency. Crosscutting associations will come—if they come—from expansion of what is sometimes called the tertiary, or voluntary, sector and from movements themselves if they are tolerated and allowed to flourish.[44] These crosscutting associations are crucial bases for the emergence of a truly pluralist public sphere, one within which a variety of different identities can be recognized as legitimate. A nested hierarchy of membership groups by itself can encourage participation and solidarity but cannot so readily facilitate discourse about or across differences. Minorities in one group, for example, cannot gain protection from links to similar minorities in other groups. The overall pyramidal structure links different interests through the center or the apex, not laterally and directly.

MASS MEDIA AND PUBLIC DISCOURSE

Most Western conceptions of democracy are rooted in the image of the classical polis with its concrete public *place*—the Athenian *agora* or Roman forum, the New England town hall. These venues of face-to-face interaction constitute the structural basis of discourse in the small city or town, a forum for interpersonal debate. Representative democracy has been seen as a necessary compromise. In modern large-scale societies, however, democracy depends on a critical public discourse that escapes the limits of face-to-face interaction. Such a discourse requires that the space-transcending mass media support of public life. It also requires that local discussions are able to feed into larger discussions mediated through technology and gatherings of representatives.

China made massive investments in television technology in the late 1980s. In 1987 the nation had a total of 112 million television sets and an estimated television audience of 600 million, or over 56 percent of the population; by 1990 the number of sets had risen to 150 million, distributed such that there was a set for every three or four people in urban areas and every eight nationwide.[45] The advantage to the government of widespread TV viewership lies in the capacity to get centrally decreed messages out to the whole country, including people in remote areas. It links the entirety of China together, fostering national integration, cultural and linguistic standardization, and central political control.

But there is a catch: Proliferation of televisions is not very effective without expansion of programming. Such expansion tends to put greater opportunity for creativity—and therefore for defiance of Party leadership—in the hands of those who produce the programs. The most celebrated case of such nonconformity was *Heshang* (*River Elegy*), the 1988 television series.[46] This powerful critical consideration of Chinese culture and China's contemporary situation was probably seen by several hundred million viewers. During the 1989 protests, news broadcasters joined in calls for press freedom. Thus, the officially ordained use of television was challenged not only by protesters in Tiananmen Square but also by broadcasters who insisted on reporting honestly about those protests.

As the aftermath of the Tiananmen massacre showed, however, the government was initially able to reassert solid control over this medium. And because it is the main medium of national communication, opposition—even clear memory of the events of April to June 1989—has been seriously hampered. Moreover, the spread of TV has not been accompanied by any comparable development of intermediate associations outside of central control. Only in such associations is it likely for citizens to engage in critical discourse.

The Beijing Spring of 1989, in short, was both intensively located in Tiananmen Square and extensively linked to diverse populations by modern communications. The occupation was among other things a way of defining a public sphere. In moving the action from the protected but only semipublic terrain of the university campuses, the occupation not only gave a spatial center to the internal discussions of the students but also seized the symbolic center of China's public realm. This physical space became also the focus of the media, whose space-transcending capacities carried the activities of the students to both domestic and international observers. From the two-fingered victory salute to the Goddess of Democracy statue, the movement's protagonists wove together symbols from a common global culture and their own specifically Chinese concerns; they consciously tried to conquer space, reaching out to audiences thousands of miles away from the center of protest. But much as students valued media coverage, they were dependent on face-to-face communication; the diverse, far-flung actors they addressed through the media had to seem remote and intangible. Thus, the movement lost coherence and intensity the farther it was removed from Tiananmen Square.

In the Square itself, where hundreds of thousands of people had gathered to protest, it was easy to believe that "the people" had spoken with a single and unanimous voice. How, one wondered, could the government withstand their will? Yet even at its peak, the Chinese democracy movement of 1989 never mobilized as much as 1 percent of China's population. Some three-quarters of the country's people are peasants. They have grievances against the government, but the protesters did not speak to them directly. A very few may have had familial connections to the protesters. Some others may also have followed the protest with interest, but the vast majority presumably did not. One of the basic facts about the prospects of democracy in China was that only a tiny percentage of the population participated in political, or even literary, discourse.[47]

Even though a crowd of a million people may be huge, it is not the *whole* people of China. One of the dangers of experiences like the Tiananmen protests is that they make it easy to imagine that a particular crowd *is* "the people." Repeatedly Chinese students told me, "The whole people of China have spoken," "The government cannot go against the will of the people." In the first place, a government may be quite able to go against the will of the people, especially if it is prepared to use violence. More generally, one must be cautious in assuming there to be a single popular voice. Leaders sometimes recognized this fact, asserting that the government needed to view the people as more differentiated, to treat them as individuals. But this recognition was often belied by the rhetoric of the movement, which was monological and authoritative.

The issue can be put another way. We eyewitnesses to the movement were overwhelmingly influenced by what went on in Tiananmen Square. Yet for most of the people of China, and for the future of democratic struggles in China, firsthand observation will be far less crucial than representations of the movement in photographs, narratives, news reporting, gossip, histories, sociological analyses, trials, speeches, and poetry. Even the eyewitness accounts are shaped by the constructions put on events in all these other contexts. And one can directly observe no more than a fraction of any major social process.[48]

For a public sphere to work on a very large scale—urban China, for example, let alone the country as a whole or the entire world—it requires communications media. In 1989 there was a lot of talk about the use of fax machines. It is true that Chinese students in the United States used faxes to stay in touch with their colleagues in the PRC. Thousands of expatriate students in the United States were linked, moreover, by a computer network (ChinaNet) that helped them spread news about the events back home.[49] Faxes primarily established long-distance connections among people who already knew each other; they were more significant in passing reassurances about who was alive and well than in distributing crucial information among activists.[50] But they also helped to spread and reinforce the sense of excitement about history in the making.

The more familiar broadcast and print media remained crucial in relaying news of the events in Tiananmen Square. China's journalists were in many ways waiting for just such an opportunity. An increasing number had university training in journalism and were familiar with Western media methods. Some had studied abroad; many others had worked in parts of the Chinese media bureaucracy that dealt with foreign media. During the reform era, Chinese journalists began to cultivate a greater sense of professionalism, and fewer were transferred into media work from unrelated occupations; group identity was strengthened by lateral connections (forged especially during university study) among journalists working in different units.[51] Writers such as Wang Ruoshi (himself a former editor of the *People's Daily*) and Liu Binyan inspired their colleagues with a sense that they could be something other than mouthpieces for the government.

During the early days of the protests, most newspapers and all television coverage continued to reflect the government's guidance. The earliest signs of media independence came not in the content or form of coverage but in its extent. After April 22 the press began to give more and more attention to the students; gradually, they also began to present more balance between official and student opinions. This objectivity was made easier by the fact that even negative reporting could get the students' message across as long as readers or viewers adjusted for the official bias. Visual media, for example, could show images of banners, signs, and marches, which were compelling regardless of the commentary. Journalists were dismayed not only by explicit government direction but also by their own sense of caution. By May 4 a large number had had enough; they created the largest sensation of that day's massive protest by marching together into Tiananmen Square. They carried signs that were pitiful as well as critical: "Don't believe what we write; we print lies," said one.

Increasing numbers of journalists joined the marches during the next week. Print and radio reporters appeared first, followed by television news readers and journalists. Workers at China Central Television sent out a mimeographed flyer offering not only a mea culpa for their previous behavior but also an indication of the humiliation they felt over their failure to stand up for their own ideals: "We painfully admit that we are a mere propaganda tool. On the evening of May 13, when our camera crew went to film the hunger strikers, the students shouted: 'Get the hell out, CCTV!' We were stunned; we were pained."[52] Journalists were visible in all the major marches of the next two weeks.

The Chinese papers and television had only a short period of relative freedom. By May 20, the infamous Yuan Mu had been put in charge of the *People's Daily*. His authority was not consolidated until troops moved into newspaper offices and television studios on May 25. Still, during the early days of martial law, as Andrew Walder notes, "the mass media openly encouraged resistance to martial law, making it appear that practically the entire country was united in opposition against it."[53] Increasingly during late May, however, the newfound "objectivity" was reduced to subtle hints—a bit more coverage to the Party power struggle than many leaders would probably have liked, rather gleeful reporting on liberalization in Hungary, an occasional use of quotation marks around a word such as "*dongluan.*" Even this was forthright compared to the radical rewriting of history that Yuan Mu would help superintend after the June 4 massacre.

Frank Tan, a former *People's Daily* reporter and editor, has called attention to the many ways in which the newspaper could hint at subversive views without expressing them directly.[54] The first was straightforwardly to report manifest facts without making any overt judgments. Simply reporting students' claims to be patriotic, for example, challenged the government's statements to the contrary. Emphatic presentations of official decrees could have the same effect. For ten days after Li Peng's May 19 speech, the front page of the *People's Daily* ran a black-bordered box headlined "Beijing on Day N of Martial Law" that contained very neutral, matter-of-fact reports of protests staged in defiance of martial law. The criticisms implicit in "factualness" were extended, Tan suggests, by balance; instead of presenting the usual monological reports of government declarations, the papers (and on some occasions also television broadcasts) explicitly paired them with reports of what students did or had to say, thus conveying the notion that there were two sides to the story. This technique is so familiar to most Westerners that it could pass unnoticed, but it was striking to Chinese audiences and readerships used to seeing the news presented not only without balance but with the attitude that such balancing was unneeded.

A closely related innovation was simple attribution. Many stories in the Chinese press lack specific identification of sources. They simply report the views the government wishes to be disseminated, as though such views involve nothing but observable facts. Consider the difference between the following reports, the first using typical PRC style and the second using attribution to suggest that there might be legitimate differences of opinion about the facts claimed:

1. Beijing's normal work and production, order, and daily routines have all been thrown into chaos.

2. In a speech of May 19, President Yang Shangkun said that "Beijing's normal work and production, order, and daily routines have all been thrown into chaos."[55]

During the protests, attribution was used to create distance between the reporters and the stories and they covered, especially the opinions they were obliged to repeat. Thus, when the *People's Daily* described the entrance of troops into Beijing as an effort to quell "a serious counterrevolutionary turmoil," it put that evaluation in quotation marks and attributed it to the *People's Liberation Army Daily* rather than representing it directly as fact. In a particularly radical act, a *People's Daily* editor ran a headline on June 5 saying that a military commander "alleged" that troops had put down the "counterrevolutionary turmoil" in Tiananmen Square.

The necessary selectivity involved in deciding what to cover in the finite space of a newspaper or broadcast sometimes allowed journalists to avoid writing stories with which they disagreed. As Tan reports, this avoidance involved a struggle between the Xinhua News Agency and the newspapers. The former is more closely tied to official Party views, and its staff members are less committed to a professional, journalistic identity.[56] In the late 1980s, it had been a matter of pride for *People's Daily* reporters to research and write their own stories rather than relying on Xinhua. But after the crackdown the paper ran many more Xinhua stories than usual, as though the journalists knew they had no choice but to publish the government's version of events but could not bear to put it in their own words. Moreover, stories the government might deem significant were often given extremely bland headlines, either to disguise them or to express the editors' distaste for them. For example, in order to avoid reinforcing the message contained in an official decree concerning the government's success in quelling the rebellion, the *People's Daily* ran it under the generic headline: "Chinese Communist Party Central Committee and State Council Notice to All Party Members and All the People of the Country." A more engaging form of avoidance was to use space for seemingly trivial or irrelevant reports. On June 6, three days after the crackdown and during the "mopping up" phase, the *People's Daily* ran no front-page stories concerning the events in Beijing. It carried instead a variety of minor reports of relatively routine events in outlying provinces, plus production reports and other filler. Sometimes journalists resorted to manipulation or distortion to sneak in editorial comments. A small story about misuse of pesticides in a rural province was given the headline: "How Long Can the Masses be Cheated?" The day after the massacre, an otherwise minor report on the successes of a handicapped athlete was headlined: "The People's Hearts Will Never Be Conquered."

Journalists also employed the traditional Chinese literary techniques of allusion and hidden metaphor. Foreign news seemingly unrelated to domestic events in China afforded journalists a convenient way to offer oblique commentary to a public skilled in reading between the lines. Early in the protest, before the papers had begun to give much overtly sympathetic coverage to student allegations of corruption, the *People's Daily* ran a story on anticorruption measures in Egypt. Shortly after martial law was declared, a routine Xinhua story was given this headline in the *People's Daily*: "Khomeini Aged and in Poor Health; Who Will Succeed Him?" A front-page article quoted the prime minister of Hungary as saying that his country had learned from sad experience that military force could not solve its problems. As troops moved into Beijing, stories about the use of force against student demonstrators in South Korea were a favorite—especially because they were submitted by a correspondent in North Korea. That friendly communist government's negative evaluation would normally have been seconded by the PRC. Beyond allegories embedded in news articles, journalists managed to print potentially controversial views by embedding them in the cultural pages of the newspapers in the form of poetry, reviews, or literary discussion.

Finally, page layout, story placement, and special graphics were used to manipulate editorial emphasis and give hints to readers willing to look be-

yond manifest content. The continuous box focusing on martial law between May 21 and 30 is an example; after the massacre a similar box was
used to set off an account of "The Night in Beijing." Moreover, the *People's
Daily* conventionally puts the day's most important story runs in the top
lefthand corner of page 1, but on May 18 Gorbachev's visit was relegated to
a small story at the bottom of the page—in fact, a reprint of the stock
Xinhua story. Thereafter, the student protest and related events dominated
page 1. For example, Li Peng's contentious meeting with students displaced
the Sino-Soviet accord on May 19. When Zhao Ziyang made his comments
during the Asian Development Bank meeting, his characterization of the
student movement as patriotic and his declaration that China was not on
the verge of great turmoil were made the focus of a huge front-page spread;
these and related remarks were excerpted for repetition and set off as sub-
heads. Tan suggests that one of the most striking examples came the day
after the massacre:

> The issue published the morning of the military crackdown has a page one
> layout that looks especially strange to the trained eye (June 4). The authori-
> tative verdict on the crackdown, and the piece with the harshest tone, is an
> editorial republished from the same day's *People's Liberation Army Daily*
> reporting on the martial law troops' "great triumph" over the "counter-
> revolutionary turmoil." This editorial is squeezed in at the bottom of the
> page and uses a very cramped typeface, as if the editors wanted to make it
> disappear. Furthermore, the editorial is surrounded by several extremely
> minor stories related to weather, agriculture and trade that easily could
> have been omitted or moved to an inside page to make more space for this
> authoritative statement—but obviously were not.[57]

In short, Chinese journalists employed a variety of techniques of resistance. Many of these actions required the tacit consent of a wide range of
newspaper employees, as various production staff had an opportunity to
suppress stories or change headlines and layouts if they wished to. These
actions certainly expressed journalists' discontent and perhaps helped them
preserve a certain sense of personal dignity and professional integrity. The
tactics may also have spread some news the state would have preferred repressed and impeded the state's ability to circulate its own stories effectively. Though interesting and significant, however, this resistance is not
the same as the creation of media adequate to sustain rational-critical debate over public issues. To the extent that such media existed in China in
the late 1980s, they operated on more restricted scales, primarily among
intellectuals (e.g., through the circulation of serious books and literary
magazines). They only occasionally broke free of these bounds—as, for

example, in the broadcast of the critical TV series *Heshang* in 1988—and then what was disseminated widely was a single intervention into Chinese culture, not the sustained discussion intellectuals engaged in during face-to-face meetings.

THE INTERNATIONAL MEDIA

In order for the students who seized China's metaphorical center to get a really wide audience (especially outside Beijing) for their actions, they had to seize the initiative in presenting their views to the international press. This they did fairly effectively, although whether those who enjoyed media attention were accurate in representing their fellows was hotly debated. By the time of the Bank meeting and Gorbachev's visit in mid-May, the student protests were receiving major television coverage.[58]

Speaking to (or performing for) the foreign press had several functions for the students. First, it mobilized international public opinion on the side of protesters and against the government with remarkable success. The "China story" was front-page news for weeks—perhaps the single most sustained visibility ever for a Third World country in the press of Western Europe and the United States.[59] The press made the Chinese students seem remarkably familiar; many portrayals played on nostalgia for the 1960s. I had to remind myself constantly that the two-fingered "V" sign meant victory, not peace, and probably came to China from the Philippines, not from the United States.

Second, the foreign press spread word of the protests throughout China, especially as people listened to reports beamed back by the BBC and the Voice of America. These were especially important sources of information after martial law was imposed; students brought transistor radios out to the barricades to tune them in the nights of May 20 and 21. These outlets broadcast in both Chinese and English, coming through at least faintly except for three days when apparent jamming made reception intermittent at best.[60]

Third, the foreign press spoke significantly to an international audience of overseas Chinese (though equally important in this regard were the reports from journalists based in Hong Kong, Taiwan, Singapore, and other Asian Chinese communities). Members of the Chinese diaspora were deeply moved, perhaps all the more so in some cases because of ambivalent feelings about their national identity. This ambivalence could be found among those newly abroad as well as those whose ancestors had left China generations before. Both citizens of the PRC residing abroad (e.g., as students) and Chinese emigrants to other states were crucial actors. Some of them had helped spread ideas about democracy in the PRC. They not only had talked to family and friends but also had written articles for newly flourishing periodicals and helped in China's massive translation programs for Western social science, literature, and criticism. Others sent financial support. Still others lobbied the governments of countries in which they resided. In this way they echoed the role played by overseas Chinese communities in Sun Yatsen's republican revolution. In 1989, however, overseas Chinese communities were larger and richer, and China was a more distant homeland for many of their members. And these communities were not as closely knit by webs of personal association as they had been early in the twentieth century. Rather, they were mobilized significantly by the media. They were addressed as a single category of people; some could mobilize associational networks for action, whereas others acted as a widely scattered set of individuals.

The foreign press coverage was often of high quality, especially its camera work. Indeed, photojournalists would prove extraordinarily brave during the violence of early June. But the coverage was not without problems.[61] Despite efforts at double-checking, reporters were often caught up in the transmission of rumor. Moreover, many journalists (and television network anchors) came with understandably superficial knowledge of the situation and were remarkably sheltered once they arrived. For example, the CBS crew took over the fifth floor at one of Beijing's best joint-venture hotels, the Shangri-La. When they went to Tiananmen Square, they often traveled in a bus or a two-ton red truck, parked it well away from the core of the protest, and ventured out only on specific forays for interviews or footage. As a result, they seemed to have little direct acquaintance with what was going on. Junior reporters found subjects and started interviews; big names such as Dan Rather were brought in for the crucial shots. Journalists kept asking other Westerners and often each other to explain things.

There was a sense in which the press fed upon itself. Near the end of May, for example, the *Hong Kong Standard* quoted the Xinhua news agency quoting the *Guangming Daily* to the effect that students had returned to classes in Beijing—a false story. One paper's rumor sometimes turned into another's "informed sources." The press's biggest advantage may have been its superior access to rumors coming from government circles. However, the elusiveness of information, the difficulty figuring out just what was going on, was palpable in Beijing. The international papers offered a synthesis of reports from many vantage points and were accordingly sought after by both Chinese and foreigners. Except during a couple of days at the peak of the resistance to martial law, one could get a wide range of Chinese and international papers (including English publications such as the *Hong Kong Standard, South China Morning Post, International Herald Tribune,* and *Asian Wall Street Journal*). My copies made the rounds of Chinese students eager to learn what accounts of their movement were reaching the rest of the world.

Though far less transparently ideological and manipulative than the official Chinese press, the Western media recast history as they tried to record it. Almost all Western reporters sought out individuals to personalize their stories, an approach that undermined the presentation of a broad social movement. Wuerkaixi and Chai Ling became the heart of the drama. One reporter told me she telexed her New York office that leadership was diffuse, not concentrated in the hands of one or two people; they telexed back that she should get on the stick and interview the real leaders.

At the same time, although their sympathies might lie with the students, many journalists felt obliged to focus some attention on the government. These reporters consistently gave the impression that the really interesting questions involved what the official political leaders were up to and who would wind up on top of the Party. This tendency was reinforced when editors supplemented such stories with commentary from "China experts," who naturally knew much less about the recent student movement than about the Party leadership.

The papers were at their best in tracing out the sequence of battles among the Party heavyweights and diagramming troop movements. They were much weaker on the questions of what made the student movement happen and what the students wanted; these got still shorter shrift on TV. After June 4, ironically, the student protesters all but disappeared from the coverage except for periodic stories of their escapes from China.

PROSPECTS

A crucial question remains: Can the public sphere be broad enough to encompass all of China and still foster rational-critical debate? Are Chinese intellectuals right in their widespread sense that the country's peasants are not yet ready for democracy and require further education by the intellectual elite?[62] Or is this elitism simply antidemocratic? To be reminded that this is a serious and difficult question, we have only to recall the difficulties faced by rational-critical opposition movements in the former East Germany, Czechoslovakia, and even Poland when they tried to move beyond small circles of activists to national electoral politics. The intellectuals and critical thinkers central to the anticommunist opposition movements lost power to more demagogic leaders in every country.

The implications of democratic inclusiveness do not exhaust questions about the potential for a large-scale public sphere in China. However important rational-critical discourse may be, it cannot plausibly be the whole of what makes the public sphere important; the public sphere is also a vehicle of change in culture and personal identity. Focusing on this aspect is crucial to understanding the 1989 events, because students set out not just to help build civil society and democracy but also to respond to a deep sense of cultural crisis.

6   Cultural Crisis

THE CHINESE IDENTITY CRISIS

At the heart of students' concerns lay basic questions about China's fate and what it meant to be Chinese at the end of the twentieth century. These were products, above all, of a shared sense of China's weakness and backwardness. When China opened to the West in the reform era, travel and television footage showed capitalist societies to be so wealthy that ordinary people drove cars, occupied huge houses, and worked in gleaming highrises. Such evidence belied the previous Maoist message that capitalism was on the skids. Although many people drew rather simple economic conclusions rooted in desire and envy, students and intellectuals asked deeper questions about what the comparison said about Chinese culture. Had China not advanced in relation to the rest of the world for a hundred years? Had it actually fallen farther behind?

Many intellectuals and even more young students responded with an out-and-out embrace of the West. As Fang Lizhi put it, for example, "I sincerely believe that if we want things to change, 'complete Westernization' is the most viable approach."[1] More dramatic and troubling were the Chinese youth who, in addition to finding no fault with the West, lost the capacity to find virtue and resources in Chinese culture. Their difficulties of self-image were manifested in everything from clothing styles to a fad for "de-Sinicizing" cosmetic surgery to an eagerness to embrace Western social science theories as solutions to China's ills.[2]

Su Xiaokang, a reporter and television documentary writer, referred to what he saw as the recurrence of a "fin-de-siècle" mentality among intellectuals during the reform era—particularly in the two "dragon" years of 1976 and 1988.[3] From popular music to learned debates, poetry to televi-

213

sion, social science research to the fad for *qigong* (breathing exercises), thoughtful citizens of the People's Republic were caught up in a "culture fever" in the late 1980s, a passionate reexamination of the strengths, failings, and possibilities of Chinese culture. Most of the more intellectually serious protagonists resisted the notion of radical Westernization, though they saw much that China could learn from the West. Many sought to revitalize traditional Chinese culture, finding the basis for dissent and reform in a distinctively Chinese heritage. Among the most important such efforts was Li Zehou's attempt to rethink the Chinese intellectual tradition (discussed briefly in the next chapter). Liang Congjie (editor of a magazine called *Intellectuals*), historian Pang Pu, and philosopher Tang Yijie of Beijing University also offered prominent reconstructions of traditional Chinese culture explicitly focused on the important role allocated to intellectuals. The newly founded International Academy of Chinese Culture provided many of these thinkers with a base and brought young scholars from all over the country to its headquarters near People's University. These more traditional scholars held great prestige in the intellectual community, but it was the Westernizers who commanded the most widespread popularity.

Indeed, the flood of new influences from the West was hard to escape. Tourists and tourist hotels brought tiny bits of Western civilization into Chinese cities. Already in the early to mid-1980s, this influx was creating a sensation. Young women schooled in Maoist modesty were now being ordered to forsake shapeless tunics for slinky "traditional style" *pipaos* to serve drinks to foreign guests. Businessmen stayed longer than the tourists and demanded even more fundamental changes. These took place very abruptly. As recently as 1984, the Jin Ling Hotel in Nanjing, one of China's first modern highrises, was such a novelty that it sold tickets to locals who might wish to glimpse its lavish lobby, its enormous ballroom, or the view from its upper floors. Otherwise the hotel resembled a sequestered foreign enclave of the colonial era, keeping ordinary Chinese out. With increasing regularity through the 1980s, Chinese television began to import foreign programs, and China's own broadcasters produced accounts of the startling developments—from supersonic jets and robotics to personal computers—that had taken place in the rest of the world. For many intellectuals, it was as though China had been sleeping (or worse) while the rest of the world shot ahead. It was hard to resist comparisons to the way in which the "feudal" regime of the imperial past had kept China backward.

Tourists, businessmen, and the mass media were only aspects, however powerful, of a more general internationalization of culture. There were exchange students moving in both directions, "foreign experts," literary translations, and scientific works. The explosion of intellectual and cultural activity in the 1980s was motivated substantially by the attempt to find China's proper place in this newly transnational context. This enterprise joined young intellectuals of the 1980s to their forebears, especially those of the 1910s and 1920s.[4]

ENLIGHTENMENT AND NATIONAL SALVATION

For generations, Chinese intellectuals have sought answers to the challenges posed by contact with the West. For a time, Chinese communism seemed to offer a plausible, if not perfect, answer. More recently, this solution has been thrown into doubt and subjected to derision. The Cultural Revolution and its aftermath radically undermined the claims of the Communist Party to offer viable and attractive leadership. This failure was followed quickly by Deng Xiaoping's policies of pursuing rapid "modernization" and importing Western technology but limiting other Western influences. The result was a profound cultural crisis.[5]

It is a crisis with old roots. Since the late Qing dynasty, Chinese people have struggled to understand their country in relation to the world—a world much larger, more diverse, and more powerful than traditional Chinese culture acknowledged. They have faced not only Western gunships, opium traders, and merchants but also Japanese invasion and Russian intervention into their communist movement. The history of popular struggle in modern China—the last 150 years—is not just a history of leveling inequality and lifting peasants out of cyclical starvation. It is also a history of a people trying to assert a viable national identity in an often hostile world.

The May Fourth movement of 1919 was sparked by the willingness of Chinese negotiators at Versailles to accept extremely disadvantageous terms of settlement after World War I. Though China had not been an enemy of the victors, the latter refused to stop the annexation of her land. The weak and corrupt Chinese government was completely ineffectual and did not even try very hard to win a better settlement. Students were as angry with their own government as with the Japanese. The May Fourth movement involved both nationalistic sentiments and a critical challenge to Chinese culture. From the self-strengthening movement of Kang Youwei through Liang Qichao, Lu Xun, and other prominent figures in the 1919 movement, Chinese intellectuals pointed repeatedly to failings in their traditional way of life; they sought to develop a new Chinese culture that would retain only certain ties to the past and would appropriate a variety of positive features from the West.[6] They wanted to identify the sources of China's weakness and to remedy them.

A division quickly formed between a focus on the technical aspects of Western knowledge—those that even conservative Chinese might hope to acquire in order to give the country strength—and interest in Western values and political processes, which were thought dangerous in official circles and by a good many others. "Chinese learning is for the essence," a prominent codification of official Confucian views went, "Western learning is for practical use" (*Zhongxue wei ti, Xixue wei yong,* or simply *"ti-yong"* in slogan form).[7] This interpretation was the ancestor of the government's more recent attempt to pursue modernization while resisting "bourgeois liberalization" and "wholesale Westernization." The familiarity of the distinction helped Party leaders to pursue the virtually impossible line of importing Western technology, economic thought, and bits of business practice without accepting any political or cultural baggage.

However, faced with national crisis, a sharp distinction between Chinese culture for essence and Western culture for utilitarian ends did not seem satisfactory. China needed change in institutions, not just new technology. In the late nineteenth and early twentieth centuries, some thinkers proposed that what mattered was not whether a particular practice or idea was Western or Chinese but whether it worked. As Yen Fu put it:

> What are China's principal troubles? Are they not ignorance, poverty, and weakness? In a nutshell, any method which can overcome this ignorance, cure this poverty, lift us out of this weakness, is desirable. The most urgent of all is the overcoming of ignorance, for our failure to cure poverty and weakness stems from our ignorance. In overcoming ignorance we must exert our utmost efforts to seek out knowledge. We have no time to ask whether this knowledge is Chinese or Western, whether it is new or old.[8]

Similarly, in 1989 Li Zehou sought to reverse the old *ti-yong* formula and work out practical Chinese ways to apply the "essence" of certain aspects of Western culture.[9]

One of the problems Chinese intellectuals faced was that they understood Chinese and Western culture too much as separate, homogeneous wholes; they had a hard time accepting that certain ideas did not fit neatly and exclusively into one category or the other. Yen was concerned above all with the preservation and strengthening of the Chinese nation and state, and to that end he was willing to abandon the definition of either in terms of Confucian cultural inheritance. Most other intellectuals of his time would not go so far. But, consciously or not, they had embarked on a program of theoretical questioning and practical reform that forced them to choose between contrasting visions of national salvation and enlightenment. Even if most linked national salvation to a more traditional, Confucian sense of Chinese identity than did Yen Fu, they could not reconcile the two goals.

The politics of national salvation (*jiuguo*) seemed to involve a subordination of all other goals to political and technical strength. Yet after the republican revolution of 1911, government was stripped of much of its Confucian rhetoric and seemed even more clearly devoted to material power. "In the guise of republican politics," wrote Chen Duxiu, a classically trained scholar-turned-vernacular writer, editor, and radical activist, "we are now subjected to the sufferings of autocracy."[10] Patriotism, the pursuit of national salvation, had turned into blind loyalty to the state. Chen even wondered whether China should be considered a nation at all, as it lacked a consciousness of the importance of autonomy.[11] Autonomy was an issue not just for the country but also for the intellectuals within the country.[12]

In 1915 Chen advised intellectuals to turn away from politics to pursue a purer study of culture. Yet he didn't really do this himself. Instead, he sought with some success to forge a cultural politics. To this end, he developed personifications of science and democracy as vehicles to spread enlightenment among the less educated in China (and thereby to strengthen the nation both domestically and internationally). Writing in *New Youth*, among the most important of all the many journals created to encourage the "new culture" of the era, Chen responded to critics:

> They accused this magazine on the grounds that it intended to destroy Confucianism, the code of rituals, the "national quintessence," chastity of women, traditional ethics (loyalty, filial piety, and chastity), traditional arts (the Chinese opera), traditional religion (ghosts and gods), and ancient literature, as well as old-fashioned politics (privileges and government by men alone).
>
> All of these charges are conceded. But we plead not guilty. We have committed the alleged crimes only because we supported the two gentlemen, Mr. Democracy and Mr. Science. In order to advocate Mr. Democracy, we are obliged to oppose Confucianism, the codes of rituals, chastity of women, traditional ethics, and old-fashioned politics; in order to advocate Mr. Science, we have to oppose traditional arts and traditional religion; and in order to advocate both Mr. Democracy and Mr. Science, we are compelled to oppose the cult of the "national quintessence" and ancient literature. Let us then ponder dispassionately: has this magazine committed any crimes other than advocating Mr. Democracy and Mr. Science? If not,

please do not solely reprove this magazine; the only way for you to be heroic and to solve the problem fundamentally is to oppose the two gentlemen, Mr. Democracy and Mr. Science.[13]

"Mr. Science" and "Mr. Democracy" (often presented not through the full Chinese terms but as the equivalent of "Mr. Sci" and "Mr. De") were widely touted as solutions to China's problems, particularly those relating to modernization and relations with the West.

The May Fourth movement was clearly nationalist, yet it was also a movement of cultural rejuvenation, "bound up with concepts of the supremacy of public opinion, people's rights, and an intellectual renaissance."[14] Though China's material poverty had become an increasing concern, illiteracy, primitive technology, and a low level of cultural attainment among the mass of the population were equally alarming. Traditional Chinese culture—the binding of women's feet, the patriarchal family, feudal relations in the countryside, the stultifying rote learning and archaic formal essay style left over from the imperial examination system—was not merely an obstacle to progress but an embarrassment.[15] Vera Schwarcz sums up:

> Precursors of the May Fourth enlightenment, in spite of the political differences among them, had all been motivated by a single-minded commitment to *jiuguo*, national salvation. Their intellectual and emotional energies had been focused on making China strong, and enabling it to survive foreign aggression. The iconoclasts [i.e. the adherents of enlightenment and New Thought], less concerned with China's political weakness, went on to probe the indigenous sources of their nation's spiritual and intellectual backwardness.[16]

This was much the same issue on which culturally conscious intellectuals departed from the government in the 1980s. The threat of foreign aggression had lost credibility; China emerged in the 1980s from more than thirty years free of foreign aggression yet was still in decline. This fact made it harder to ignore questions about the deeper spiritual and intellectual sources of backwardness. In both the 1920s and the 1980s, enough people embraced a more robust notion of learning from the West to give ulcers to the Chinese government and the moderate reformers attached to it.

Yet Western culture provoked great anxiety at the same time that it excited a powerful attraction. Many intellectuals were unable to reconcile their opposing feelings and vacillated from one side to the other. They were also disillusioned with political involvements, as once-idealistic regimes always seemed to turn corrupt. This disenchantment with politics is another link between 1989 and 1919 and a key reason why students took the lead in protests. As Schwarcz puts it, students "were free of the weight of disappointment that still burdened their older contemporaries in the spring of 1919."[17] Virtually the same could be written about the 1989 movement.

Moreover, the debate about national salvation versus enlightenment was still very much alive in 1989. In a provocative and very widely read essay, Li Zehou had suggested that the turn away from enlightenment and toward blind passion for national salvation—which Chen Duxiu had decried seventy years earlier—was a recurrent problem. Democracy, he said, must be more scientific.[18] The theme was taken up by protesting students during the Beijing Spring, as seen in this late May poster:

> Li Zehou has said that well: after May 4th, in the democratic movement, the struggle for national salvation replaced the introduction of Enlightenment, the fundamental democratic mechanisms were not effectively understood, and each time the democratic movement had to start again at zero. Drawing the lessons of history, we must place the mission of introducing Enlightenment and the promotion of fundamental democratic mechanisms at the center of our preoccupations.[19]

THE ART OF DISSENT

Chinese radicals and reformers had long seen literary efforts as central to the basic changes they wanted to produce. As Liang Qichao wrote in 1902: "To renovate the people of a nation, the fictional literature of that nation must first be renovated. . . . to renovate morality, we must renovate fiction, to renovate manners we must first renovate fiction . . . to renew the people's hearts and minds and remold their character, we must first renovate fiction."[20] In the Chinese case, reform of language itself was crucial, so much was it tied up with Confucianism and imperial rule. Yu Pingbo, a veteran of the May 4 protest, wrote in a commemorative poem in 1979, "We did not worry if our words were sweet or bitter/We just wrote in the newly born vernacular."[21] The Communist Party attempted to harness literature to class struggle and the task of building socialism, but after Mao's death, unauthorized writings critical of the Party surfaced. During the Democracy Wall movement in 1978, for example, a ninety-four-page wall poster, the "God of Fire Symphonic Poems," spoke of a monstrous idol that suffocated the Chinese people and subjected them to a "war of spiritual enslavement":

> The war goes on in everyone's facial expression.
> The war is waged by numerous high-pitched loudspeakers.
> The war is waged in every pair of fearful, shifting eyes.[22]

Poetry and fiction remained controversial throughout reform-era China. Authors had experimented with new styles, from a sort of vague, evocative poetry (known as "misty" or "obscure" poetry) to stream-of-consciousness novels.[23] The most important common thread in this literature was a new preoccupation with the distinctiveness of individual experience—a theme previously forbidden in communist China. A debt to Western modernism was also apparent. The new sort of poetry written by individuals such as Bei Dao, Shu Ting, and Jiang He (particularly that which appeared in the journal *Today*, founded during the 1978–79 democracy movement) was widely understood to carry simultaneous political, cultural, and personal messages. But the messages were seldom blunt. For example, the opening and closing verses of Shu Ting's famous 1982 poem "The Wall" read:

> I have no means to resist the wall,
> Only the will.
>
> Finally I know
> What I have to resist first:
> My compromise with walls, my
> Insecurity with this world.[24]

A factory worker as well as a poet, Shu was initially celebrated in part for the particular female strength she brought to her writing. In the late 1980s, younger poets criticized her for making accommodations with the literary and Party establishment. This complaint itself suggests the demand for radical authenticity.

The pursuit of authenticity was linked to both reflection on individual experience and an unwillingness to subordinate art to political ends. These characteristics did not mean, as some critics charged, that there was no socially decipherable point to the art; "accustomed to message-hunting, critics do not realize that having no message is itself a kind of message."[25] A focus on "mere" sensory perceptions could carry implicit statements about the importance of the perceiving self and of the art that records the perception—both distinct from the socially recognized custom of evaluating poetry by instrumental criteria.

Older poets such as Ai Qing attacked the new poetry, likening it to an intellectual version of the Red Guards, even calling it the "Beat and Smash Poetic School."[26] Indeed, it did have roots in the Cultural Revolution—in the intensity of young participants' commitment, in their later disillusionment, and in the wounds with which so many Chinese people were left. It was also this poetry, more than any directly political texts, that established the crucial link between the protesting Chinese students of 1989 and their predecessors of 1978–79.[27] Protesting students in 1989 frequently quoted Jiang He's "Motherland, O My Motherland" and Bei Dao's "The Answer," particularly the stanzas reading:

> Baseness is the password of the base,
> Honour is the epitaph of the honourable.
> Look how the gilded sky is covered
> With the drifting, crooked shadows of the dead.
>
> I come into this world
> Bringing only paper, rope, a shadow,
> To proclaim before the judgment
> The voices of the judged:
>
> Let me tell you, world,
> I—do—not—believe!
> If a thousand challengers lie beneath your feet,
> Count me as number one thousand and one.
>
> I don't believe the sky is blue;
> I don't believe in the sound of thunder;
> I don't believe that dreams are false;
> I don't believe that death has no revenge.[28]

On May 4, 1989, I saw a marcher heading from Haidian toward Tiananmen, carrying aloft a sign with no words—simply a piece of paper, a bit of rope, and a cut-out shadow.

Novelists and short-story writers of the same era as the misty poets were perhaps less radical and less able to strike to the very heart of their readers, but they were also influential. "Exploring" writers such as Jiang Zilong, Chen Rong, and Liu Xinwu (editor of *People's Literature*) took up the implicit critique of the Cultural Revolution and remaining "leftist" tendencies and tried to rehabilitate a certain individualism. In his famous "Black Walls," Liu has his protagonist paint the apartment entirely black, only to confront the puzzlement and ultimately the hostility of his neighbors. The point is apparent even to an orthodox literary critic who claims he cannot find it:

> A certain fellow by the name of Zhou—a man recognized as being a little "odd"—paints the walls and ceiling of his apartment black without providing the slightest explanation. An egotistical "indulgence" of this nature can hardly be seen as normal or acceptable. . . . the problem, however, is that the author . . . regards the "abnormal" as "normal," and is critical of the attempted suppression of Zhou's desire to express his quirky individuality.[29]

The stifling of individuality was linked to the stifling of artistic and literary creativity. As Wang Ruowang put it, turning government condemnation on its head, "[W]e should say that those people who opposed the freedom of creativity are themselves the greatest source of contamination in spiritual pollution."[30]

The young literary critic Liu Xiaobo brought much of this sensibility to the 1989 protests. A popular teacher among many of the protesting students and a bridge to the generation of the misty poets, he was an enthusiastic Westernizer, an antitraditionalist radical, even something of a self-conscious enfant terrible.[31] In this context, "traditional" meant a good balance of emotion and rationality, an emphasis upon the social responsibility of the artist. "Radical," by contrast, meant a focus on the expression of personal feeling and individuality, (auratic art, to borrow Benjamin's term), an insistence upon the autonomy of artistic production and its independence of national particularity in the modern metropolitan culture. Notes Geremie Barmé, "It is this stance as the 'angry young man,' a bohemian and his anti-social truculence that made him so popular with audiences of Chinese university students since 1986."[32] It is no accident that Liu Xiabo's participation in the 1989 protests (as one of the last four hunger strikers) seemed so evocative of nineteenth-century European romanticism yet struck a chord among so many Chinese. As Barmé puts it, "Liu Xiabo expressed the desire for people to participate in protest as part of a civil action of redemption."[33]

"REPORTAGE LITERATURE"

In the post-Mao period, literature rooted in authentic self-expression was indeed "renovating" Chinese culture, but not always with Liang Qichao's focus on practical social ends. The resulting tension was played out in differences between "creative writers" and "reportage writers." The latter were investigative journalists of a sort, positioned between social scientists and literary writers. The Communist Party saw them as central to literature, holding that social reportage (particularly reportage emphasizing the moral side of socialist society) was the main responsibility of writers. Many young poets and authors disagreed, wishing to claim the turf of literature entirely for art. Paradoxically, the call of "art for art's sake" was not apolitical at all. In "The Life of an Artist," for example, Bei Dao described "the betrayal of the artist to the cultural orthodoxy,"[34] presenting himself at the end as "a doctor, a large syringe in hand," pacing "up and down the hallway to while the nights away." The point, Michelle Yeh suggests, is that "in a society that operates on absolute authority (assigning jobs with little regard for personal ability or proclivity) and rigid conformity, the artist—the artist who insists on creative freedom and pursues personal ideals—has no place."[35] The misty poets portrayed alienation as a product of the socialist People's Republic of China, whereas the official position of the PRC was that alienation was "the product of the decayed capitalist system only."[36]

This focus linked the misty poets to the more prosaic efforts of theorists such as Su Shaozhi, who at the same time was attracting attention with his explorations of the writings of the young Marx and raising the forbidden question of whether there might be alienation in socialist China. Though there was sometimes a politics to the individualism and aestheticism of the misty poets—as, for example, there had been a politics to European existentialism—it clashed with the more immediately practical politics imagined by the government but also by many of the government's most famous critics.

Wang Ruowang and Liu Binyan were the senior statesmen of China's reportage writers.[37] Though both were long-standing Communists who wielded considerable influence in official periodicals, Wang and Liu were attacked repeatedly as rightists and periodically accepted Party discipline (including, in Liu's case, temporary expulsion) throughout their careers. The two played enormously popular roles as gadflies of authority and a sort of conscience of the nation. Yet even in their most critical writings, they retained a remarkable commitment to the beliefs that made them Communists in the first place. In one of his articles, for example, Liu spoke of "another kind of loyalty" to the Party, one that put ideals and the interests of the people ahead of the dictates of the bureaucracy and the hierarchy.[38] He tied his efforts very much to the reform branch of the Communist Party exemplified by Hu Yaobang. After the fall of the Gang of Four, the project of rediscovering the forward momentum of Chinese liberation seemed urgent and seemed also to depend on uncovering the various ways in which old leftists clung to power despite rectification campaigns.

From 1979 on, Wang became increasingly bold and unrepentant with his admittedly "heterodox" views.[39] He was one of the few writers willing to look seriously at the implications of Deng's policies embodied in the slogan, "To get rich is glorious." Class polarization, he argued, was an inevitable consequence of the program. Wang argued not for reversing the reforms but for seriously addressing their effects: "If we go on emphasizing that we don't want inequalities to develop, we may as well attack the economic reforms and turn everything back to the egalitarians. Let them carry on their highly authoritarian management. Let them decisively and fearlessly cut down to size those who were so bold as to get rich sooner than others."[40]

Ultimately Wang was dismissed from the Party for his refusal to recant such views; Deng was determined to maintain an egalitarian myth even as he opened up a market economy with hints of capitalism. Yet Deng had a serious problem. One of the main ideological difficulties China faced in the spring of 1989 was that the government had neither developed—nor allowed a public discourse capable of developing—a rationale for economic inequality. Nearly all serious and novel wealth differentials looked to many ordinary people like corruption.

Liu was (and is) even more famous than Wang. In the 1980s, he developed an enormous popular following for his stories documenting official corruption and abuses of power. Predictably, he came under recurrent Party pressure. More troubling in some ways to Liu, however, was a shift in the fashion and commitments of younger writers: "In recent years, with the exception of a very small number, writers with a similar set of experiences as mine have turned their attention to subjects that are less politically or socially sensitive, devoting themselves to the pursuit of art. Consequently, even more than ever I have stood as the odd man out."[41] He added that "fewer and fewer Chinese writers think they should use their writing to help the Chinese people to reorganize society. One common view is that it would destroy the artistic purity of their work and cause it to lose the value of timelessness."[42]

Liu regarded writers and artists who turned away from "reality" as people whose sense of mission had never been strong and who turned to commercialism, the ideology of "art for art's sake," or the pursuit of a Nobel Prize partly out of timidity in the face of hostile authority.[43] As far as he was concerned, the purpose of writing, for a person of conscience, was social improvement. At a conference in California in April 1989, Liu (already living in the United States) clashed with Bei Dao over just this issue, as recorded by Perry Link:

> "Our job is to tell the truth," said Bei Dao, "and if we don't, we indeed *are* inferior to bean curd vendors, who do their jobs quite well." But there was no consensus on how much an intellectuals' independence should be devoted to social action as opposed to pure scholarship or art. "I see a terrible incongruity," said Liu Binyan. "On one side, 500,000 people massed in Tiananmen Square; on the other, in our literary magazines, essentially a blank—*avant-garde* experiments, read only by a few, understandable sometimes by none."

Bei Dao bluntly disagreed. "True art does not ask about its own 'social effects.' We will understand this problem more adequately only when we understand why foreign writers, unlike Chinese writers, sometimes commit suicide. . . . It's because they're concerned with life itself, not social engineering."[44]

Liu Binyan's style is simple and straightforward, often a flat recitation of facts punctuated by occasional condemnations in the strongest terms. Readers were never likely to miss the point of his articles, even when references were oblique out of political necessity. His pieces were simultaneously reports for the Party and publications for the people. The official definition of "social reportage" fits him well (and reveals what Bei Dao found so stifling about expectations for writing in China): "Reportage literature is a literary genre, a type of prose; also an umbrella term for sketches and *texie* [feature stories]. It is a fast and timely representation, with adequate artistic processing, of the real people and the real events that are drawn directly from and regarded as typical of the real life. As such it serves the current political agenda and is said to be the 'light cavalry' of literary production."[45] In a sense, then, Liu was the sort of socially responsible writer that communist activists said they wanted, the type they praised—until they were in power and apt to bear the brunt of the criticism. To label Liu a bourgeois individualist was merely to say that he insisted on civil rights and liberties—including his own right to publish the truth as he saw it and the rights of the victims of Party excesses about whom he wrote. The new poets and younger fiction writers, however, have often expressed something much more akin to the "bourgeois individualism" of the West, an emphasis on self-expression as an end in itself and an understanding of art as the product solely of inner consciousness.

It is nonetheless important to realize that the sense of a Chinese cultural crisis and concern for the fate of the nation did drive these younger, less political writers as well. Liu Binyan, for example, reports on the young scholar Liu Xiaobo:

Liu Xiaobo was not very interested in politics; in fact, he despised and hated politics. After Hu Yaobang died, Liu published an article in the *China News Daily*, a Chinese-language New York newspaper, in which he said he did not think much of the student movement. His opinions were unusual: For instance, he thought Hu Yaobang was only the leader of the Party, and that we should not honor him so. Instead, we should honor Wei Jingsheng, who had been imprisoned by the Communist Party ten years earlier for fighting in the Democracy movement.[46]

Nonetheless, Liu Xiaobo did return to Beijing and was one of the four intellectuals who caused a stir by announcing a hunger strike only days before the massacre. He was arrested and reportedly tortured.

The work of Liu Binyan and similar investigative reporters no doubt loomed much larger in the Chinese national consciousness than did the experimental, often obscure poetry and fiction of the 1980s (or Liu Xiabo's related criticism). Yet in the student movement, the two influences merged. Students responded both to a straightforward account of the corruption of the communist regime and to a more nebulous rendering of cultural crisis—and potential. They responded both to simple logical arguments for civil liberties and human rights and to mystical literary expressions based on a claim to those rights. Democracy was not just a preferable form of government but also the symbolic answer to China's economic backwardness—and Chinese intellectuals' wounded cultural pride.

Many young and middle-aged intellectuals also responded to the student movement with enthusiasm—or at least, as in the cases of Chen Ziming and Wang Juntao, with a mixture of interest, respect, anxiety, and frustration—rather than with the hesitancy of most of their colleagues. As Liu Binyan and Xu Gang remarked:

> Literary critics could be seen shouting in streets and alleys, calling people to block army vehicles; famous writers ran around in a sweat, buying urinals for students. Scholars of the Chinese Academy of Social Sciences were also very active. Groups of people from many research institutes came to join the movement. University professors plunged in, also abandoning their usual discreet and retiring behavior.[47]

HESHANG (RIVER ELEGY)

The sense of crisis in Chinese culture profoundly influenced students' identities and ideas, including their understanding of democracy. The discourse flourished in innumerable poems, essays, books, magazine articles, and debates over the dinner table, as well as in Hou Dejian's enormously popular song, "Descendants of the Dragon." But the most influential manifestation of this sense of crisis was the television series *Heshang* (*River Elegy*), shown in the fall of 1988.

Produced by a group of prominent young intellectuals and well-educated television journalists, this was an explicit attempt to bring the elite literary-cultural-historical debate to a broader audience. Su Xiaokang, the key intellectual figure in the production, recounted the "sales pitch" he had made to secure the participation of philosopher and historical theorist Jin Guantao:

I recall that later on, after we had created the scenario, we went to call on Jin Guantao and Liu Qingfeng in order to invite them to participate. Both husband and wife wore pained expressions. They too probably feared that television was not a medium for high culture. At that point I got anxious and blurted: "Mr. Jin, these days you are famous overseas and have published a great deal, but have you ever wondered how many people here in China know of your 'super-stable structure' theory? And what would the effect be if you were to go on TV and say a few words yourself to an audience of several hundred millions?" Jin Guantao's eyes sparkled with an interest that could not be concealed.[48]

Remarkably enough, *Heshang* did reach and galvanize an audience of several hundred million in each of two showings. Though it had a pronounced aesthetic sensibility, the series was in a sense a television version of reportage literature.[49] Su Xiaokang, indeed, had gained his reputation mainly as a reportage writer; in 1987, for example, he had published a study on educators entitled, "The Teachers' Lament." A lecturer in the Beijing Broadcast Institute as well as a writer, Su had interviewed middle school teachers around Beijing and reported that many suffered from ill health, poor housing, and poverty in general. He wrote also on mental illness, unhappy marriages, wife abuse, male/female tensions, the housing crisis in Beijing, and even such openly political topics as infringements of civil rights.[50] Su represented a younger generation of reportage writers than that of Liu Binyan and Wang Ruoshi—more impatient, more theoretical, eager to go beyond questioning corruption to asking basic questions about China's political system and culture.

The *Heshang* producers took as the basis for their film extensive footage from a Japanese-produced travelogue about the Yellow River. Adding their own commentary and a wide variety of archival footage, they transformed the travelogue into a kind of critical cultural analysis. The Yellow River is traditionally seen as the heart and source of China. But instead of praising the Yellow River as the cradle of Chinese civilization, *Heshang* criticized its frequent floods and the soil erosion that gave it its color. The film conveyed a sense of mourning, as reflected in the title: *He* means river, and *shang* means something like "to die ahead of one's time."[51] It has been translated variously as "River Dirge," "River Elegy," "The River Dies Young," and "Deathsong of the River."[52] Playing deliberately on viewers' familiarity with glorious images of the Yellow River, the makers of *River Elegy* turned the stream into the symbol of an inward-looking culture, characterized by mud and erosion, disastrous floods, and unfortunate human interventions. A dominant motif was the contrast between "blue" and "yellow" cultures—the former portrayed as ocean-exploring and open, the latter as riverine and closed.[53] Dozens of images played on these contrasting colors, perhaps most strikingly with aerial shots of the Yellow River meeting the blue sea—and being swallowed by it.

This was the culminating image of the series, and it invoked a well-established symbol. In Bei Dao's poetry, the sea often suggests freedom, openness, and the possibilities of the future. In "The Life of an Artist," the image of the missing sea is linked to that of missing enlightenment:

> Oh, sea, where are you?
> —a drunkard asks
> Why have all the street lights exploded?
> —I wonder[54]

In Su Xiaokang's words, from part 1 of the *Heshang* filmscript:

> For thousands of years, the Yellow River civilization was under constant attack from the outside but never fell. We have always appreciated its great power to assimilate other cultures. But today at the end of the twentieth century, even though external attacks are no longer accompanied by cannons and iron hooves, our ancient civilization can no longer resist.
> It has grown old and feeble.
> It needs a transfusion of new blood for its civilization.
> Oh, you heirs of the dragon, what the Yellow River could give us has already been given to our ancestors. The Yellow River cannot bring forth again the civilization that our ancestors once created. What we need to create is a brand new civilization. It cannot emerge from the Yellow River again. The dregs of the old civilization are like the sand and mud accumulated in the Yellow River; they have built up in the blood vessels of our people. We need a great tidal wave to flush them away.
> This great tidal wave has already arrived. It is industrial civilization. It is summoning us![55]

Wang Luxiang, the writer of part 2, "Destiny," kept the ocean metaphor going and picked up the theme of intellectuals torn between xenophobic national salvation and enlightened modernization:

> This tidal wave from the West in no way resembled the nomadic culture which descended from the Mongolian plateau like a flood and then quickly retreated without a trace. What came by sea was a new sort of civilization which the ancient Chinese agricultural civilization could no longer assimilate. And so a threat to our race and a crisis for our civilization broke out simultaneously.
> To save our nation from danger and destruction, we should try to keep the foreign pirates at bay beyond our country's gates; and yet to save our civilization from decline, we should also throw open our country's gates, open up to the outside, and receive the new light of science and democracy. These extremely contradictory antiphonal themes of national salvation and

modernization have taken turns over the past century in writing China's abnormally-shaped history; as complexly intertwined as myriad strands of hair, they can neither be trimmed by the scissors nor untangled by the comb, a situation which has caused the Chinese people to pay an immeasurably heavy price! [56]

Heshang gained much of its rhetorical power by asking in various ways how China, a nation with such a great past, could have such a problematic present. "Why was it that the light of Chinese civilization, which had led the way for more than a thousand years, dimmed after the seventeenth century?" the filmmakers wondered. "Why has such a smart people become so slow-witted and decrepit? What was it, after all, that we possessed yesterday yet whose loss we have only discovered today?" [57] Indeed, the West had been able to use great Chinese inventions such as printing, gunpowder, the axial rudder, and the magnetic compass in its modernization, but these innovations had made little impact in China. "If the light of China's science, technology, and culture could help the West create a new era in history, then why is it that the light of culture and science from foreign parts has always flickered on and off in China?" read the script in part 3, "The Light of the Spirit." Wang Luxiang's answer was clear-cut: "When the most advanced and learned persons of a people are so ignorant and when the people's soul—her intellectuals—are abandoned by the times, then what hope does this people still have?" [58]

Being the soul of the people is an attractive self-image for intellectuals, even if it comes with accusations of not having lived up to the role. Conversely, the authors of *Heshang* were predictably harsh on what they understood as the mentality of the Chinese peasant:

> When we asked this youth in this northern Shaanxi village why he remained at home in poverty and didn't go out to seek his fortune, he responded, "My mom and dad didn't give me the guts to do so!"
>
> In the vast, backwards rural areas, there are common problems in the peasant makeup such as a weak spirit of enterprise, a very low ability to accept risk, a deep psychology of dependency and a strong sense of passive acceptance of fate. No wonder that some scholars sigh with regret: faced with the [psychological] makeup of people such as this, not to mention the many limitations of government policy, even if a great economist like Keynes were to come back to life, what could he do about it? [59]

Zhang Gang's and Su Xiaokang's script for part 4 combines this critique of peasants with an attack on the Communist Party they see as perpetuating it. Nonetheless, it conveys another version of the elitism of intellectuals.

A montage of shots likened China to "primitive" Africa—a shocking statement for proud and racist Chinese. Revered relics of early dynasties—for example, the terra-cotta warriors left in Xian by the Qin emperor who first unified China—were visually juxtaposed with the Egyptian pyramids, hinting that both cultures were equally dead. The heritage of four thousand years of civilization was characterized more as a trap than a resource. The communist era was just a continuation of the old patterns, *Heshang* suggested; like previous dynasties, the Communists had hoped to make the Yellow River run clear but failed. In part 5, "Sorrow and Worry," Mao Zedong was shown standing at the top of Mangshan, a small mountain in Henan, gazing into the distance at the Yellow River. The narrator intoned: "When the greatest man of contemporary China faced this huge river, what might he have been thinking? . . . Mao Zedong, a man of great talent and bold vision, had said many daring things in his life, and it was only the Yellow River about which he spoke sparingly and carefully."[60]

Glamorous shots of skyscrapers represented the attractions of the West, and shots of Hong Kong stressed that such glories were within the reach of the Chinese people if only they would accept change.

> New China for a while was indeed able to make Chinese all over the world swell with pride; but who would have thought that after a mere thirty-some years, when we had awakened from a civil turmoil in which we had tried to strangle ourselves, that we would discover ourselves in the company of poor nations such as Tanzania and Zambia; that even South Korea, Singapore and Taiwan would have outpaced us, and that the Japanese would have come back laughing, bearing their Toshibas, Hitachis, Toyotas, Kokans, Yamahas, and Casios?[61]

In part 6, "Blueness," Xie Xuanjun and Yuan Zhiming suggested that China's intellectuals, faced with similar failures of modernization, had often retreated into Confucianism:

> Even in the 1980s, in the midst of our great debate stirred up by the "passion for studying Chinese culture," people still continue the century-old inconclusive argument over the strong and weak points of Chinese versus Western culture. No matter whether it is the fantasy of "wholesale Westernization" or the fervent wish for a "third flowering of Confucian civilization," it all seems to be going over the same ground as before. No wonder some young scholars say with a sigh that their tremendous cultural wealth has become a tremendous burden, that their feeling of tremendous cultural superiority has become a feeling of tremendous cultural inferiority; and this we cannot but admit is a tremendous psychological obstacle standing in the course of China's modernization.[62]

"China is pondering," *Heshang* told its viewers. "Young people are questioning History."[63] History gave innumerable lessons in how difficult it was to escape the dynastic cycle and achieve meaningful modernization.

> But History did give the Chinese people an entirely unique group: its intellectuals.
> It is very difficult for them to have economic interests in common or an independent political stance; for thousands of years they have been hangers-on.
> Nor can they become a solid social entity that employs a steel-hard economic strength to carry out an armed critique of the old society.
> Their talents can be manipulated by others, their wills can be twisted, their souls emasculated, their backbones bent, and their flesh destroyed.
> And yet, they hold in their hands the weapon to destroy ignorance and superstition;
> It is they who can conduct a direct dialogue with "sea-faring" civilization;
> It is they who can channel the "blue" sweetwater spring of science and democracy onto our yellow earth![64]

According to *Heshang*, intellectuals faced two major obstacles in carrying out this historical mission. The first was simply their weakness: They were able to discover the faults of tradition but, reduced to poverty and ignored by the communist leadership, they lacked the ability to change it. It was crucial that they form common cause with entrepreneurs, who were bringing new social energy and greater practical strength to China. The second obstacle was the intellectuals' own identity crisis: "The greatest difficulty of reform lies perhaps in that we are always worrying: 'Are the Chinese people still Chinese?' "[65] This cultural concern informed both the students' initial, very moderate message—essentially "take us and our ideas seriously, give us a voice"—and their subsequent determination to persist as government recalcitrance made their movement more radical.

Heshang attracted a remarkably large audience on Chinese television, probably several hundred million, and was shown twice before the authorities had second thoughts about their liberalness in allowing it to be aired.[66] The series also sparked strong responses among viewers. Watching television was almost always a social experience in China, one shared with family, neighbors, and friends.[67] Viewing was thus often accompanied by active dialogue, debate, and collective interpretation. It was not only university-trained intellectuals who held discussions on *Heshang*, then, but also millions of ordinary Chinese at neighborhood and family gatherings; a broad public was prepared to engage in a critical discourse about China's future (though surely many found the film's more unkind comparisons and evaluations shocking and offensive).[68]

Heshang's popularity dramatized the centrality of the problem of culture for thoughtful Chinese in the late 1980s. Few doubted the desirability of economic modernization, though what form it should take was debated. But how was economic change to relate to culture? What did it mean to be Chinese in a world of computers and fax machines, tourists and joint ventures, the internationalization of commodity flows and culture? Maoist communism had offered an alternative source of pride and national identity (incorporating some aspects of tradition, rejecting others). But Maoism had also depended on closing China off from the rest of the world. What elements of Maoism or Confucianism could provide a vision for the twenty-first century? Or had both decisively failed the tests of modernity? Did that mean wholesale Westernization was the only solution, or were there still the resources for an authentic Chinese path? All but the most technocratic or cautious and Party-loyal Chinese intellectuals felt that China's modernization was in need of a cultural vision. However real the economic gains might be, they were in jeopardy, even pernicious, if not accompanied by a sound rejuvenation of Chinese society and culture.

This was essentially where most students and intellectuals thought they had a crucial role to play. Some were primarily trained to perform technical functions in modernization, as engineers or doctors or demographers, yet many had worries about creating a larger vision. For humanists and the more culturally oriented social scientists, these worries were much more acute, and they were coupled with a sense that the government lacked respect for them and failed to let them contribute fully to China's modernization and strengthening. Not all of the students had a strongly political conception of what to do, of how far an insurrection could go, of what role the Communist Party might play, of whether multiparty elections were possible or good, or of what form decentralization of bureaucratic power should take. But the political ideas of nearly all the active leaders, as well as the sentiments of rank-and-file participants in the protest, were deeply shaped by this sense of cultural crisis and impoverishment. It was at the heart of the students' talk of democracy, at least as central as any imported Western specifics about the mechanics of liberal democratic rule.

Indeed, in commenting on the 1986–87 student demonstrations, the authors of *Heshang* pointed to a concern that would remain at the core of the 1989 dissent: "[T]he form of direct dialogue between government officials and students which was established in the course of calming down the movement in fact attained the objective of the vast majority of college students who participated in the student movement: that is, greater 'transparency' in government and policy-making."[69] Transparency (*toumingdu*) was in a sense China's equivalent to glasnost, a general call for the workings of the government to be open to the people; it was also a phrase associated especially with Zhao Ziyang. This passage from *Heshang* thus suggests something of a common denominator to a wide range of different political orientations. Whether they favored technocratic or cultural remedies for China's ills, all intellectuals wanted increased transparency—an aspect of "blueness," according to *Heshang*. Transparency was a goal both of those who would be happy simply with continued gradual reform and of those who wanted more radical change. It was a central feature of democracy.

THE "IN-BETWEEN" GENERATION

Su Xiaokang, Jin Guantao, Liu Qingfeng, and many of the others involved in making *Heshang* were part of the famous "in-between" generation of Chinese intellectuals. More specifically, they belonged to the crucial cohort of "worker-peasant-students" who entered higher education in 1977 and 1978.[70] These students formed a bridge between the Cultural Revolution (in which many were Red Guard activists) and the Deng Xiaoping era (in which they persistently prodded the government to push reform beyond the economic and technological realms to include cultural and political dimensions). They were largely undergraduates during the Democracy Wall movement of 1978–79. Many of the misty poets were among them.

This generational identity, especially the issue of relationship to the Cultural Revolution, evoked a powerful symbolic concern in China but one difficult to address openly. The Cultural Revolution was often cast as antithetical to rational-critical discourse, indeed as the very embodiment of irrationality. This stigma all but disqualified from such discourse anyone who would recall the Cultural Revolution's genuinely democratic aspects or claim an element of rationality in parts of its program. Such exclusion created great tension for those who were young during this period, people now in their thirties and forties. However, this generation was a very important source of inspiration, ideology, and advice for the protesters of 1989.

In this regard, there is a yet another link between the intellectuals who participated in the 1989 protests and those involved in the May Fourth movement of seventy years before. The latter were transitional in an important sense: They had been born under the old imperial regime but would live their adult lives in a postrevolutionary China. Many were raised in Confucian households and struggled with tensions between the expectations of their fathers (e.g., for arranged marriages and conventional careers) and their own desires. Similarly, in the 1980s a special role was played by a transitional generation, which first appeared in the guise of the Red Guards, the true faithful of the Cultural Revolution, but later experienced a series of setbacks—the disillusionment of discovering that the Cultural Revolution had been manipulated from above, the shock of finding their seeming heroism condemned, and the difficulty of integrating into post-Mao China.

Much of the continuity between the protests and crises of 1976, 1978–79, and 1989 was provided by intellectuals who identified themselves with this "in-between" generation, which linked the radical democratic aspirations of the Cultural Revolution to the era of economic reform. Those who were principals in all three of these major mobilizations are sometimes termed "athletes of three events" and particularly feared by the Chinese government. Ren Wanding was perhaps the most prominent example in the Square itself, but his influence was limited because so few students actually recognized him or remembered his role in 1978–79. (Even so, the government chose to punish him harshly.) Ren spoke on several occasions, but his most important contribution was in having helped keep the issue of human rights alive over the years. Ren seemed to accept that he was closer to the age of the protesters' parents: "They are my kids," he told a reporter in May. "I respect them, and they are brave, but they don't really understand human rights."[71]

Wang Juntao and Chen Ziming had a greater impact than Ren. As the proprietors of a prosperous correspondence college and the Beijing   al and Economic Sciences Research Institute, they were in a position tc provide organizational support and links to government reformers, but they were not able to offer direct guidance.[72] Though it engaged in little outright activism in the Square, the "in-between" generation paved the way for the movement by raising enduring issues.

What it was "between" was the last generation of Communists, whose ideals were bankrupt, and the current youth, who before 1989 were thought to be apathetic and apolitical. In the late 1980s there emerged a widely circulated conception of China's "four generations," starting with the old revolutionaries of Deng Xiaoping's vintage, followed by those who came of age in the 1950s (e.g., Li Peng), those who were youth leaders during the Cultural Revolution, and those who were young in the late 1980s. The "in-between" generation was indeed lost in this scheme. Though its members may have been child activists in the Cultural Revolution, most were too young to have been leaders. They came of age somewhat rootlessly in the aftermath of the Cultural Revolution and the uncertain early years after Mao. As Wang Luxiang put it:

I wonder what generation I am? I've tried very hard to think of what generation I belong to, but in the end I had to give up. . . . The members of these four generations all have a sense of belonging to their own generation, and so their lives all have a home base. But as for me? And my age mates? We have no slot to fit into, we have lost any sense of a "generation" to belong to, we have become drifters unable to find our fixed place in history on this continent. And yet we are very numerous, for we all happened to be born in the first "baby boom" after the founding of the People's Republic, and of that famous group who started college in 1977 and '78 we number about half. At present, a significant number of the active young intellectuals on the mainland belong to our group of generationless "historical drifters." Perhaps it is precisely the deep-rooted fear created by this sense of the loss of a historical home to belong to that has made us so active in this critical age. To lack a sense of belonging is to lack anything to rely on or to hold on to. Perhaps we were born to be critics, because we don't fit in, because we are transitional figures between generations, because History has not set aside a time for us to be builders.[73]

Although the issue of generations could be articulated in a general way, the Cultural Revolution itself was much harder to introduce into the state-dominated public sphere of China. One of the most shocking elements of *Heshang* was that it broadcast footage of the mass adulation of Chairman Mao.[74] Such scenes were virtually never seen in the reform-era People's Republic, and they created a sensation. Su Xiaokang received this letter from a fifteen-year-old girl attending an elite Beijing high school:

When I lived through the "Great Cultural Revolution," I was still very, very small, and couldn't remember things, so that now I don't have any impression of it at all. But when I saw in *Heshang* some scenes reflecting the conditions of that time, I urgently wanted to know what the China of that time was like. When I saw some of those scenes on TV, such as: young people waving the little red book and yelling "Long Life!" upon seeing Chairman Mao, so moved that hot tears filled their eyes; or the "fervor" of people at a criticism meeting; or the situation during the "Great Leap Forward"—I felt I didn't understand them at all, didn't understand why they were that way.

Su remarked:

> This passage indeed shocked me far more than did those articles upbraiding *Heshang* for "historical nihilism" [a charge from progovernment historians]. Though less than twenty years have passed, the children of today are as ignorant of the Cultural Revolution as if it belonged to another century; they find it extremely strange as well as inconceivable—this fact sends shivers down my spine. When I recall how I was a Red Guard myself in those days, I would have found it very hard to predict whether at any time in the future Chinese young people would ever again madly rush onto the streets under the incitement of a revolutionary slogan.[75]

7 Claiming Democracy

NOTHING TO THEIR NAMES

Western journalists and academics have recurrently expressed surprise at the frequency with which protesting Chinese students sang the "Internationale."[1] This old socialist song was taught to them by the Party they now attacked, observers noted; wasn't it odd that the students sang it again and again? Was this a sign of their continued loyalty to some less corrupt vision of communism? Did the students sing the "Internationale" only with a well-developed sense of irony? Were they merely forced to sing this song because they knew so few in common?

Oddly, these commentators fail to consider the possibility that the song was inherently appealing. Certainly the fact that every protester was sure to know the "Internationale" was an advantage, and certainly it was useful that authorities could hardly punish someone for singing a song the Party itself had made popular and still played on official occasions. Here, as in many other ways, students appropriated an aspect of everyday life under Communist rule for use in protests aimed in part at Communist rulers. This tactic so aggravated some Communist leaders, in fact, that they attempted to ban all impromptu singing of the "Internationale."[2]

Yet in singing the "Internationale," the students were not simply making ironic use of a communist form on an anticommunist occasion. In the first place, the protests were not primarily anticommunist. The specific leadership of government and Party was blamed for China's problems much more frequently than was the system or communist ideology as such (though these received no ringing endorsements and a good bit of criticism). Indeed, the message of the "Internationale" was one with which every protesting student could agree—all irony aside—and that expressed

237

a great deal of the ideological orientation of the movement.[3] The words to the song were thus repeated and paraphrased in innumerable *dazibao*.[4] There can be little doubt that the ideas of the "Internationale" were themselves taken seriously; the song was not just convenient. Here is a literal translation of the Chinese words to the "Internationale":

> Arise, poverty-stricken slaves;
> Arise, all suffering people of the world;
> The blood in our hearts is boiling,
> Let us fight for truth.
> Smashing the old world into pieces,
> Arise slaves, arise!
> Do not say we possess nothing,
> We will be masters under heaven.
>
> There has never been a Savior,
> Nor should we rely on gods and emperors.
> To create happiness for human kind,
> We must rely on ourselves.
> We will seize back the fruits of our labor
> And break through the cage of old thoughts.
> Let us be quick and set the stove-fire burning;
> We can only succeed by striking [while the iron is] hot.
>
> Who are the creators of the human world?
> It is us the working masses.
> Everything should belong to the laborers.
> Why should we tolerate the parasites?
> They are the most hateful poisonous snakes and brutal beasts.
> They drink up our blood and eat up our flesh.
> Once they are wiped out,
> The fresh and red sunshine will brighten up the whole world.
>
> This is the last struggle.
> Get united for tomorrow,
> *Internationale* will surely come.[5]

The students of 1989 were not much interested in the specific claims of the working masses, to be sure, but they were very much interested in the idea that the aged leadership of the Communist Party of China had become parasites living well on the labor of others. Indeed, this accusation joined the students to the "working masses" and the bystanders who observed their protests.

The idea that no savior was coming, originally intended as a critique of Christian and feudal disengagement from immediate social struggles, was readily transmuted by the protesting students into a suggestion that the

Communist Party could be relied on neither to save China nor to provide for ordinary happiness. This was not a new thought. During the Democracy Wall movement, Wei Jingsheng had made it a central part of his call for a "Fifth Modernization" (democracy, freedom, and happiness): "The leaders of our nation must be informed that we want to take our destiny into our own hands. We want no more gods and emperors. No more saviours of any kind."[6] Placard upon placard likened Deng Xiaoping to an emperor (or to the Empress Cixi) and mocked his pretensions to be China's savior; it was not a far stretch to see the idolatry of Mao as an attempt to enshrine a new god between ordinary humankind and the achievement of its happiness. In their June 2 declaration of a new hunger strike, Liu Xiaobo, Zhou Duo, Hou Dejian, and Gao Xin had echoed the thought as well as the phrasing of the "Internationale": "For several thousand years, Chinese society has been living in a vicious cycle of a new emperor replacing an old emperor. History has proven that the stepping down of some unpopular leader and the assumption of power by some very popular leaders cannot solve the essential problems of Chinese politics. What we need is not a perfect savior, but a perfect democratic system."[7] The image of breaking through the cage of old thoughts, reminiscent of the New Culture movement of the 1920s, suggested the conservatism of China's leaders as they faced Western ideas and domestic innovations in the 1980s.

The "Internationale" dates from the Paris Commune of 1871.[8] This origin in itself made the song appropriate to the Beijing Spring, for few Western historical events more closely prefigured the 1989 student protests than the doomed struggle of the communards. As we saw above, the analogy to 1871 was in fact made by some Chinese students in the middle of the protests, especially when barricades were first erected against the threatening army. They were familiar with the Paris events from Marx's essay "The Civil War in France" or its more generic summaries in Chinese texts on the history of communism.

Last but not least, it is worth noticing how closely the end of the first stanza of the "Internationale" parallels that most popular of late-1980s Chinese pop songs, Cui Jian's "Nothing to My Name." Cui Jian linked personal to social and cultural bankruptcy when he sang, as much to China as to a girlfriend:

> I want to give you my hope
> I want to help make you free
> But all you ever do is laugh at me, 'cause
> I've got nothing to my name.[9]

The song was perhaps the most popular of the late 1980s among Beijing students. Such songs gave encapsulated, often repeated expression to grievances and desires. The very style of Cui Jian's music—as close as Chinese performers came to hard rock—combined elements of Westernization with countercultural critique.

The sense of being left without opportunities, resources, and possessions, and therefore without the chance to live an autonomous individual life was palpable among Chinese students in the late 1980s. In Cui Jian's song and in everyday life, it extended into the most intimate and emotionally powerful relations. Cui Jian sings of his expectation that the girl of his dreams will forsake him because he has nothing to offer her (and implicitly curses the system that left him in that situation). So, too, did Chinese students smart under the constraints of material scarcity: Marriages were postponed, spouses had to live apart because it was too expensive for both to live near school in Beijing, and single males hoping to find (in the male view) potential girlfriends found them more interested in *getihu*, young businessmen who had the money to show women a nice time. The students' aspiration to be masters, at least of their own lives, was powerful.

DEMANDS: PATRIOTIC AND PARTICULARISTIC

So what did the students want? Democracy, certainly, though within a wide range of understandings; a degree of autonomy and recognition; the sort of civil rights that might guarantee a richer public life and protect some realm of privacy; an end to corruption; and a richer China, and a better share of those riches. Western observers have had a hard time making sense of student aspirations because those observers have started by asking, "Did they really understand democracy?" or that seldom-voiced question that has rested just beneath so many other inquiries: "Did they want to be just like us?"

Student demands initially reflected their particularistic concerns rather closely: recognition of an autonomous students association, improvement of a variety of conditions in universities, and more choice and meritocracy in the assignment of jobs to graduates. Yet once the protest took root, a variety of deeper, longer-range ideas came to the fore. Grievances specific to students and intellectuals flowed together with a discourse about democracy, modernization, and China's cultural crisis.

The students who protested in Tiananmen Square were young or budding intellectuals. They all saw China's problems through lenses that focused attention on their own role. But they were genuinely concerned with

China's fate, not only seeking their own interests; they saw existing government policies as denying them not only privileges and income but also a proper chance to help meet the country's challenges. For most students, cultural and technocratic intellectual visions were intertwined with both traditional and more radical cultural thinking. However, the protesters did not sort out these two different dimensions—if indeed they could have. But both worked to shape the movement.

Technological improvements and economic reforms certainly required intellectual expertise, and students felt the government did not invest enough in preparing them or paying them for this role. More basically, democracy required a public discourse, and students saw intellectuals as playing a central role in this arena—as watchdogs for government accountability, proposers of policies, interpreters of the demands and desires of the inarticulate masses. More than anything else, the sense that China was wracked not just by material underdevelopment but also by cultural crisis seemed to call for contributions that intellectuals alone could make.

The leadership of the Tiananmen Square occupation issued a list of demands and attempts at self-definition at the end of May. This list converted previous broader claims into specific tactical concerns and, in the face of immediate military threat and martial law, focused on the Party and the government rather than on the students themselves. It also reflected the movement's earlier shift from focus on students' particularistic interests toward identification with the Chinese people as a whole. The list reiterated in various forms the centrality of two themes—patriotism and democracy. It did little to define either theme; they were mainly evoked, not explicated (which was enough for the immediate purpose). The document read:

1. The spontaneous student movement has developed into a widespread, patriotic campaign for democracy. Because the movement has already ignited political struggles within the Party, the democratic forces it represents will not be stopped.

2. Whoever takes power in the government must be in accord with the people, set democracy as his starting point, and reform the political system to make it democratic.

3. Future leaders of China will be judged by their attitudes toward democratic patriotism. Pro-democratic leaders will be supported by the people; those who are against democracy will be abandoned.

4. It is not wise for Li Peng, He Dongchang, Yuan Mu, and Li Ximing to adopt a negative attitude toward the patriotic and democratic student movement. They have demonstrated their inability to serve as China's major leaders. Having Li Peng in office is a great danger to the safety of workers, urban citizens, officials, and those Party members who have shown their support of the student movement.

5. Zhao Ziyang, the general secretary of the Party, is supportive of the movement; he should remain in his office.

6. No official who loses his office because of his negative attitude toward the movement should hold a grudge toward the students.

7. This movement is, as stated, a spontaneous campaign, patriotic and democratic in nature, by the students and the people. It is by no means a political struggle inside the Party.

8. Whatever the outcome of the Party struggle, martial law must be lifted, the army must be withdrawn from the city of Beijing, the April 26 editorial by the *People's Daily* must be refuted as must Li Peng's speech on May 20, 1989, and an emergency meeting of the Standing Committee of the People's Congress must be held immediately to discuss the proposal to remove Li Peng from office.

9. On May 30, the eleventh day after martial law was ordered, we shall withdraw from Tiananmen Square after a mass rally.

10. April 27 should be observed as a Day of Democracy and Liberty for China.[10]

The protesters joined the ideals of patriotism and democracy not just in response to the April 26 editorial, in which the Party leadership condemned the students as antipatriotic. This conjunction was a basic motivation and theme of the whole movement, a continuation of the discourse on enlightenment and national salvation. Indeed, though nearly all signs in Western languages and pronouncements to the foreign press stressed democracy, placards and speeches in Chinese placed at least equal emphasis on patriotism and national advancement.[11] Patriotism meant not just pride in being Chinese—a pride that was injured by unfavorable comparisons with the West. It meant also that China should aspire to great things and achieve the wealth to offer ordinary happiness to its people. Being patriotic meant speaking for China as a whole. As one student put it in mid-May, "I am speaking as a Chinese and also as a student. I think this student movement has aroused the masses of people so that we can all help save our own country from disasters."[12] For many students and others in China, the project of democracy has been understood to follow from these patriotic aspirations. It appeared not only as a good end in itself but also as a crucial ingredient of modernization. Democracy (*minzhu*, or "people rule") meant that the interests of ordinary people should be served by the government. This notion is distinct from the idea that ordinary people should *run* the government. Moreover, the pervasive critique of corruption fit closely with the call for national pride and solidarity. The parasitical government, students argued, bred the corruption with which everyone in China was familiar from daily life. Because of this corruption, the government thwarted the common goals of national strength and economic development.

These same two issues of national strength and development infused the meaning of the slogan "Democracy and Science," which linked the students of 1989 to the intellectuals who created the May Fourth movement of 1919. "I believe it will benefit everyone to establish a system of democracy and to make use of science to save the country," wrote Chai Ling.[13] Students at Beijing University sold "Democracy and Science" t-shirts in May 1989. "Democracy is the prevailing trend for China," one student volunteered; "the Chinese people have been awakened. But we lack a political party that is capable of leading the movement of democracy." At least as common were calls for awakening a population passive about its own fate: "I believe that true democracy in China should be built upon a fundamental change in the people's outlook; in other words, the people should have a strong sense of democracy." And from another: "The reform of our political and economic systems should speed up and the masses of people should be awakened." This awakening and an emphasis on the importance of enlightenment and reason against the forces of superstition and ignorance remained the main referents of the "science" part of the slogan. It also continued to have a special resonance, predictably, among young intellectuals.

But what of democracy? The declarations of student leaders tended to treat the term as transparent, as though it had an obvious, incontestable meaning. They focused on strategy, on tactics, on specific grievances and specific freedoms. But by themselves, the formal public pronouncements of the leadership did not say much about how students understood the meaning of democracy. Not only were they intended for specific public relations purposes, they were the views of an elite within the student movement. We need to ask how widely these ideas were shared, as well as what deeper understandings of democracy lay behind them.[14]

THE MEANING OF DEMOCRACY

Around May 16, several of my Chinese graduate students and I were marching along Chang'an Boulevard on our way into Tiananmen Square. A reporter for a California newspaper strode alongside us and asked me to tell her what the students really wanted. "Ask them yourself," I said, "they speak English." She asked one, who replied simply, "Democracy." "What do you think democracy means?" she asked, as though of a child. My student responded with exaggerated humility, "Oh! You come from America. What does democracy really mean to you?" The reporter stammered. "Well, er, um, you know, elections, I guess." "Ah," said the student, "yes. But I think more in terms of Rousseau and the model of direct participation." Of course, Chinese understandings of democracy varied quite widely, as one might expect, and few students would have cited Rousseau. But the point of the story is really that our own conceptions of democracy are no more precise than the Chinese students'. The poverty of the reporter's answer is perhaps more remarkable than the cleverness of my student's. In the late 1980s, democracy may have been a more vital topic of discussion at Beijing University than at the University of California. Moreover, the reporter's reply—"elections"—is symptomatic of the thin understanding of democracy that informs Western thought about the transformations of communist and authoritarian regimes.

Seeking more systematic information about just what the protesters wanted, a student (I will call him Xu after his favorite poet, Xu Zhimo) and I went to Tiananmen Square with questionnaires that I had formulated and he had translated. We had pretested them and debated translations with some other graduate students, then had them photocopied by a private vendor who gave us a radical discount "because he believed in the student movement."

Simply as an event, the survey would have warmed the heart of any American public opinion researcher. It went contrary to all accounts we were offered of survey research in China and to the common belief that the Chinese are unwilling to divulge information or share opinions even under ordinary circumstances, let alone discuss controversial information at a time of some risk. Far from having any difficulty finding respondents, we discovered that people clamored for the chance to fill out the forms. Some wanted their pictures taken with me; most thanked us for giving them the opportunity to voice their opinions. We had planned to get five to ten responses from the camps of up to fifteen smaller schools, then fifteen to twenty responses from each of the four main Beijing universities. This plan went fine for several hours, until we had two schools left. As we were searching for the Beijing University and People's University camps, however, we were besieged by a crowd of people from a wide range of schools—together with a few hangers-on—demanding that we give them forms. There was great dismay when we ran out. We had to get more copies made and come back for the two major schools.

But that wasn't the height of the survey craze. I had prepared a separate questionnaire for bystanders, and Xu and I went to a sidewalk in front of the Museum of the Chinese Revolution (just east of Tiananmen) to give them out. We were going to do one at a time, and Xu started with a middle-aged man. Suddenly a second man appeared and insisted on getting a survey, too—and immediately. In a few seconds there was a crowd; people were snatching forms out of each other's hands, ripping them in the process. With increasing violence, people tried to reach into Xu's shoulder bag. It looked like a rugby scrum: Xu passed the bag out to me, and I was instantly besieged by fifteen people pulling at the bag, my shirt, and the papers in my hand. I made like an American football player, pushing through the crowd and over a small fence into the street. They didn't follow, and I was left alone wondering what to do. Everyone stared, a few yelled, but no one seemed brave enough to make an approach in open territory. Then a few people began to call timidly to me, waving the forms they had completed during the melee and wanting to turn them in! Xu escaped with no real injury, and we decided to try interviewing bystanders later—and elsewhere.[15]

The results of the survey were not in and of themselves startling, but taken together with the protesters' verbal responses they helped to clarify just what democracy and the movement meant to ordinary students. We asked both questions rather directly. Table 1 gives the breakdown of students' answers when asked to name the three most important goals of the movement.

Responding to a different version of the survey, 109 students indicated what they considered the three most important aspects (the translation said literally "parts") of democracy. As Table 2 indicates, these responses were not altogether different from those about the goals of the movement, but an even stronger emphasis on civil liberties or the "rights of man" came to the fore.

The results in Table 2 clearly contradict the widespread notion that Chinese students had no "real" understanding of democracy. The first four responses offer a plausible account of what democracy might mean to citizens of North America and Western Europe: a mixture of civil liberties and institutional conditions for informed public decisionmaking and free elections. Indeed, by perceiving that free elections require the support of free public discourse and the capacity to organize, the Chinese respondents displayed a more advanced conception of democracy than the California reporter (whose unreflective views are all too characteristic of the complacency of Western democratic populations). However, only half the number of students who cited free elections as a defining characteristic of democracy stressed that such elections would regularly change the incumbent

Table 1. Goals of the Student Movement

Goal	%
An end to corruption	71
Accurate news reporting	69
Freedom of expression	51
More respect for intellectuals	46
Help modernize China	35
Free elections	33
Change in senior government officials	31
Improve the economy	21
Free and independent associations	16
Others	3

$N = 112$

Table 2. Characteristics of Democracy

	%
Accurate news reporting	89
Free expression	83
Free elections	68
Free and independent associations	47
An end to corruption	38
More participation of intellectuals in government	34
Change in senior government officials	17
Strengthening the Chinese nation	14
Free economic activity	10
Others	6

$N = 109$

government officials. When students talked about democracy, they often disappointed Westerners who expected them to place their greatest emphasis on multiparty elections. In the first weeks of the protest, only one person spontaneously mentioned elections to me as an important part of democracy or as a significant goal of the movement. Moreover, that student thought the road to free elections in China lay through the intermediary stage of a military coup d'état and caretaker government. This point of view changed somewhat after the crackdown; certainly, fewer people looked forward with any optimism to the thought of military rule. Yet even then some hoped that seizure of power by a "friendly" army (e.g., the Thirty-eighth) would prove a way out of the crisis.

The crisis of governmental authority in 1989 made students think further about how leaders were chosen. The episode was, after all, occasioned by the death of a former official leader and heir apparent to the real leader, then exacerbated by the jockeying over succession to Deng Xiaoping. But, like many of the Chinese intellectuals of 1919, a number of students harbored doubts about whether the Chinese people were "ready" for elections.[16]

Many students thought elections a good thing, to be sure, but civil liberties loomed much larger in their immediate vision of democracy. In calling for recognition of their own independent student organization they affirmed, at least indirectly, the right of free association. This demand was echoed by workers' attempts to create free trade unions. Students supported journalists struggling for freedom of speech and of the press; sought freedom of association, especially in their autonomous unions; and ultimately demanded greater freedom in conducting the affairs of their own lives. As budding intellectuals, they sought to carry on a discourse about the future of China, to offer the government advice and have it be heard. In short, they emphasized the right of self-expression, not just for political (let alone policymaking) purposes but as a general principle. Students were fond of repeating the title line from a popular song by the Taiwanese singer Su Rui called "Follow Your Own Feelings." As in the 1960s in the West, a host of different sorts of feelings found followers in China during the Beijing Spring.

ENDING CORRUPTION

It was neither the desire for democracy per se nor the idea of following one's own feelings that linked the students most strongly to the general population of Beijing. The goal they shared most was bringing an end to corruption. This was the objective cited most often by both students (see Table 1) and bystanders in our survey (see Table 3).

Here the question asked was, "Which goals do you think are most important to achieve by these demonstrations?"[17] Overall, the answers were not dramatically different from those given by students. Just as many bystanders as students wanted to see more respect for intellectuals, for example, and civil liberties were also just as prominent. Ordinary people cer-

Table 3. Bystanders' Impressions of Movement Goals

Goal	%
An end to corruption	82
An end to official profiteering	59
Accurate news reporting	50
More respect for intellectuals	48
Freedom of expression	46
Change in senior government officials	38
Help modernize China	30
End price hikes	30
Improve the economy	28
Free elections	25
Better wages/salaries	14
Free and independent associations	8
Improved public security	5

$N = 111$

tainly declared themselves to be in favor of democracy when asked, and 93 percent indicated strong or very strong support for the movement.[18] Perhaps their greatest difference from the students lay in an even stronger call for an end to corruption.

If pressed to name further grievances, most people outside the ranks of students and intellectuals would note a sense of economic injustice and anxieties brought about by changing institutions.[19] They wanted an end to the inflation that ate away at the purchasing power of their relatively fixed salaries. Though not high by Third World standards, this inflation was unprecedented in the People's Republic of China. People also talked about the distribution of wealth. The government had implemented reforms that enabled some people to get rich, and it had praised the idea of getting rich, but it had not offered a broadly understood rationale for why some should enjoy this opportunity and others should not. This omission may have been part of the reason bystanders supported the goal of more respect for intellectuals. Why should entrepreneurs become millionaires and doctors not? Why should taxi drivers make several times the income of engineers? Why should teenagers lucky enough to get jobs in a joint-venture hotel make more than the most senior university professors? In short, the economy seemed to lack order; its results did not make sense to ordinary people. This seeming randomness might well have unsettled most Chinese even if growth had been continuous and inflation nonexistent; the economy's recent troubles only worsened suspicions that something was amiss. At one level, of course, people simply wanted more wealth, but they also wanted the distribution of wealth to make sense. The Party had abandoned the extreme but clear egalitarianism of its earlier policies without offering a new legitimating message. In one sense the public's perception of an unfair distribution of income was ironic, for it is not clear that inequality had actually increased. The rise of rural incomes relative to urban had probably *reduced* overall inequality during the last decade of reform. But changing relations among economic sectors and the visibility of new displays of substantial wealth made people feel inequality acutely.

The sense of economic injustice reinforced complaints about corruption. These, like corruption itself, had several faces. Some corruption was built into the transitional economy and was not altogether "dysfunctional."[20] The policy of reducing but not eliminating detailed central economic planning created a variety of imbalances. Vital goods might be in short supply in one region, whereas another might have an excess of goods but an absence of either documents or cash for any transaction. A number of businessmen moved into the breech as black-market "fixers" who helped overcome the contradictions of the system. They might organize a barter deal among three regions, each one having too much of something another one wanted. Or they might arrange for the sale of a good at a price triple the official one, with only the controlled price being reported. Fixers were thus useful in maintaining a technically illegal trade in nonmarketized commodities. When official prices for lightbulbs, to take an example from early 1989, were set so low that manufacturers could not afford the market-priced tungsten needed to make them, fixers stepped in to arrange a barter trade between lightbulb manufacturers and tungsten suppliers, bringing alternative goods from the former's state-rationed stockpiles to those who had tungsten to sell.

People resented the fortunes made in this way, but they generally saw such manipulations as simply a part of the mercantile practice of buying cheap and selling dear, shady but not the sort of corruption on which they focused. The visible and offensive faces of corruption were the displays of officials and their children, who were rich enough to drive foreign cars, indulge in bourgeois hobbies such as golf, and pay the everyday bribes necessary to get a passport, an apartment, or any of a dozen supposedly free public services. It was also the role of officials, rather than the illegality of market-fixing as such, that made this corruption potentially so dysfunctional. Officials artificially reduced the number of suppliers through nepotism and by playing favorites. This type of corruption tended to provide windfall profits for those with connections, exclude others, and raise prices for everybody.[21]

Bringing an end to corruption would require curtailing official profiteering (guandao), stopping the favoritism shown to the children of top leaders, and lessening the importance of connections in getting things done. Of course, there was nothing new about the advantage of having connections (guanxi) in opening up backdoor opportunities; there was a long-standing pattern of investment in personal relationships as a kind of social capital.[22] But the guanxi system grated in the late 1980s for three reasons. First, it was directly contrary to the vaunted rationalism and egalitarianism of communist ideology. The Communist Party, ironically, had taught people to despise as a corrupt feudal inheritance a set of practices that its own bureaucratic and inefficient administration now made ubiquitous. Second, reliance on guanxi had become more prominent and widespread in the 1980s. Party cadres and petty officials displayed less of the ideological commitment and puritan values they exhibited (albeit in varying degree) in earlier decades.[23] At the same time, the opening of a more active and monetarized market created new opportunities and new resources for graft.

But the third reason guanxi rubbed people the wrong way in the 1980s was perhaps the most potent: the system was becoming commodified, reduced to a business sustained by cash transactions. Instead of resting on personal connections cultivated through kinship, neighborhood, or longstanding friendship, guanxi was becoming increasingly a matter of simple bribery. It had always been easier to get an airplane ticket, say, if you knew someone with a relative in the airline's office; now the relatives were acting as "professional" brokers and allegedly keeping seats off the open market. Moreover, payment was made on the spot, in cash; there was no expectation that the favor would be returned (perhaps to one's kin or children, not directly to oneself) and certainly no satisfaction at not being a debtor in the system of cultural credit. Rather than encouraging and reinforcing a web of social relations that helped to maintain solidarity, the monetarized system placed relationships at the mercy of ability to pay. A "connection" no longer meant something binding; it was simply a matter of access to someone who controlled scarce resources.

Guandao went beyond guanxi, however.[24] Government officials revealed great ingenuity and minimal conscience in putting their positions to work for private profit or for the advantage of their family members. Both Zhao Ziyang and Li Peng had sons working as executives on Hainan Island, one of the new enterprise zones in the south. Everyone assumed that these young men not only owed their good jobs to their fathers but also could skim money from local ventures with impunity. Deng Xiaoping's son not only profited in the new free market but also gained financially from his leadership of the China Welfare Fund for the Handicapped. Reference to this sort of abuse was ubiquitous; it was the subject of innumerable *dazibao* and *xiaozibao* (small character) posters, many of them long and full of detailed stories of the crimes and privileges of this or that "young prince" of the Communist Party. Almost all stressed how, in perpetuating their privileges, Party bosses were making their families a hereditary elite; a few posters echoed the "new class" analyses current in Eastern Europe a generation before. The corollary was that in monopolizing the best opportunities, Party leaders denied others their legitimate chances in life. Sometimes the comment was terse: "Down with the official profiteers! Oppose the system of lifetime leadership!"

Official profiteering sometimes manifested itself in another form of corruption involving much larger transactions. It was practiced by official units as well as private businessmen and entailed a variety of under-the-table quid pro quos—padded payrolls, attempted price manipulations, toleration for inferior products or materials, demands for foreign exchange certificates in payment for work that should have been compensated in domestic currency. This kind of problem is familiar worldwide. It is hard to know if it was unusually prevalent in China in 1989, though everyone seemed sure that it had grown. The high proportion of government businesses made it more likely that such shady antics would be seen as official corruption rather than simply as unsavory capitalism. *Guandao* was seen as contributing directly to inflation and other economic woes. "The main goal, it seems to me," wrote one bystander on a copy of our survey, "is to oppose rising prices and eradicate official profiteers and corruption." Indeed, as Tony Saich suggests, students may have been able to appeal to other Beijing residents partly because they appeared less corrupt than most other social groups.[25]

However, there is no guarantee that the protest movement, had it not been crushed, would have been able to develop an analysis of China's current situation that would adequately link democracy to plans for economic reform. It is not obvious that democracy by itself can lessen corruption, though many students had faith that it would. Nor is it obvious that a democratic transition in China could be managed without serious economic problems—an issue the student leaders had not really addressed.

In any case, complaints about corruption reflected not just annoyance at having to pay but dismay at the inefficiency it brought to the economic system and to the activities of everyday life. This sentiment helped make a crucial link to the ideas of democracy and development. Corruption appeared to be a roadblock, a source of inefficiency that stood in the way of progress. The Communist Party had always proclaimed as much, despite the actions of its representatives. Of course, not every critic of the Communist Party or corruption was a friend of capitalism. "We must get rid of corruption," one respondent said, expressing the views of many, "in order to build a better socialist country."

For students and intellectuals, corruption was especially intolerable because it created blockages to meritocracy—that is, blockages to the efficient use of ideas and talent (not to mention the efficient career promotion of those possessing the ideas and the talent). It prevented the greatest effort from being put to work for the Chinese people. Thomas Gold has noted the salience of the comparison to East Asia's "Four Dragons," the rapidly developing economies of Hong Kong, South Korea, Singapore, and Taiwan. These countries were hardly democratic in most senses of the word, but "political repression was traded off for genuine opportunities for mobility through education and business."[26] The Chinese system was inefficient because it was corrupt, in other words, and corrupt partly because positions of responsibility were not filled on the basis of qualifications and capacities. Many protesters looked to democracy to end this sort of corruption, which helps explain why 38 percent of students listed ending corruption as one of the three most important aspects of democracy and why another 34 percent suggested that democracy meant more participation of intellectuals in government. As one student engaged in the occupation wrote at the bottom of his questionnaire:

> We came from Henan Province to lend our support to the student movement in Beijing. Our objectives are:
>   1. To support the patriotic movement of Beijing university students;
>   2. To eradicate bureaucracy and political corruption and demand freedom of the press;
>   3. To demand greater attention to science and education and more money for education.

In short, the broad ideas of civil liberties and an end to corruption were closely linked in the democratic imagination of the students and many others. This was so in good part because the Communist Party depicted democracy as the image of what the government was *not*. As the latter was corrupt and denied civil liberties, fairness and civil rights were taken as joint aspects of democracy by the students. Changing the government (or at least speeding up its reform) would necessarily bring progress on both fronts. And if such transformation served the particular interests of students and intellectuals as well as the general interest of the country by bringing more support for science and education, so much the better.

THE QUEST FOR ORDINARY HAPPINESS

Both the critique of corruption and the desire for civil liberties were rooted in an "affirmation of ordinary life," an assertion of the value of everyday personal and family routines, of simply being happy. This theme was celebrated in Chinese pop songs, poetry, short stories, and novels. After decades of deferring gratification to the higher ends of the Communist Party and the building of socialism, many Chinese—especially those in younger generations—simply wanted more food, more fun, and more freedom. They were prepared, moreover, to defend these as real values, not merely personal desires.

Charles Taylor coined the phrase "the affirmation of ordinary life" as part of an account of changing moral values and ideas of self in early modern Europe. Christian thinkers shifted their moral sensibilities away from a sharp separation between "higher moral goods" and "base human existence" and toward a directly positive evaluation of "those aspects of human life concerned with production and reproduction, that is, labour, the making of the things needed for life, and our life as sexual beings, including marriage and the family."[27] I borrow the phrase here to call attention to a somewhat parallel development in reform-era China. The leaders of communist China's first thirty years did not take second place to any Protestants in their praise of productive labor. They were not like medieval Catholics or ancient Greeks, oriented to a spiritual ideal rather than the material realm. All in all, they were rather more reminiscent of Puritans. Though affirming the importance of ordinary life in general, the Puritans, like the citizens of the People's Republic in its first thirty years, were called upon to renounce purely personal enjoyments that would turn attention away from dedication to the general good and duty before God. They were expected to subordinate their affirmation of ordinary life to transcendental goals.

In Maoist China, socialist realist art glorified everyday life and material production, with paintings of rosy-cheeked peasants cheerfully laboring in their fields and eager factory workers smiling as new tractors rolled off assembly lines. A wide range of concrete policies sought to improve the everyday lives of ordinary people by housing them better, feeding them better, and providing better health care. This approach was a striking departure not only from the transparent greed of the early republican and warlord years but also from the ancient imperial system, which drew resources from ordinary people so that elites might enjoy extraordinary luxuries, refinements, and intellectual pursuits. But Maoist ideology did not see gains in everyday life as merely private benefits. They were public goods, to be achieved and enjoyed collectively. Personal desires were to be held in check, not only so that there would be enough and as good for others but also so that the people as a whole could flourish, could build socialism, and make China strong. Chinese communism, like Puritan capitalism, developed into a system of "worldly asceticism" (though without an equally productive investment of the surplus retained). Maoist communism was also famously "puritanical" with regard to sexuality and other pleasures. In one sense it outdid its European religious counterpart, regarding even the family as suspect and emphasizing loyalty to groups higher than this crucial locus of ordinary life.

In the reform era, Deng renounced much of communist Puritanism. "To get rich is glorious," he proclaimed, and though he may have meant mainly the *accumulation* of wealth, he and his colleagues in the leadership gradually legitimated greater and greater freedom in its consumption and eventually (especially after the Tiananmen massacre) its ostentatious display. But just as the affirmation of ordinary life in early modern Europe eventually outran Puritan and other strictures against hedonism, so a similar affirmation escaped the grasp of Deng and his fellow leaders.

The affirmation of ordinary life gained strength in the "literature of the wounded," in which victims of the Cultural Revolution recounted their torments and tried to rebuild their shattered lives. Children who had been forced to betray their parents, wives who had willingly or unwillingly condemned husbands, and parents whose disgrace had been visited on their children all sought to rebuild family life. In doing so—especially in cities—they not only restored ancient Chinese values but also made the family the object of a new kind of attachment. Instead of simply being regarded as the ubiquitous unit of lineage, it was now seen as a small cluster of cherished relationships among individuals. This transformation paralleled the emergence of friendship as a special and basic value. Such developments were a sharp change from the Maoist era, when "the Party and the state did not shine kindly on unauthorized personal relationships."[28] The ideology of romantic love spread widely through the population—nowhere more prominently than among students. The idea that marriage should bring personal fulfillment, including sexual satisfaction, reinforced the idea that the basic happiness of ordinary people was a fundamental value.[29]

New consumption patterns also responded to and encouraged a new emphasis on enjoyment in the here and now.[30] The government actively boosted some of this consumerism in order to create motivation for harder work and, perhaps most importantly, to draw money hidden under mattresses back into circulation. In addition to driving the economy, increased personal consumption kept people's attention focused on economic ends rather than on politics or other, more dangerous domains. However, it seemed that the more individuals focused on satisfying their material wants, the more they wanted. Indeed, some of the student protests in the early days of the movement were motivated by dissatisfaction with standards of living. Students who lived better than their counterparts of five or ten years ago nonetheless chafed at lacking the material goods they could increasingly see around them.[31]

Students chafed also at the lack of privacy, at being jammed four or six to a room. They were no longer subject to the intense scrutiny that had been characteristic under Maoism and immediately after. But because they no longer believed in the ideals that had justified the Maoist intrusions, and because they were rapidly developing stronger claims to individual autonomy, they found even modest levels of surveillance and involuntary publicness intolerable. Most would agree with Sun Longji's argument about the pernicious effects of Maoism's refusal to recognize any realm of purely private life: "This intrusion into and control of private lives has no other function than to eradicate individual personality."[32]

In clamoring for better standards of living, then, students were demanding not only more material possessions but also more respect for their privacy. They were voicing the idea that it was all right to care about themselves, about lovers and friends, and about day-to-day pleasures. They had not renounced the rhetoric of selflessness and sacrifice; on the contrary, they adopted it with the hunger strike. But even then, numerous speeches, placards, and interviews noted that this was not simply routine selflessness such as that the Party felt entitled to demand of all citizens. Rather, the students had valuable ordinary lives and aspirations that they were unwilling to sacrifice for the sake of the Party—but *were* prepared to sacrifice for the sake of the *country*. As Chai Ling put it in her late May interview, "I wanted to live a very peaceful life with children and small animals all around."[33]

The value of ordinary life was celebrated publicly in the Square through

the marriage of Li Lu and Zhao Ming.[34] This theme was not explicitly political, but it was an important ground for some of the students' more directly political ideas and actions. It underpinned their claim to speak as
autonomous citizens joining together in a public discourse, rather than as
an undifferentiated mass. The affirmation of everyday life and happiness
offered straightforward criteria for assessing the performance of the government. Giving weight to ordinary life also implied giving weight to the
experience and feelings of ordinary people. Though students were (perhaps
unconsciously) ambivalent, torn between their affirmation of "the common man" and their own sense of superior access to knowledge, this affirmation nonetheless amounted to a very large step in the direction of
democracy.

EXPECTATIONS AND ASPIRATIONS

Most of the students Xu and I surveyed were cautiously optimistic about
the prospects for democracy. Of 109 who were asked, "Do you think China
will achieve democracy?" only 1 answered "never." A quarter thought democracy would come "soon," 49 percent expected it within the next twenty
years, and 18 percent thought it would arrive "in the distant future." A
handful said they didn't know. Asked whether they expected the protest to
succeed in its goals, 44 percent said "very much" and 46 percent said
"somewhat." There was one outright cynic who wrote, "I doubt that this
movement will succeed in achieving the above-mentioned goals because
the government and the Party are already hopeless." A number of others
may have been voicing their hopes as much as their real expectations. As
one told us, "I have chosen the answer 'very probable' for the question
whether this movement will achieve its goals, though I am convinced it
might take a considerably long while." Men may have been especially vulnerable to the impulse to claim more confidence than they felt; in any case,
they declared themselves substantially more optimistic than did their female classmates. Only 16 percent of women said they thought democracy
would come soon, whereas nearly 29 percent of men offered the same
claim. Over 40 percent of women saw China as achieving democracy only
in the distant future, a view voiced by only 12.5 percent of the men. It is
not fair to say that women didn't *want* democracy (though they were less
unanimous than men on that score, apparently seeing democracy as a
somewhat lower priority).[35] Nor is it true that women had very different
conceptions of democracy than did men; they were slightly more likely to
name "free economic activity" or "an end to corruption" as elements of it,

but otherwise their views were hard to distinguish from those of men. But just as men accounted for the vast majority of protesters (as much as 80 percent), so perhaps they also voiced a more unswerving faith in the efficacy of their actions. Noting this difference shouldn't overshadow the general sense of confidence and enthusiasm the students exuded in mid-May. Though their overall spirits would be worn down by the end of the month, at this point they were exuberant about what they were doing.

The bystanders were less likely to be caught up in the excitement of the movement than the students—especially in mid-May—and were accordingly more cautious in predicting meaningful changes in society. Although 80 percent had visited Tiananmen Square to see (or perhaps participate in) the demonstrations, and although 93 percent said they supported the demonstrations either strongly or very strongly, only 29 percent indicated "very much" confidence in their success, and only 40 percent "somewhat" expected success.[36] As one commented, "I fully support the students' movement. But it will come to no avail. It is too difficult to get anything done in China." A number of bystanders offered variations on this theme: "I'm rather pessimistic about the future of this student movement because the feudal forces in China are too powerful." Many more offered comments such as, "I *hope* the university students will win," rather than echoing the confident declarations commonly made by students: "we will win," "victory is in sight," "the day will soon break." A few bystanders focused neither on the hope for success nor on the fear of repression. For them a different disaster seemed imminent: "This student movement is, if allowed to develop, bound to stir up turmoil in spite of its good intention. We should now do everything possible to safeguard unity and stability and allow no turmoil to affect the whole country." This view was echoed by a retired senior army officer, perhaps himself echoing the view the leadership wished to encourage: "The enthusiasm shown by the student movement is commendable, but its methods and approaches are not. It will probably lead to turmoil throughout the country."[37] "What the society needs, first and foremost," said another man, "is stability."

Worries about stability were linked to the question of whether Chinese democracy should somehow be different from that in the West. Many students associated the idea that democracy needed specifically "Chinese characteristics" to work in China with the government's attempts to limit reform. "Democracy is just democracy," one wrote, "it knows no national bounds! We must attain a firm grasp of the genuine meaning of democracy." In the survey, 25 percent of respondents indicated that democracy in China should be like that in the West, whereas 60 percent answered that it should be tailored for Chinese conditions (the remainder offered no opinion). One student tried to find a middle ground: "In essence, the democracy we want is different from that of the West. But in form, we have a great deal to draw on from the system of checks-and-balances. Our goal is not to depose one individual leader so-and-so, but to boost up the development of democracy, and to bring about, by means of publicity campaigns, a social milieu in which democracy and constitutional government take deep roots in the hearts of the people."[38]

Several students took pains to argue that democracy was broader than any particular set of political mechanisms. Wrote one, "What is crucial to democracy in China is not a choice between one-party and multi-party rule. It is, rather, the building of an effective system of democracy to be complete within the realm of political life within the party or the country, and the detachment of the army from the political scene." Though a specific focus on electoral politics was relatively unusual, calls for political pluralism in a broader sense were common. One student even told me, "We should invite the KMT [the Taiwan-based nationalists] to Beijing and establish a multiparty coalition with the KMT and CPC [Chinese Communist Party] playing a prominent role." It is not entirely accidental that this student advocated a multiparty *coalition* rather than competition between multiple parties in elections. Most students I talked to were concerned that different views should be heard and combined in an appropriate balance. They criticized the Communists not just for being dictatorial or for keeping power without a majority mandate but also for failing to listen to and represent the views of the people. Limiting the power of top leaders and increasing the opportunities for intellectuals and others both to have their views heard and to exercise oversight seemed more important than having a regular system of electoral shifts from one party to another. As one student wrote, "The centuries-old history of China has proved that a dictatorial ruler really always takes to a fascist government. So the power of the higher leaders should be limited." The goal was to prevent dictatorship and encourage responsiveness.

The more sophisticated students understood democracy as a matter of degree, not something that was simply present or absent. "People pursue higher and higher goals as they continuously improve their knowledge of democracy. Democracy is such that it usually moves to a higher and higher realm with every step ahead. 'Give me liberty or give me death' should be changed to 'Struggle for freedom or wait for death.'" Over and again students reminded themselves—and their listeners—that the movement was just a step in a longer struggle, though this recognition was at odds with the enthusiasm of the moment. Sometimes caution and excitement were joined in the thought that the current dictators could be toppled immediately even though democracy would take a long time to build afterwards. Noted one survey respondent, "We should, after dismissing the octogenarian party leaders, and still maintaining the party rule, embark on a large-scale movement of democratization and guide this process into sustained and gradual orbit, and eventually bring about genuine and modern democracy characterized by pluralist politics."

The belief that the Party might be the agent of democratic reform was not uncommon. Even more widespread was the arrogant but virtually unchallenged assumption that the "knowledgeable elements"—i.e., students and intellectuals—would need to guide the rest of the Chinese people through some period of tutelage before full democracy could be achieved.

"Putting emphasis on education is the precondition to the realization of democracy," declared one survey participant. Students did not seem to have considered that the election process itself could be a matter of political education (though their own movement ought to have shown them how political action can work this way). Rather, they envisaged education as something to be accomplished first, before elections could work. And most (somewhat undemocratically) regarded education as something that they—the intellectuals—should provide *to* the people, rather than something that would happen naturally, as a direct outgrowth of a participatory political process. This view was a continuation of an older way of thinking. The May Fourth intellectuals, argued literary theorist Liu Zaifu, saw themselves as the "subject," or those who did the enlightening, in relation to the "object," the people they wished to enlighten.[39] The Communists had demanded the subject role, and now the intellectuals were demanding it back. The political philosopher Gan Yang, author of the May 25 declaration, made a similar complaint. The problem with Chinese intellectuals, he said, lay in their obsessive determination "to speak for others and to speak the truth to others who have not seen the truth."[40]

Similarly, democracy seemed to be spoken of more as something that people might *have* than as something people might *do*; the perception of it as a *process* was not well developed. Democracy meant having a government that took the interests of its people seriously, acted for their benefit rather than that of its cadres, listened to expressions of popular opinion, and was fair in its dealings with ordinary people.[41] The idea of democracy as a form of popular rule was much less well developed. The crucial forms of participation the students sought to guarantee were extensions of the tradition in which officials (and to a lesser extent ordinary people) might remonstrate with the emperor, hold him to his responsibilities, and tell him what he needed to know in order to be a good ruler. Thus, a greater role for intellectuals was central to their vision of democracy. Whereas Americans tend to emphasize the role of elections to the point of forgetting the importance of social movements and other less mechanical forms of democratic participation, Chinese thinkers have often pointed to the weaknesses of electoral democracy in the West and the problems of reliance on elections in a backward, undereducated country. Thus, students implicitly postponed universal suffrage elections to a later stage, after the raising of popular consciousness, and put the role of intellectuals in the forefront, thereby making their own actions the precondition of democracy.

For many, democracy turned not simply on who was in power but on whom those in power consulted. A sound system of government called for top officials to listen to the advice of intellectuals and experts. Of course, the same could be true for traditional imperial government; the difference lay largely in the method of proffering advice. Under democracy, intellectuals did not just make private consultations or send memorials to the emperor or Party secretary; they communicated their ideas in a public sphere, an arena of open discussion and cultural production. This perspective is a key reason that freedom of the press figured so prominently among student demands. Valuing this discourse made them democrats, and as democrats they knew they needed such a public arena.

As we have seen, free expression and a free press were widely valued. But just as corruption was clearly the first concern of ordinary people, intellectuals had a special sort of "elective affinity" for press freedom and the rights of public discourse. After all, who wrote the articles and conducted the discussions? For many students and intellectuals, one of the principle attractions of democracy lay in the possibilities of speaking without fear, of gaining due attention and respect, and of contributing to the progress of Chinese culture. In this desire for the voice they thought proper to themselves, students did indeed express the elitist aspirations and self-image of intellectuals. But though elitist, this self-image was not simply self-interested.[42] It was an identity that could be expanded beyond their own interests to embody a sense of speaking for the Chinese nation as a whole. Students might or might not fairly represent the thoughts or aspirations of all Chinese people, but they certainly did (to paraphrase John F. Kennedy's famous paraphrasing of Rousseau) ask not solely what their country could do for them, but also what they could do for their country.

Conclusion
To Be Worthy of the Cause

The Beijing Spring has not yet ended; it will reverberate in historical memory. As students of 1989 were shaped by distant images of Tan Sitong (and their elders by the more recent travails of Wei Jingsheng), so future protesters, future democrats will be inspired by the martyrs of 1989.

BRAVERY BEYOND REASON

The sense of acting on behalf of the Chinese nation was a powerful motivator for protesting Chinese students. Part of the power of the rhetoric of nationalism comes from its capacity to join the living and the dead as members of the same people.[1] The vocabulary of national identity also enabled students to affirm the higher purposes of democracy and freedom and to rise above their more narrowly self-interested claims and desires. "We defy death to win life for the nation," Chai Ling and her colleagues wrote in the Hunger Strikers Declaration.[2] On the night of June 3 and the morning of June 4, indeed, students in Tiananmen Square knowingly risked—arguably even courted—death at the hands of government troops.

Students took these risks without belief that in the near term their actions would improve their own or their fellows' circumstances or effect the political changes they sought. They did so despite the availability of apparent alternatives. Yet these were not habitual risk-takers. Some of those who died had been too cautious to identify themselves publicly with the boycott of classes only a month before. Many of those who risked death the night of the crackdown have gone to great lengths to avoid attack or arrest in succeeding months. But at the crucial moment, they were brave to the point of apparent foolishness. Why?

The question is not idle. Were it not for this extraordinary courage, the Chinese protest movement would not be remembered as it is. Were it not for similar cases elsewhere, revolutions would not have been made, battles won, rescues attempted. We cannot reduce heroic events to the mere exercise of interest and still make sense of history.[3] At the same time, we grasp heroism poorly if we treat it as simply a static attribute of certain persons rather than a broader human potential realized only when situations and social processes lead normally prudent people to take on seemingly unreasonable risks. At the heart of the stunning courage displayed by Chinese protesters in 1989 lies a question of representation or articulation, of how people arrive at an understanding of who they are.

The importance of identity and bravery poses challenges for attempts to explain the movement in terms of students' selfish interests. Early in the movement, to be sure, the students' self-image was unquestionably elitist, and many of their concerns were self-centered. They came almost entirely from urban families, and those from academic universities were the products of a selection system that allowed only a little more than 1 percent of their age-mates such an educational opportunity. During the April 27 march on Tiananmen Square, the demonstrators had their first direct confrontation with soldiers, most of them young men from peasant families. "Go home to your fields," the students taunted. "You have no business here." Similarly, when Han Dongfang, the workers' leader, stood up to speak at the Monument to the People's Heroes on May 30, students shouted him down. "Who is this guy?" "We are the vanguard!" "Get down, leave!"[4]

Six weeks later, some of these same arrogant, self-important students were willing to die for those peasant soldiers and rebel workers, as well as for their fellow students, for one reason: They were willing to die for the Chinese nation. How are we to reconcile the risk-takers of June 3–4 with the students who began the movement so disdainful of peasants, workers, and officials?

CLASS INTERESTS OF INTELLECTUALS?

To be a student, an intellectual in the making, was not a casually adopted role; it was a matter of basic personal identity. It had resonances going back thousands of years in Chinese history, and it was manifest in the way people spoke, dressed, and carried themselves. The students' selfhood was bound up with and indistinguishable from their participation in a whole variety of social relationships that were colored and shaped by reciprocal recognitions of class identity.

From the self-strengthening movement of the 1890s through the 1919 protests, the ebbs and flows of republicanism, and early stages of Chinese communism, intellectuals took on a stronger and stronger sense of their own crucial role in China's modernization. In the 1980s, Deng Xiaoping and other Communist leaders had courted intellectuals as important agents of reform. This new respect and tolerance, however, encouraged intellectuals to resume their advocacy of "science and democracy" and more generally of national salvation and enlightenment, which had long been on their collective agenda. On May 4, 1989, the unauthorized Federation made it clear in its declaration that it wanted to "Let Our Cries Awaken Our Young Republic!"

> Seventy years ago today, another group of students gathered here before Tiananmen. That was the beginning of a new, great chapter in the history of China.
> Today we are gathered here not only to commemorate that great day, but also to carry on and develop the spirit of democracy and science upheld by the May 4th Movement. Standing before Tiananmen—the symbol of our ancient nation—we proudly declare to the people of the nation: We are worthy of the cause advanced by our predecessors seven decades ago.
> For more than a century, the elitist elements of the Chinese people have been ceaselessly exploring the way to modernize their ancient and degenerating nation.[5]

Along with this relatively new cause, students and intellectuals reclaimed the older idea of their responsibility to remonstrate with an emperor (though fulfilling that responsibility had never matured into a right to be free from punishment). A scholar, tradition held, should be ruled most basically by his ideals. This view was sometimes transmuted into a more modern notion of authenticity, of being true to oneself. In any case, when Chinese students in 1989 claimed to be acting as "the conscience of the nation" and said this was a responsibility they had to live up to, they were speaking in line with a long tradition.

Students were different from other intellectuals not only in their youth, the lesser development of their ideas and skills, and their relative freedom from the discouragement of past failures but also in the fact that they did not have families to support or jobs to risk (at least in the immediate sense). They were therefore understood to be freer than their elders to act through public protest. Spatial concentration; subject, class, and cohort organization; and the web of communication among universities provided students with structural facilitation for mobilization. More senior intellectuals offered advice, tried to protect young activists, and pushed for change in quieter ways (though special respect was paid to those elders who did put themselves on the line in public protest).

Of course, the students had their own complaints. They lived in dormitories of poured concrete (often not even reinforced against earthquakes) with blank walls and floors. Undergraduates lived as many as six or eight to a room; M.A. students were privileged to share with only three others, and Ph.D. students were considered lucky to have only one roommate. Stipends were inadequate, and good jobs were scarce after graduation. Students had little control over whether they would be assigned to remote teachers colleges or to major universities; all they could do was toe the line within the system and perhaps work the corrupt game of *guanxi*. And students shared in the broader frustrations of the intellectual class. The government seemed not to listen, public respect was not forthcoming, pay was poor. As a colorful saying went, "The doctor earns less than the old woman selling baked potatoes at the entrance of the hospital, and the barber who cuts a person's hair earns more than the surgeon who operates on the brain beneath it."[6]

To many Chinese observers, it seemed at first that the striking students were mainly interested in themselves. Demonstrating that students—as intellectuals—were prepared to makes sacrifices for the interests of the Chinese people and the Chinese nation was in fact one of the major functions of the hunger strike. When the ordinary people of Beijing rallied to protect the hunger strikers starting on May 19, they did so not only because they shared the students' ideals but also because they respected the students' unselfishness. Here again, as so often happened, 1989 directly echoed 1919. On May 26, 1919, in the first article to speak of the May Fourth "movement," Luo Jialun wrote:

> This movement shows the spirit of sacrifice of the students. Chinese students used to be eloquent in speech and extravagant in writing, but whenever they had to act, they would be overly cautious. . . . This time, and only this time, they struggled barehanded with the forces of reaction. . . . The students' defiant spirit overcame the lethargy of society. Their spirit of autonomy (*zijue*) can never be wiped out again. This is the spirit which will be needed for China to be reborn.[7]

Even when their concerns were for China and not simply themselves, however, students and intellectuals understood China's needs in ways shaped by their participation in intellectual life. They were guided both by their belief that intellectuals were important and should be paid more and by their visions of the nature of China's crisis and the role they were destined to play in resolving it.

Certainly the students were elitist, and their positions in economic and prestige hierarchies influenced their participation in the movement. Certainly some part of the content of their "democratic" consciousness was focused on their identity as students and/or intellectuals and what that identity ought to mean in China. But we cannot explain the student protest movement simply in terms of the self-interested consciousness of intellectuals. The consciousness of the students changed in important ways during the course of the protest, and the consciousness of Chinese intellectuals was changed by the movement and by its repression. These processes of change cannot be grasped through an understanding of consciousness that focuses on the recognition of interests.[8]

The basic self-identification of the protesting students in Tiananmen Square was transformed, and at least for a time radicalized, by six weeks of activism. Their consciousness expanded beyond particularistic interests to include national concerns and universal ideals. As these themes evolved, it became possible for those in the movement, participants and observers alike, to identify emotionally with a general category—the Chinese people—instead of focusing on their distinctions from the rest of the population.

HONOR AND IDENTITY

With startling heroism and perhaps unreasonable optimism, student protesters demonstrated that the government could be challenged, if not yet toppled, and that neither students in particular nor today's Chinese in general have given in to apathy or selfishness quite so completely as has sometimes been argued. This heroism was not just a given attribute of China's students and can hardly be explained by rational self-interest. It was forged in the movement itself because students cared deeply enough and threw themselves wholly enough into the action for constructions of personal identity itself to be at stake. We cannot altogether make sense of the risk-taking without some idea of the sense of honor that motivated individuals and the sense of collective identification that made them more than mere individuals. Both of these were subject to remaking during the course of the movement. Not only is life always social, living is always a matter of action, not of statically possessing an identity or set of attitudes prior to action. What one does defines who one is, both for others and especially for oneself. Risky and unusual collective action places one's identity on the line in an especially powerful way.

Put another way, very risky actions, such as standing in front of a tank rolling down Chang'an Boulevard, depend on a sense of who one is as a person and what it means to go on living with oneself, a sense that is inextricably social as well as personal and that is sufficiently powerful to outweigh what might ordinarily be paramount prudential concerns.

To take the opposite example, when *I* stood in Tiananmen Square the evening of June 3, prudential considerations won out. I felt a rush of adrenalin at early stages of the fighting, a macho impulse to be where the action was, and deep anger at the government's decision to attack the protesters. I also felt all sorts of good reasons for not being there, including personal safety, and ultimately withdrew. I did so in large part because my sense of who I was had not been put on the line. I was not Chinese; it was not my government or my army that was beginning to attack. I was not even a journalist whose professional identity involved commitment to getting a story or a photograph; I was more committed to being a husband and father and to finishing my book on critical theory. However, none of these aspects of my identity was fixed and immutable. By early June I identified with the student protesters more than I had in mid-April, largely because I had been with them around the clock for six weeks. But I had not been on hunger strike, I had not made speeches, I had not put my career in jeopardy. In other words, I had not been through nearly so transformative an experience as had many Chinese students. Perhaps in some basic sense I was not as brave as they were. But on June 3, some students were brave enough to risk death—students who a month before had not been brave enough to participate openly in the boycott of classes.[9]

Still another side of heroism is the goading of the crowd, as Lu Xu   w in the case of Qiu Jin.[10] She was clapped to death, he wrote, and s) too everyone who demanded escalation, the next jolt of adrenalin, the next shocking challenge to those in power must share in the responsibility for the deaths of 1989. We need to understand heroism and understand the momentum of a social movement that can produce it, but we need not wholeheartedly and uncritically endorse it. It was not a good thing that students were unable to organize an earlier tactical retreat from Tiananmen Square.

At least one observer, Jane MacCartney, has described the students as being caught up in a "cult of the hero." She cites their adulation for Fang Lizhi, the near deification of Hu Yaobang, and an eagerness to achieve heroism for themselves. "The hero was important to the students because they needed someone to look up to but also they each wanted a share of the limelight, the glory of action," she writes.[10] "The yearning for heroism extended to the ultimate sacrifice, an almost hysterical desire for blood."[11] MacCartney's comments are offered in a biting tone, but they certainly capture an aspect of what was going on. Many students tried on the mantle of heroism, making melodramatic declarations on the eve of the April 27 march or at the start of the hunger strike. Just as the classic Chinese psychology of "thought reform" turns on getting individuals to begin to behave in "appropriate" ways even before they have altogether internalized the values, so the recurrent writing of "last testaments" and discussions of possible "ultimate sacrifices" served as rehearsals for the real thing. But it is an exaggeration to say that as a group "the students were almost eager to attain the glory of death."[12] Superheated rhetoric can help prepare one for sacrifice, but is not an altogether reliable indicator of readiness to face death.

Though rehearsals for heroism were important, students (and workers) were not just reading from scripts already written. They were improvising, making up their roles as they went along. Martyrdom became plausible because they had thrown their identities so completely into the movement. Little of them was invested in other relationships, in everyday activities, or at least these other investments seemed to pale besides the magnitude of their cause and the radical commitment they made to it through weeks of fasting, shouting, living fear and excitement and trying on the idea of being a hero.

As we improvise each action, we constantly construct and reconstruct our identities.[13] We do this always in social and cultural contexts. The commonplace events of everyday action—shopping, flirting, asking questions in class, developing a style of dress—all have innumerable possible contemporary models. Even without innovation the range of choice is wide and multiplied by print and electronic media which extend the proliferation of examples beyond one's direct observation. Unfortunately, the number of available models for how to challenge the legitimacy of the government, face the threat of military repression, or suffer execution is fairly small. This makes historical examples such as those provided by Qin Jin and Tan Sitong all the more important. They offer scripts for action in the midst of radical struggle. Moreover, protesters who back down in the face of repression do not live on as positive role models, much less as heroic legends. Our daily lives are full of examples of caution, but our narratives of revolution and popular struggle contain far more tales of bravery rather than of prudent common sense. As a movement takes participants beyond the range of usual experience, they are thrown back more and more on such heroic images in their struggle to find acceptable guidelines for action.

An important part of these images is often the notion of honor. It stresses not only reputation and the esteem of others but also a particular type of self-evaluation that is deeply wrapped up in archetypal patterns of behavior.[14] The judgment of honor is holistic; it does not break down into separable justifications of specific acts as readily as do calculations of interests or evaluations of guilt and innocence. Constructions of honor draw on commendable models that generally come in the form of prefabricated scripts linking together a whole series of actions and events.

Other distinctive features of social identity are reliant on the notion of honor. As Peter Berger has remarked, "the obsolescence of the concept of honour is revealed very sharply in the inability of most contemporaries to understand insult, which in essence is an assault on honour."[15] No such inability hindered the 1989 student movement. Government descriptions of their protests as "turmoil," accusations that they were led or manipulated by a tiny band of foreign agitators, and charges that they were hooligans engaged in antisocial (or antisocialist) behavior all offended them deeply. On the night of May 19, I watched students dither in uncertainty about whether to march yet again to Tiananmen Square, only to be galvanized into immediate action by Li Peng's speech declaring martial law. Amid their tears and shouts they repeated over and over their sense of anger and outrage at his insulting tone. "He lectures us like naughty children." "He speaks like a bad, old-fashioned teacher." "He is so arrogant." Earlier, students had felt similarly insulted by the People's Daily editorial of April 26 condemning their protests as unpatriotic. One of the central student demands became the call for an apology and an official recognition of student patriotism. To a Westerner this demand seemed oddly abstract amid the more substantive calls for freedom of press, freedom of association, or an end to corruption, but it was emotionally central to the protesters themselves (though they were well aware that the other sorts of demands were more fundamental long-term goals).

The rhetoric of salvation and redemption through blood sacrifice had been deployed at many times in the 1989 movement. Liu Xiaobo specifically characterized protest as a civic ritual of redemption. As Barmé puts it, "there was something about these young people who had pledged themselves to death for the sake of a cause that now had as much to do with honor and self-esteem as anything; it was reminiscent of that 'splendid death' (rippa na shi) pursued by the Japanese shimpu pilots."[16]

Honor is linked to the primacy of social hierarchy and at odds with a conception of the world in which individuals are essentially equivalent.[17] Honor (like shame) derives not only from personal reputation but also from the evaluation of collective niches in the hierarchy; one's group must defend its honor against presumption from below and slights from above. These notions are clearly incompatible with the "all men are created equal" ideal evoked most commonly in Western liberalism. Certainly Chinese protesters were drawn to much of Western liberalism and individualism, but they were also moved by a more social notion of the individual person that made possible a stronger sense of collective responsibility. In explaining why he had taken the huge risk—one enormously fateful for his life—of reading *xiaozibao* aloud for the crowd in 1976's Tiananmen incident, for example, Chen Ziming cited *ting shen er chu*—a phrase from classical Chinese literature meaning "show resolve, strike the posture of the hero, stand up and be counted."[18] Chen's action helped lead him into a career of dissent and attempts at reform from outside the system. It changed him from being one of the many members of the crowd to one who stood out for taking risks; it rerouted his personal trajectory from that of more conventional academic life to that of fame (or infamy) and activism. Something of the same consciousness, I think, must have informed the thoughts of Chen's friend Wang Juntao when he wrote from prison to thank his lawyers for being brave enough to defend him at his show trial:

> I feel sad when I see that so many leaders and sponsors of the movement, when facing the consequences, dare not shoulder their responsibility. They will certainly suffer less as a result. But what about the dead?
>
> The dead are unable to defend themselves. Many of them intended to fight for China and her people, for truth and justice. I decided to take my chances to defend some of their points, even if I did not agree with all of them all the time. I know that my penalty was more serious because of all this action. But only by doing so can the dead rest in peace . . . The trial has brought me a sort of relief and consolation. I once again have a clear conscience. . . .
>
> Yet what I am most concerned about is the loss of spirit and morality of our nation. . . . What I value is whether a human spirit has nobility—a noble and pure soul.
>
> In China, even intellectuals lack it.[19]

During the spring of 1989, Chinese student protesters—and some older intellectuals like Wang and Chen—went through a series of experiences that shaped and reshaped the identities of many. They moved from small statements such as marches to more overt acts such as boycotts, petitions, and hunger strikes. They made speeches—simply to each other as well as on television—that affirmed the primacy or even irreducible priority of certain values. They linked these values—freedom, national pride, personal integrity or honor—to their positional identity, seeing them as the particular responsibility of intellectuals. But their actions were more than a reflection of positional interests. Students joined the protest movement largely in blocks of classmates, so their primary immediate social network supported the process of redefinition of identity. Indeed, it seems that those more centrally placed in everyday social networks—e.g., class monitors and other leaders at school—were more active in the movement and felt more obligated to hold themselves to high standards of committed behavior.[20]

Of course, various factors besides the honorable defense of identity underpinned expressions of bravery. Not least of all, I suspect, were largely arbitrary situations the night of June 3 that presented demands for heroism. Nonetheless, though the student protesters of China's Beijing Spring began their protest with a consciousness shaped by their class position and concrete material concerns, the risks they took, the sacrifices they made, and the moral example they provided for the future of democratic struggles in China cannot be understood primarily in terms of that positional identity. We have to see how, for some of the students, participation in the protest contributed at least temporarily to a transformation of personal identity. They not only identified with a larger whole—the Chinese people—or with democratic or other ideals; crucially, these students understood *themselves* in entirely new ways. They held themselves to such high standards of courage and struggle that failing to accept the danger would have meant a collapse of personal identity. That so many rose to the challenge of their own ideals was crucial to giving the events of 1989 their enduring significance.

Glossary

Beida	short for Beijing University
Beigaolian	short for the Beijing Federation of Autonomous Students Unions
Beiwai	short for Beijing Foreign Studies University
chuanlian	to link up
danwei	work unit
dazibao	large character poster
dongluan	turmoil; making chaos
duihua	face-to-face conversation, dialogue
feihudui	"Flying Tigers" (same as *gansidui*)
gansidui	"dare to die" squads
getihu	small-scale entrepreneurs
guandao	official profiteering
guanxi	connections (i.e., influential friends)
hutongs	alleys
jiuguo	national salvation
laobaixing	ordinary people ("hundred old names")
luandong	free-form dancing *or* aimless drifting
minzhu	democracy
pipao	form-fitting traditional female dress
putonghua	"common people's language" (PRC name for Mandarin)
qigong	breathing exercises linking traditional medicine and martial arts
qimeng	enlightenment

Renda	short for People's University
renmin	"the people" (i.e., the masses)
shimin	city people
texie	feature stories
tomingdu	transparency
Waigaolian	short for Federation of Students From Outside Beijing
wenhua re	passion for studying culture
xiaozibao	small character poster
zhendan	live fire
zhishifenzi	intellectuals
zifa	spontaneous
zui	small (as in "small number of people")

Notes

1. See Schwarcz (1992: 111).

2. There are literally scores of published "eyewitness accounts" of the 1989 events. I read all I could find and drew on many in preparing this study. But I have chosen not to try to take these on in academic debate as though they were competing historical analyses. For the most part these early accounts were honorable efforts to "tell the world the truth about us," as students constantly urged Westerners in Beijing to do. None is fully authoritative, partly because no eyewitness can be everywhere. The lack of agreement between sources need not be the occasion for picking quarrels so much as for trying to use all the available sources to make the story—and the analysis—as accurate as possible. Further research has allowed me to improve on my own previously published accounts of the student protest movement, so none is incorporated directly into the present book. Nonetheless, the earlier publications brought me helpful exchanges with other scholars and with many Chinese students who sent me their own observations and reflections. Pages that follow reflect, with greater or lesser modification, articles that originally appeared in *Society, Dissent, Partisan Review, Actes de la récherche en sciences sociales, Praxis International,* and *Public Culture*. I am grateful to the various editors and to the anonymous reviewers for the University of California Press.

INTRODUCTION

1. Quoted in Che Muqi, *Beijing Turmoil: More than Meets the Eye* (Beijing: Beijing Foreign Languages Press, 1990) 102.

2. Later, one of the same group of students added another anniversary he considered significant: Hitler's hundredth birthday.

3. In this they echoed a very common theme of the late 1980s, summed up most famously by figures such as Li Zehou and Su Xiaokang. The former described the two social roles of intellectuals as those of "public conscience" and "enlightener" (see chapter 6).

4. See Dirlik (1978: chapter 6).

5. Schrecker (1991).

6. This was a prominent theme of the influential television series *Heshang* (see chapter 6 for in-depth discussion).

7. In Yu and Harrison (1990: 84).

8. As Tarrow (1989) has argued, social movements in general need to be explained in terms of political opportunity structure, not solely in terms of their internal features (see chapter 4).

9. See Perkins (1990) for a concise discussion. Broader perspectives on reform and its problems are provided in several of the essays in Baum, ed. (1991), Harding (1987), Lin (1989), Shirk (1989), and in Vogel's (1989) study of Guangdong, the province where reform moved most rapidly. Hartford (1990) relates the political economy of reform directly to the student movement.

10. See Walder's (1989: 34–35) concise summary; also discussion in chapter 7 herein.

11. Almost everyone in China belongs to a *danwei*, and many of the crucial decisions affecting one's life are controlled by this unit. *Danwei*s provide housing and often health care as well as work and income. Ranging from peasant communes to universities, hospitals and factories, *danwei*s are a central building block of social organization in communist China and the principal locus of official identity (an ID card presents an individual as a member of a *danwei*).

12. On the shifting fortunes of intellectuals, see Goldman (1981), Shapiro and Heng (1986), Spence (1981), Thurston (1987), Tu (1987), and White and Cheng (1988).

13. There is a substantial literature on the collective history of Chinese intellectuals during this period. See, among many, Chang (1987), Gasster (1969), Greider (1981), Levenson (1959, 1968), Li and Schwarcz (1983–84, which gives a brief English summary of some of Li's major work in Chinese), Rankin (1971), Schwartz (1964), and Schwarcz (1986). On the idea of a public sphere, see chapter 5 herein.

14. Though their analytic orientations differ substantially, Cheek (1988, 1992), Goldman (1987), Goldman, Cheek and Hamrin (1987), Link (1986, 1992), Link, Madsen and Pickowicz (1989), Schell (1988), Su Shaozi (1988), Suttmeier (1987), and various essays in Hicks, ed. (1990) all fill in parts of the general picture of Chinese intellectuals in this period. Useful selections are translated in Barmé and Minford (1988), Barmé and Jaivin (1992), and Link (1983).

15. Fang (1988a: 68–69); see Fang (1988d).

16. Fang (1987b: 137). "Democracy has a very clear definition, which is different from just relaxing a little bit here and there in a controlled society. What democracy means is the basic rights of the people, or human rights" (Fang 1988c: 89). Fang (1991) collects and introduces a number of his writings. Useful commentary can be found in Kelly (1991), Link (1990), Buckley (1991, which is particularly good in illustrating the link between Fang as scientist and Fang as dissident), and Kraus (1989, which offers a salutary critical perspective). See also Fang's interviews (1986, 1987a).

17. The declaration is reprinted several places, including Bachman and Yang, eds. (1991: 158–59). This is a good source on Yan Jiaqi. See also the intellectual autobiography and translations of Yan's work in Yan (1992).

18. The essay is reprinted in Bachman and Yang (1991: 9–18).

19. Bachman and Yang (1991: 85–86).

20. Ibid., 104–5.

21. See Liu (1988, 1990).

22. Liu (1990: 52)

23. Nonetheless, Liu can be self-promoting in his own way. His rhetoric is that

of "a simple writer," but his message is that he has struggled against mighty odds to make things right. Many younger Chinese intellectuals mistrust him as someone ultimately still too close to the Party, one who believes in the same sort of monological truth the Party promotes, albeit different in particulars.

24. Han (1990: 14).

25. See Schell (1988)

26. See Zha (1990) on the founding of one of these. In addition to various PRC publications, several journals helped break down the barrier between mainland and overseas Chinese. *Overseas Chinese Voice (Hai Nei Wai)*, published in the United States; *Jiuzhou*, published in Hong Kong; and *Intellectuals (Zhishifenzi)*, published initially in the United States with Liang Heng as editor, then transferred to mainland China under Liang Congjie (no relation to Liang Heng, but a descendent of Liang Qichao), then brought back to the United States after June 4. Each of these magazines published articles by Chinese scholars from the mainland, Taiwan, Hong Kong the United States and elsewhere; overseas PRC students were particularly prominent in the first and last.

27. For a discussion of "political opportunity structure," see chapter 4.

28. This has been a central theme of resource mobilization theory. See Zald and McCarthy, eds. (1979), Tilly (1978), and the review by McAdam, McCarthy, and Zald (1988).

29. McAdam (1982); see also Eyerman and Jamison (1991).

30. This is not to say that there is complete agreement among accounts or a fully adequate narrative already available. Nearly all the narratives of the movement were written almost immediately after its conclusion. Most reflect their authors' reliance on limited personal observation and sources. I believe the present narrative is the first that attempts to synthesize what is known from the available secondary literature with the author's own firsthand experience and to supplement both with interviews with a range of participants.

31. See especially Bourdieu (1976, 1990) and Bourdieu and Wacquant (1992).

CHAPTER 1

1. Li (1987).

2. Fang (1988c: 93)

3. Fang (1988b: 85)

4. Fang (1991: 169); italics in original.

5. See further discussion in chapter 6.

6. See Black and Munro (1993: 133–35). We know about this meeting now partly because the government bugged and monitored it. But the government was not a simple "enemy"; after all, the organizers were able to rent and use a State Council facility. State and civil society were thus intertwined.

7. Chang (1989: 1). Chang comments that this letter "marks the first time since the founding of the Chinese Communist regime that mainland intellectuals have dared to publicly raise their collective voice despite the possibility that they might be subjected to persecution as a result. It signifies a growing independent political activity among mainland intellectuals." Individuals had previously dissented, of course, and sometimes paid a high price for it, but the collective sponsorship of this letter is noteworthy. It is also significant that the letter was signed by intellectuals of all three of China's main generations, "old, middle aged, and young."

8. Chong (1989).

9. Link (1989: 41). The letters and petitions are briefly summarized by Kelly (1990: 37). Fang Lizhi, though prominent as an individual, was not part of any of the groups signing collective letters or petitions.

10. Quoted in Black and Munro (1993: 370). Black and Munro translate *zhishifenzi* as "intelligentsia" because they think it reduces the ambiguity caused by the differences between Chinese and English meanings.

11. Chong (1989: 4).

12. Shen (1990). See discussion in Chong (1990), which stresses (perhaps exaggerates) the specific interest shown in the work of Karl Popper by many in these discussion groups.

13. See discussion in Zha (1990); also Lee (1990: 95).

14. The colleges had generated some ten million yuan in profit; see Black and Munro (1993: 89–90).

15. Wasserstrom (1991) shows a similar pattern of small discussion groups and voluntary organizations behind student protests in Shanghai between 1919 and 1949.

16. Shen Tong (1990), for example, has chronicled how he was drawn into abortive protest in 1988, how he formed his discussion group, met Wang Dan and other activists, and later became a leader of the protests. His narrative is perhaps the best by any of the students, revealing clearly the unfocused restlessness that was harnessed by the movement in 1989. At the same time, a little skepticism toward such autobiographical accounts is warranted. Both Shen's and Li Lu's (1990) autobiographies are co-authored, ghosted and/or translated, with the collaborators' effect on the story unknown. Both Shen and Li placed themselves firmly at the center of the story and dramatized their "adventure." They were not free of pressure to dramatize; Shen is more prominent in exile than he was in China, partly because the William Morris agency became his publicist.

17. On the May Fourth movement see, among many, Schwarcz (1986); Chow (1960); Goldman, ed. (1977). There is further discussion in chapter 6.

18. "An Open Letter to Beijing University Authorities," April 3, 1989, in Han (1990: 16–17).

19. Ibid., 18.

20. "The Star of Hope Rises in Eastern Europe," March 4, 1989, in Yu and Harrison (1990: 37–8). Wang referred not only to the Polish and Hungarian reform movements and Khrushchev's secret revelations but also to China's "Hundred Flowers Movement," which briefly gave intellectuals license to offer heterodox opinions and criticisms of the Party. All were followed, Wang noted, not by increasing liberalization but by "military-autocratic rule."

21. "Open Letter," in Han (1990: 17).

22. In a China where few details of public events are not meant to be interpreted symbolically, it was no accident that Hu's funeral marked the first occasion in recent years for which China's senior leaders all turned out in Mao suits, specifically eschewing Western suits in mourning a man associated with them.

23. Shen (1990: 166–67).

24. "Why Did the Rally in memory of Hu Yaobang Turn Into a Democracy Movement?" Speech of April 21, 1989, in Yu and Harrison (1990: 42). Ren, a radical leader of the 1970s, still claimed a socialist vision. This orientation was less common among the younger students who made up the bulk of the movement in 1989.

25. But see the very warm appreciation in the reportage-style memoir by a former colleague writing under the name Pang Pang (1989).

26. Interview conducted by another activist during the May hunger strike (in

Yu and Harrison 1990: 154). Note Wuerkaixi's surprising apparent use of the term chaos (*luan*) to describe the events.

27. In Han (1990: 6–7).

28. Quoted from Yi and Thompson (1989: 15).

29. "Open Letter," in Han (1990: 17).

30. Shen (1990: 157–161).

31. Shen (1990: 172).

32. Francis (1989: 905).

33. Translation in Ogden et al. (1992: 84).

34. Gunn (1990: 244) reports, for example, that the first display of protest in Shenyang followed the news late April 20 of the Xinhuamen beatings; see also Esherick (1990), Chan and Unger (1990). Francis (1989) gives an insightful account of the "reactive" nature of the protests.

35. Ironically, according to Feigon (1990: 145) it was students from the Party History department at People's University who played a crucial role in planning this move against the Party's leadership.

36. Han (1990: 72); see further discussion in chapter 6.

37. Ogden, et al. (1992: 87).

38. In Simmie and Nixon (1989: 28)

39. Esherick (1990) suggests that it was not clear whether the rioting that formed the pretext for police retaliation and repression was instigated by agents provocateurs or by young, perhaps unemployed urban workers joining the protests on their own.

40. This act not only followed imperial precedent but also reproduced a common element from protest scripts of the first half of the twentieth century, when radicals had seized on the same dramatic trope (Esherick and Wasserstrom 1990; Wasserstrom 1991). It is not clear however, that students made this connection; to my knowledge, none of the posters defending the act of kneeling do so.

41. Translation in Ogden, et al. (1992: 104–5).

42. "Tragedy of the Age," poster from the Beida Geology Department, April 22, 1989, in Han (1990: 64–65).

43. In Human Rights in China (1990: 53–54). Wuerkaixi's memory of the number of representatives is at odds with the accounts of other witnesses. It also fails to square with photographs; some of these show him stooping slightly but not kneeling.

44. To be strictly accurate, those who say that no organization was allowed outside the direct control of Party and/or state exaggerate. During the reform era, various sorts of business organizations were allowed, and some—for example, the Stone Computer Corporation, with its private research institute—were of considerable stature and public influence. Even before that there were "democratic" parties, a handful of largely docile political parties with which the Communist Party cooperated and that were sometimes even allowed representation at quite high governmental levels. Nonetheless, these were exceptions that proved the rule (or in the former case, challenged it). In general, communist China did not tolerate autonomous public organizations. As Fang Lizhi reported concerning the early organizing at Beijing University: "There were certainly discussions of a multiparty system on big character posters, but the main question was the demand that their autonomous organization be regarded as legal. That is very important, for it relates to the future development of independent organizations." Interview translated in Yu and Harrison (1990: 166).

45. Shen (1990: 197).

46. Li (1990: 123).

47. Shen (1990: 188) gives an account of the news center in chapter 7 of his book.

48. The account in Shen (1990: chapters 7 and 8) nicely evokes the fluid composition of the leadership and the confusion around selection processes.

49. Simmie and Nixon (1989: 31)

50. In Tong and Chan, eds. (1990: 28).

51. See Han (1990: 85–88) for several versions of this rumor, including the slightly milder one Han (a pseudonymous Hong Kong observer) thinks closest to the truth: "There are now 60,000 students boycotting classes; 100,000 students are not striking. We must protect and support those 100,000. Also, of the 60,000 boycotting, the majority can be won over. Workers and peasants side with us; cadres side with us, the democratic parties are also good. We have several million army troops!" Despite the secrecy of top Communist Party and government meetings, key statements always seem to circulate in gossip. Indeed, the functioning of the Party and government depend in part on this unofficial reporting to supplement and provide interpretative frameworks for official proclamations.

52. Note this repeated phrase, which Fang Lizhi recalled as a bit of rhetoric pioneered in the Cultural Revolution. Where the translation reads "an extremely small number of people," the original repeats the adjective "*zui*," as in "a very, very small number." Such repetition was a common way of amplifying abuse or praise in the Cultural Revolution. Interview in Yu and Harrison (1990: 163–64).

53. "We Must take a Firm Stand Against Turmoil," in Han (1990: 83–85). This document has been reprinted in several other translations as well. The correctness of the editorial was reaffirmed in the government's official "report on checking the turmoil and quelling the counter-revolutionary rebellion" issued after the massacre by Chen Xitong, the mayor of Beijing (Chen 1989: 16–20).

54. Han (1990: 63).

55. "A Review of the *People's Daily* Editorial," in Han (1990: 86–87).

56. "Choosing Between the Demands of Party Spirit and the Dictates of One's Conscience," quoted from Han (1990: 90–91); also translated in Yu and Harrison (1990: 121–22).

57. Shen (1990: 197–98).

58. Quoted in Human Rights in China (1990: 61–62).

59. In Chen and Thimonier (1990: 95).

60. Quoted in Shen (1990: 199–200).

61. And as Wasserstrom (1991; also Esherick and Wasserstrom 1990) points out, it was a form of theater used by earlier Chinese student protesters as well.

62. Shen (1990: 203).

63. "My Views on the Success of the April 27 March," in Han (1990: 93).

64. One effect of this tactic was to draw a sharp line between students and other citizens. As Chan and Unger (1990: 272) point out, this may have reflected an elitism on the part of students who "felt ambivalent about the 'lower' social strata joining *their* protest movement." The division, so strongly implied early in the movement, later had to be overcome as the "students' movement" was redefined as a "people's movement."

65. "My Views," in Han (1990: 94).

66. In Han (1990: 93–95).

67. Students had begun to discuss how to bring the movement successfully to a close as early as April 22 (see Shen 1990: 185); the issue resurfaced after every major event. It reappears in this narrative; see discussion in chapter 4.

68. Shen (1990: 263). I have to admit the connection didn't occur to me.

69. In Han (1990: 136).

70. Slogans reported in *Ming Pao* (1989: 43). The *Ming Pao* article and many others give the number of journalists as five hundred; Shen Tong estimated eight hundred (1990: 220). The group looked smaller to me.

71. As Francis (1989: 909) notes, this created a lasting tension between Qinghua leaders and others in the Federation. The representative from Qinghua was the only member of the standing committee of the Federation who failed to attend its founding ceremony on April 26.

72. "The State Council Proposes Dialogue; Qinghua University Students Reject," *HuaQiao Ribao* April 26, 1989, p. 1. Quoted in Francis (1989: 909).

73. "Students on New Dialogue Rules," *Hsin Wen Pao* (Hong Kong), in FBIS, DR/CHI May 1, 1989, p. 59. Quoted in Francis (1989: 910–911).

74. "Dialogues with Students Continue," *China Daily*, May 9, 1989, p. 4.

75. "Yuan Mu Holds News Conference 3 May," Beijing Television Service, FBIS, DR/CHI, May 3, 1989, p. 23. Quoted in Francis (1989: 911). Yuan Mu spoke, of course, of one of the banes of democracy, putting it in its most disreputable light by attaching it to the Cultural Revolution and echoing age-old arguments for centralization.

76. Fang (1987b: 135).

77. Shen Tong's account of the Dialogue Delegation (1990: chapter 9) gives the impression that it was somewhat more closely linked to reformist government advisers than were the Preparatory Committee or the Federation. The Dialogue Delegation seems to have attempted moderation partly on the counsel of senior intellectuals with ties to Zhao Ziyang who hoped to bring off a negotiated end to the protests that would both keep the peace and save Zhao and the official reform program.

78. In Human Rights in China (1990: 63); see also alternative version in Han (1990: 197–99). Chai Ling's remarks are translated from the tape of an interview in late May. Niming (1990) has also noted the phases of students' "learning how to protest."

CHAPTER 2

1. Shen (1990: 236).

2. Quoted in Shen (1990: 237)

3. Quoted in Han (1990: 197–98).

4. Ibid. It is not clear precisely who from the Federation actively opposed the hunger strike. After the fact, nearly all claimed credit for it, including especially Wuerkaixi, the Federation's head:

> [T]he hunger strike, which started on May 13, was initiated by six people, including Wang Dan, Ma Shaofang, myself, and three others. We first came up with the idea around May 8 or 9, and on May 10 we decided to go ahead with it. We held a meeting in a small, shabby, two-table restaurant. After the meeting, we put our money together—a total of twenty yuan—and had a meal. Our call for a strike was immediately answered by Beijing University, Beijing Normal University, the University of Politics and Law, and other schools (in Human Rights in China [1990: 65]).

Some graduate students I knew had argued against the idea, but they were not leading officers of the Federation. In interviews, some students have disputed that Wuerkaixi played a central role and have said that Wang Dan at first urged caution. However, these students agree that both leaders joined in the strike from the beginning.

5. Shen Tong's (1990) account nicely captures his skepticism toward the initial idea of the hunger strike—his uncertainty that the goals were worth dying for and that the hunger strike was the best way to win concessions from the government and build a democratic movement. However, his memoir also conveys the extent to which he was moved by Chai Ling and by the hunger strikers' determination to make a sacrifice.

6. Han (1990: 199–201).

7. Ibid., 203.

8. Ibid., 202.

9. On Tuesday I gave my last lecture at Beiwai. Thereafter the boycott of classes was renewed (though not, I think, because of what I had to say about Max Weber, the origins of capitalism, and its failure to develop in China), and I began going to Tiananmen every day and some nights, usually with one or another group of students.

10. I have checked this impression in several interviews, often getting assent but not with enough clarity to be sure. Han (1990: 199) reaches the same impressionistic conclusion. See discussion in chapter 5 herein.

11. Shen (1990: 234).

12. Wang and Chen were among the most important of all intellectuals working behind the scenes on behalf of the protesting students. Both had been active in pursuit of democracy through China's reform era—indeed, since 1976. See discussion in Black and Munro (1993).

13. In Han (1990: 207–8). The signatories constituted a veritable "who's who" of reform-oriented intellectuals: Dai Qing, Yu Haocheng, Li Honglin, Yan Jiaqi, Su Xiaokang, Bao Zunxin, Wen Yuankai, Liu Zaifu, Su Wei, Li Zehou, Mai Tianshu, and Zhou Tuo. These figures are writers, editors, social scientists, a chemist, and a philosopher. All were more "insiders" than Chen Ziming and Wang Juntao.

14. Shen (1990: 242).

15. Ibid., 243.

16. The Politburo had apparently held secret meetings on May 10 and 11, giving Zhao Ziyang a cautious endorsement for his attempt to arrive at resolution to the crisis by peaceful means. More conservative figures may nonetheless have tried to undermine these efforts.

17. In addition to Shen Tong's (1990: 238–254) account, the People's University Autonomous Student Union printed a detailed statement on a poster (cited in Han 1990: 204–6). Shen tells of one interesting sideline to the abortive dialogue. Zhou Yongjun, the original head of the Federation, showed up at the United Front Building hoping to participate in the dialogue. The delegates from his own school adamantly rejected him, and he was kept out—a *dazibao* had even branded him a traitor for trying without proper authority to end the class boycott on May 4. Whether noted or not, his was a cautionary tale for leaders who would try too hard to be moderating forces. Leaders who called without authority for acceleration of action were never punished—only those who tried to put on the brakes.

18. Shen (1990: 256).

19. The adoption of such military titles has a long precedent—back to the genuinely military Taiping rebellion but more pointedly to the student protests of the nationalist era (see chapter 4). As Wasserstrom (1991) notes, this use of titles was among other things a usurpation of a government prerogative and thus an implicit challenge to authority, not just innocent mimicry.

20. Shen (1990: 262).

21. Zhao may have been trying to prod Deng into siding with the reformers, or he may have been distancing himself from decisions Deng had already backed.

22. Han (1990: 222).

23. In ibid., 219–221.

24. Black and Munro (1993: 183).

25. In Han (1990: 221–22). See note 13 above.

26. Ibid.

27. I marched with the Beiwai contingent, at first uncomfortable about whether I really belonged in this protest; not being Chinese and standing a head taller than almost anyone else, I was highly visible. I decided that democracy was an international goal, however, and observed that the government seemed bent on blaming a "small number of foreign agitators" anyway, even when there weren't any. So I shouted "Long live democracy!" and signed my name on countless shirts proffered by their owners in what became the primary mode of souvenir creation throughout the occupation of Tiananmen Square. Foreign signatures seemed to be particularly sought after, though one wonders whether these shirts did not become rather dangerous souvenirs in the ensuing repression. The Beiwai students were proud of me and of the other, equally obvious Westerner in our group (a blond English professor from San Diego) and kept thanking us "for winning us much more applause than we would have received otherwise." We also bought them lunch.

28. Black and Munro (1993: 188). Erbaugh and Kraus (1990) suggest that in Fujian the students reached out even less to workers.

29. Black and Munro (1993: 201).

30. The very anonymity of the non-Beijing students is perhaps an indication of their marginalization within the movement—and by journalists, who had already formed contacts with those they considered the "established leaders."

31. See Li (1990).

32. Shen (1990: 140).

33. Shen (1990: 276). See also Shen's description of his difficult first meeting with Li Lu (297–99).

34. In exile, Li became perhaps the best English-language public speaker among the Chinese students and thus an especially visible reminder of the 1989 protests and the democracy movement in China, though not organizationally central to the field of exiled activists.

35. The dialogue has been transcribed and translated on more than one occasion. An edited version appears in *Ming Pao* (1989: 81–85); a fuller version is in Chen and Thimonier (1990: 143–53).

36. A Chinese phrase referring to later reprisals.

37. *People's Daily*, May 19, 1989; also in Chen and Thimonier (1990: 154–55).

38. Shen (1990: 281–82) implies that the story about Wang was false and was being spread by Wuerkaixi's supporters to justify his actions.

39. Shen (1990: 281).

40. Quoted in Fathers and Higgins (1989: 74).

41. Ibid.

42. Shen (1990: 287).

43. The specific term "sit-in" was widely used that day and the next, both in English and in Chinese (it also appears in Li Lu's account [1990: 164]). The use of this term self-consciously echoed the American student movement; a few students knew also of the precedent in the civil rights movement. To nearly everybody, the connection with broader, international traditions of protest was important.

44. Li (1990: 164).

45. The speech was printed in the *People's Daily* and is translated in several anthologies, including *Ming Pao* (1989: 93–95).

46. Li may have thought the army had already effectively moved into Beijing

when he spoke. The formal orders imposing martial law indicated that it would begin at 10 A.M. the next morning, May 20.

47. In Han (1990: 258).

48. Ibid., 259–60.

49. See discussion in chapter 7.

50. A rumor later circulated that this was in fact the plan of Qin Jiwei, the defense minister, who advocated a softer line on students and was subsequently condemned with Zhao Ziyang as part of the counterrevolutionary clique.

51. A May 20 Beijing University flyer analyzing the declaration of martial law reported that Wan Li "had given Zhao Ziyang his firm support and had called a meeting of the Standing Committee of the NPC, where almost all [NPC] vice chairmen rejected the . . . decision of the Politburo. Li Peng threatened to punish Wan on the basis of party discipline." In Tong and Chan (1990: 21–22).

52. Simmie and Nixon (1989: 147).

53. It was never clear to me to what extent the apparent reference to the U.S. pilots who aided the Chinese (under Guomindang direction) in World War II was recognized by or significant to either the motorcyclists or their admirers. "Dare to die" (*gansidui*), a term with older Chinese precedents, was associated with Tan Sitong, the student-martyr of 1898 and with republican-era protests.

54. Shen (1990: 305).

55. Gold (1989b) has remarked on the low self-esteem of the *getihu*. Chan and Unger report on the prominence of *getihu* in the protest mobilization in Chongqing, Sichuan, but also report the suspicion and sense of distance that shaped students' attitudes toward them.

56. See Shen Tong's (1990) account of the difficulties involved in establishing and maintaining any links with workers (and also the pressure brought to bear on workers who protested); this is discussed further in chapter 4. Early statements of the BAWU are translated in Yu and Harrison (1990: 107–108ff) and Tong and Chan (1990: 49–60). The best source on workers' organizing in 1989 is Black and Munro (1993).

57. Yu and Harrison (1990: 114).

58. Béja et al. (1991: 223).

59. Handbill of the standing committee, May 21, 1989, in Han (1990: 274).

60. See discussion in chapter 7 of the protesters' emphasis on "ordinary happiness," as against the "higher" virtues of loyalty to or sacrifice for the nation, the Party, and so on. I am indebted to Taylor's (1989) analysis of how the moral elevation of claims to ordinary happiness figured in the rise of the modern Western notion of the self and the reconfiguring of morality in the era of nascent capitalism and democracy.

61. This account is based on Li's recollection (1990: 173–75) and my discussions with him.

62. *Ming Pao* (1989: 114).

63. Guo Haifeng was named general secretary; Zhang Lun was in charge of security (commander of the pickets); and Wang Dan and Wang Chaohua joined them as members at large of the standing committee. In relation to the larger consultative body, Wang Dan was to be coordinator of the students and Bao Zungxung coordinator of the intellectuals. Feng Congde and Zhang Lun both gave this summary of the leadership in interviews; it is also consistent with what Li Lu reports (1990: 175). Li adds that Lao Mu headed a propaganda section and Liu Suli headed a liaison section. I heard slight variations on the composition from other students, though none were as well placed to know.

64. From a brief statement by Chai Ling in May, printed in Yu and Harrison (1990: 173–175); see also Han (1990: 327–28).

65. A text appears in Béja et al. (1991: 325).

66. Li (1990: 176).

67. Two different, nearly homophonic Chinese terms (*gong* with different tones) are translated as "public." One means "collective" in the sense of public property or state affairs; the other means "generally shared." Neither was a prominent term of address for the common people in 1989. On the idea of "public," see chapter 5.

68. The statement is translated in its entirety in Béja et al. (1991: 314–16) and quoted in Black and Munro (1993: 212–13).

69. See further discussion in chapter 5.

70. Quoted in Black and Munro (1993: 223). The *"gong"* in *"gongren"* is yet another homophonic character, though not usually translated as public.

71. Ibid.

72. Béja et al. (1991: 303–5).

73. The phrasing is Li Lu's (1990: 178); he also reports the vote (179).

74. Simmie and Nixon (1989: 152).

75. See *Ming Pao* (1989: 123).

76. Human Rights in China (1990: 112–115; with Cunningham's introduction, 106–112); Han (1990: 327–28).

77. Human Rights in China (1990: 114).

78. Cao Xinyuan, in Human Rights in China (1990: 116–121); this is one of the best accounts of the creation and erection of the statue. See also brief coverage in "Talk of the Town," *New Yorker*, September 16, 1989. A more sustained analysis of the statue in relationship to the history and significance of Tiananmen Square and its monuments can be found in Wu (1991).

79. Shen (1990: 312).

80. As Wu (1991: 109) notes, "this image-making movement began by portraying a new, public hero (Hu Yaobang) in protest against the old, official hero (Mao Zedong)." The placement of the statue was a logical continuation of the pattern.

81. Li Lu hinted at this when I interviewed him later.

CHAPTER 3

1. I used this phrase in the first account I wrote after leaving Beijing in June; I have since found it with remarkable frequency in the descriptions of a range of observers and participants.

2. *Ming Pao* (1989: 129).

3. Han (1990: 356).

4. Munro (1990: 813).

5. *Ming Pao* (1989: 132).

6. *Ming Pao* (1989: 131).

7. Wu (1991: 112–13).

8. Quoted in Simmie and Nixon (1989: 165).

9. Barmé (1990: 59).

10. Ibid., 66.

11. *Ming Pao* (1989: 137–40); all quotations in this discussion are from this text.

12. Quoted in Fathers and Higgins (1989: 90).

13. See the brief discussion in Han (1990: 348); there is also mention of the

opening ceremony in Chai Ling's narration of the night of June 3 in Han (1990: 361–67) and *Ming Pao* (1989: 151–55); see also below.

14. Chen (1989: 40–41).

15. Ibid., 41.

16. Han (1990: 359)

17. Black and Munro (1993).

18. Fathers and Higgins (1989: 110).

19. Actually, the tomb houses a poor peasant woman who was honored by a Ming emperor for taking good care of him when he stopped at her home while traveling. The legend in a sense pays tribute to an emperor with "the common touch."

20. This report is confirmed by Robin Munro's careful research (Black and Munro 1993: 238). Munro puts the first serious violence at 10:30; I thought the confrontation started a little earlier. Another careful attempt at reconstruction of the army's violent advance is presented by Brook (1992), who broadly supports Munro's account (with much more detail, though largely in the form of quotations from sources whose reliability is hard to judge). Brook argues that the numbers killed ran into the thousands.

21. The aftermath of this scene is recorded on Cable News Network's film of the events. See also Munro (1990: 816) for several eyewitness accounts.

22. Simmie and Nixon (1989: 183–84).

23. Chen (1989: 43–44).

24. Fathers and Higgins (1989: 115).

25. Yu Shuo (a People's University professor) in Human Rights in China (1990: 147).

26. Cai Chongguo in Human Rights in China (1990: 132).

27. Munro (1990: 814); Black and Munro (1993: 239).

28. Munro's conclusion is, "Once the troops saw that their initial terror tactics clearly had failed to subdue the crowds, they feared for their lives, and as they advanced along the great east-west artery of Chang'an Boulevard they responded by escalating the level of terror" (Black and Munro, 1993: 239).

29. Comparable but less severe. Westerners must be careful not to imagine that democracy came easily in the West or that government terrorism is rooted in civilizational differences. The repression of the Paris Commune of 1871 was unquestionably more brutal than that of the 1989 Beijing protesters, resulting in more deaths during the fighting itself and more executions afterward.

30. Interview in Béja et al. (1991: 503).

31. Ibid. Unaccountably, Yi and Thompson (1989: 84) describe Yan as delivering his speech "amid gunshots on Changan Avenue."

32. Human Rights in China (1990: 130).

33. From Chai Ling's narration of the massacre, *Ming Pao* (1989: 151); alternative (but still melodramatic) translations appear in Han (1990: 362) and Béja et al. (1991: 375).

34. Black and Munro (1993: 241). In telling their stories of the massacre, students usually portray themselves as counseling persuasion and pacifism; the workers come across as the ones prone to violence. There are likely elements of both truth and class stereotype in the students' recollections.

35. Human Rights in China (1990: 126).

36. *Ming Pao* (1989: 151).

37. E.g., *Time* (1989: 57–58). I first heard this story from students the morning of June 4.

38. Quoted in Munro (1990: 818).

39. Human Rights in China (1990: 165), from the transcript of a recording made by a German journalist. Chen's (1989: 47–48) official account quotes from this text; it is also recorded by Fathers and Higgins (1989: 120).

40. Human Rights in China (1990: 165).

41. Munro (1990: 818).

42. Ibid., 817–18).

43. Hou Dejian, in Human Rights in China (1990: 159).

44. *Ming Pao* (1989: 152).

45. Ibid.

46. Human Rights in China (1990: 158),

47. Munro (1990: 819).

48. Ibid.

49. Hou Dejian in Human Rights in China (1990: 159–162).

50. Human Rights in China (1990: 166–169). It is not clear that the vehicles referred to in the transcription as tanks were actually tanks; they may have been armored personnel carriers or other vehicles with noisy tracks.

51. Chai Ling's narrative in Han (1990: 364).

52. Hou Dejian in Human Rights in China (1990: 163).

53. Cao Xinyuan in Human Rights in China (1990: 179).

54. See, e.g., Yu Shuo's account in Human Rights in China (1990: 176).

55. Munro (1990: 819).

56. These quotations come from the account as reprinted in Yu and Harrison (1990: 176–80).

57. Quoted in Munro (1990: 819).

58. Chen (1989: 48); see also the government pamphlet, "VOA Disgraces Itself" (Chicago archive).

59. Human Rights in China (1990: 168), quoted above. As Rosemont (1991: 22) sums up, "By all non-ideological estimates, at least eight times as many workers and civilians were killed as students in the bloody aftermath." See also Black and Munro (1993).

60. Quoted in Link's narrative in Human Rights in China (1990: 191).

61. Chen (1989: 47).

62. The commander, General Xu Qinxian, was later court-martialed (Black and Munro 1993: 363).

63. *Ming Pao* (1989: 167).

64. Béja et al. (1991: 561).

65. *Ming Pao* (1989: 167).

66. Warner (1990: 306).

67. *Ming Pao* (1989: 167); *Time* (1989: 217). *Ming Pao* claimed that thirty people were killed; another Hong Kong paper, *Wen hui bao*, claimed eight dead and thirty injured (cited in Warner 1990: 310); *Time* claimed only six dead.

68. *Time* (1989: 217).

69. Deng's speech is translated in Yi and Thompson (1989: 188–94).

70. Black and Munro (1993: 260).

71. Esherick (1990: 231).

72. Chen (1989: 46–47).

73. See Wasserstrom (1992) for a description of several of the "myths" that have been constructed and circulated about the protest.

74. Chen (1989: 46–47).

CHAPTER 4

1. The important concept of "political opportunity structure" is generally understood to include not only such transient "windows of opportunity" but also the whole range of features of a political system that makes it open to or inhibiting of social movements. Good sources include Klandermans, Kriesi, and Tarrow (1988); Tarrow (1988, 1989); McAdam (1982); McAdam, McCarthy and Zald (1988).

2. More than most commentators, Walder (1989) notes that although students' motivations and grievances were important, they alone cannot explain the movement, partly because they were long-standing whereas the movement was a brief episode. He sees two factors as crucial: the splits within the Party and the relatively new willingness of intellectuals to support public protest. In different ways, both reflected breakdowns in the Party-state authority structure during the reform era; intellectuals, for example, ceased to be persuaded by Deng Xiaoping's implicit argument that protest could only make things worse and his preferred willingness to exchange a greater advisory role for public quiescence.

3. Quoted in Manion (1990: xxxvii).

4. Wasserstrom (1992b) illustrates several different versions of romantic and tragic narrations of the 1989 events. He sees the tragic form mainly in the narratives of Western observers, whereas Chinese students cast themselves, in his view, as romantic heroes. There is something to this, but I don't think the correlation is so clear. In any case, I want to suggest the qualities of openness and closure rather than the specific complexes of features that make narrative forms romantic or tragic. This said, Wasserstrom is clearly right to see the students portraying themselves as heroic innocents in several of their narrative reconstructions. It is also the case, I think, that foreign observers were drawn not just into the narrative form of tragedy but into a view of the protest that focused on the government and not the students, the outcome and not the movement.

5. See further discussion of this theme in the conclusion.

6. Indeed, Jin Guantao and other Chinese historians writing about the "superstable" structure of Chinese society were among the important intellectual voices paving the way for the movement, as students mounted an attack on that very "immobility" (to borrow Alain Peyrefitte's [1990] phrase for the same phenomenon). See Kane (1989).

7. In Ogden et al. (1992: 203).

8. Ogden et al. (1992: 265).

9. In Han (1990: 18).

10. Jia (1990: 19).

11. The claim to spontaneity is a version of what Adorno (1973) termed "the jargon of authenticity" in his analysis of Heidegger and existentialism; it is both widespread in the modern era and congruent with ancient Chinese praise for intellectuals who sought forceful expression for their inner convictions and remained true only to their own ideals.

12. Li Qiao et al. (1990: 16–17).

13. In interviews during 1987 and 1988, for example, "a number of intellectuals specifically referred to Hu's dismissal as marking a key turning point in their belief that the regime was capable of reforming itself. Zhao Ziyang was not seen as a leader who had a high regard for issues of intellectual freedom" (Saich, 1990: 183).

14. See Bourdieu (1976, 1990) on misrecognition—such as that involved in seeing the exchange of gifts at Christmas as disinterested and spontaneous rather than

shaped by calculations as to the status and likely actions of recipients. Misrecognition is actually a kind of partial recognition and not just a false consciousness.

15. Han (1990: 218–21).

16. Wasserstrom (1991: 320–21).

17. See Wasserstrom's (1991: 208) discussion of Li Jianmin's research on the May 30 protests of 1925.

18. On the idea of a repertoire of protest, see Tilly (1978).

19. See Shen (1990) and Francis (1989).

20. "School protest groups decided, nonetheless, to form special brigades of "monitors" (*jiucha*, sometimes translated as 'pickets'), whose main task was to step in where self-discipline failed" (Wasserstrom 1991: 64). Not all 1989 protesters were aware that the term "*jiucha*" or the translation "pickets" had roots in 1919. Some must have made the connection explicitly, whereas others simply recognized *jiucha* as the appropriate term or learned it from fellow protesters. Many also presented "pickets" as the appropriate translation, though a number of these were not quite sure whether it was a reference to fenceposts or placard carrying labor protesters or something else.

21. Israel (1966), Wasserstrom (1991).

22. Kuhn (1970).

23. Manifesto in Ogden et al. (1992: 316).

24. See discussion in Black and Munro (1993: 204–13).

25. Varieties of constitutional claims were prevalent throughout the protest. One of the key notions—mistaken, alas—was the idea that an appeal to the National People's Congress would offer a way around the monopoly of power in the hands of the Party central committee and top government officials. Thus, the thirty-three intellectuals who in February joined Fang Lizhi's call for the freedom of Wei Jingsheng addressed their petition to the NPC. Nathan (1990: 171) dates to the Li Yizhe group of early 1970s dissidents the introduction of "what was to become a consistent strategy of Chinese democrats, namely, attempting to ameliorate or circumvent one-party dictatorship by taking seriously the provision, found in every constitution of the People's Republic of China (PRC), that the National People's Congress is the supreme organ of government."

26. Kuhn (1970: 24).

27. Wasserstrom (1991: 283); see Esherick and Wasserstrom (1990) for a more general discussion of "political theater" in China's recent prodemocracy movements.

28. See further discussion in chapter 7. Black and Munro (1993) perhaps exaggerate the importance of Wang Juntao, Chen Ziming, and other persevering democratic activists from the 1970s.

29. See Schwarcz (1992) on how problems of historical memory shaped the 1989 movement.

30. Hannah Arendt (1951) analyzed this volatility as a crucial ingredient of totalitarianism, one of the means by which it was perpetuated as well as a by-product of the presence of multiple contending power centers within the state bureaucracy.

31. This has been apparent in the West as various "new social movements" have in recent years sought to establish older lineages for themselves—for example, as feminists have traced roots through campaigns for suffrage back to Mary Wollstonecraft and earlier, and as African Americans have reminded themselves that black struggles for civil rights began not in the 1950s but long before the end of slavery. History offers a sense of shared oppression, ongoing resistance, occasional gains, and some lessons, both tactical and moral.

32. The term is McAdam's (1982); the idea is of course much older, figuring in

a general way in nearly all enlightenment thought—in a more specific sense, in the lineage of modern dialectical thought, notably Marx's, and centrally in the tradition of critical theory. See Calhoun (1995).

33. Zhou (1993: 54). To be fair to Zhou, his essay is not mainly on 1989 but on the Hundred Flowers period and the student protests of 1986; he considers 1989 only in passing. In any case, the "large numbers" phenomenon may coexist with more organized collective action rather than be seen as a mutually exclusive account.

34. Ibid.

35. Many of these officials were linked to Zhao Ziyang and to the various networks of radical reformers he had nurtured and protected. To this extent, their action could be seen as part of a more concerted effort, an ongoing project. But many officials also protected students and other dissidents.

36. Zhou (1993: 58).

37. Ibid.

38. My vocabulary of category and network here is indebted to Harrison White; it was introduced into sociological usage through unpublished lectures and used by Tilly (1978). See White (1992) for more recent discussion.

39. Zhou (1993: 59).

40. Marx (1852).

41. I have argued the latter point at greater length in Calhoun (1983).

42. This is far from unique to communist societies; such categories are also generated within capitalist societies. Categories of consumers may have few lateral links but very similar propensities for individual action. Conversely, many large categories are crosscutting. Race, class, and gender are all important, but race and gender divide the rich, whereas class and racial divisions make it hard to achieve organizational unity among women. How salient any one category remains despite being crosscut by the others is a crucial empirical variable. One of the points of the "new social movement" literature was to show what a diverse range of identities and interests move people to collective action in the modern West (see discussion and a suggestion that this pattern is not as new as the label suggests in Calhoun 1993).

43. As with Australian mateship, this discourse of Chinese friendship addressed primarily male bonding (*gemer yiqi*) or a "buddy" spirit.

44. In sociological jargon, students' ties were "multiplex" rather than single-stranded.

45. Ties formed as early as middle school often retain lifelong salience for Chinese people—even those who go on to advanced education and highly mobile careers.

46. See Wasserstrom (1991).

47. Excerpt from interview, translated in Han (1990: 327). Wuerkaixi attracted even harsher criticism in exile when he not only claimed the limelight but engaged in an unproductive and ill-conceived dalliance with Taiwanese agents.

48. From the French translation in Béja et al. (1991: 353–59); quoted passage on 354.

49. Beja et al. (1991: 356–57).

50. In Han (1990: 327); see Ogden et al. (1992: 344) for an alternative translation. Shen (1990: ch. 7) discusses some of the Beida wranglings.

52. An aspect of this that struck me especially forcefully was most students' refusal to use Marxist and/or Maoist rhetoric in their slogans. Only a handful of explicitly Marxist critiques of Li Peng and his colleagues figured in *dazibao*, and

most of these appeared early in the movement and did not really catch on. For example, on April 24 an anonymous author suggested that Chinese "democracy" was as illusory as the capitalist democracy to which Kautsky had been sympathetic, thus bringing Lenin's ringing rebuke. An even smaller class of Party leaders dominated China than the class of capitalist exploiters that dominated bourgeois countries, the writer argued: "Democracy and freedom have been seriously trampled on, and the people's legal rights have been severely violated. The ideas of Lenin have been defiled, and Lenin is crying in the nether regions" (in Ogden et al., 1992: 111).

If there was a general rhetorical frame for criticism, it was the attack on "feudalism," which was shared with but not limited to Chinese Marxism. Even students who did use some Marxist categories in their analyses during small group discussions, and who might acknowledge abstractly the rhetorical force of using the government's own language against it, never made any effort to develop this in their public pronouncements. I was never certain whether this absence simply indicated that Marxism had been made boring by mandatory political study classes taught from translated Soviet manuals, that it had been deradicalized by its use as an official ideology, or that it had been more deeply discredited by its role in Maoist rule. But protesters did not accuse elites of class rule. Students who in the classroom were keen to discuss Marx's writings on alienation (and who regarded the government's dismissal of these "immature works" as merely an attempt to avoid the charge that alienation continued under socialism) did not use this language in movement gatherings. In this, the 1989 protesters differed substantially from those of 1978–79, who made considerable use of Marxist texts, even using "The Civil War in France" as a basis for conceptualizing democracy. Perhaps the most important reason for avoidance of such writings was simply the much readier availability of other languages of discourse after a decade of Western influence and internal reform.

53. Wang Dan's April 5 meditation "On the Opposition's Freedom of Speech" was an exception: "Truth is not absolute or monolithic. The proletariat may possess the truth, but so may the bourgeoisie or the minority. This is what is meant by 'everyone is equal before the truth' " (Tong and Chan 1990: 78). Of course, this was written before the movement and with the tacit assumption that the only illegitimate attempt to monopolize truth would be the Party's.

54. Todd Gitlin's (1988) extraordinary combination of memoir and analysis is probably the best source on this. Gitlin rightly stresses the role of the media in extending the mobilization beyond the reach of the organization; this too was a factor in China.

55. Qiu Jin is discussed in Rankin (1971) and Spence (1981). I discuss this and other aspects of her example and some of the themes it raises in Calhoun (1991).

56. Lu Xun's comment also stresses the way in which personal identity may be transformed in the course of public action so as to foreclose the options of moderation and retreat (see the Conclusion, below). Qiu Jin's death, like that of many martyrs, fits well into Durkheim's (1895) account of altruistic suicide. See accounts by Rankin (1971) and Spence (1981).

57. Gramsci (1971).

58. By comparison with Poland, say, China's nascent public sphere has few domestic hiding places. It is harder to run seminars in people's apartments.

59. Not only was linking workers, students and other citizens a problem, but links from one city to another and from the cities to the countryside were minimal. Earlier democracy movements had faced this problem as well. Near the end of the Democracy Wall movement, for example, workers began to try to organize links

among those speaking up in different parts of China. A shipyard worker named Hu Qiu called for a nationwide network of unofficial journals (Black and Munro 1993: 60). This threat of linking up—*chuanlian*—was one of the reasons Deng Xiaoping and other Party leaders decided to crack down harshly on the Democracy Wall activists they had earlier tolerated and even encouraged.

60. Erbaugh and Kraus (1990: 151) cite Rod Curnow's report on a visit to a village above Fuzhou on June 6: "The villagers had heard news of the massacre, but were indifferent."

61. Black and Munro (1993: 159, 183, 201–2). See more general discussion in chapters 2 and 3.

62. See Erbaugh and Kraus (1990) on Fujian.

63. See Wilson (1990) for a broader discussion of how the "Polish lesson" figured in China during the 1980s.

64. China's economic planners seem to regard the economy as dangerously "overheated" in the early 1990s but appear unwilling to rein it in for fear of domestic unrest. So long as rapid growth continues, the talk on the streets of Beijing is of getting rich, not of getting democracy.

CHAPTER 5

1. See Wu (1991) on the transformations of the Square in the transitions from imperial to republican rule and then, above all, to the communist era.

2. Emile Durkheim (1915) argued that in order to maintain their cohesion and solidarity, societies required rituals or other means of communication that would reaffirm and reproduce members' sense of moral commitment to the whole. Maoist ritual performances offer models of such communication at least as apt as the religious rituals from which Durkheim drew his examples. Chinese scholars of the 1980s commonly made the link between Maoism and religion. Thus, Wang Luxiang commented about the Red Guards of the Cultural Revolution: "In a country such as China which lacks a religious life, they are perhaps the only group of people who in the depths of their hearts have experienced the religious emotions of worshipping a superhuman man-god and his power" (translated in Wan [1991: 75]). But the moral drawn was often precisely about the weakness of a solidarity achieved in this way, whether in the old tradition of a "great unity" (*datong*) or through Mao's cult of personality. As the May 16 declaration of Beijing intellectuals remarked, "A society with only one voice is not a stable society" (in Li Qiao et al. [1990: 45]).

3. Wu (1991) helpfully situates the Goddess of Democracy statue in relation to the political history of Tiananmen Square and the monuments placed there.

4. Habermas (1989: 8).

5. On the continuing importance of ritual in the construction of Chinese cultural identity, see Watson (1992).

6. Such a conception is echoed in Marx's notion of class consciousness, which he describes as not being a question "of what this or that proletarian, or even the whole proletariat at the moment regards as its aim. It is a question of *what the proletariat is*, and what, in accordance with this being, it will historically be compelled to do" (Marx [1845: 211]). It is also integral to much nationalist rhetoric; see Anderson (1991) and Calhoun (1993). On Mao and Rousseau, see Schwartz (1970).

7. Nationalism, in the sense of presuming and seeking to defend the integrity of a categorical identity, is more helpful than strategic considerations in understanding why neither the People's Republic nor the Republic of China (Taiwan) can give up its claim to authority over all China—and why British rule over Hong

Kong has to be seen as fundamentally illegitimate. Though a more traditional authority structure, such as that of the Chinese emperors, might not have liked having an autonomous kingdom off its coast and might have persisted (as was the case with Japan) in fictions that it was still a tributary subject, it could have tolerated the Taiwan regime more easily than the PRC can, because capacity to exercise authority simply attenuated with distance and military obstacles. The government in Taiwan has been a galling challenge precisely because the communists are committed to a nationalist understanding of Chinese identity.

8. In European political history, the separation of state from society, now celebrated in analyses of Eastern European struggles for Western-style liberalism, was prefigured crucially by the contrast between "descending" and "ascending" authority. Though the first treated authority as devolving from God onto Pope and emperor and thence to lesser lords, the second stressed the role of the community (especially in the Germanic tradition of tribal *Volk* and *Gemeinde*) in recognizing or granting authority to the "best" or "strongest" of its members. See Ullman (1970), Gierke (1934, 1959).

9. Habermas recognizes the classed and gendered construction of the classical bourgeois public sphere but passes it by almost without comment. Even when Habermas later acknowledges the importance of gender inclusion/exclusion, he has a hard time seeing the issue as anything other than a matter of the representation or nonrepresentation of one interest group among many; he does not acknowledge the notion that the exclusion of women raises more basic categorical issues. See, however, his discussion of this point—particularly in response to challenges from Nancy Fraser—in Calhoun (1992).

10. This is not just a casual count but based on the results of the survey described in chapter 7. I attempted a count of marchers only once, on May 15; the marchers were somewhat over 70 percent male. Erbaugh and Kraus (1990) report that protest marchers in Fuzhou were 90 percent male. They also remark on the striking inattention of protesters to women's issues that were becoming increasingly urgent—for example, women were being pushed out of the work force as part of drives to "streamline" enterprises (1990: 151). Feigon (1992) offers one of the few discussions of gender in the 1989 protests.

11. See discussion in chapter 6.

12. This is a problem for Habermas's (1989) classic analysis and a number of studies influenced by it. See Calhoun (1995), chapters 7 and 8.

13. Though the European rhetoric of nation and nationalism did not emerge until the nineteenth century, and although there was significant continuity within Chinese imperial institutions, it is not unreasonable to see the resistance to Qing rule as involving something close to nationalism and national identity from the time of the collapse of the Ming dynasty (see, e.g., Spence [1991]).

14. Li (1987); see also the similar remarks in Su (1989b) and the discussion by Zhu (1989).

15. This was already true in the late Qing and early republican eras, as intellectuals might identify with the strengthening of the navy as much as with the production of "New Culture."

16. Student leaflet translated in Cherrington (1991: 217).

17. Gunn (1990: 251).

18. This is a point that Habermas (1989) does not fully recognize. In his theory the combination of private life and identity formation in civil society provide for the formation of individuals as capable participants in the public sphere. See Fraser (1992) and Calhoun (1994).

19. In this sense, the claim to absolute authority involved in the rhetoric of personal authenticity (the pure expression of the inner self) is also problematic for

a rational-critical discussion, even if it is granted that all individuals have an equal opportunity to such claims.

20. There are, of course, more directly cultural discussions of national identity, but the goal of a single Chinese state remains powerfully evocative.

21. This claim is familiar in Eastern Europe, especially in the writings of Agnes Heller, Ferenc Feher, and a number of other dissident social theorists of the 1960s and 1970s. In the wake of the transformations of the 1980s, the discourse of civil society became a virtually ubiquitous feature of Western discussions of what was distinctive about Western democracy—and, by implication, needed in Eastern Europe. See the collection edited by Keane (1988) and discussion in Cohen and Arato (1992) and more critically in Taylor (1991) and Seligman (1992).

22. This sense of what "totalitarianism" means informs Arendt's (1951) classic usage.

23. Quoted in Chow (1960: 59). A number of recent writers have used the concepts of civil society and public sphere to open up fruitful new inquiries concerning social change in modern China. A burgeoning literature on China's late imperial and early republican periods, for example, draws on Habermas but often equates the "public activity" of elites—especially the creation, transformation, and running of local "civic" organizations—with a political public sphere (see Strand [1989, 1990]; Rowe [1989, 1990, 1993]; Rankin [1986, 1990, 1993]; Madsen [1993]; Chamberlain [1993]; Huang [1993]; and the critical survey by Wakeman [1993]). Though such studies offer insight, they are often less closely linked to the issue of democracy than they may at first appear, especially as they fail to consider both the quality of discourse and the potential to organize effective public discourse at the level of state power. Similarly, in using the concept of civil society to inform discussions of China's 1989 events, it is important not to identify civil society simply with nonstate business institutions and media proliferation per se and to clarify relations among economic, political, social, and cultural dimensions of analysis. See Strand (1990), Gold (1990), Nathan (1990); Whyte (1992); Sullivan (1990); and several essays in Wasserstrom and Perry (1992), including the particularly theoretically sensitive usage in Anagnost (1992).

24. Quoted in Black and Munro (1993: 98).

25. This is a renewal of an older discourse, indebted not only to recent Eastern European and Western discussions of civil society but also to debates on the nature of and supports for "civic virtue" (*gongde*) in the late Qing and Republican eras. Anarchism both struck a chord with earlier Chinese themes and helped this discourse to flourish. See Zarrow (1990) and Dirlik (1986).

26. Such estimates (which are repeated in guidebooks to Beijing) seem to include the streets immediately around the Square. The space officially demarcated as the Square proper seems "only" to hold six hundred thousand people, and to enclose fifty-some acres. See the discussion in Wu (1991).

27. Intermediate associations—groups, networks, and organizations joining people beyond the range of personal connection but below the scale of the state—are a crucial dimension of civil society: they were crucial to Tocqueville's (1840–44) argument about what made democracy sustainable. I refer to intermediate associations specifically rather than civil society in general because the latter term evokes so many different forms of nonstate social organization, including in some usages markets, which are a different matter.

28. See Calhoun (1988).

29. See, e.g., Gold (1990), Nathan (1990), Anagnost (1992), Strand (1993).

30. For the latter argument, see Zhou (1993). Walder (1989: 40) notes the misleading nature of the state-society opposition, citing especially the narrowness and ephemerality of the social reach of movement organization. The 1989 events in

China, he suggests, were more like those of 1956 in Hungary than like the decade-long struggle of Poland's Solidarity union.

31. Consider also, though, the Huaxia Publishing Company, which was a central part of the network of institutions Chen Ziming created to push reform from outside the party. Though Chen was not enough of an insider—and was politically too suspect—to be admitted to the Beijing Young Economists Association, he succeeded in having Huaxia registered under the auspices of the China Welfare Fund for the Handicapped. This was a state-sponsored charity headed by Deng Xiaoping's son, Deng Pufang.

32. For recent works in the international discussion, see Cohen and Arato (1992), Seligman (1992), Taylor (1991), Keane (1984) and the winter 1993 special issue of *Public Culture*.

33. See Black and Munro (1993).

34. On entrepreneurs, businesses and civil society, see Gold (1990, 1991). Just as we ought not to dwell exclusively on markets as such, it is not the mere presence of entrepreneurs that provides for a politically significant civil society, but rather roles that entrepreneurs *can* play if they choose to do so.

35. From the script for *Heshang*, part 6 (in Bodman and Wan [1991: 219]).

36. Some journals, such as the important *New Enlightenment*, were publishable only because they were registered under the legal status provided for book series (Nathan [1990: 181]).

37. And, as one student asked me after a lecture, could China move immediately into the stage of postmodernity, or would it have to be modern first?

38. The so-called "fifth generation" filmmakers associated with the Xian Film Studios—Zhang Yimou, Chen Kaige, and Wu Tianming—were especially influential. Films such as *Red Sorghum* and *Yellow Earth* had presented implicit or explicit critiques of either the Cultural Revolution or more general and ongoing aspects of the Chinese system. Perhaps the most remarkable instance was the television series *Heshang* (*River Elegy*), discussed at length in chapter 6.

39. Like civil society the theme of a public sphere is a revival of an older discourse. It has roots in many different classical and modern distinctions of public from private and is revitalized by new readings of Hannah Arendt (esp. 1958) and by modern feminist theory but perhaps above all by the work of Jürgen Habermas (1989); see also Calhoun, ed. (1992). Distinguishing public sphere from civil society and avoiding the state-versus-society formulations may help to address some of the problems Wasserstrom (1992) notes with the assumption that civil society automatically produces democracy.

40. Fang Lizhi had stressed this ideal against more monological notions of the speech of authorities:

> I hope we may all benefit from this interchanging discussion method. I don't want you to listen to me only. . . . I think, if I have said something wrong, you may refute me. Thus, we shall advance toward democracy. I must stress this. I insist on expressing my own opinion. When I see something wrong, I say it. If my criticisms are incorrect, you may always refute me. This [expression of one's own opinion] may be gradually realized when "both sides are not afraid of each other." I think, democracy is still far away, but at least, outspoken criticisms may create a democratic impression. I mean, we intellectuals are able to play a certain role in democratization (1987b: 135).

41. In Chen and Thimonier (1990: 153). Similarly, a poster offered "An Evaluation of the 'Dialogue' of the Afternoon of April 29": "We have to inquire: was this really a dialogue between equals? or was it merely a father's lecture to his children?" (Han [1990: 113]).

42. Chen (1989: 25); translation in Oksenberg, Sullivan, and Lambert (1990: 70). The government thus used the same sort of contrast that Habermas and other Western theorists have used to describe how the public sphere may "degenerate" from rational-critical discourse among various participants to mere attempts at negotiation among interest groups. The latter, considered typical of welfare-state politics (and discussed by political scientists under labels such as "consociationalism" and "corporatism"), is a degeneration because the parties no longer seek by discussion to discern their greatest common interest but simply seek compromises among the self-interests they had already established prior to interaction.

43. Thus members of different work units marched together under the banners of the *danweis* or hung banners from windows. They were recruited not as discrete individuals but as members of these groups. On block recruitment as a general phenomenon in social movements, see Oberschall (1973). Shi (1990) and Niming (1990) discuss the importance of *danweis* as units of action; Shi stresses also the limited extent to which *danweis*—outside those composed disproportionately of intellectuals—were mobilized.

44. However, the CCP should be recognized as a significant crosscutting association, albeit one skewed toward government. In single-party political systems the party itself always becomes the setting for political contestation and at least some diversity. Although open factions were not tolerated in the Chinese Communist Party, networks certainly linked individuals with shared backgrounds or views— and to a significant extent worked to protect those who had expressed minority opinions and others out of favor at any one moment.

45. Wan (1991: 65); Lull (1991: 23).

46. See chapter 6.

47. Chinese intellectuals are apt to point out that the peasants are not "politically active" in China—an irony for the country in which Mao pioneered the idea of peasant revolution. It is unquestionably true, however, that in China urban people have more political clout. Throughout the Third World, urban people tend to have more power than their rural compatriots. This is a key reason they are usually better fed: Urban food riots threaten to topple regimes; rural people simply starve. An infrastructure of effective transportation and communications may begin to change this state of affairs by allowing people in remote locations to receive information about what the government is up to and to put pressure on officials. Only with some of the reforms of the 1980s have China's peasants begun to eat well (and acquire a variety of consumer goods) on a regular basis—sometimes even exciting the envy of city dwellers.

48. The day after the Tiananmen massacre my friends and I began to feel an acute deprivation of news. We talked to everyone we could, especially anyone adventurous enough to have ridden into the center of Beijing to see the army deployments and the remnants of struggle. We tried to sort through the many rumors. But we suffered for lack of television and newspapers; we huddled around radios trying to hear the BBC or Voice of America above the static and squeals of the jamming. Only two weeks earlier we had enjoyed the freest press in the history of the People's Republic. Now it was almost impossible to find out anything. The television played irrelevant soap operas and Kung Fu movies; there were no news broadcasts, not even lies. Even telephone service from our university to different parts of Beijing was interrupted. What we could know firsthand had, perhaps, a special veracity but was hardly the whole story.

My foray to the Shangri-La with two friends (see chapter 3) was an attempt to pick up a "complete" view through the use of telephones and mass media. We lived crucially in both the physical space of Beijing and the formless space of the international information flow. The army had made the first cease to function as a sphere of public discussion, as citizens retreated into private spaces and private conversations in the face of public terror. The second become all the more important, if more problematic at the same time.

49. Black and Munro (1993) even report that Wang Juntao and Chen Ziming used beeper services to keep in touch with their colleagues at the Beijing Social and Economic Sciences Research Institute.

50. Money sometimes flowed through those same channels. Electronic banking technology was useful in transferring donations from abroad quickly to the students mounting the occupation of Tiananmen Square. This capacity contributed to the acceleration of the events; earlier in the twentieth century it had often taken weeks for donations to reach Sun Zhongshan's (Sun Yatsen's) revolutionaries.

51. "In the field of journalism, numerous developments of the post-Mao reform period have heightened the importance of knowledge and training, intensified group identity among news workers and brought the public service ideal to the fore" (Polumbaum 1993: 297). See also Berlin (1993) and Tan (1993).

52. In Tong and Chan (1990: 47).

53. Walder (1989: 39).

54. Tan (1993: 285–91). The following account adapts Tan's analytic categories; some, though not all, of the examples are also his. See also the brief discussion in Faison (1990).

55. Part of Yang Shangkun's speech is translated in Han (1990: 258).

56. Xinhua also monitored journalists and intellectuals for the Party, supplementing the efforts of the Public Security Bureau. See, e.g., Black and Munro (1993: 39) on Xinhua's forwarding of "black reports" concerning Chen Ziming.

57. Tan (1993: 290).

58. So powerful was this story that it represented a major coup for Dan Rather and CBS, which had committed to heavier coverage of the Gorbachev visit than either of the other major U.S. broadcast networks. After the massacre, ABC's Ted Koppel and NBC's Tom Brokaw rushed to Beijing to try to catch up with Rather's scoop. Perhaps the most consistent coverage came from Cable News Network (whose prestige rose enormously as a result).

Though the American media were prominent, they were far from the only major international press organizations covering Beijing. The BBC and Independent Television News from Britain were both active, along with a number of British print journalists; French, Spanish, German, Italian, Finnish, Danish and a host of other European correspondents moved among the protesters. From Japan came both employees of the main news organizations and freelancers (some of the latter partly because of their own backgrounds in Maoist-inspired left-wing activity). Several of the Japanese freelancers, along with Hong Kong Chinese, were among the most courageous in video-recording the massacre and attendant events. And a central role was played by Chinese reporters who came from Hong Kong, Taiwan, Singapore, North America, and elsewhere outside the PRC. Much of the coverage that excited interest in Eastern Europe came from the wire services and the Western media, but of course a number of Russian journalists were also in Beijing to cover Gorbachev.

59. Consider, by contrast to the number of Westerners who have heard of Tiananmen, how few have heard of Kwangju—where South Korean government troops killed at least two hundred prodemocracy demonstrators in 1980 and which has since been the scene of major annual protests.

60. Gunn (1990: 251) reports that in Shenyang, finding the stations was a matter of trial and error because of the jamming, but one station or another was always audible somewhere on the airwaves.

61. Harvard's Barone Center on the Press, Politics and Public Policy (1992) has published a fairly extensive analysis of U.S. press coverage.

62. As Fang Lizhi put it, "You can go travel in the villages and look around; I feel those uneducated peasants, living under traditional influence, have a psychological consciousness that is very deficient. It is very difficult to instill a democratic consciousness in them; they still demand an honest and upright official; without an official they are uncomfortable" (quoted and translated by R. Kraus [1989: 298]; see also Fang [1988c]).

CHAPTER 6

1. Fang (1991: 138; 1987b: 127). The phrase "complete Westernization" had been in use since Tan Sitong and the rebellion of the *jinshi* examination candidates in 1895.

2. Orville Schell (1988) nicely documents much of this.

3. Su (1989a: 273).

4. The process started centuries ago with missionaries, traders, and soldiers. It reached a dramatic focus in the early twentieth century. See Schwarcz (1992), which includes also a useful discussion of the role of "commemoration" of earlier events in the drama of 1989.

5. See Lee (1990) and Watson (1992).

6. Spence (1981) is an excellent introduction to this history. See also Lee (1987) and Chow (1960).

7. This formula has numerous variations in translation, such as "Chinese learning as the goal, Western learning as the means." It was coined by Zhang Zhidong in 1898. The division of "essence," or fundamental structure of values and spirit, from "practical use," or mere utilitarian skill, reflected an opinion about Western knowledge in relation to Chinese. It also reinforced a classical division between Confucian scholarship and moral elevation, on the one hand, and the merely practical skills of craftsmen, astronomers, engineers, and so forth, on the other hand. The achievements of the latter were deemed narrowly utilitarian, rooted in the accomplishment of some external result rather than the cultivation of personal qualities. Japanese thinkers had used somewhat similar formulas in their attempts to distinguish a Japanese cultural essence from the enormous range of Chinese imported knowledge: "Japanese spirit, Chinese skill" is attributed to Sugawara Michizane (A.D. 845–903). There are brief discussions in Chow (1960: 13–14) and Schwarcz (1986: 5–6); see Levenson (1968) for a more sustained discussion of the Confucian context for this formulation.

8. Quoted in Schwartz (1964: 49).

9. Schwarcz (1992).

10. Quoted in Schwarcz (1986: 37).

11. Ibid., 38; see also Feigon (1983).

12. In 1988 Xu Jilin wrote an essay called, "On the Independent Personality of Intellectuals," a title echoing Chen Duxiu's concern with autonomy. It was published in the "New Enlightenment Series," a further reminder of the link to the New Culture movement of the republican era—as well as to the Western Enlightenment. Xu argued that intellectuals were called upon to play two roles, enlightener and public conscience, the latter a more critical version of the national salvation ideal (see Bodman [1991: 72–73]. Like many other translators of this discussion, Bodman uses the term "cultural luminary" instead of "enlightener." Though the French *lumière* might work, this term does not convey quite the right sense in

English. Xu and others were not speaking of being famous (a contemporary English implication of "luminary") so much as of bringing light. The Chinese term in question is the same used to refer to the eighteenth-century European Enlightenment, *qimeng*.

13. Quoted in Chow (1960: 59)

14. Ibid., 5.

15. It is worth noting, however, that in the 1919 protests, "science and democracy were widely accepted goals but conspicuously absent from the slogans of May Fourth, which voiced more immediate political demands" (Israel [1992]). By 1989 these words had both come to symbolize the May Fourth–era protest and taken on a new significance as a way to liken the now devalued communist regime to its own hated precursors. If the government of the PRC was "feudal" in 1989, as students charged, then it was likened not only to the imperial dynasties but to the warlords and to Chiang Kaishek.

16. Schwarcz (1986: 36).

17. Ibid., 38.

18. Schwarcz (1992: 114). Conversely, and demonstrating how frequently the two terms were invoked together, Su Shaozhi had said in 1986, "Without a spirit of democracy, there will be no spirit of science" (quoted in Gittings [1989: 212]).

19. Translated in Béja et al. (1991: 335–41; quotation from 336).

20. Quoted by Schwarcz (1986: 33), following Sato Shin'ichi.

21. Ibid., 20. Yet this is not altogether unique to China. Writing in the vernacular, rather than in Latin, was one of the crucial developments that paved the way for the European enlightenment; a figure as modern as Hobbes was a pioneer in this regard. In the European enlightenment, and in the development of modern consciousness more generally, literature played a central role. Similarly, in nationalist and other radical movements throughout the Third World, literary production may be *the* central means by which elite intellectual ideas are circulated and introduced into broader discussions.

22. Quoted in Black and Munro (1993: 42). The poems were written by Huang Xiang, a former Red Guard and sent-down youth who was a member of the "lost" or "in-between" generation so prominent in China's cultural and political struggles. Huang Xiang later started a mimeographed magazine called, like so many landmarks in the history of modern Chinese intellectuals, *Enlightenment*.

23. The "misty poetry" (*menglongshi*) was the most celebrated—and most widely attacked. Discussion and translations appear in Barmé and Minford (1988); see also McDougall (1985), Tay (1985), and Yeh (1990).

24. Translation from Barmé and Minford (1988: 18).

25. Yeh (1990: 6).

26. Beijing University critic Xie Mian became a minor hero for standing up against the old poets and defending the "misty" poetry as an authentic and important part of modern Chinese literature.

27. The Democracy Wall protests were the most important of the previous popular struggles of the reform era. They were mounted largely by intellectually alert young workers and veterans of the Cultural Revolution, including most famously Wei Jingsheng, Wang Xizhe, and Xu Wenli. One dimension of their protest was a call for China to live up to some of the democratic ideals that had been promulgated in the early years of the Cultural Revolution itself but that seemed betrayed by both the later history of the Cultural Revolution and successor regimes.

28. Barmé and Minford (1988: 236). Bei Dao's poetry was only occasionally political, though its iconoclastic individualism made it nearly always fairly radical and moving to young people. Though he was not personally flamboyant in the

same way, and his style is not the same, his artistic stance is in some ways reminiscent of Xu Zhimo's seventy years before.

29. The story is translated in Barmé and Minford (1988), and the criticism reprinted on p. 29. The critic goes on to suggest that in this story Liu "has revealed that he lacks a firm basis in life, and that he is out of step with the world around him."

30. Interview in Guan (1988: 44).

31. See Barmé (1990).

32. Ibid., 57.

33. Ibid., 76.

34. McDougall (1985: 238).

35. Yeh (1990: 10).

36. Wang Qingpan, quoted by Yeh (1990: 12).

37. In Zhang's (1990: 2) words, reportage literature is "a new genre of narrative that cuts across the conventional borders between fiction and journalism, fiction and history, and fiction and politics, and thus invites us to rethink critical concepts such as fact, fiction and history." In some ways similar to American "investigative journalism," reportage writing includes much more fictionalizing of its subjects, even though it is meant to deal directly with actual conditions.

38. See Schell (1988); Liu (1990).

39. Guan (1988).

40. Quoted in Schell (1988: 173).

41. Liu (1988: 33).

42. Liu, Ruan, and Xu (1989: 25).

43. Liu (1990: 171).

44. Link (1989: 40)

45. Quoted in Zhang (1990: 3); Zhang continues with an interesting discussion of this definition, focusing not only on its claims about "the real" but also on its interesting image of the "light cavalry."

46. Liu, Ruan, and Xu (1989: 25). Liu Xiaobo and Liu Binyan had clashed repeatedly.

47. Liu, Ruan and Xu (1989: 25–26).

48. Su (1989: 277–78).

49. Su Xiaokang (1988) attempted to coin a new term, or perhaps to name a new genre of televised political commentary, *dianshi zhenglun pian*.

50. See discussion in Bodman (1991, esp. 38–40).

51. The *shang* term in the title takes its meaning partly from allusion to third century B.C. poem, *Guoshang*, ascribed to Qu Yuan. It is a lament for soldiers who died in battle. As Bodman (1991: 3) notes, moreover, Qu Yuan is a Cassandra figure, the archetype of the loyal minister whose prophecies of doom go unheeded by his king. This is an allusion that would be understood by many educated viewers but not by the entire public reached by *Heshang*. It thus offers an example of the many levels on which the series can be grasped.

52. By Wakeman (1989), Lee (1989, 1990), Yi (1989), and Bodman and Wan (1991), respectively. Each translation shifts the English connotations slightly; I will henceforth generally use *Heshang*, but the reader should keep in mind the complexity of interpretations of the Chinese title.

53. This general framework reached back before Marx to Hegel; the theoretical framework of the film was also indebted to Toynbee, Wittfogel, and others who had analyzed China as a "hydraulic" society dominated by the need to control floodwaters and achieve irrigation. Jin Guantao's theory of a "super-stable" society was a synthesis of such views. The emphasis of this Chinese appropriation, however,

was slightly different from that of most of its Western predecessors. The Western literature followed from thinkers like Montesquieu, who in his *Spirit of Laws* had asked what explained variations in patterns of legitimacy and power and offered an answer that turned largely on climate and geography. Hegel picked up this idea, shifting attention even more to geography. But what the Western thinkers were attempting to explain was primarily "Oriental despotism," an important motif in their efforts to distinguish the liberties they took to be characteristic of Western societies. This political result was the central focus of their accounts of China's arrested development. The Chinese authors shifted the emphasis to the arrested development itself, putting the political implications more in the background. It was precisely China's super-stability, its incapacity for progressive change, that Jin and others lamented. They sought political liberties (or democracy) as an aspect of openness, of forward historical movement and a break with the cycles of the past, even more than as an end in itself.

The actual historical analysis in *Heshang* is problematic, though that is not our concern here. See discussion and references in Bodman and Wan (1991) and Wakeman (1989). Not only is Chinese history presented in a tendentious fashion, but "the West" is collapsed into a highly simplistic and uniform phenomenon—as is common in Chinese thought.

54. Translated in Yeh (1990: 7); see discussion of Bei Dao's use of the image of the sea in McDougall (1985).

55. This and all future quotations from the script are from the Bodman and Wan (1991) translation. This quotation is from p. 116.

56. Bodman and Wan (1991: 133–34) note that the metaphor of hair that can neither be cut nor combed both comes from an ancient poem and can be read as a play on words suggesting the simultaneous futility and inescapability of both efforts to bring order (*li*) and turmoil (*luan*).

57. Ibid., 140.

58. Ibid., 152–53.

59. Ibid., 169–70.

60. Ibid., 190.

61. Ibid., 276.

62. Ibid., 210–11.

63. Ibid., 153.

64. Ibid., 219.

65. Ibid., 212.

66. Though my analysis has focused on the content of *Heshang*, and though this content was exciting and even startling, it cannot account by itself for the success and influence of the series. *Heshang* was also technically surprising and sophisticated—especially by Chinese standards. It worked mainly through montage, with extremely rapid cuts from scene to scene (influenced, I suspect, by Hong Kong film fashions and reminiscent of recent trends in American TV advertisements and music videos). In the space of a few seconds, a viewer might see the Great Wall, the Gobi Desert, Confucius, the blue Mediterranean, Venice, clipper ships, the Houses of Parliament, and John Locke. *Heshang* intentionally purveyed more information than any viewer could take in at one showing, especially more than he or she could assimilate within received categories. It thus left the viewer with a welter of unresolved impressions. The voice-over provided only a partial framework for understanding. The film's real message, which was left just short of explicit, was heavily dependent on visual images. As Gunn (1993: 258) remarks, "If the series is verbally a modernist work, it is visually postmodernist."

67. See discussion in Lull (1991: 67ff).

68. The series, moreover, did less than it might have to present varying views as a support for discussion. As Leo Lee (1990: 94) has remarked, *Heshang* has shown that "post-Mao political discourse remains essentially in the Maoist mode even as most of the intellectuals are becoming vehement anti-Maoists. In other words, their rhetoric in "monologic[al]."

69. Bodman and Wan (1991: 219).

70. Among the makers of *Heshang*, the two principal writers (Su Xiaokang and Wang Luxian) and their coauthors (Xie Xuanjun, Yuan Zhiming, and Zhang Gang) were of this crucial generation. The director, Xia Jun, was a little younger. Bodman (1991) and Wan (1991) offer very helpful discussions of the background to the film, including the generational issue. See also Gunn (1993). My discussion of the film is greatly indebted to their annotated translation of the film script (Bodman and Wan, 1991). There are other translations, mostly of relatively small fragments, but none approaches the Bodman and Wan version with regard to either care or provision of contextual information. I am also grateful to Leo Ou-fan Lee, Benjamin Lee, and other members of the "Center Forum" at the Center for Transcultural Studies with whom I first viewed *Heshang* in 1988 and whose commentaries were very insightful.

71. Wu Dunn (1990: 32).

72. See Black and Munro (1993).

73. Quoted by Wan (1991: 76). Wan offers a very helpful discussion of this issue of generational identities; see also Kelly (1990: 42).

74. Bodman (1991: 23) elaborates: "The classes that entered college in 1977 and '78 consisted of many students who had been forced to wait ten years for the opportunity, and the entrance examinations were particularly competitive. Ten years later it would be this group of graduate students and young professors who would be most active in the movement to reevaluate traditional Chinese culture and from whom many of the authors and advisors of *Heshang* would be drawn."

75. Su (1989a: 290–91). The girl who wrote the letter was born when the Cultural Revolution was all but over; she could hardly be said to have lived through it.

CHAPTER 7

1. Just to give an idea of how frequently the song was sung, here is the account of student presence at Hu Yaobang's memorial service produced by Li Qiao and other intellectuals shortly after the event:

> At 8:00 that evening more than 100,000 students marched out through the gates of Beijing's universities carrying banners and heading for Tiananmen Square. Along the way they were cheered on by several hundred thousand citizens, who formed two great walls on either side of the column of marching students. Many chimed in when the students sang the "Internationale," and many were moved to tears. . . . Around midnight, after some five hours of marching, the demonstrators, representing all the institutions of higher learning in Beijing and Tianjin's Nankai University finally reached Xinhuamen. They shouted the slogan,, "Remember Hu Yaobang," sang the "Internationale" and the national anthem, formed themselves into ranks, and proceeded in orderly fashion to Tiananmen. . . . At 3:00 A.M. . . . standing in the chill of early morning, the lightly clad students shivered in the breeze. Their enthusiasm undaunted, they continued shouting, "Long Live Freedom! Long Live Democracy!" and sang the "Internationale" at the top of their lungs. At 7:25 A.M. . . . after the national anthem, the "Internationale" was heard again. Just past 8:00 A.M. on the steps in front of the Great Hall and behind the wall of troops there began to appear those

officials and representatives of all walks on life who were invited to the official memorial service. At that moment, two hundred thousand voices joined to sing the "Internationale" (Li 1990: 25–27).

The "Internationale" was sung no less than five times in the twelve hours chronicled. It was sung at least three times during the students' last hour at the Monument to the People's Heroes, before they withdrew from the Square the morning of June 4.

2. Forward (1990: 297).

3. It follows, of course, that the ideals of the protesters were not altogether hostile to those of international socialism and the early Chinese communist movement, despite their feelings about the current regime.

4. See, e.g., "Uproot Obscurantist Rule, Live Again as Chinese," translated in Ogden et al. (1992: 313), which develops the theme of the need for the Chinese people to depend on themselves and not hope for a savior.

5. The Chinese version was translated from the Russian by the early communist leader Qu Qiubai in 1921 and published in *The New Youth* (a key communist magazine of the "new culture" era). The Chinese version differs in several particulars from both the original French and the Russian (as well as the almost unsingable English). The images of "gods [literally, 'celestial beings'] and emperors" and "poisonous snakes and brutal beasts" are traditionally Chinese, the latter a common label for targets of popular resentment. In the last line, "*Internationale*" is not translated but given Chinese characters designed to simulate the French pronunciation of the word so that singers in China could share with those everywhere else a single word evoking a common ideal. It is "L'internationale" in French and "the International Party" or "International Union" in English. Significantly missing from the Chinese version is the claim of the French and English versions that "the International Party shall be the human race" ("L'internationale sera le genre humain"). The call to "break through the cage of old thoughts" in the second stanza is also distinctively Chinese, an echo of May Fourth–era emphasis on "new culture." The line in French and English evokes a characteristic religious heritage, "to free the spirit from its cell" ("pour tirer l'esprit du cachot").

6. In Barmé and Minford (1988: 277).

7. Translation in Ogden et al. (1992: 358).

8. The words were written by Eugene Pottier in June 1871 as the army closed in on Paris; Pierre Degeyter set the words to music for an 1889 labor congress.

9. Translation in Barmé and Minford (1988: 400–401).

10. *Ming Pao* (1989: 123); this is a somewhat condensed translation. I have changed the term 'civilians' to 'urban citizens,' which more accurately captures the students' sense.

Note the tension between the claims of the second sentences of points 1 and 7. They are not strictly contradictory because the emphasis falls on the extra-party *origin* of the movement, but point #1 betrays the widespread tacit assumption that what happened in the Party was the true determinant of the future. Points 4, 5 and 8 go on to take sides in intra-Party struggles.

11. These two ideals have been joined in the West as well. The ideal of national self-rule could be simultaneously an articulation of the rights of "the people" as against a monarch and of the nation as against others. In countries like France and the United States, the political ideals of republican government and democracy were part of the definition of nationhood as something achieved by revolutionary political action (rather than claimed on the basis of inherited culture or ethnicity as in Germany). See discussion in Calhoun (1993; 1995, chapter 8).

12. This quotation and others without specific citation in the following paragraphs come from my interviews in May and June. On several occasions in mid to late May, I invited students and others in the Square to respond to open-ended questions or simply to write down anything they would like to communicate about the movement. Translations of the statements were made by other Chinese students, and checked later in the U.S.

13. In Ogden et al. (1992: 345).

14. The most sustained English-language inquiry into contemporary Chinese understandings of democracy is in Nathan (1985); see also Nathan (1990). It should be said that there is no reason to doubt that by some definition of the term, the idea of democracy enjoyed widespread support in China. In 1988 the Opinion Research Center of China, a branch of the Beijing Social and Economic Sciences Research Institute, conducted a survey that found that 72 percent of those polled agreed that "Democracy is the best form of government," and 79 percent disagreed with the proposition that "If we implement democracy in our country now it will lead to chaos" (Black and Munro, 1993: 132).

15. As this story should make clear, our survey was hardly a perfect exemplar of representative sampling or other virtues of scientific accuracy. However, we have looked for evidence of systematic biases in the data and not found much. Representation of colleges and universities is extremely broad, for example. Still, the data—which in any case are not enormous in scope because we intentionally kept the instruments very brief—should be treated as suggestive and/or confirmatory, not the source of an objective final answer.

The first version of our student survey was completed by 112 people, the second version by 109. In each case, all but four (i.e., over 96 percent) indicated that they were full-time students; of the eight others, three simply did not answer and four gave other occupations. All were with student groups in the Square at the time of the survey (and we have included them in the results reported here, though in fact their responses make no material difference). We took the "bystanders" survey into the field on two successive days, gathering responses first near Tiananmen and second at a major intersection several miles away.

16. In 1919, intellectuals pointed to machine politics and other examples of the problematic nature of elections in the West; I heard no similar comparisons in 1989.

17. Again, respondents could name up to three goals. This question elicited some of the most active debate and rewording in the pretest period as students worried about whether it would be understood accurately as asking the respondents for their own evaluation of importance or for their guess as to what the students thought most important. Whether respondents definitely understood and responded to the former question is still subject to some doubt.

18. People out and about enough to be interviewed as "bystanders" were more likely to be supportive of the movement than a representative sample of the Beijing population would have been. They included twenty-five workers, fifteen officials, eighteen private business people, six teachers, four farmers, four clerks, four people "waiting for work," two journalists, and sixteen students at various levels.

19. Chan and Unger (1990: 268) report that in Sichuan students emphasized issues like honesty in government, while "the demands of workers' representatives concerned job security, pay, and welfare benefits."

20. Johnston (1986) contrasts "integrative" to "disintegrative" corruption; see also Meaney (1991) for a consideration of this distinction in the specific context of 1989.

21. Meaney (1991) rightly stresses how the dual economy of plan and market increased corruption generally, and also how nepotism made some corruption par-

ticularly disintegrative. Meaney also makes a good point by indicating how the rapid influx of overseas Chinese capital contributed to higher levels of (often disintegrative) corruption. Solinger (1991) and Oi (1991) also discuss the place created for corruption by the partial transition from plan to market.

22. See Gold (1985).

23. Debunking the image of upright communist officials has become a major occupation for both Chinese and Western writers in recent years. The numerous reports of profiteering and oppression exercised by local party bosses and officials both petty and grand do not, however, provide evidence that there has not been a substantial increase in grasping behavior, in its tacit acceptance and even its public recognition.

24. The ideas of official profiteering and corruption might seem equivalent to a Western reader, and indeed I had not made this distinction in my initial draft of the questionnaire, but in China these are distinct concepts—if closely related—and distinct terms, so we included both in the question.

25. Saich (1990: 191).

26. Gold (1989a: 9).

27. Taylor (1989: 211). Taylor emphasizes the importance of the Protestant Reformation, and in a sense, his account of the affirmation of ordinary life is a reworking and expansion of themes treated by Max Weber in *The Protestant Ethic and the Spirit of Capitalism*, with less emphasis on "worldly asceticism." Praise for sober and disciplined production might have been the first prominent version of the new affirmation, but it was far from the only way the affirmation could find expression.

28. Schell (1990: 420).

29. In the 1980s, any number of short stories, novels and pieces of reportage explored the new themes of sexual fulfillment, marriage for love versus disastrous forced marriages, the acceptability of divorce, and similar themes. For discussion and a few samples in translation, see Barmé and Minford (1986: 199–231) and Barmé and Jaivin (1992: 293–311). This theme has a significant history and like so much else in the 1980s, a resonance with the 1920s. See Decker (1993).

30. No works describe the immediate human quality of this new consumption better than Orville Schell's (esp. 1984, 1988).

31. The link between protest and the sense of relative deprivation amid rising affluence has been widely recognized; see Davis's (1962) famous "J-curve" explanation of revolutions.

32. Quoted by Schell (1990: 423) in an article that gives a good brief introduction to this theme.

33. In Han (1990: 198).

34. Discussed in chapter 2 above; see Li (1990: 173–5).

35. Only one man of seventy-five answering the question, "Do you agree with the goal of democracy for China?" said "Somewhat"; none said "Not much/a little" or "Not at all." Five of the twenty-eight female respondents gave one of those three answers, three of them "Not much/a little."

36. The least optimistic groups were members of the armed forces and officials, particularly the former.

37. Even this army officer indicated some support for the movement; only one respondent (another army officer) out of 107 answered that he did not support the student movement at all.

38. Of course, not every student would make the same distinction between deposing specific leaders and building democracy. To many the two seemed inextricably linked: "This is a life-or-death struggle between democracy and totalitarian-

ism. We want to overthrow Deng Xiaoping because we see him as the last dictator in the centuries-long history of China. This is precisely what the present movement really focuses on!"

39. Discussed in Lee (1990: 92)

40. Quoted in Lee (1990: 93–4).

41. As Nathan notes, this understanding of democracy is in accord with long-standing Chinese tradition. Nineteenth century thinkers interpreted the Western notion of democracy initially through the Confucian-Mencian tradition of seeing "people as the basis" (*minben*) of rule. "The people's only claim in the Mencian conception of government was for welfare, and even this was not a right they could demand but a responsibility the ruler was urged to shoulder for both moral and prudential reasons." Gradually, the notion of people-as-the-basis was supplemented by those of people's rights (*minquan*) and people's rule (*minzhu*). But the older heritage kept the focus (a) on the advantages popular participation could bring to public projects, and (b) rights of appeal or opportunities for seeking correction of state policies, not rights to run the state as such. "In short, democracy was seen as a highly efficacious means of tapping the vast energies latent in the masses to propel the country out of backwardness and into a position of world power fitting for a nation with rich natural resources and an enormous population" (Nathan 1985: 127–8).

42. Erbaugh and Kraus (1990) suggest that in Fujian (and perhaps more generally outside Beijing or the other major urban centers) the movement remained more narrowly elitist and self-interested, with less involvement of workers or other non-students. "Fuzhou students seemed mostly concerned with improving their own economic situations" (1990: 153).

CONCLUSION

1. See Anderson (1991).

2. From text in *Ming Pao* (1989: 57).

3. I have argued this case at greater length in Calhoun (1991).

4. Quoted in Black and Munro (1993: 231).

5. Translation in Tong and Chan (1990: 15–17). The word "elitist" may give an unfortunate impression in the translation and perhaps should be rendered simply "elite." In any case, the students clearly meant to speak of themselves as an elite; they go on to repeat the term.

6. Chong (1989: 17).

7. Quoted in Schwarcz (1986: 22)

8. This is equally true of rational choice theory and much traditional Marxism.

9. McAdam (1982, 1988) has shown a similar process at work among participants in 1964's "Freedom Summer," part of the U.S. civil rights movement. More generally, he shows how participation in the longer-term civil rights movement nurtured an intense identification with that movement, supported by webs of relationships with fellow activists. These relationships in turn encouraged participation in the specific high-risk and high-cost actions of Freedom Summer.

10. MacCartney (1990: 7).

11. Ibid., 10. MacCartney tends to present the whole movement through a sketch of the hysterical few; she also neglects the temporal dimension to the production of heroes and martyrs. Students were not simply sitting around for months or years before the movement admiring Fang Lizhi (or envying his fame and courage).

12. Ibid.

13. This is part of what Pierre Bourdieu evokes through the concept of "habitus." Bourdieu's (1976, 1990) use of the notion of "habitus" is an attempt to grasp this constant process of improvisation, where conscious and unconscious strategizing is constant but where the play of the game involves more than merely strategy and identity becomes an embodied sensibility as well as a set of assumed social roles.

14. Campbell (1964), Taylor (1989).

15. Berger (1984: 149).

16. Barmé (1990: 78).

17. Montesquieu's *Spirit of Laws* is a classic locus for this argument. See also Dumont's (1982) more recent theorization of this issue.

18. Black and Munro (1993: 25).

19. Quoted in Black and Munro (1993: 314).

20. A somewhat distinct account of selective pressures is needed to explain the preponderance of students from outside Beijing in the Square just before the crackdown. These had overcome greater obstacles (for example, traveling farther) to participate. They had a special need to demonstrate their own radical commitment, their comrades from Beijing having already proved theirs through the hunger strike and other earlier actions (and being enrolled in more prestigious and traditionally radical universities). Perhaps most important, it was much harder for them simply to leave as danger grew.

Select Bibliography

Adorno, Theodor W. 1973. *The Jargon of Authenticity*. London: Routledge and Kegan Paul.

Anagnost, Ann. 1992. "Socialist Ethics and the Legal System," in Jeffrey N. Wasserstrom and Elizabeth J. Perry, eds., *Popular Protest and Political Culture in Modern China: Learning from 1989*. Boulder, CO: Westview Press, 1992, pp. 177–205.

Anderson, Benedict. 1991. *Imagined Communities*. London: Verso (revised edition; original 1983).

Arendt, Hannah. 1951. *The Origins of Totalitarianism*. New York: Meridian.

———. 1958. *The Human Condition*. Chicago: University of Chicago Press.

Bachman, David, and Dali L. Yang. 1991. *Yan Jiaqi and China's Struggle for Democracy*. Armonk, NY: Sharpe.

Barmé, Geremie. 1990. "Confession, Redemption, and Death: Liu Xiaobo and the Protest Movement of 1989," in G. Hicks, ed., *The Broken Mirror: China After Tiananmen*. Chicago: St. James Press, pp. 52–99.

Barmé, Geremie, and John Minford, eds. 1988. *Seeds of Fire: Chinese Voices of Conscience*. New York: Hill and Wang.

Barmé, Geremie, and Linda Jaivin, eds. 1992. *New Ghosts, Old Dreams: Chinese Rebel Voices*. New York: Times Books.

Barone Center on the Press, Politics and Public Policy. 1992. *Turmoil at Tiananmen: A Study of U.S. Press Coverage of the Beijing Spring of 1989*. Cambridge, MA: Harvard University, John F. Kennedy School of Government.

Baum, Richard, ed. 1991 *Reform and Reaction in Post-Mao China: The Road to Tiananmen*. New York: Routledge.

Béja, Jean-Philippe, Michel Bonnin, and Alain Peyraube. 1991. *Le Tremblement de Terre de Pékin*. Paris: Gallimard.

Benhabib, Seyla. 1992. "Models of Public Space: Hannah Arendt, the Liberal Tradition, and Jürgen Habermas," in C. Calhoun, ed., *Habermas and the Public Sphere*. Cambridge, MA: MIT Press, pp. 73–98.

Berger, Peter. 1984. "On the Obsolescence of the Concept of Honor," in Michael

Sandel, ed., *Liberalism and its Critics*. New York: New York University Press, pp. 149–58 (original 1970).

Berlin, Michael J. 1993. "The Performance of the Chinese Media During the Beijing Spring," in Roger Des Forges, Luo Ning, and Wu Yen-bo, eds., *Chinese Democracy and the Crisis of 1989: Chinese and American Reflections*. Albany, NY: State University of New York Press, pp. 263–76.

Bishop, Robert L. 1989. *Qi Lai! Mobilizing One Billion Chinese: The Chinese Communication System*. Ames, IA: Iowa State University Press.

Black, George, and Robin Munro. 1993. *Black Hands of Beijing: Lives of Defiance in China's Democracy Movement*. New York: Wiley.

Bodman, Richard W. 1991. "From History to Allegory to Art: A Personal Search for Interpretation," in R. W. Bodman and P. P. Wan, *Deathsong of the River: A Reader's Guide to the Chinese TV Series Heshang*. Ithaca, NY: Cornell East Asia Series, pp. 1–62.

Bodman, Richard W., and Pin P. Wan. 1991. *Deathsong of the River: A Reader's Guide to the Chinese TV Series Heshang*. Ithaca, NY: Cornell East Asia Series.

Bourdieu, Pierre. 1976. *Outline of a Theory of Practice*. Cambridge: Cambridge University Press.

———. 1985. "Social Space and the Genesis of Groups," *Theory and Society* 14: 723–44.

———. 1987. *Homo Academicus*. Stanford, CA: Stanford University Press.

———. 1990. *The Logic of Practice*. Stanford, CA: Stanford University Press.

Bourdieu, Pierre, and Loïc Wacquant. 1992. *Toward a Reflexive Sociology*. Chicago: University of Chicago Press.

Brook, Timothy. 1992. *Quelling the People: The Military Suppression of the Beijing Democracy Movement*. New York: Oxford University Press.

Buckley, Christopher. 1991. "Science as Politics and Politics as Science: Fang Lizhi and Chinese Intellectuals' Uncertain Road to Dissent," *Australian Journal of Chinese Affairs* 25: 1–36.

Calhoun, Craig. 1983. "The Radicalism of Tradition: Community Strength or Venerable Disguise and Borrowed Language?" *American Journal of Sociology* 88 (5): 886–914.

———. 1988. "Populist Politics, Communications Media, and Large Scale Social Integration," *Sociological Theory* 6 (2): 219–41.

———. 1991. "The Problem of Identity in Collective Action," in J. Huber, ed., *Macro-Micro Linkages in Sociology*. Beverly Hills, CA: Sage, pp. 51–75.

———, ed. 1992. *Habermas and the Public Sphere*. Cambridge, MA: MIT Press.

———. 1993. "Nationalism and Ethnicity," *Annual Review of Sociology* 19: 211–39.

———. 1995. *Critical Social Theory: Culture, History and the Challenge of Difference*. Oxford: Blackwell.

Campbell, J. K. 1964. *Honor, Family and Patronage*. Oxford: Oxford University Press.

Chamberlain, Heath B. 1993. "On the Search for Civil Society in China," *Modern China* 19 (2): 199–215.

Chan, Anita, and Jonathan Unger. 1990. "Voices from the Protest Movement, Chongqing, Sichuan," *The Australian Journal of Chinese Affairs* 24: 259–79.

Chang, Chen-pang. 1989. "The Awakening of Intellectuals in Mainland China," *Issues and Studies* 25 (3): 1–3.

Chang, Hao. 1987. *Chinese Intellectuals in Crisis: Search for Order and Meaning, 1890–1911.* Berkeley: University of California Press.

Cheek, Timothy. 1988. "Habits of the Heart: Intellectual Assumptions Reflected by Mainland Chinese reformers from Teng T'o to Fang Li-chih," *Issues and Studies* 24 (3): 31–52.

———. 1992. "From Priests to Professionalis: Intellectuals and the State Under the CCP," in J. N. Wasserstrom and E. J. Perry, eds., *Popular Protest and Political Culture in Modern China: Learning from 1989.* Boulder, CO: Westview Press, pp. 124–45.

Chen, Lichuan, and Christian Thimonier, eds. 1990. *L'Impossible Printemps: Une Anthologie du Printemps de Pékin.* Paris: Editions Rivages.

Chen, Xitong. 1989. *Report on Checking the Turmoil and Quelling the Counter-Revolutionary Rebellion.* Beijing: New Star Publishers

Cherrington, Ruth. 1991. *China's Students: The Struggle for Democracy.* London: Routledge.

Chong, Woei Lien. 1989. "Present Worries of Chinese Democrats: Notes of Fang Lizhi, Liu Binyan and the Film 'River Elegy,' " *China Information* 3 (4): 1–20.

———. 1990. "Petitioners, Popperians, and Hunger Strikers: The Uncoordinated Efforts of the 1989 Chinese Democractic Movement," in T. Saich, ed., *The Chinese People's Movement: Perspectives on Spring 1989.* Armonk, NY: M. E. Sharpe, pp. 106–25.

Chow, Tse-tung. 1960. *The May 4th Movement: Intellectual Revolution in Modern China.* Cambridge, MA: Harvard University Press.

Cohen, Jean, and Andrew Arato. 1992. *The Political Theory of Civil Society.* Cambridge, MA: MIT Press.

Davis, James C. 1962. "Toward a Theory of Revolution," *American Sociological Review* 27: 5–19.

Decker, Margaret H. 1993. "Living in Sin: From May Fourth via the Antirightist Movement to the Present," in E. Widmer and D. D. Wang, eds., *From May Fourth to June Fourth: Fiction and Film in Twentieth-Century China.* Cambridge, MA: Harvard University Press, pp. 221–48.

Dirlik, Arif. 1978. *Revolution and History.* Berkeley: University of California Press.

———. 1986. "Vision and Revolution: Anarchism in Chinese Revolutionary Thought on the Eve of the 1911 Revolution," *Modern China* 12: 123–65.

Duke, Michael S. 1990. *The Iron House: A Memoir of the Chinese Democracy Movement and the Tiananmen Massacre.* Layton, UT: Gibbs-Smith.

Dumont, Louis. 1982. *Essays on Individualism.* Chicago: University of Chicago Press.

Durkheim, Emile. 1895. *The Rules of Sociological Method.* New York: Free Press.

———. 1915. *The Elementary Forms of Religious Life.* New York: Free Press.

Erbaugh, Mary S., and Richard Curt Kraus. 1990. "The 1989 Democracy Movement in Fujian and its Aftermath," *Australian Journal of Chinese Affairs* 23: 145–60.

Esherick, Joseph W. 1990. "Xi'an Spring," *The Australian Journal of Chinese Affairs* 24: 209–35.

Esherick, Joseph W., and Jeffrey N. Wasserstrom. 1990. "Acting Out Democracy: Political Theater in Modern China," *Journal of Asian Studies* 49: 835–65.

Eyerman Ron, and Andrew Jamison. 1991. *Social Movements: A Cognitive Approach.* Cambridge: Polity.

Faison, Seth. 1990. "The Changing Role of the Chinese Media," in T. Saich, ed., *The Chinese People's Movement: Perspectives on Spring 1989.* Armonk, NY: M.E. Sharpe, pp 145–63.

Fang, Lizhi. 1986. "Intellectual and Intellectual Ideology" (interview with Dai Qing), *Beijing Review* (December 15): 16–17.

———. 1987a. "Interview with Tiziano Terzani," *The Far Eastern Economic Review*, October 22, 1987.

———. 1987b. "Intellectuals and the Chinese Society," *Issues and Studies* 23 (4): 124–42.

———. 1988a. "The Social Responsibilities of Young Intellectuals Today," *Chinese Law and Government* 21 (2): 68–74 (original December 1986).

———. 1988b. "Intellectuals and Chinese Society" (speech of November 15, 1986; alternative translation of 1987), *Chinese Law and Government* 21 (2): 75–86.

———. 1988c. "China Needs Modernization in All Fields—Democracy, Reform, and Modernization" (speech of November 18, 1989), *Chinese Law and Government* 21 (2): 87–95.

———. 1988d. "Intellectuals Should Unite," *Chinese Law and Government* 21 (2): 96–102 (original February 1987).

———. 1991. *Bringing Down the Great Wall: Writings of Science, Culture, and Democracy in China.* New York: Knopf.

Fathers, Michael, and Andrew Higgins. 1989. *Tiananmen: The Rape of Peking.* London: Doubleday.

Feigon, Lee. 1983. *Chen Duxiu: Founder of the Chinese Communist Party.* Princeton: Princeton University Press.

———. 1990. *China Rising: The Meaning of Tiananmen.* Chicago: Ivan R. Dee.

———. 1992. "Gender and the Chinese Student Movement," in J. N. Wasserstrom and E. J. Perry, eds., *Popular Protest and Political Culture in Modern China: Learning from 1989.* Boulder, CO: Westview Press, pp. 165–76.

Forward, Roy. 1990. "Letter from Shanghai," *Australian Journal of Chinese Affairs* 24: 281–98.

Francis, Corinna-Barbara. 1989. "The Progress of Protest in China," *Asian Survey* 29 (19): 898–915.

Fraser, Nancy. 1992. "Rethinking the Public Sphere: A Contribution to the Critique of Actually Existing Democracy," in C. Calhoun, ed., *Habermas and the Public Sphere.* Cambridge, MA: MIT Press, pp. 109–42.

Gasster, Michael. 1969. *Chinese Intellectuals and the Revolution of 1911: The Birth of Modern Chinese Radicalism.* Seattle: University of Washington Press.

Gierke, Otto von. 1934. *Natural Law and the Theory of Society.* Cambridge: Cambridge University Press.

———. 1959. *Political Theories of the Middle Age*. Cambridge: Cambridge University Press.

Gitlin, Todd. 1988. *The Sixties: Years of Hope, Days of Rage*. New York: Bantam.

Gittings, John. 1989. *China Changes Face: The Road from Revolution, 1949–1989*. Oxford: Oxford University Press.

Gold, Thomas B. 1985. "Personal Relations in China since the Cultural Revolution," *The China Quarterly* 104: 657–75.

———. 1989a. "Neo-Authoritarianism Won't Create Economic Miracle," *Los Angeles Times* (June 30) p. II-9.

———. 1989b. "Guerrilla Interviewing Among the *Getihu*," in P. Link, R. Madsen, and P. G. Pickowicz, eds., *Unofficial China: Popular Culture and Thought in the People's Republic*. Boulder, CO: Westview Press, pp. 175–92.

———. 1990. "The Resurgence of Civil Society in China," *Journal of Democracy* 1 (1): 18–31.

———. 1991. "Urban Private Business and China's Reforms," in R. Baum, ed., *Reform and Reaction in Post-Mao China: The Road to Tiananmen*. New York: Routledge, pp. 84–103.

Goldman, Merle, ed. 1977. *Modern Chinese Literature in the May Fourth Era*. Cambridge, MA: Harvard.

———. 1981. *China's Intellectuals: Advise and Dissent*. Cambridge, MA: Harvard University Press.

———. 1987. "Dissident Intellectuals in the People's Republic of China," in V. Falkenheim, ed., *Citizens and Groups in Contemporary China*. Ann Arbor: University of Michigan Press, pp. 159–88.

Goldman, Merle, Timothy Cheek, and Carol Hamrin, eds. 1987. *China's Intellectuals and the State: In Search of a New Relationship*. Cambridge, MA: Harvard Contemporary China Series, no. 3.

Gramsci, Antonio. 1971. *Selections from the Prison Notebooks*, trans. Q. Hoare and G. Nowell Smith. New York: International.

Greider, Jerome. 1981. *Intellectuals and the State in Modern China: A Narrative History*. New York: Free Press.

Guan, Yuqian. 1988. "Wang Ruowang Discusses Literary Policy and the Reform," *Chinese Law and Government* 21 (2): 35–58.

Gunn, Anne. 1990. "'Tell the World about Us': The Student Movement in Shenyang, 1989," *The Australian Journal of Chinese Affairs* 24: 243–58.

Gunn, Edward. 1993. "The Rhetoric of *River Elegy*: From Cultural Criticism to Social Act," in Roger Des Forges, Luo Ning, and Wu Yen-bo, eds., *Chinese Democracy and the Crisis of 1989: Chinese and American Reflections*. Albany, NY: State University of New York Press, pp. 247–62.

Habermas, Jürgen. 1989. *The Structural Transformation of the Public Sphere*, trans. T. Burger. Cambridge, MA: MIT Press (original 1962).

Han, Minzhu (pseudonym), ed. 1990. *Cries for Democracy: Writings and Speeches from the 1989 Chinese Democracy Movement*. Princeton: Princeton University Press.

Harding, Harry. 1987. *China's Second Revolution: Reform after Mao*. Washington, DC: Brookings Institution.

Hartford, Kathleen. 1990. "The Political Economy Behind Beijing Spring," in T. Saich, ed., *The Chinese People's Movement: Perspectives on Spring 1989*. Armonk, NY: M. E. Sharpe, pp. 50–82.

Hicks, George, ed. 1990. *The Broken Mirror: China After Tiananmen*. Chicago: St. James Press.

Huang, Hui. 1993. "China's First Returned Students," M.A. thesis, University of North Carolina at Chapel Hill.

Huang, Philip C.C. 1993. "Public Sphere/'Civil Society' in China? The Third Realm between State and Society," *Modern China* 19 (2): 216–40.

Human Rights in China. 1990. *Children of the Dragon*. New York: Macmillan.

Hung, Wu. 1991. "Tiananmen Square: A Political History of Monuments," *Representations* 35: 84–117.

Israel, John. 1966. *Student Nationalism in China, 1927–1937*. Stanford, CA: Hoover Institution.

———. 1992. "Reflections of 'Reflections on the Modern Chinese Student Movement,' " in J. N. Wasserstrom and E. J. Perry, eds., *Popular Protest and Political Culture in Modern China: Learning from 1989*. Boulder, CO: Westview Press, pp. 85–108.

Jia, Hao. 1990. "Historical Trends and the 1989 Democracy Movement," in Jia Hao, ed., *The Democracy Movement of 1989 and China's Future*. Washington, D.C.: The Washington Center for China Studies, pp. 19–26.

Johnston, Michael. 1986. "The Political Consequences of Corruption: A Reassessment," *Comparative Politics* 18 (4): 463–73.

Kane, Daniel. 1989. "Jin Guantao, Liu Qingfeng and their Historical Systems Evolution Theory," *Papers on Far Eastern History* 39: 45–73.

Keane, John. 1988. *Democracy and Civil Society*. London: Verso.

Kelly, David. 1990. "Chinese Intellectuals in the 1989 Democracy Movement," in G. Hicks, ed., *The Broken Mirror: China After Tianmen*. Chicago, St. James Press, pp. 24–51.

———. 1991. "Introduction to 'The Dissident,' " Part Four of Fang Lizhi, *Bringing Down the Great Wall*. New York: Knopf.

Klandermans, B., H. Kriesi, and S. Tarrow, eds. 1988. *From Structure to Action: Comparing Movement Participation Across Cultures*. Greenwich, CT: JAI Press.

Kraus, Richard. 1989. "The Lament of Astrophysicist Fang Lizhi: China's Intellectuals in a Global Context," in Arif Dirlik and Maurice Meisner, eds., *Marxism and the Chinese Experience*. White Plains, NY: Sharpe, pp. 294–315.

Kuhn, Philip A. 1970. *Rebellion and Its Enemies in Late Imperial China: Militarization and Social Structure, 1796–1864*. Harvard: Harvard University Press.

Lee, Leo Ou-fan. 1987. *Voices from the Iron House: A Study of Lu Xun*. Bloomington, IN: Indiana University Press.

———. 1989. "Towards an Azure Culture," *Times Literary Supplement* (April 28–May 4), pp. 454–58.

———. 1990. "The Crisis of Culture," in A. J. Kane, ed., *China Briefing, 1990*. Boulder, CO: Westview Press, pp. 83–105.

Lee, Leo Ou-fan, and Benjamin Lee. 1989. "The Goddess of Democracy Deconstructed," *New Perspectives Quarterly* 4: 58–61.

Levenson, Joseph. 1959. *Liang Ch'i-ch'ao and the Mind of Modern China*. Berkeley: University of California Press.

———. 1968. *Confucian China and Its Modern Fate*. Berkeley: University of California Press.

Li, Lu. 1990. *Moving the Mountain: My Life in China from the Cultural Revolution to Tiananmen Square*. London: Macmillan,

Li, Qiao, et al. 1990. "Death or Rebirth? Tiananmen: The Soul of China," trans. H. R. Lan and J. Dennerline, in M. Oksenberg, L. R. Sullivan, and M. Lambert, eds., *Beijing Spring, 1989: Confrontation and Conflict*. Armonk, NY: Sharpe, pp. 7–54.

Li, Zehou. 1987. "The Dual Variation of Enlightenment and National Salvation," in *A Collection of Essays on Modern Chinese Intellectual History*. Beijing: East Publishing House, pp. 7–49.

Li, Zehou, and Vera Schwarcz. 1983–84. "Six Generations of Modern Chinese Intellectuals," *Chinese Studies in History* 17 (2): 42–57.

Lin, Cyril Zhiren. 1989. "Open-Ended Economic Reform in China," in V. Nee and D. Stark, eds., *Remaking the Economic Institutions of Socialism: China and Eastern Europe*. Stanford, CA: Stanford University Press, pp. 95–136.

Link, Perry, ed. 1983. *Stubborn Weeds: Popular and Controversial Chinese Literature After the Cultural Revolution*. Bloomington, IN: Indiana University Press.

———. 1986. "Intellectuals and Cultural Policy after Mao," in A. D. Barnett and R. N. Clough, eds., *Modernizing China: Post-Mao reform and Development*. Boulder, CO: Westview Press, pp. 81–102.

———. 1989. "The Chinese Intellectuals and the Revolt," *New York Review of Books* 36 (11): 38–41.

———. 1990. "The Thought and Spirit of Fang Lizhe," in G. Hicks, ed., *The Broken Mirror: China After Tianmen*. Chicago: St. James Press, pp. 100–14.

———. 1992. *Evening Chats in Beijing*. New York: Norton.

Link, Perry, Richard Madsen, and Paul G. Pickowicz, eds. 1989. *Unofficial China: Popular Culture and Thought in the People's Republic*. Boulder, CO: Westview Press.

Liu, Binyan. 1988. "Self-Examination," *Chinese Law and Government* 21 (2): 14–34 (original October 1986).

———. 1990. *Another Kind of Loyalty*. New York: Pantheon.

Liu, Binyan, with Ruan Ming and Xu Gang. 1989. *"Tell the World": What Happened in China and Why*. New York: Pantheon.

Lull, James. 1991. *China Turned On: Television, Reform, and Resistance*. London: Routledge.

MacCartney, Jane. 1990. "The Students: Heroes, Pawns, or Power-Brokers?" in G. Hicks, ed., *The Broken Mirror: China after Tiananmen*. Chicago: St. James Press, pp. 3–23.

Madsen, Richard. 1993. "The Public Sphere, Civil Society, and Moral Community: A Research Agenda for Contemporary China Studies," *Modern China* 19 (2): 183–98.

Manion, Melanie. 1990. "Introduction: Reluctant Duelists: The Logic of the 1989 Protests and Massacre," in M. Oksenberg, L. R. Sullivan, and M. Lambert, eds.,

Beijing Spring, 1989: Confrontation and Conflict. Armonk, NY: Sharpe, pp. xiii–xlii.

Marx, Karl. 1845. *The Holy Family,* in Karl Marx and Friedrich Engel, *Collected Works,* vol. 4. London: Lawrence and Wishart, 1976, pp. 5–211.

——. 1852. "The 18th Brumaire of Louis Bonaparte," in Karl Marx and Friedrich Engels, *Collected Works,* vol. 11. London: Lawrence and Wishart, pp. 99–197.

McAdam, Doug. 1982. *Political Process and the Development of Black Insurgency, 1930–1970.* Chicago: University of Chicago Press.

McAdam, Doug, John D. McCarthy, and Mayer Zald. 1988. "Social Movements," in N. J. Smelser, ed., *Handbook of Sociology.* Newbury Park, CA: Sage, pp. 695–737.

McDougall, Bonnie S. 1985. "Bei Dao's Poetry: Revelation and Communication," *Modern Chinese Literature* 1: 225–52.

Meaney, Constance Squires. 1991. "Market reform and Disintegrative Corruption in Urban China," in R. Baum, ed., *Reform and Reaction in Post-Mao China: The Road to Tiananmen.* New York: Routledge, pp. 124–42.

Ming Pao News. 1989. *June Four: A Chronicle of the Chinese Democratic Uprising.* Fayetteville: University of Arkansas Press.

Munro, Robin. 1990. "Who Dies in Beijing, And Why?" *The Nation* (June 11): 811–22.

Nathan, Andrew. 1985. *Chinese Democracy.* Berkeley: University of California Press.

——. 1990. *China's Crisis: Dilemmas of Reform and Prospects for Democracy.* New York: Columbia University Press.

Niming, Frank. 1990. "Learning How to Protest," in T. Saich, ed., *The Chinese People's Movement: Perspectives on Spring, 1989.* Armonk, NY: M. E. Sharpe, pp. 83–105.

Oberschall, Anthony. 1973. *Social Conflict and Social Movements.* Englewood Cliffs, NJ: Prentice-Hall.

Ogden, Suzanne, Kathleen Hartford, Lawrence Sullivan, and David Zweig, eds. 1992. *China's Search for Democracy: The Student and the Mass Movement of 1989.* Armonk, NY: M. E. Sharpe.

Oi, Jean C. 1991. "Partial Market Reform and Corruption in Rural China," in R. Baum, ed: *Reform and Reaction in Post-Mao China: The Road to Tiananmen.* New York: Routledge, pp. 143–61.

Oksenberg, Michel, Lawrence R. Sullivan, and Marc Lambert, eds. 1990. *Beijing Spring, 1989: Confrontation and Conflict, The Basic Documents.* Armonk, NY: M. E. Sharpe.

Pang Pang (pseud.). 1989. *The Death of Hu Yaobang,* trans. Si Ren. Honolulu: University of Hawaii Center for Chinese Studies.

Perkins, Dwight H. 1990. "The Prospects for China's Economic Reforms," in A. J. Kane, ed., *China Briefing, 1990.* Boulder, CO: Westview Press, pp. 25–46.

Peyrefitte, Alain. 1990. *La tragédie chinoise.* Paris: Fayard.

Polumbaum, Judy. 1991. "Making Sense of June 4, 1989: Analyses of the Tiananmen Tragedy," *The Australian Journal of Chinese Affairs* 26: 177–86.

——. 1993. "'Professionalism' in China's Press Corps," in Roger Des Forges,

Luo Ning, and Wu Yen-bo, eds., *Chinese Democracy and the Crisis of 1989: Chinese and American Reflections*. Albany, NY: State University of New York Press, pp. 295–312.

Rankin, Mary B. 1971. *Early Chinese Revolutionaries: Radical Intellectuals in Shanghai and Chekiang, 1902–1911*. Cambridge, MA: Harvard University Press.

———. 1986. *Elite Activism and Political Transformation in China*. Stanford, CA: Stanford University Press.

———. 1990. "The Origins of a Chinese Public Sphere," *Etudes Chinoises* 9 (2): 1–60.

———. 1993. "Some Observations on a Chinese Public Sphere," *Modern China* 19 (2): 158–82.

Rosemont, Henry Jr. 1991. *A Chinese Mirror*. La Salle, IL: Open Court.

Rowe, William T. 1989. *Hankow: Conflict and Community in a Chinese City, 1796–1895*. Stanford, CA: Stanford University Press.

———. 1990. "The Public Sphere in Modern China," *Modern China* 16 (3): 309–29.

———. 1993. "The Problem of 'Civil Society' in Late Imperial China," *Modern China* 19 (2): 139–57.

Saich, Tony. 1990. *The Chinese People's Movement: Perspectives on Spring, 1989*. Armonk, NY: M. E. Sharpe.

Schell, Orville. 1984. *To Get Rich Is Glorious*. New York: Anchor Books.

———. 1988. *Discos and Democracy: China in the Throes of Reform*. New York: Anchor Books.

———. 1990. "The Re-emergence of the Realm of the Private in China," in G. Hicks, ed., *The Broken Mirror: China after Tiananmen*. Chicago: St. James Press, pp. 419–27.

Schrecker, John. 1991. *The Chinese Revolution in Historical Perspective*. New York: Praeger.

Schwarcz, Vera. 1986. *The Chinese Enlightenment: Intellectuals and the Legacy of the May Fourth Movement of 1919*. Berkeley: University of California Press.

———. 1992. "Memory and Commemoration: The Chinese Search for a Livable Past," in J. N. Wasserstrom and E. J. Perry, eds., *Popular Protest and Political Culture in Modern China: Learning from 1989*. Boulder, CO: Westview Press, pp. 109–23.

Schwartz, Benjamin, J. 1964. *In Search of Wealth and Power: Yen Fu and the West*. Cambridge, MA: Harvard University Press.

———. 1970. "The Reign of Virtue: Some Broad Perspectives on Leader and Party in the Cultural Revolution," in J. W. Lewis, ed., *Party Leadership and Revolutionary Power in China*. Cambridge, MA: Cambridge University Press, pp. 149–69.

Seligman, Adam. 1992. *Civil Society*. New York: Free Press.

Shapiro, Judith, and Liang Heng. 1986. *Cold Winds, Warm Winds: Intellectual Life in China Today*. Middletown, CT: Wesleyan University Press.

Shen, Tong, with Marianne Yen. 1990. *Almost a Revolution*. New York: Houghton Mifflin.

Shi, Tianjin. 1990. "The Democratic Movement in China in 1989: Dynamics and Failure," *Asian Survey* 12: 1186–1205.

Shirk, Susan. 1989. "The Political Economy of Chinese Industrial Reform," in V. Nee and D. Stark, eds., *Remaking the Economic Institutions of Socialism: China and Estern Europe*. Stanford, CA: Stanford University Press, pp. 328–62.

Simmie, Scott, and Bob Nixon. 1989. *Tiananmen Square: An Eyewitness Account of the Chinese People's Passionate Quest for Democracy*. Seattle: University of Washington Press.

Solinger, Dorothy J. 1991. "Urban Reform and Relational Contracting in Post-Mao China: An Interpretation of the Transition from Plan to Market," in R. Baum, ed., *Reform and Reaction in Post-Mao China: The Road to Tiananmen*. New York: Routledge, pp. 104–23.

Spence, Jonathan. 1981. *The Gate of Heavenly Peace: The Chinese and their Revolution, 1895–1980*. Baltimore: Penguin.

———. 1991. *In Search of Modern China*. New York: Norton.

Strand, David. 1989. *Rickshaw Beijing: City People and Politics in the 1920s*. Berkeley: University of California Press.

———. 1990. "Protest in Beijing: Civil Society and Public Sphere in China," *Problems of Communism* 39: 1–19.

Su, Shaozhi. 1988. *Democratization and Reform*. Nottingham: Spokesman.

Su, Xiaokang. 1988. "Arousing the Whole Nation to Self-Questioning," trans. in R. W. Bodman and P. P. Wan, eds., *Deathsong of the River: A Reader's Guide to the Chinese TV Series* Heshang. Ithaca, NY: Cornell East Asia Series, 1991, pp. 93–99.

———. 1989a. "The Distress of a Dragon Year—Notes on *Heshang*," trans. in R. W. Bodman and P. P. Wan, eds., *Deathsong of the River: A Reader's Guide to the Chinese TV Series*, Heshang. Ithaca, NY: Cornell East Asia Series, 1991, pp. 271–99.

———. 1989b. *The Memorandum of Freedom*. Beijing: Beijing Publishing House.

Sullivan, Lawrence R. 1990. "The Emergence of Civil Society in China, Spring 1989," in T. Saich, ed., *The Chinese People's Movement: Perspectives on Spring 1989*. Armonk, NY: M. E. Sharpe, pp. 126–44.

Suttmeier, Richard P. 1987. "Riding the Tiger: The Political Life of China's Scientists," in V. Falkenheim, ed., *Citizens and Groups in Contemporary China*. Ann Arbor: University of Michigan Press, pp. 123–58.

Tan, Frank. 1993. "The *People's Daily* and the Epiphany of Press Reform," in Roger Des Forges, Luo Ning, and Wu Yen-bo, eds., *Chinese Democracy and the Crisis of 1989: Chinese and American Reflections*. Albany, NY: State University of New York Press, pp. 277–94.

Tarrow, Sidney. 1988. "National Politics and Collective Action: Recent Theory and Research in Western Europe and the United States," *Annual Review of Sociology* 14: 421–40.

———. 1989. *Struggle, Politics and Reform: Collective Action, Social Movements and Cycles of Protest*. Ithaca, NY: Cornell University Press (Western Societies Papers No. 21).

Tay, William. 1985. "Obscure Poetry: A Controversy in Post-Mao China," in J. C.

Kinkley, ed., *After Mao: Chinese Literature and Society, 1978–1981*. Cambridge, MA: Harvard University Press, pp. 133–57.

Taylor, Charles. 1989. *Sources of the Self*. Cambridge, MA: Harvard University Press.

———. 1991. "Modes of Civil Society," *Public Culture* 3 (1): 95–118.

Thurston, Anne. 1987. *Enemies of the People: The Ordeal of the Intellectuals in China's Great Cultural Revolution*. Cambridge, MA: Harvard University Press.

Tilly, Charles. 1978. *From Mobilization to Revolution*. Reading, MA: Addison-Wesley.

Time Magazine. 1989. *Massacre in Beijing: China's Struggle for Democracy*. New York: Warner Books.

Tocqueville, Alexis. 1840–44. *Democracy in America*. New York: Schocken.

Tong, James, and Elaine Chan, eds. 1990. "The Democracy Movement in Beijing," *Chinese Sociology and Anthropology* 23 (1) (special issue).

Tu, Wei-ming. 1987. "Iconoclasm, Holistic Vision, and Patient Watchfulness: A Personal Reflection on the Modern Chinese Intellectual Quest," *Daedalus* (Spring): 75–94.

Ullman, Walter. 1970. *Medieval Political Thought*. Harmondsworth: Penguin.

Unger, Jonathan. 1990. *The Democracy Movement in China: The View from the Provinces*. Armonk, NY: M. E. Sharpe.

Vogel, Ezra. 1989. *Guangdong Under Reform*. Cambridge, MA: Harvard University Press.

Wakeman, Frederick. 1989. "All the Rage in China," *New York Review of Books* (March 2): 19–21.

———. 1993. "The Civil Society and Public Sphere Debate: Western Reflections on Chinese Political Culture," *Modern China* 19 (2): 108–38.

Walder, Andrew G. 1989. "The Political Sociology of the Beijing Upheaval of 1989," *Problems of Communism* (September–October): 30–40.

Wan, Pin P. 1991. "A Second Wave of Enlightenment? Or an Illusory Nirvana? *Heshang* and the Intellectual Movements of the 1980s," in R. W. Bodman and P. P. Wan, trans. and eds., *Deathsong of the River: A Reader's Guide to the Chinese TV Series, Heshang*. Ithaca, NY: Cornell East Asia Series, pp. 63–89.

Warner, Shelley. 1990. "Shanghai's Response to the Deluge," *The Australian Journal of Chinese Affairs* 24: 299–314.

Wasserstrom, Jeffrey N. 1991. *Student Protests in Twentieth-Century China*. Stanford, CA: Stanford University Press.

———. 1992a. "Student Associations and Student Protest in China: Reflections on Events of the Recent (and Not-so-recent) Past," paper presented to the Conference on Urban China, Washington, D.C.

———. 1992b. "History, Myth and the Tales of Tiananmen," in J. N. Wasserstrom and E. J. Perry, eds., *Popular Protest and Political Culture in Modern China: Learning from 1989*. Boulder, CO: Westview Press, pp. 244–80.

———. 1993. "Putting 1989 in Historical Perspective: Pitfalls and Possibilities," *Working Papers in Asian/Pacific Studies*, Durham, NC: Duke University.

Wasserstrom, Jeffrey N., and Elizabeth J. Perry, eds. 1992. *Popular Protest and Po-*

litical Culture in Modern China: Learning from 1989. Boulder, CO: Westview Press.

Watson, James L. 1992. "The Renegotiation of Chinese Cultural Identity in the Post-Mao Era," J. N. Wasserstrom and E. J. Perry, eds., *Popular Protest and Political Culture in Modern China: Learning from 1989.* Boulder, CO: Westview Press.

White, Lynn, and Li Cheng. 1988. "Diversification among Mainland Intellectuals," *Issues and Studies* 24 (9): 50–77.

Whyte, Martin King. 1992. "Urban China: A Civil Society in the Making?" in A. L. Rosenbaum, ed., *State and Society in China: The Consequences of Reform.* Boulder, CO: Westview Press, pp. 77–101.

Wilson, Jeanne L. 1990. "'The Polish Lesson': China and Poland, 1980–1990," *Studies in Comparative Communism* 23 (3/4): 259–80.

Wu Dunn, Sheryl. 1990. "The Prisoners of Tiananmen Square," *New York Times Magazine* (May 13): 28–34.

Wu, Hung. 1991. "Tiananmen Square: A Political History of Monuments," *Representations* 35: 84–117.

Yan, Jiaqi. 1992. *Toward a Democratic China.* Honolulu: University of Hawaii Press.

Yeh, Michelle. 1990. "Debunking Official Ideology: The Controversy over Contemporary Poetry," Paper presented to the First Annual Conference of the American Association of Chinese Comparative Literature, Duke University, Durham, NC.

Yi, Jiayan (pseud.). 1989. "What Does 'The River Dies Young' Advocate?" *Beijing Review* (August 21): 14–21.

Yi, Mu, and Mark V. Thompson. 1989. *Crisis at Tiananmen: Reform and Reality in Modern China.* San Francisco: China Books.

Yu, Mok Chiu, and J. Frank Harrison, eds. 1990. *Voices from Tiananmen Square: Beijing Spring and the Democracy Movement.* Montreal: Black Rose Books.

Zald, Mayer N., and John D. McCarthy, eds. 1979. *The Dynamics of Social Movements.* Cambridge, MA: Winthrop.

Zarrow, Peter. 1990. *Anarchism and Chinese Political Culture.* New York: Columbia University Press.

Zha, Jianying. 1990. "Notes on the Emergence of a Counter-Public in China," unpublished paper. Chicago: Center for Transcultural Studies.

Zhang, Yingjin. 1990. "Narrative, Ideology, Subjectivity: Chinese Reportage Literature as a Socially Symbolic Act," Paper presented to the First Annual Conference of the American Association of Chinese Comparative Literature, Duke University, Durham, NC.

Zhou, Xueguang. 1993. "Unorganized Interests and Collective Action in Communist China," *American Sociological Review* 58 (1): 54–73.

Zhu, Yongtao. 1989. "American Culture as Seen by Chinese Intellectuals Today," *Journal of American Culture* 12 (4): 35–42.

Index

Compositor:	G & S Typesetters, Inc.
Text:	10/13 Aldus
Display:	Aldus
Printer and Binder:	Thomson-Shore, Inc.